INDUS CIVILIZATION

LANGUAGE & SCRIPT

THAKUR A. K. SINHA

PREFACE

During childhood days, my curiosity and inquisitiveness about space, time and astral bodies was very high and I used to wonder how systematically the astral bodies, planets and stars are moving in cyclic manner within star dynasties and how much precision they maintain regarding their position and periods of movement in space. I found many correlations between seven stars of U. Minor, seven stars of U. Major, seven colors of spectra, seven types of sound waves, seven crystal systems, seven matter and anti-matter zones, seven body systems in living beings, seven sacks in animal body, seven holes in skull of human beings, movement of energy within seven color regions, formation of anions and cations up to seven points, creation of elements in rounds containing seven elements starting from metallic elements and ending at non-metallic elements. Every turn of planets and stars about axis creates elements and increases their mass and size gradually due to Rotation-linked movement, Revolution-linked movement and Precession-linked movement along three axes in space.

The atomic theory of magnetism is based on arrangement of atoms of $^{56}_{26}Fe$ in fixed pattern inside ferromagnetic axle along three axes inside every planet and star. Compaction of one crystal of atom of $^{56}_{26}Fe$ by fourteen outside crystals creates ferromagnetic axle along three axes inside every planet and star which connects micro-world of element with macro-world of planets and stars in the universe. Thus, fourteen matter zones inside astral bodies and fourteen anti-matter zones outside astral bodies, planets and stars in space exist to the maximum for every astral body. The time is round in shape which controls, captures and stores mass of space inside round time frame. Time and space relationship exists as outer covering and inner mass. In root values, the time retrogresses and tries to contract mass in crystallized form inside astral bodies while in square, cubic and higher values time progresses and increases the ellipticity of elliptical orbit of astral bodies. Time is the biggest arbiter for contraction of mass and expansion of orbit of movement of all astral bodies, planets and stars. Smallest level of space-time relationship is observed in e- and e+ particles where smallest quantity of mass is contracted by outer geometrical time frame. Highest level of space-time relationship is observed in biggest Red Star where highest quantity of mass as matter is enclosed inside spherical time frame.

The energy of electromagnetic waves in the range of seven colors, i.e., 4000 Å to 7500 Å converts into electrical energy due to electromagnetic effect. The electric energy produces oppositely charged particles, i.e., e- and e+ initially and then produces bigger particles (e- and p+). Prominence of red color produces positively charged particles whereas prominence of blue color produces negatively charged particles. Positively charged particles emit red color rays whereas negatively charged particles emit blue color rays. Both charged particles encapsulate neutral mass particles and produce solid nucleus in crystallized form inside atoms. The structure of atom shows that positively charged particles shape axial ratios and contract dark matter particles inside nucleus through axial ratios whereas negatively charged particles shape axial angles of nucleus. In this process, a 'set of three fundamental particles' contract energy and produces atoms of 118 elements on all planets and stars in seven periods, fourteen rounds and twelve blocks.

Science and religion are two faces of the same coin. Stellar evolution takes place in monarchical manner and not in democratic way and creates hot bodies, spiral stars and planets during cycle of evolution. Three axes attachment is the biggest arbiter for all astral bodies in the universe. Time Cycle or Age Cycle takes birth, lives in equilibrium and dies after fixed time period. Every star dynasty, Solar System, planets, plants and animals have their own Age Cycle. Time cycle always moves forward and never moves backwards. Atomic theory of languages is based on periodic table of elements and letters of Sanskrutam are produced as atoms of elements by human bodies within atmosphere of planet. The ladder of evolution and ascendance of planets and stars takes place within seven colors cycle in the universe. Life and science with present level of intelligence existed on earth about 43.2 lakh years ago and it has proliferated for the second or third time on planet earth.

Mass is contracted in root values starting from $\sqrt{m}$ to $^{252}\sqrt{m}$ inside astral bodies, planets and stars in the universe. Energy of electromagnetic waves in the range 4000 Å to 7500 Å is stored with mass particles as both charges of electric energy inside spherical time frame. The momentum of spherical astral body increases in $10^{84} \times 10^{84} \times 10^{84} = 10^{252}$ Time units (Along three axes) x $\sqrt{m}$ x Electromagnetic energy in the range 4000 Å to 7500 Å. It culminates at $^{252}\sqrt{m}$ x Electromagnetic energy in the range 4000 Å to 7500 Å x 10^{252} Time units which shows highest contraction of crystals mass inside elements and compounds along three axes and highest expansion of orbit of movement of biggest red star. Every individual life form, planet and star has fixed Time cycle or Age cycle. It takes birth, lives during equilibrium and dies within that Age cycle. Space and universe have endless existence. New Time cycles take birth with every individual living being, planet and star in space every time and die after completing cycle in fixed time period.

The signs of next catastrophe and reshuffling are visible with two moons of Mars, i.e., Phobos and Deimos. Phobos is getting closer to Mars and will collide and merge with Mars during movement while Deimos will flee away with increased compounding velocity from the orbit of Mars. Phobos is spiraling in towards Mars with increased orbital velocity and will collide with Mars. Bereft of moons, Mars planet will fail to exist without moon. Mars planet will lose three axes attachment and magnetic balance. A "Lunar Vacuum" will be created around Mars which will compel Mars to move towards Jupiter. This vacuum may make Mercury and Venus to collide with each other and earth will collide with our own moon due to imbalance in Universal Magnetic Balance. Huge wobbling will take place on planets which will cause plenty of changes in magnetic axis of attraction of moons and planets along three axes. One planet may become moon of Jupiter and any moon of Jupiter may become planet in Nine Planets System creating new sequence around Sun. Finally, only four planets, i.e., Jupiter, Saturn, Uranus and Neptune will remain around Sun. At last, four bigger planets will also collide and finally merge with Sun. The sequence of evolution takes place in ascending order of colors of electromagnetic waves and never in descending order.

The magnetic balance of our Sun exists along three axes with nine planets system, fourteen stars of Ursae Minor and Ursae Major and twelve constellations of stars in our star dynasty. Our Solar system is in process of losing ninth planet, i.e., Pluto and it will create "Planetary Vacuum" around Sun. Rest eight planets will collide in future producing four planets and finally entire mass of solar system will be assimilated in Sun. Our middle-aged Sun will evolve in the ladder of ascendance of colors and finally convert into biggest Red Star. There will be shift in Magnetic Axis of Attraction of all planets and change in the magnetic balance of nine planets system due to reshuffling in relation to Sun, constellations of twelve stars and Pole Star.

THAKUR A. K. SINHA

CONTENTS

1

EVOLUTION OF LANGUAGES

Language is a powerful tool of intellect and creativity in all living beings, which allows for almost infinite recombination of letters and words to generate new communication skills and ideas out of atoms of elements. Language plays a big role in human brain for processing the reasoning, ideas and helps in making judgments. It helps how we decide visual attention, remember events, differentiate objects, decipher smells and musical tones, stay oriented about time, perform mental exercises, prefer to listen desired languages, make proper decisions, experience and express our feelings and emotions etc. The experience with speech, language and hearing increases the decision making capacity of brain. There are many languages developed and spoken by different living beings in different communities of the world. The languages with different phonetics depend upon the characteristic features of body, size, shape and degree of evolution of animals and human beings. Many languages like Elamite, Sogdian,Nahuati and Greek etc have been overtaken by other languages due to migration, conflict, change of religion and power etc throughout the world.

There is linguistic theory that all the languages of world originated from single Proto-Indo-European language. Inferences have been drawn basing upon evidences, such as fossil records, archaeological evidences, contemporary languages of the area, studies of language acquisition and comparisons between human languages and their systems of communication existing among different mammals especially primates. Most of the languages are defined by rules and they are not static rather they evolved over period of time and place. Some old languages have evolved very less over time, as for example, Icelandic, which resembles its parent old Norse. Many languages have evolved by incorporating elements of other languages prevalent throughout the world. Only one language, i.e., Sanskrit has evolved on scientific lines from Spinal Nerves of human body. Many languages have developed and emerged as artificial intelligence throughout the world. Sanskrit is language of naural intelligence becuse it emits from nerves of human body. Thr actual script of Sanskrit language are 118 atoms of elements created in periodic table. Thirty two consonants are based on 32 classes of crystal symmetry and half its value are created as vowels of alphabet.

Sanskrit or *Sanskrut* or *Samskrutam* or *Sanskrutam* language is bound by rules that determine its syntax and semantics without any ambiguity.The sound waves emitted from the vocal cords of lower animals are spontaneous and are guided by climatic, ecological and biotic factors. The emission of sound waves in lower animals generally corresponds to group activity, group migration, alarm signals, group protection, mating partners and availability of food etc. Higher animals languages become slightly refined and phonetics and trends relating to groups, family, isolated patches, control and community type approach develops. The languages of isolated patches of human beings living on islands, hilly terrains, dense forest areas and closed ethnic groups on earth are small, compact and feeble having less number of alphabets. Their languages are need based without having any scientific background. The languages of human beings depend upon their personal requirements, dominance over other people, community desires, community dominance, latitude, altitude and religious practices that they follow on earth. Languages are created by animals and human beings in different ways:

1. **Vocal Emissions:** Lower animals and invertebrates often emit different sounds or languages but their languages are highly unsymmetrical. Definite signals cannot be derived out of their language and animal species fail to communicate and interact among

themselves. Common examples are animals of Protozoa, Porifera, Coelenterata, Annelida. Arthropoda, Mollusca, Echinodermata and small fishes.

2. **Unsystematic Languages:** Lower animals and vertebrates often emit different voices but their languages and vocal expressions are not symmetrical. Individual animals derive some signals out of the language and group of animal species respond, communicate and interact among themselves. Common examples are repeating sound, chirping, common movement of small fishes, some amphibians, reptilians, mammals and aves. These "vocal emissions or languages" are associated with body expression, combined movement and group signals and they do not have alphabets.

3. **Systematic Languages with alphabets:** They are created by human beings in different regions of the world. The language has less number of alphabets which may be associated with expression for a particular and common cause. The letters of alphabets combine to create words and it was copied and preserved on leaf papers, stone edicts, metallic plates and currencies of many civilizations.

4. **Systematic Languages with fixed number of vowels and consonants:** They are created by human beings in different region of the world. The language has fixed number of vowels and consonants. Vowels generally correspond to light expression and help in joining consonants during formulation of words. Words were created with letters and preserved from generation to generation by listening (*shrutis*) and memorizing (*smritis*). Scholars and intellectuals in different parts of the world helped in preserving knowledge and culture of different places throughout the world with the help of papers of leaf, books, stone edicts, metallic plates, currencies, alma maters and institutions. Prevailing social customs, racial groups and local civilization decided the type of language and its alphabets.

5. **Systematic Languages based on development of cervical nerves, spinal nerves, human body parts, systems, organs and central nervous system along three axes:** These languages have been created by human beings in different regions of the world taking into account evolution of thirty two pairs of spinal nerves, twelve pairs of cranial nerves and nine body systems inside human body. Vowels generally correspond to development of vocal cord around cervical vertebrae whereas consonants are associated with development of spinal nerves. Nine body systems develop due to nine colors (white + seven colors + black) and help in development of letters in the multiples of nine inside body. Systematic languages have evolved on the pattern of periodic table of elements which creates elements in the multiples of thirty two along one axes, in the multiples of twelve along second axis and in the multiples of nine colors (white + seven colors + black) along third axis. Example is Sanskrit language where thirty two classes of crystal symmetry create periods of elements as thirty two spinal nerves.

The growth of human body is different along three axes depending upon position of life form on planet. The impact of pressure, volume and temperature decides the size and shape of individual living being on planet. Every living being maintains individual thermodynamic equilibrium on planets. The thermodynamic equilibrium of living body depends upon four forces and combined action of pressure (p), volume (v) and temperature along three axes on living body. Basing on points of places of articulation, letters can be divided into different types, e.g., Glottal or Laryngeal, Pharyngeal, Uvular, Guttural, Cerebral, Palatal, Alveolar, Dental, Labio-dental and Bilabial.

6. **Systematic Languages created due to Religion, Religious Principles, concentration of power, tone and accent:** Worship of particular religion changes the voice, accent and phonetics of language spoken by particular group of people. Worship of particular religion and concentration of power brings changes in their speech, opening of mouth, tongue position, voice emission and response by people of that community. It also shapes the number of alphabets, vowels, consonants and creation of jumbled words spoken by followers of that particular religion. It is easily spoken, audible and understood by the people of that community whereas its audibility may be difficult for people of other communities. One language of particular religious community may not be understood by the people of other community professing other religion. In the speech; tongue alignment and shape of mouth along with audible apparatus of human beings play distinct role in creation of languages. Many religions are common throughout the world in different pockets and the speech and voice of people in that area resembles particular religion. The number of alphabets, i.e., vowels and consonants are decided and shaped by people of that particular religion and community. The language of that particular religion is clearly audible and understood by people professing the same religion. That language is easily deciphered by people of same religion and same community.

Many communities have reduced the number of alphabets in their languages for sake of clear and easy understanding. Communication becomes faster when number of alphabets are reduced from 36 to 32 and then to 26 alphabets. Highest binding energy of atom of element at atomic number 26 makes English language clear and fastest. Number of alphabets are decided by the choice of every community and depends upon latitude, longitude and altitude. Change in religion of person shows changes on the accent and pronunciation of words.

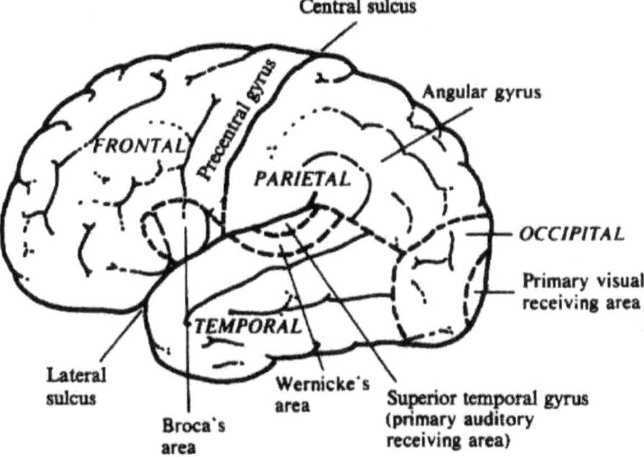

CEREBRAL HEMISPHERE SHOWING SOUND RECEIVING AREA. DIFFERENT TYPES OF NEURONS DEVELOP COORDINATION BETWEEN VOICE AND LANGUAGE AND AUDIBLE CAPACITY OF EAR IN BRAIN.

Fig. 1.1

Opening and closing of vocal cord decides the type of letters emitted by human being. Vocal cord generally remains open during inhalation. During exhalation the vocal cord becomes slightly narrow and voice coming out is 'voiceless'. During emission of sound wave packets, air faces friction and produces letters. The friction decides volume of sound, intensity and pitch. Partial opening and partial closure of vocal cord produces 'whispering' and 'murmuring' type of sound waves in different religion. Glottis is the open space of vocal cord and helps in inhaling and exhaling of air. Below the root of tongue, one epiglottis is available which moves forward and backward and helps in pronunciation of letters. Above glottis is the open area which is called pharynx and pharyngeal cavity can be narrowed down for control of pronunciation which comes out either through mouth or through nasal passage. At this juncture is found uvula. Soft palate and uvula in combined form produce different types of sound waves. In normal conditions the uvula rests with soft palate. In active state, Uvula obstructs nasal passage and common vowels and consonants are produced. When uvula remains in the middle, it effects out coming air and nasal consonants are produced. The position of uvula produces different letters of different religions. Upper portion of Mouth cavity contains teeth, alveolar ridge, hard palate, palate and soft palate.

Tongue helps in emission of sound and during speaking it comes in contact with different places of mouth cavity. It helps in emission of many vowels, consonants and words. Tongue position changes in mouth of people of different religions and emits different types of sound waves. The outermost part of tongue which generally comes out from mouth is the blade. It helps in emission of letter, e.g., *sa*. Front of tongue is located below hard palate. It helps in production of *Talabya* sound waves. The change in position of front of tongue produces different types of letters. It produces palatal (*Talabya*) and front (*Agrya*) sound. The sound produced from front, middle and back portion of palate is called Pre-palatal, Mid-palatal and Post-palatal. Back and root portion of the tongue produces many types of vowels and consonants. The sound produced is called as *Kanthaya* and can be divided into Pre-velar, Mid-velar and Post-velar.

7. **Languages are effected due to impact of longitude, latitude and altitude:** The production of voice and speech from mouth of animals and human beings is very much effected by longitude, latitude and altitude of place. People residing along Tropic of Cancer are generally soft spoken whereas people residing along Tropic of Capricorn are harsh and rough in their tone and speech. The human being near equator become taller and thinner in size. The human beings near both the poles become smaller, round and compact in size and shape.

Change in altitude, latitude and longitude effects the accent of speaking of human beings. The uttering and voice changes and shows some difference from the earlier language.The metallic elements inside human being help in changing longitude whereas non-metallic elements effect position of human being from place of birth. Human beings will shift in position either towards east or west or towards north or south from place of his or her birth. Wearing and use of metals by human beings changes the direction and position of human beings. The ferro-magnet made up of $^{56}_{26}Fe$ makes the man sit in north direction because Ferro-magnet faces towards north. The human being near equator will be taller, hefty and dark complexioned and these features will decrease gradually towards both the poles.

'Mass Extinctions' took place many times on earth and life evolved on scientific lines again and again on planet. In ancient times, many dialects and proto-languages emerged and developed with local languages in different parts of the world. Sanskrit and Indo-European languages spread and flourished due to trade and migration to different places. Following languages were commonly found in different continents.

1. AFRICA

Phoenicia became trading and colonizing state by 12th century BC and spread its language in present Libya, Tunisia, Morocco, Spain, Algeria and Cyprus etc. Phoenician alphabet is old Abjad consonantal alphabet which is ancestor of Latin alphabet. Proto-Bantu spoken earlier in central and western Africa splitted from Bantoid languages in different states. Proto-Berber and Berber languages spread in many places. Nubian civilization became prominent along Nile river and Meroitic was common language at that time. Later on Swahili became prominent language.

2. AMERICA

Alaska's native language shows that Eskimo and Aleut were common among people. The Zapotec Script is not well deciphered and was probably oldest Mesoamerican literature and writing. Many mixed new dialects emerged in America and Canada and vanished with time due to change in rulers and kingdoms. Many kingdom developed bi-lingual and tri-lingual dialects.

3. ASIA

Proto-Dravidian and Indo-Aryan were common before Sanskritization from about 1500 BC onwards. During later trade period Tokyo Edo dialect became common in Japan. Mixed dialects developed at many places throughout Asia.

4. EUROPE

Proto Indo-Eropean languages were common alongwith other local languages. Greek and Latin with many variants in different portions emerged. Later on, Danish became common language. Evidences of Sign languages were noticed in some parts.

5. OCEANIA INCLUDING AUSTRALIA

Pama-Nyungan and Hawaiian languages alongwith other languages were common in earlier civilizations.

Many 'dialects and languages' developed in different princely states, regions, kingdoms and countries throughout the world due to intermixing during course of time and tried to make their existence. Sanskrit was the only language which developed on scientific lines from nerves of human body. During studies of anatomy and nervous system of human beings, it is observed that letters oscillate from guttural, palatal, retroflex and dental to labial in mouth. Letters are shaped by different parts of mouth in which tongue plays definite role in articulation and produces different letters in separate religions. The front, middle and rear portion of tongue help in creation of pronunciation. At different latitudes, the part of tongue used for emission of letters and words depends upon the opening of mouth cavity. Partial opening, half opening and full opening decides the type of letter emitted by mouth. Position of tongue and lips varies at different latitudes and longitudes producing different types of languages.

Opening and closing of vocal cord decides the type of letters emitted by human being. Vocal cord generally remains open during inhalation. During exhalation the vocal cord becomes slightly narrow. During emission of sound waves, air faces friction and produces letters. The friction decides volume of sound, intensity and pitch. Partial opening and partial closure of vocal cord produces 'whispering' and 'murmuring' type of sound waves. Glottis is the open space of vocal cord and helps in inhaling and exhaling of air. Below the root of tongue, one epiglottis is available which moves forward and backward and helps in pronunciation of letters. Above glottis is the open area which is called pharynx. The pharyngeal cavity can be narrowed down for control of sound of pronunciation which comes out either through mouth or through nasal passage. At this juncture is found uvula. Soft palate and uvula in combined form produce different types of sound waves. In active state, Uvula obstructs nasal passage and common vowels and consonants are produced. When uvula remains in the middle, it effects out coming air and nasal consonants are produced.

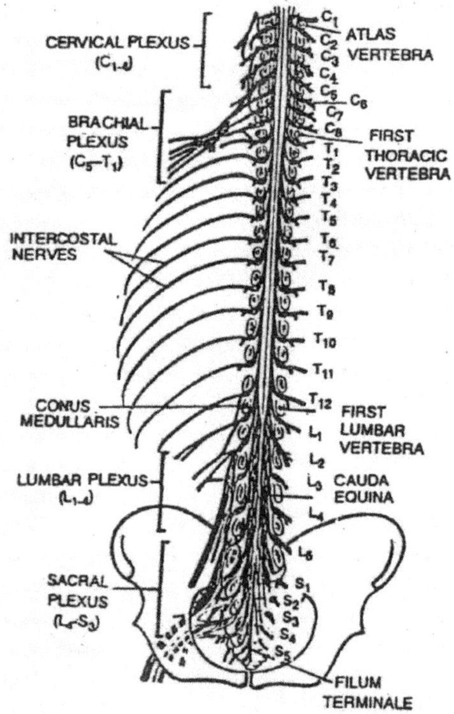

FIGURE SHOWS SPINAL NERVES IN RELATION TO SPINAL CORD AND VERTEBRAL COLUMN. EIGHT PAIRS OF CERVICAL NERVES STARTING FROM C1 TO C8 EMIT THE VOWEL LETTERS STARTING FROM *A, AA, I,*

EE, U, OO, RHI, RHEE, LRI, LREE, E, AI, O, AU, AM TO *AH*. THE VOWELS MULTIPLIED WITH CONSONANTS CREATE 32 X 16 = 512 TYPES OF SOUND WAVE PACKETS IN HUMAN BEINGS. THE FIRST LETTER, KA MIXED WITH SIXTEEN VOWELS GRADUALLY CREATES SIXTEEN TYPES OF SOUND WAVE PACKETS LIKE, *KA, KAA, KI, KEE, KU, KOO, KRI, KREE, KRLRI, KRLREE, KE, KAI, KO, KAU, KAM* AND *KAH*. SIMILAR UTTERING IS OBSERVED FOR ALL 32 CONSONANT LETTERS.

Fig. 1.2

Upper portion of Mouth cavity contains teeth, alveolar ridge, hard palate, palate and soft palate. During pronunciation of vowels and *ka, kha, ga* etc, soft palate moves up and closes nasal passage. During pronunciation of nasal sound, soft palate comes down and closes mouth cavity. During sleep, soft palate vibrates and produces snoring sound in human being. Teeth are thirty two in number and upper two teeth are very important for emission of sound.

Tongue is very important for emission of sound and during speaking it comes in contact with different places of mouth cavity. Depending upon structure, it is divided into following parts:

(a) Tip of Tongue: Tip or Apex of tongue is the front portion which is most active. It helps in emission of many vowels, consonants and words.

(b) Blade of the Tongue: The outermost part of tongue which generally comes out from mouth is the blade. It helps in emission of letter, e.g., *sa.*

(c) Front of Tongue: Front of tongue is located below hard palate. It helps in production of *Talabya* sound waves. It stops air flow and produces tenth consonant,e.g., *Eina.* The change in position of front of tongue produces different types of letters. It produces palatal (*Talabya*) and front (*Agrya*) sound. The sound produced from front, middle and back portion of palate is called Pre-palatal, Mid-palatal and Post-palatal.

(d) Back of tongue, Dorsum and Root of Tongue: Back and root of the tongue produces many types of vowels and consonants. The sound produced is called as *Kanthaya* and can be divided into Pre-velar, Mid-velar and Post-velar.

The growth and development of body is different along three axes depending upon position of life form on planet. The impact of pressure, volume and temperature decides the size and shape of individual living being on planet. Every living being maintains individual thermodynamic equilibrium on planets. The thermodynamic equilibrium of living body depends upon four forces and combined action of pressure (p), volume (v) and temperature along three axes on living body. Basing on points of places of articulation, different types of letters are produced by different communities and religious people.

(a) Glottal or Laryngeal (*Swarayantramukhi*): This sound wave emerges from Glottis.

(b) Pharyngeal (*Upalijihwiya*): This sound wave emerges in pharynx near uvula.

(c) Uvular (*Jihwamuliya or Alijihwya*): It emerges from back of tongue or root of tongue.

(d) Guttural or Soft Palatal (*Kanthaya*): This sound wave is produced when back portion of tongue touches soft palate.

(e) Cerebral (*Murdhanya*): This sound wave is produced when tongue bends and touches cerebrum.

(f) Palatal (*Talabya*): They are pronounced from hard palate.

(g) Alveolar (*Vartasya*): The tip of tongue when touches alveolus produces these sound waves.

(h) Dental (*Dantya*): The tip or front portion of tongue touches teeth and produces these sound waves.

(i) Labio-dental (*Dantoshthya*): The sound wave packet produced by combination of upper teeth and lower lips.

(j) Bilabial (*Dwayoshthya*): The sound wave packet produced with the help of both lips.

The letters oscillate from guttural, palatal, retroflex and dental to labial. Letters are shaped by different parts of mouth in which tongue plays definite role in articulation. The front, middle and

7

rear portion of tongue help in pronunciation. The part of tongue used for emission of letters and words depends upon the opening of mouth cavity. Partial opening, half opening and full opening decides the type of letter emitted by mouth. Size and position of lips also varies and it may be fully rounded, partially rounded and un-rounded.

All the planets containing multi-cellular life forms will maintain an outer atmosphere full of life supporting gas bound by outer covering (ozone in case of Earth) for protection from outer radiations. Every planet has different pressure associated with atmosphere, volume of growth and temperature and development of life forms is guided by these factors along three axes. If the temperature increases, volume may decrease or atmosphere may become thinner affecting the mass, size and shape of life forms.

The increase in gravity of planet increases the accumulation of mass inside living body. On the contrary decrease in the gravity reduces contraction and compaction of mass inside body of living beings. The living beings will not survive longer on planets having less gravity and mass accumulated inside tissues of their body will decay. The interaction of fundamental particles takes place along three axes due to pressure, volume and temperature effect of atmosphere. Neutrons effect pressure, protons effect temperature and electrons control volume of letters or '*Akshars*' within atmosphere of planet. Creation of letters like atoms of elements are controlled by temperature, volume and pressure along three axes on planets having atmosphere.

Human beings at higher altitudes will be soft spoken and their language will have more vowels than consonants. Seven *Swaras* or *Suras* create all the voices and speech in human beings. The impact of Sa (Do with frequency 256 Hz), Re (Re with frequency 324.7 Hz), Ga (Mi with frequency 363.4 Hz), Ma (Fa with frequency 407.2 Hz), Pa (Sol with frequency 439.5 Hz), Dha (La with frequency 464.3 Hz) and Ni (Ti with frequency 491.5 Hz) is observed gradually on change of latitude. These waves show increase of energy towards Arctic and Antarctic on earth. The voice and tone of people near equator is harsh and rough whereas the voice becomes sweet and soft towards both the Poles due to use of less consonants and more vowels. Example is tribal languages and languages spoken by isolated people on islands. Atomic theory of sound waves is based on periodic table of elements. Intermixing of sound waves creates words on the pattern of compounds of elements inside atmosphere of planet. Power wave packets possessing mass of atoms of elements behave as 'Sound Wave Packets'.

Sanskrit is the eternal language of nerves of human body and all other languages have emerged from it due to change in number of alphabets. Different languages accepted different number of vowels and consonants in their alphabets. The living beings of different sizes and shapes develop on earth due to inter-relationship among pressure, temperature and volume and their balance along three axes on planet. The earth develops thick ozone layer around atmosphere and contains plenty of oxygen and water at 18°C. The inter-relationship among pressure, volume and temperature of life forms on other planets may be different and different planets show growth of life forms of different sizes and shapes along three axes on planet. The growth pattern and development of internal parts and systems along three axes will remain the same for all species on all planets but the size and outer shape of life forms will depend on pressure, volume and temperature prevailing on that planet. In case temperature of planet increases then volume of living body will decrease and simultaneously pressure will also decrease. In case oxygen, water and ozone layer of planet decreases then size and shape of living body may also decrease along three axes and species with different characteristics may be produced.

Sanskrit is a scientific language. The languages of human beings living in plain areas, valleys and human habitations close to glaciers and snow-fed mountains gradually became refined and complex with emphasis on vowels. The developed and advanced human societies created their own languages depending upon structure and physiology of their body. Many languages developed depending upon twelve pairs of cranial nerves of brain, thirty two pairs of spinal nerves in spinal column and nine body systems. The gravity caused due to pressure, volume, temperature and thirty two classes of crystal symmetry effect the body of human beings along three axes and plays major role in creation of phonetics. Languages develop links with nervous system of body, spiritualism, faith, will power and requirements of self and community. Production of sound is controlled by brain and neuro-linguists study the correlation between brain damage, speech, language deficits and specific linguistic theories. Specific neuro-anatomic structures generally of the left hemisphere are vital for speech and language. For most individuals the left cerebral hemisphere is dominant for language in human beings. Evolution of languages takes place due to impact of spinal nerves, cranial nerves and nine body systems along three axes in every human body.

'Sound wave packets' are power waves containing neutral mass particles of smallest size with charged particles. Spherical wave packets containing neutral mass particles in it create sound waves in power wave region of electromagnetic waves. Sound wave packets are round in shape controlled by three axes attachment within atmosphere. The +Ve charges and -Ve charges effect sound wave packets. Sound wave packets effect animal and human body along three axes. In the absence of charges, both +Ve and -Ve, the sound wave packets are unable to act in vacuum and in space. The sound waves are not audible in space, vacuum and low density areas. Language is developed by every animal and human being depending upon availability of 32 pairs of spinal nerves, 12 pairs of cranial nerves and nine color systems inside body. Creation and development of particular language by human beings effects body parts, organs and systems of animals and human beings.

What underlies the continuous flow of human speech is a sequence of articulatory configurations that can be represented by a series of discrete units. The basis of sound component of human language is a discrete combination that is smeared together in the overlapping fashion. The writing system uses symbols that represent for the most part the sounds produced by particular configuration of vocal tract. A symbol such as 's' therefore represents the vocal tract configuration in which the tongue tip and blade are lightly pressed against the roof of the mouth near the teeth ridge so that when air from the lungs passes between tongue and teeth ridge and strikes the teeth, a hissing sound is produced. All human languages have a regular and consistent set of distinct sound that can be represented phonemically. Some of the symbols common in linguistics are stops, fricatives and affricates etc which is mentioned below:

1. Stops are sounds produced when the airflow is completely obstructed during speech.
2. Fricatives are sounds produced when the airflow is forced through a narrow opening in the vocal tract so that noise created by friction is created.
3. An affricate is a single but complex sound beginning as a stop but releasing secondarily into a fricative.
4. Nasals are voiced oral stops similar to the voiced stops produced with a complete obstruction in the oral cavity. With nasals the airflow and sound energy are channeled into the nasal passages due to lowering of the velum.
5. Liquid sounds are found in the overwhelming majority of the world's languages. The term liquid is a non-technical expression indicating that the sound is smooth and flows easily. Liquids share properties of both consonants and vowels. In the articulation of certain consonants, tongue blade is raised towards the alveolar ridge and in the articulation of vowels air is allowed to pass through the oral cavity without great friction.
6. Glides are vowel-like articulations that precede and follow true vowels. The term glide is based on the observation that the sequence of a glide and a vowel is smooth and continuous gesture.

Language is the outcome of sound waves from living body and emission of symbols synchronizes with development of body parts of living body. The letters of different languages up to number 26 are protective in nature and contain highest energy of elements of periodic table. The letters from number 27 and onwards show destructive trend because the inherent energy starts decreasing. The proponents of Maya dynasty included letters up to 25 (*ma* letter of Devanagari) in their languages and did not include letter 26 and beyond 26 in their languages. In many languages, letters up to 25 and below 25 are created to limit the words within creative and protective regions. Languages with 26 letters were created because element at atomic number 26 possesses highest binding energy. Languages with more number of letters, e.g., 27 and above become destructive in character and were avoided in many languages of tribes and western civilizations. The combination of vowels and consonants of a language create words with specific meaning.

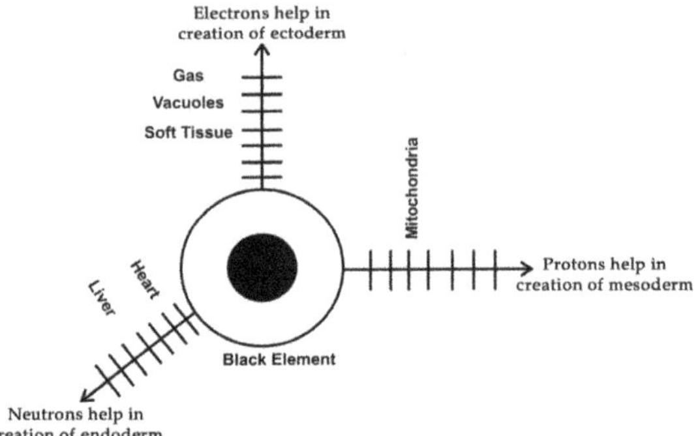

DEVELOPMENT OF CHARACTERS TAKES PLACE INSIDE ANIMAL BODY AND HUMAN BODY ALONG THREE AXES AND HELPS IN CREATION OF VOWELS AND CONSONANTS.

Fig. 1.3

Every nerve of the brain of animal body has link with one star group in the universe at particular wavelength of electromagnetic wave. The planets and stars group are created for every wavelength of electromagnetic waves and in similar manner nerves are created inside human body having attachment with energy of electromagnetic waves. Seven places of Articulation are generally accepted as mentioned below:

(a)   Bilabial

(b)   Labiodental

(c)   Interdental

(d)   Alveolar

(e)   Alveopalatal

(f)   Velar

(g)   Glottal

Speech is continuous and the phonetic segments overlap, yet speakers have little trouble accepting that speech and can be represented by a writing system that uses discrete and linearly written symbols. In Sanskrit the fundamental sound units of a language are consonants and vowels which have persisted since time immemorial and biological and anatomical features of body have shown that consonants and vowels are in turn composed of more basic units called distinctive features of organs inside human body. Phonology is the field of linguistics that studies the structure and systematic patterning of sounds in human language. The term phonology is used in two ways. On one hand, it refers to a description of sounds of particular language and the rules governing the distribution of those sounds. Thus we can talk about the phonology of English, German or any other language. On the other hand it refers to that part of the general theory of human language that is concerned with the universal properties of natural language sound systems.

Every living animal and human being emits words made up of vowels and consonants with definite grammatical arrangement. The impact of body parts, systems and organs along three axes in human body creates many words with different combinations. As improves the alphabets and languages of human beings so increases the receptive capacity of ear of that living being. The differentiation of sound waves by ear improves gradually and language reception by nerves of ear also increases in equal proportion.

The phonemes of all languages may be described in terms of differing subsets of the universally available set of distinctive features. Although all languages draw from the same universal set of features, individual languages differ in the groups of features that make up their phonemes. For example, the features like coronal, lateral, affricate and distributed are found in English, but they never occur together in a single phoneme. In contrast, in Navajo as well as in many other Native American languages of North America, these features do occur together in a single consonant called a lateral affricate; the Navajo word *'tlah'* "ointment" begins with this phoneme, which is represented by two letters *tl* in the Navajo writing system. To take other example, English does not have the feature of rounding in front vowels but many European languages do among them and French, German, Hungarian and Finnish are common. Thus, the widely differing sounds occurring in the world's languages are actually based on different combination of relatively small and restricted set of features.

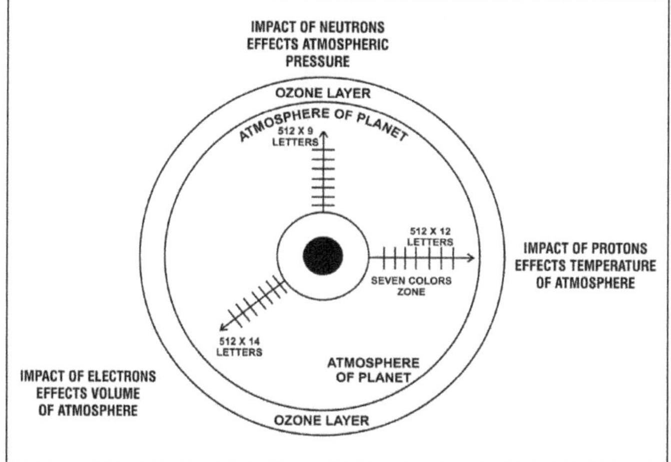

SOUND WAVE PACKETS EXIST WITHIN ATMOSPHERE SURROUNDED BY OZONE LAYER OF A PLANET. POWER WAVES IN THE FREQUENCY RANGE 256 Hz TO 512 Hz CREATE "SOUND WAVE PACKETS' OR LETTERS OR 'AKSHARS' LIKE ATOMS OF ELEMENTS WITHIN ATMOSPHERE OF PLANET EARTH. THE ENERGY OF ELECTROMAGNETIC WAVES OF THREE FUNDAMENTAL SUB-ATOMIC PARTICLES, i.e., ELECTRONS, PROTONS AND

Fig. 1.4

Despite the fact that languages draw upon different features to make up their phonemes, there is high amount of convergence in the sound systems of human language. There are minor differences in pronunciation of letters and words and the consonant systems of many languages throughout the world around same regions of articulation. There are evidences that these particular points of articulation are regions of acoustic stability. For example, the sound produced by tongue-tip contact in the dental and alveolar region is relatively stable acoustically. It is constant regardless of minor shifts in the position of the tongue within this region. The regions of articulation between commonly occurring points of articulation, i.e., region on the border between dental or alveolar region and the palatal region are regions of acoustic instability. Here even a small shift in the position of tongue leads to radical changes in acoustic properties of the sound. It is articulation made in the vocal tract regions of acoustic stability that there is considerable "leeway" for tongue position. This leeway permits rapid speech and co-articulation effect when the target area is larger because an exact articulatory target is not necessary. There are many important differences between languages spoken throughout the world. The set of distinctive features is a set that is available to all languages and all features and combination of features are actually not found in each individual language.

The consistency and regularity of the correspondences among daughter languages of the Indo-European language family establishes their historical relationship. None of the descendant languages preserve all the phonetic features of hypothesized proto-language for the words under consideration. Sanskrit is wholly conservative language in terms of preserving the original consonants. Sanskrit language contains 32 consonants and 16 vowels which are related to twelve body parts, fourteen types of organs with ions and nine systems inside human body. Language reconstruction and establishment of language relatedness involves many features like, longitude, latitude, altitude, geographical features of earth and evolution of human race at particular point of time. It is said that Khmer languages has highest letters. Khmer language (Cambodian) has highest 74 number of letters. The alphabet consists of 33 consonants, 23 vowels and 18 independent vowels.

We can shed light on the ultimate origin or ancient history of human language through analytical techniques and comparative methods. Most of the languages show independent origin and maintained their individuality at many isolated places and pockets on earth. Many languages originated basing on their religious practices. Many languages having independent and isolated origin gradually mixed with other languages due to inter-marriages between different tribes, groups, clans and races. Many tribal languages having independent and isolated origin gradually mixed with other languages due to migration of different tribes, groups, clans and races. On flat lands and civilizations developing near major rivers the languages having independent and isolated origin gradually mixed with other languages due to acculturation between different tribes, groups, clans and races. The languages having independent origin but spoken by majority of the groups gradually mixed with other languages due to integration between different tribes, groups, clans and races. Languages are always changed by communities and their transmission and ultimate sharing of changes among speakers is observed in many linguistic communities. The ultimate changes in the languages of speakers bears the impact of temperature, climate, altitudinal conditions and religion of that community.

Sanskrit language has evolved on scientific lines of vocal cord, spinal nerves, cranial nerves and seven body systems developed on seven colors system. The language based on nerves of human beings accompanied with chanting of words of particular frequency evolved in mountainous snowy areas of northern countries and Central Asia called as Sanskrit with *Devanagari* script and was common among group of intelligent people or *'Aryans'* or intellectual people in ancient times.

Evolution of languages begins with creation of vowels and then alphabets are created by living animals. Vowels are created due to anti-matter force acting on animals. The number of vowels increases from one and may reach up to sixteen in number. Simultaneous to development of anti-matter vowels, matter waves create consonant letters which are heavy as matter waves and create complex and jumbled words. Consonants are generally double the number of vowels due to anti-matter and matter force acting on animals and human beings. The complexity of living animal body and human body increases during evolution and so increases the number and complexity of letters of alphabets. The highest level of evolution of vowels and consonants is observed in the living body having nine body systems, twelve pairs of cranial nerves and thirty two pairs of spinal nerves. Evolution of body parts takes place along three axes inside animal body in the similar pattern of nucleosynthesis of elements of periodic table in the universe.

If a change begins in one area, it is possible to follow its progress through time and space as it moves in wave-like manner through a community of speakers. The change and modification in language is always perceived as group and community approach. When two separate areas are sources of changes, the changes spread in an overlapping manner and inter-mix both the languages. Differences are often noticed in pronunciation of languages by different groups of the same community. It may happen due to change in climatic conditions, altitude, longitude, latitude, temperature and geographical conditions. The speakers of one area may have an influence on neighboring speakers and features of language, e.g., pronunciation, vocabulary, morphology and syntax can be assimilated by neighboring groups in course of time. The neighboring groups in turn can pass on above features to further neighbors so that the rule appears to move wave-like through successive groups of speakers in different communities.

Two important facts decide the efficacy and acceptance of any language in the world. One is its attachment with nervous system of human body and other is number of alphabets in that language. The nervous connection decides the efficacy of language, e.g., Sanskrit language. The number of alphabets in that language links it with binding energy of alphabets and relationship of four forces with time, e. g. English language. The languages originate in different areas and gradually spread, meet, cross and overlap to create new languages in different communities subject to their survival and acceptance in that community.

At present it can be said that English language has established its acceptance throughout the world in different communities and countries. English language has survived in different pockets of the world and has been accepted by many communities as common language. English language with 26 letters has proved its acceptability by different groups of people throughout the world. It bears the impact of Fe element with highest binding energy having atomic number 26 and occupying core and center of the planet and centre of human body in compound form. The sound waves coming out from the vocal cord of human beings are like smaller 'wave packets' of alphabets, letters and words made up of power waves within atmospheric covering of earth. These 'wave packets' of alphabets, letters and words with lower wavelengths and higher energy act as electromagnetic waves and their energy effects and shapes the human body. It is the reason for saying that sound wave packets made up of smaller packets of power waves are more powerful than energy of electromagnetic waves of seven colors which creates life forms on planets. The tongue position inside mouth of human being changes according to number of alphabets in the language and religion of that community. Thus pronunciation and phonetics of one particular community will be different from pronunciation of other communities. The number of alphabets in different civilizations vary and some may have 118 letters in their language in total. Some example of common languages spoken in different countries of the world are as follows:

(a) **Spanish: Spanish language is common in Europe. Spanish language is written with 26 Latin letters of English alphabet and 27th letter is ene, n. In total it contains 27 letters.**

(b) **English: English language is created with 26 letters in alphabets.**

(c) **Pali: The language was common in eastern India in the past. Pali or Magadhan is a middle Indo-Aryan liturgical language native to the Indians. Pali is normally written in Sinhala, Khmer, Burmese, Devanagari, Lao or Thai scripts. The current script has shapes based on those of ancient Brahmi and Pallava, which were the ancestors of Indian scripts.**

(d) **Hindi: The language having 36 consonants and 16 vowels.**

(e) **Sanskrit: The language having 32 consonants and 16 vowels.**

(f) **Greek: The language is common in Europe. It contains 24 letters including seven vowels and all of its letters are capitals. It is actually the fore bearer of all European alphabets.**

(g) **Chinese: The language is common in China and many other countries. Chinese characters are logograms used in writing of Chinese and other languages.**

(h) **Urdu: The language common among Islamic people in India. The Urdu alphabet has up to 40 letters in total. 39 basic letters of Urdu alphabet is written in calligraphic Nastaliq script whereas Arabic is more commonly in Naskh style.**

(i) **Arabic: The language common in western Asia. The Arabic alphabet has 28 letters and all represent consonants. It is written from right to left. Twenty two of the letters are those of Semitic alphabet from which it descended and rest six letters represent sound not used in language written in the alphabet.**

(j) **Old Indian languages: Some languages have 118 alphabets based on number of elements in the Periodic Table. Some have** many different numbers of consonants and vowels in old tribal areas.

(k) French: The language is common in France. The French alphabet is based on 26 letters of Latin alphabet, upper case and lower case with five diacritics and two orthographic literatures.

(l) German: The language is common in Germany. German alphabet consists of 26 letters in total. There are combined letters and three umlauted forms. An umlaut is the pair of dots placed over certain vowels in German.

(m) Persian: The language common in West Asian countries. Persian language is written in version of Arabic script with 28 letters and is one of the old languages of world. Words are written from right to left and numbers are written from left to right.

(n) Bangala: The language common in eastern India. There are 51 letters in Bengali alphabet which contains 11 vowels and 40 consonants.

(o) Japanese: The language common in Japan and Eastern Asia. In modern Japanese, hiragana and katakana contain 46 basic characters or 71 characters including diacritics.

(p) Telugu: The language spoken in Andhra Pradesh. There are 56 Telugu letters in total.

(q) Tamil: One of the oldest languages of the world and common in Tamil Nadu. There are 247 letters in Tamil language.

(r) Malayalam: The language spoken in Kerala province. Malayalam script is Brahmic script common in Kerala. It has 56 Malayalam letters.

(s) Kannada: The language common in Karnataka. Kannada Varnamala consists of 49 letters which contains 13 vowels.

(t) Mandarin: It is common in China and adjoining countries.

(u) Russian: It is commonly spoken in Russia.

(v) Cantonese: This language is common in China,

(w) Korean: It is common language in North Korea and South Korea.

(x) Vietnamese: A common language of Vietnam.

(y) **Tagalog: It is common language in Philippines.**

(z) **Armenian: It is common language of Armenia.**

(aa) **Gurmukhi: Gurmukhi alphabet was developed by the Sikhs. Gurmukhi script contains 41 letters.**

1.1 CREATION OF LANGUAGES

The languages are created and produced by different animals and human beings depending upon their position, place, time and degree of evolution in any community. The degree of civilization of any community helps in developing and refining the language spoken by that community and determines the number of alphabets, consonants and vowels. The musical scale with seven frequencies have particular pleasing effect on the human ear. A widely used musical scale, called diatonic scale, has eight frequencies covering an octave. Each frequency is called a note. In the covered places or objects, absorption and reflection of sound waves is clearly observed. The sound waves can reach a listener directly from the source as well as after reflection from wall, covering or ceiling. The vocal cords of animals and human beings produce sound waves as 'wave packets'. The frequency of wave packets emitted by different animals varies from one animal to other and constitutes building blocks of different languages. Most of the languages show independent origin and maintain their individuality at many isolated places and pockets on earth.

The words are created by vocal cord and mouth parts of every animal under the guidance of nervous system and all body parts of animal and human being. The words are expression of a particular cause or sentiment with specific meaning for every animal. The words emitted by vocal cord and mouth of animal and human being effect the body parts and organs of every living body within atmospheric covering of planet. The words are made up of wave packets of sound waves and show definite impact on body of every living being through energy of electromagnetic waves. The sound waves inherent in language create words or wave packets at particular frequency which acts as electromagnetic waves of low frequency effecting the body of living beings. During evolution of languages, it is observed that the language having 26 alphabets is extremely strong, durable, acceptable and easiest mode of conversation and understanding. As much is the number of alphabets in a language so high is the complication inside body of living animals and human beings. Similarly, reduction in the number of alphabets increases vocal efficiency of animal body subject to a minimum of 26 alphabets in the language. Development of languages can be categorized in following manner.

1.1.1 CREATION OF LANGUAGE BASED ON POSITIVE CHARGE OF ATOM (CATIONS)

Any community may develop language and alphabets depending upon the positive charge associated with atoms of elements, words and alphabets. It will help in strengthening the community, migration to better places and improvement of health of that community. It is observed as worship of lion, elephant, black god, male gods, father and grand father etc with tough words, harsh language and tough accent. It is associated with positive charge of atoms of elements and it will increase fat, cancerous growth and outgrowth of body parts in human body. This language develops in communities having worship of father, grandfather, son and grandson or male deities etc. This may lead to reduction in number of alphabets of language of that community.

1.1.2 CREATION OF LANGUAGE BASED ON NEGATIVE CHARGE OF ATOM (ANIONS)

Any community may develop language and alphabets depending upon the negative charge associated in atoms of elements, letters, words and alphabets. It is observed as worship of female idols, animals and female goddess with sweet and soft language, accent and tone. It will help in strengthening the community, migration to better places and improvement of health of that community. It is associated with negative charge of atoms of elements and it will reduce fat, cancerous growth and outgrowth of body parts in human body and produce lean and thin body. This language develops in communities having emphasis and accent on mother, grandmother, daughter, grand daughter and female deities etc. This type of community develop more number of alphabets in their language.

1.1.3 CREATION OF LANGUAGE WITH FIXED ALPHABETS

The seven colors cycle moves for one day each due to rotation of earth and makes a cycle of seven days week. The inner mass remains locked in 24 hours time frame of a day and its relationship is seen in crystal structures found on astral bodies. Every day in a week has fixed 24 hours time period but its mass component is variable due to different wavelength of colors in seven colors cycle. In the universe time frame being fixed is more powerful than the mass component, which is variable and remains locked inside time frame. The 24 hours time period of a day is the timekeeper for earth and it acts as point of stagnation for our solar system. The time period of movement of stars and planets above 24 hours and below 24 hours may show variable value but period of movement at 24 hours remains constant around pole star. Due to seven types of ions, seven color electromagnetic waves, seven energy levels of elliptical orbits and seven crystal systems, movement of time takes place in cycle of seven days of 24 hours rotation each on earth. It may be the reason that Greek language has 24 letters in total. Twenty four consonants, from *Ka* to *Bha* create majority of the words and sentences because they maintain equilibrium of movement with planets. Example is *Bharat* with 24 spokes (eight fold formation of octet in 8 *prahar* yielding *bha + ra + ta*) for perfect rotation of any particle, living body and astral body etc. Time period moves in eight *prahars* of three hours each during every rotation. Spinal nerves are fixed for every animal and human being and number of alphabets of their language depends upon religion, phonetics and pronunciation of that community.

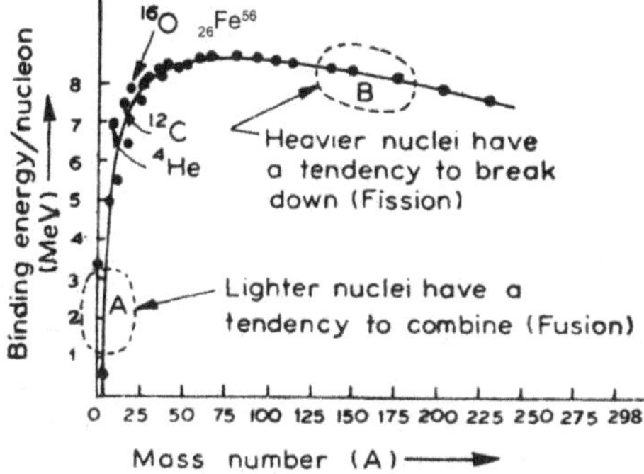

IN ENGLISH LANGUAGE TWENTY SIX LETTERS ARE COMMON DUE TO BINDING ENERGY OF ELEMENTS. Fe ELEMENT HAVING HIGHEST BINDING ENERGY OCCUPIES CENTER OF HUMAN BODY AND BEYOND 26

Fig. 1.5

1.1.4 CREATION OF LANGUAGE BASED ON 26 ATOMIC NUMBERS WITH 26 ALPHABETS

Any community may develop language and alphabets depending upon the positive charge associated with elements, words and alphabets. It will help in strengthening the community, migration to better places and improvement of health of that community. One of the example is English language which makes community hardy, robust, cosmopolitan and long lasting. Ferro-magnet with Fe element having atomic number 26 has definite impact on human body because Fe element has highest binding energy.

The English language has 26 letters, e.g., a, b, c, d, e, f, g, h, i, j, k, l, m, n, o, p, q, r, s, t, u, v, w, x, y and z. These letters have profound impact on settlement of matter with highest binding energy inside body of human beings on the patterns of binding energy of elements of periodic table. Highest binding energy is experienced at atomic number 26 and this element tends to shift towards core and centre of all plants, animals, human beings, astral bodies, planets and stars. The language contains five vowels and 21 consonants. Geomagnetism, geomagnetic field (GMF), Bio-magnetism, Magneto-biology and electro-magneto-biology are terms which deal with cure of disease by ferromagnetic and geomagnetic activity of earth. The realization started with interaction between GMF and life processes. Research works have proved that (a) disturbance in the level of GMF significantly influences many physiological parameters, i.e., haematological, cardiovascular, endocrine, neural activity and EEG etc and (b) many patients with chronic disorders such as rheumatoid arthritis, osteo-arthritis, spondylosis, who had poor response to various forms of therapy, when exposed to Pulsed Magnetic Fields, experienced permanent relief. The effect of will power drags all the breath in human being towards brain and due to higher energy value pituitary gland releases secretions which increases kinetic energy of the human body. The centre and hub of every animal, human being, planet and star are occupied by $^{56}_{26}Fe$ element in crystalline compound form.

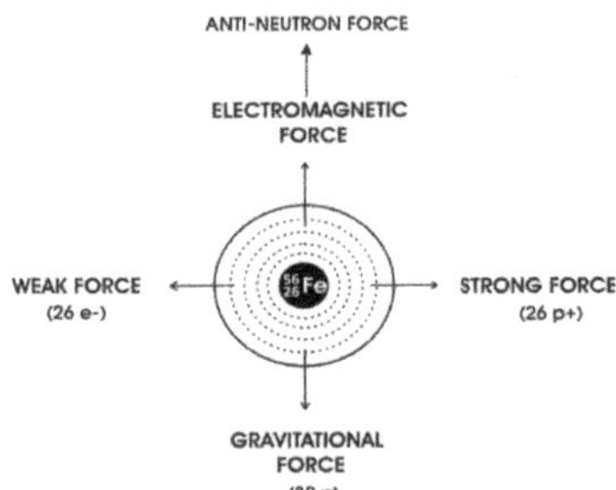

'*YA*' IS THE 26TH LETTER OF SANSKRIT LANGUAGE. BOTH COMBINED TOGETHER SHOW THAT ATOM OF $^{56}_{26}Fe$ ELEMENT EXPERIENCES FOUR FORCES EQUALLY ALONG FOUR DIRECTIONS. THE MAGNITUDE OF SPIN OF SUB-ATOMIC PARTICLES OWING TO ANTI-CLOCKWISE MOTION AND CLOCKWISE MOTION BECOMES EQUAL TO EACH OTHER AT ATOMIC NUMBER 26 IN ELEMENT. POSITIVE CHARGE AND NEGATIVE CHARGE ON ATOMS OF Fe HAVING EQUAL MOMENTA HELP IN CREATION OF FERROMAGNETIC AXLES ON EVERY PLANET AND STAR. ALL THE PLANETS AND STARS MOVE ON THEIR AXLES AND SHOW AXILIARY MOVEMENTS ALONG THREE AXES IN SPACE. THIS AXILIARY MOVEMENT CONNECTS THEM WITH THEIR ADJOINING PLANETS AND STARS IN SPACE. FULL LENGTH OF AXLE IS PROJECTED AS HYPOTHETICAL AXLE INSIDE PLANETS AND STARS FOR AXILIARY MOVEMENT OF ALL PLANETS AND STARS ON THEIR AXLES IN SPACE. AXLES ACTUALLY EXIST AS SMALLER PIECE OF FERROMAGNET INSIDE PLANETS AND STARS ALONG THREE AXES. IN THE FERROMAGNET, ATOMS OF Fe MAY REPEL EACH OTHER BUT IT IS SUPPRESSED DUE TO MAGNETIC LINES OF FORCE ON ACCOUNT OF ELECTRIC CHARGE OF 26 e- AND 26 p+ PASSING THROUGH NORTH POLE AND SOUTH POLE. MAGNETIC LINES OF FORCE BALANCE WEAK FORCE AND STRONG FORCE THROUGH ELECTRIC CHARGE OF 26 e- AND 26 p+ OF ATOM. ELECTROMAGNETIC FORCE AND GRAVITATIONAL FORCE BALANCE EACH OTHER THROUGH MAGNETIC AXIS OF ATTRACTION PASSING THROUGH NORTH POLE AND SOUTH POLE AND CREATE MAGNETIC DOMAIN. SPIN OF THE ATOM OF $^{56}_{26}Fe$ CREATES MAGNETIC AXIS OF ATTRACTION IN SPACE DUE TO ELECTROMAGNETIC FORCE AND GRAVITATIONAL FORCE. MAGNETIC AXIS OF ATTRACTION CONNECTS NORTH POLE WITH SOUTH POLE OF ALL PLANETS AND STARS.

Fig. 1.6

The outside Ferro magnet and its magnetic field try to bring human body to normalcy in relation to iron element. One end of Ferro magnet on earth tries to align itself with Pole Star whereas other end of magnet aligns with centre, core and hub. The head of human being, when kept in north direction, aligns itself with Pole Star and brings human body parallel to rotation of earth about its axis. The storage of time is balanced inside all cells of human beings and age of human being is limited by oxygen retaining capacity in solid, liquid and gas forms. The English language with 26 alphabets is highly robust language and can survive in difficult terrains of the planet. The black center of human body containing black element links this language with hub of body. It is the reason that English language becomes hardy, aggressive and cosmopolitan. Due to Fe having 26 atomic number in the center and hub of body. This language becomes body language and dominates over other languages. Reduction in the number of alphabets increases efficiency of human body and human body acts more effectively upto 26 number of alphabets.

1.1.5 CREATION OF LANGUAGE BASED ON 30 ATOMIC NUMBER WITH 30 ALPHABETS

Some languages develop with 30 letters in alphabet. Reduction in number of alphabets depends upon tongue position and speaking capability of that community.

1.1.6 CREATION OF LANGUAGE WITH 32 ALPHABETS

Some languages develop with 32 letters in alphabet depending upon 32 classes of crystal symmetry.

1.1.7 CREATION OF LANGUAGE BASED ON 32 CONSONANTS AND 16 VOWELS

Sanskrit language has developed on scientific lines of vocal cord, spinal nerves, cranial nerves and seven body systems developed due to seven colors in human body. It produces the most symmetrical body structure on earth. The language based on nerves of human beings accompanied with chanting of words of particular frequency developed in snowy mountains and Central Asia called as Sanskrit with *Devanagari* script (so called language of gods) and was common among group of intelligent people or Aryans or intellectual rhishis in ancient times. It was given different names by different communities and gradually mixing with other languages it spread to all countries in the world. Any community may develop language and alphabets depending upon the charge associated with elements, words and alphabets. It will help in strengthening the community, migration to better places and improvement of health conditions of that community. Sanskrit language is the original language developed with following:

(1) Vowels: Vowels are sixteen in number emitted by eight pairs of Cervical nerves,

(2) Consonants: Consonants are thirty two in number emitted by thoracic nerves.

The 'sound wave packets' like power wave packets, which are emitted from the vocal cord of animals and human beings, move towards atmosphere, ozone layer, space and convert into electromagnetic waves of higher frequency and low energy. These wave packets effect the animal body and groups of different genus and species on planets and effects growth of animal body along three axes. The sound waves are of different types emitted by different organs of animals and human beings, e.g.,

(a) Gutturals (*kanthaya*): (*Ka - Varga : Ka to Anga*) - These letters are pronounced with the help of throat.

(b) Palatals (*talabya*): (*Cha - Varga : Cha to Eina*) - These letters are pronounced with the help of jaw.

(c) Cerebrals (*murdhanya*): (*Ta – Varga : Ta to Na*) - These letters are pronounced with tongue hitting the roof of the mouth.

(d) Dentals (*dantya*): (*Ta – Varga : Ta to Na*) - These letters are pronounced with the help of teeth.

(e) Labials (*oushthya*): (*Pa – Varga : Pa to Ma*) - These letters are pronounced with the help of lips (upper and lower lips should meet each other).

(f) Soft Consonants (*Antastha*): (*Ya* to *Va*) - Four letters from *Ya* to *Va* are emitted from mouth as Soft Ungrouped Consonants.

(g) Sibilant Consonants (*Oushma*): (*Sha* to *Sa*) - Three Hard consonants from *Sha* to *Sa* are created with a hissing noise. They are known as *Aghosh Sangharshi*.

The periodic motion of waves gives birth to circular motion which engulfs mass particles and creates sub-atomic particles, atoms of elements, astral bodies, planets and stars. The contraction of waves leads to production of particles of smaller size and its gradual culmination into black region. Particles appear out of waves by "Self Gravitation" process due to change in density of the medium at different places in space in the universe. Thirty two consonants of this language correspond to *ka, kha, ga, gha, anga, cha, chha, ja, jha, iena, ta, tha, da, dha, anda, ta, tha, da, dha, na, pa, pha, ba, bha, ma, ya, ra, la, va, sha, sha, sa* (32 consonants in the form of 32 vertical groups of elements). The 16 vowels of this language correspond to *a, aa,, i, ee, u, oo, rhi, rhee, lri, lree, e, ai, o, au, am* and *ah*.

Vowels - अ आ इ ई उ ऊ ऋ ॠ ऌ ॡ ए ऐ ओ औ अं अः

Consonants -
क ख ग घ ङ
च छ ज झ ञ
ट ठ ड ढ ण
त थ द ध न
प फ ब भ म
य र ल व
श ष स

Emergence of vowels and consonants from nervers of human body was well known to people in the past. They had clear idea about production of words from letters and pattern of formation of words are similar in all languages of the world in all religions. Father, brother and related words are produced from *Pa, Pha, Ba* and *Bha* letters of Sanskrit languagage. Papa, father, brother, *pappa, bapa, bhai, bhaia, bhaijaan, fufa, abbajaan, bhaiajaan, pater* and *pitashree* etc have emerged from four consonants *Pa Pha, Ba* and *Bha*. Similarly, Mama, Mummy, Mumshe, *Amma, Ammijaan, Matashree, Mater, Maousi* and *Sita,* etc have emerged from *Ma* consonant and onwards up to *Sa* as last letter. Words were created from letters produced by nerves and this fact was well known to people throughout the world in the past.

Sanskrit and Hindi mixed languages are based on emissions of 32 pairs of spinal nerves, 12 pairs of cranial nerves and nine body systems along three axes. Nerve-made languages control the nerves of animal body or human body like buttons of piano or musical instruments. The languages show impact on particular and specific nerves of every body part, organ and system and can be used for cure of diseases of living body. The fact of emergence of language from spinal nerves of human body was well known to people living on earth long back. The civilization of human being was finished many times by asteroids, diseases and wars. Knowledge and science with present level of intelligence was known to human beings and it emerged again and again on earth during period of one cycle of 43.20,000 years on earth. People learnt about science and knowledge again and again.

The nervous origin of language was known to people in every part of earth and that is the reason that many words are common for many things, e.g, father and mother etc. Creation of consonants begins with Ka having lowest energy and goes up to *Pa, Pha, Ba* and *Bha* (24th consonant) having highest energy. Letters from one to twenty four show movement of energy in 24 parts of the sphere froming crystals with attachment along three axes. From twenty fifth letter onwards up to thirty two letters, crystal symmetry weakens and produces crystals with less symmetry. From 25th letter, *Ma* onwards, energy goes down and produces feminine sound and electronegative energy. From *Ma* onwards up to *Sa* the consonant letters show prominence of negative energy. Masculine representations and male figures are emitted by *Pa, Pha, Ba* and *Bha* in all the languages throughout the world. Similarly, feminine representations and female figures with female sound are emitted by Ma onwards up to Sa in all the languages of the world.

Combination of letters of Sanskrit language with letters of other languages are found everywhere. Conjugations of *tla, tsa, kham, arr* and similar mixed letters are seen in many languages throughout the world. It shows that nervous origin of letters was known to people in all the parts of the world and Sanskrit was accepted as language in some form or other in every community of the world.

All spoken human languages have sound systems made up of consonants and vowels. The languages vary greatly in the number of these sound types. All the languages function successfully as communication systems in spite of their extremely different numbers of speech sounds. Despite numerical differences the vowels found in the world's languages are often quite similar and are produced in similar portions of the mouth. A group of sounds that may be unfamiliar to speakers of English and of European and Asian languages are the so-called click sounds found in several African languages. In the production of clicks, the tongue makes a closure with roof of the mouth not just at one point but at two points (both at the velum and at one other point farthest forward). The primary airflow is created by making the sealed-off space larger, creating a partial vacuum, usually by lowering the tongue and jaw. When the front stoppage is released and air rushes into the partial vacuum, a click sound results. Some click sounds are made by English speakers and although they are not part of the English language itself, they are still used for communication.

1.1.8 CREATION   OF   LANGUAGE WITH 33 ALPHABETS

Sanskrit is the human body language and it relates to human nerves. Science developed at many places throughout the world and different branches got prominence at many places. In Central Asia, knowledge of Astronomy, Astrophysics, Planetary Science, Spherical Astronomy, dimensions and their inter-relationship with other branches developed. Panini, Patanjali, Pingala and many other Sanskrit grammar experts developed their arena of writings and produced many texts on different subjects. Panini wrote Sanskrit with 33 letters which included '*Ha*' as last letter of consonants. Thirty three letters were related to 33 crores of Gods. Language developed with 33 letters in alphabet and gave relationship with other sciences. People came to know about sphere, *Pi* (22/7), eleven dimensions and its application along three axes producing 33 letters in consonants. Scientists like Aryabhatta and Bhaskar Rao etc have considerable impact on development of languages and grammar at that point of time. Improvement of knowledge about space, time and dimensions (11 x 3) had high impact on development of different languages throughout the world. Panini and other contemporary Sanskrit experts knew about geometry, trigonometry and programming of language.

1.1.9 CREATION   OF   LANGUAGE WITH 34 ALPHABETS

Some languages developed with 34 letters in alphabet depending upon 17 x 2 symmetry.

1.1.10 CREATION OF LANGUAGE BASED ON 36 CONSONANTS AND 16 VOWELS

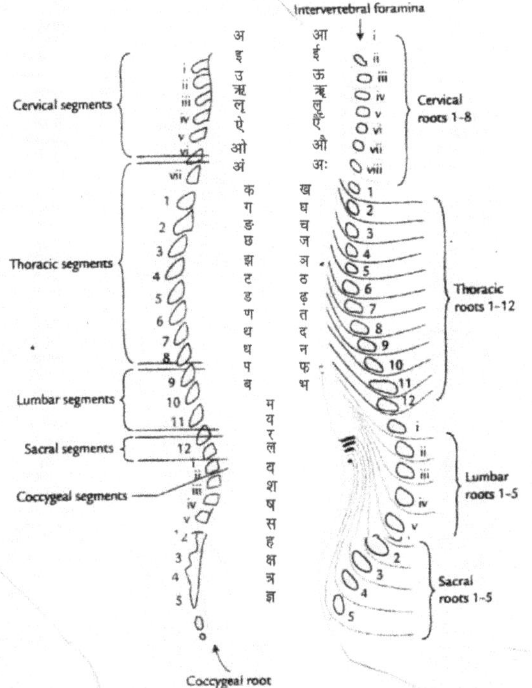

IMPACT OF VOWELS AND CONSONANTS ON CERVICAL AND SPINAL NERVES OF HUMAN BODY
Fig. 1.8

The human body science tallies with language science, number of nerves, impact of nerves on different parts of body and creation of 118 elements of periodic table in the universe. Nothing has developed in isolation in the universe and emission of 'sound wave packets' is guided by pressure, volume and temperature along three axes within atmosphere of planet earth. The ideas of Sanskrit language narrated are generally accepted because it tallies with other parallel sciences of the universe.

23

Different Sanskrit grammar scholars have given their opinion regarding number of vowels and consonants and their link with nerves. Many grammarians have opined that vowels are 16 and consonants are 36 in number as given below.

Vowels - अ आ इ ई उ ऊ ऋ ॠ ऌ ॡ ए ऐ ओ औ अं अः

Consonants -

क ख ग घ ङ
च छ ज झ ञ
ट ठ ड ढ ण
त थ द ध न
प फ ब भ म
य र ल व
श ष स ह
क्ष त्र ज्ञ

The impact of letters created with consonants and vowels on spinal nerves is shown below:

अ	आ	इ	ई	उ	ऊ	ए	ऐ	ओ	औ	अं	अः
क	का	कि	की	कु	कू	के	कै	को	कौ	कं	कः
ख	खा	खि	खी	खु	खू	खे	खै	खो	खौ	खं	खः
ग	गा	गि	गी	गु	गू	गे	गै	गो	गौ	गं	गः
घ	घा	घि	घी	घु	घू	घे	घै	घो	घौ	घं	घः
च	चा	चि	ची	चु	चू	चे	चै	चो	चौ	चं	चः
छ	छा	छि	छी	छु	छू	छे	छै	छो	छौ	छं	छः
ज	जा	जि	जी	जु	जू	जे	जै	जो	जौ	जं	जः
झ	झा	झि	झी	झु	झू	झे	झै	झो	झौ	झं	झः
ट	टा	टि	टी	टु	टू	टे	टै	टो	टौ	टं	टः
ठ	ठा	ठि	ठी	ठु	ठू	ठे	ठै	ठो	ठौ	ठं	ठः
ड	डा	डि	डी	डु	डू	डे	डै	डो	डौ	डं	डः
ढ	ढा	ढि	ढी	ढु	ढू	ढे	ढै	ढो	ढौ	ढं	ढः
ण	णा	णि	णी	णु	णू	णे	णै	णो	णौ	णं	णः
त	ता	ति	ती	तु	तू	ते	तै	तो	तौ	तं	तः
थ	था	थि	थी	थु	थू	थे	थै	थो	थौ	थं	थः
द	दा	दि	दी	दु	दू	दे	दै	दो	दौ	दं	दः
ध	धा	धि	धी	धु	धू	धे	धै	धो	धौ	धं	धः
न	ना	नि	नी	नु	नू	ने	नै	नो	नौ	नं	नः
प	पा	पि	पी	पु	पू	पे	पै	पो	पौ	पं	पः
फ	फा	फि	फी	फु	फू	फे	फै	फो	फौ	फं	फः
ब	बा	बि	बी	बु	बू	बे	बै	बो	बौ	बं	बः
भ	भा	भि	भी	भु	भू	भे	भै	भो	भौ	भं	भः
म	मा	मि	मी	मु	मू	मे	मै	मो	मौ	मं	मः
य	या	यि	यी	यु	यू	ये	यै	यो	यौ	यं	यः
र	रा	रि	री	रु	रू	रे	रै	रो	रौ	रं	रः
ल	ला	लि	ली	लु	लू	ले	लै	लो	लौ	लं	लः
व	वा	वि	वी	वु	वू	वे	वै	वो	वौ	वं	वः
श	शा	शि	शी	शु	शू	शे	शै	शो	शौ	शं	शः
ष	षा	षि	षी	षु	षू	षे	षै	षो	षौ	षं	षः

स	सा	सि	सी	सु	सू	से	सै	सो	सौ	सं	स:
ह	हा	हि	ही	हु	हू	हे	है	हो	हौ	हं	ह:
क्ष	क्षा	क्षि	क्षी	क्षु	क्षू	क्षे	क्षै	क्षो	क्षौ	क्षं	क्ष:
त्र	त्रा	त्रि	त्री	त्रु	त्रू	त्रे	त्रै	त्रो	त्रौ	त्रं	त्र:
ज्ञ	ज्ञा	ज्ञि	ज्ञी	ज्ञु	ज्ञू	ज्ञे	ज्ञै	ज्ञो	ज्ञौ	ज्ञं	ज्ञ:

CONSONANTS MIXED WITH 12 VOWELS ARE SHOWN ABOVE
Table 1.1

However, others do not agree with this view because sixteenth vowel letter '*Ah*' is repeated as '*Ha*' in 33rd consonant letter. Further, last three consonant letters, '*Aksha*', '*Tra*' and "*Jnana*' are mixed letters prepared by combination of two or more letters.

The electromagnetic waves from 4000Å to 7500Å behave as waves and make the perceptible world of color waves with electrons moving out from solid particles as waves. In this range mass particles move in the form of floating energy as waves and behave as 'wave packets'. The sound waves emitted by animals and human beings form electromagnetic waves. The sound waves can convert into electromagnetic waves in any medium in space. They show their impact on visible spectra (4000 Å to 7500 Å) of electromagnetic waves. The sound waves effect the growth and development of body parts in living animals and human beings. The electromagnetic waves in the wavelength range 1×10^4 - 1×10^7 having frequency between 256 Hz to 512 Hz effect body organs of living human beings. The voice box in the mouth of human beings is one of the prominent sources of sound. It can produce sound waves having frequency range between 100-1100 Hz.

Life forms will be the same on all planets in terms of chemical composition, building blocks, biochemistry and genes etc. The actual shape, size and mass of life forms will be decided by expansion and contraction of matter along three axes on planets. The size, shape and mass of life forms on earth and their inner and outer features will always be dictated by three axes contraction of matter and simultaneous three axes expansion of human body.

1.1.11 CREATION OF LANGUAGE BASED ON ATOMIC NUMBERS WITH 54 LETTERS

Some languages develop with 54 letters in alphabet. It is due to 23 pairs of chromosomes which produces 46 consonant letters and 8 vowel letters. In total it becomes 54 in number.

1.1.12 CREATION OF LANGUAGE BASED ON ATOMIC NUMBERS WITH 86 LETTERS

Some languages develop with 86 letters in alphabet. Increase in number of alphabets above 52 is rarely found.

1.1.13 CREATION OF LANGUAGE BASED ON 118 LETTERS

Any community may develop language and alphabets depending upon charge associated with elements, words and alphabets. It will help in strengthening the community, migration to better places and improvement of health of that community. The alphabet may contain 118 vowels and consonants and their impact will be observed on entire body of living being.

1.1.14 CREATION OF LANGUAGE BASED ON 12 BLOCKS, 16 (1 + 7 + 7 + 1 = NINE SYSTEMS ON COLORS) AND 14 MATTER ZONES (2 + 6 + 10 + 14) IN GROUPS AS PERIODIC TABLE OF ELEMENTS (DEVELOPMENT OF LETTERS AND WORDS OF SANSKRIT LANGUAGE)

The present day prevalent Sanskrit is based on above factors and characteristics which shape the human body. The human body is effected along three axes and impact of different forces is observed along three axes.

Sanskrit is the language of intellectuals who migrated probably from places full of snow and protect life forms for millions of years inside snow. The corpse remains protected inside cold snowy mountains and after getting heat becomes active and vibrant. Ancient people emerged from these areas who contained knowledge about development of body parts along three axes. Sanskrit language is based on emissions of 32 pairs of spinal nerves, 12 pairs of cranial nerves and nine body systems along three axes. This language controls the nerves of animal body or human body like buttons of piano or musical instruments. The language shows impact on particular and specific nerves of every body organ and system and can be used for curing the diseases of living body. Sanskrit has emerged and developed on scientific lines and shows links with all parallel disciplines of science.

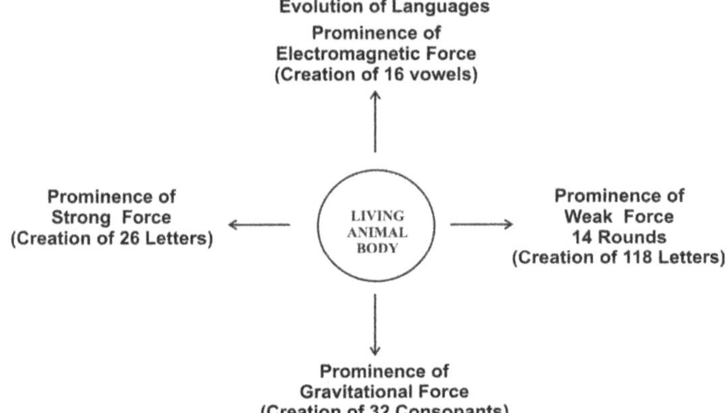

EVOLUTION OF LANGUAGE AND BODY PARTS OF LIVING ANIMAL BODY AND HUMAN BODY TAKES PLACE DUE TO IMPACT OF FOUR FORCES. THE HIGHEST EVOLVED ANIMAL BODY WILL SHOW ABOVE PATTERN OF GROWTH OF VOWELS AND CONSONANTS. WORDS ARE CREATED FROM LETTERS AS 'WAVE PACKETS' BY VOCAL CORDS OF ANIMALS AND HUMAN BEINGS. ARRANGEMENT OF LETTERS INTO 32 X 16 = 512 LETTERS IN JUMBLED FORM CREATES MANY WORDS WHICH EFFECT HUMAN BODY. CREATION OF WORDS AS 'WAVE PACKETS' TAKES PLACE DUE TO THREE AXES ATTACHMENT OF ANIMALS AND HUMAN BODIES. THIRTY TWO CONSONANTS IN ASSOCIATION WITH SIXTEEN VOWELS CREATE 512 LETTERS WHICH IS EMITTED BY VOCAL CORD OF

Fig. 1.9

Sanskrit is a systematic language of nerves developed on the basis of body parts along three axes and 'jumbled words' developed in Sanskrit effect body parts of human beings.

Development of modern Sanskrit language is based on:

> **32 Consonants or nerves (expansion of periodic table of elements in periods**
>
> **on 32 classes of crystal symmetry from 'Ka' to 'Sa')**
>
> x **16 Vowels emitted through throat – Cervical Plexus from 'Aa' to 'Ah' (1 + 7 + 7 + 1)**
>
> x **12 Times contraction of Mass in Geometrical Progression in twelve blocks.**
>
> x **7 Crystal Systems**
>
> = **32 classes of crystal symmetry x 9 colors cycle x 12 times contraction of mass**
>
> x **7 crystal systems = 24,192 Nerves and its multiples.**

Any community may develop any type of language and alphabets depending upon the positive charge and negative charge associated with elements, words and alphabets. It will help in strengthening the community, migration to better places and improvement in health conditions of that community. Languages can play positive role in giving proper shape and size to human body and maintaining health of human body in particular and community in general.

The instruction of nervous system produces Voices, letters, alphabets and Language under impact of Spinal nerves and Cervical nerves through vocal cords inside Life forms. Vowels are produced under impact of cervical nerves whereas consonants are produced under impact of spinal nerves of nervous system. Children of human beings at the time of birth cry and make sound like 'K...A..........H......A'. The child emits first letter of sound wave packet, i.e., *Ka* from nerves of spinal cord. It continues from ka, to kha, ...to last vowels of the cervical nerve, i.e., An,.....Ah of spinal cord of human body. It reaches its climax at 16th vowel *Ah* of cervical nerve of human body. This crying confirms that formation of spinal nerves and cervical nerves in the infant is correct and perfect. The infant begins emission of sound from mouth from first consonant of spinal nerves, i.e., *Ka* and stretches up to last vowel, i.e., *Ah* of cervical nerves.

Ancient people knew about physiology of human body and developed and spoke Sanskrit language which was based on anatomy and physiology of human body. Evolution of languages depends upon pressure due to gravity, temperature and atmospheric volume of individual planet. The development of living body along three axes decides the type of language which will be emitted by vocal cord of that living body. Since time immemorial, human beings have developed '*Mantras*' or cluster of jumbled words from Sanskrit alphabets which effect different parts of body and systems and help in curing the diseases. They used to chant '*Mantras*' and make camp fires or sacrificial fires (*Havanas*) during worship. They migrated to different parts of world including India. They were intellectual race and spread knowledge among local people. Depending upon historical, cultural and geographical conditions, different dialects, sub-dialects and idiolects developed at many places throughout the world at different points of time. Different communities developed different number of alphabets in their languages. All the languages of world have emerged from Sanskrit language, i.e., from nerves of human body.

1.2 PHONETICS AND PHONEMIC TRANSCRIPTION

People speaking different languages develop cognitive skills depending upon structures and patterns of vowels and consonants of their languages. Languages in different modalities, e.g., spoken language and signed language develop differences in cognitive abilities outside the boundary of language. Generally the speakers of sign languages develop different visuo-spatial attention skills. The vocal cords of animals and human beings produce sound waves as 'wave packets'. The frequency of wave packets emitted by different animals varies from one animal to other and constitutes building blocks of different languages. Most of the languages show independent origin and maintain their individuality at many isolated places and pockets on earth. Many languages originated basing on their religious practices. Many languages having independent and isolated origin gradually mixed with other languages due to inter-marriages between different tribes, groups, clans and races. Many tribal languages having independent and isolated origin gradually mix with other languages due to migration of different tribes, groups, clans and races. It is the branch of linguistics that deals with analysis, description and classification of speech sounds. It includes both the physiological processes or articulation and physical attributes or acoustics which is study of the system of sound in a language.

Sound waves are produced by collision of planets and stars in space. It is also produced by thunderstorm during lightning in sky and waves in the range of power waves are produced on planets and stars. Collision of meteorites and asteroids also produces sound waves on planets and stars. The movement of planets and stars and emission of solar flares also produces sound of iron element like fast movement of iron wheel on railway track of steel. Sound waves are produced by all animals and it depends upon deposition of cells, tissues, hard tissues and bones inside animal body which varies along three axes. The movement of organs and appendages of animal body along three axes is highest in mammals. Depending upon deposition of tissues inside body, different types of genus and species of animals are produced from protozoa to aves on different planets. The animal forms vary in size, shape, musculature, features and degree of evolution depending upon their three axes movement on planets. The deposition of cells, tissues and bones inside animal body along three axes remains the same on different planets but the external features of life forms may vary from planet to planet depending upon pressure, volume, atmosphere and temperature equilibrium of particular planet. Every living being maintains its own thermodynamic equilibrium with reference to pressure, volume and temperature of that planet.

The time frame experiences the impact of all three particles along three axes. If the impact of negatively charged particles is higher than the structure will become weak, voluminous, elongated and unstable, e.g., weak and anaemic human being. If the impact of neutral mass particles will be high than the structure will become stable, compact, solidified and highly voluminous, e.g., fatty and hefty body of human being. If the impact of positively charged particles is high than the structure will tend to become compact, solidified and dense in character, e.g., solid body of human being.

The growth and development in body of invertebrates, pisces, amphibians, reptiles, mammals and aves improves gradually during evolution. The animal bodies of vertebrates are highly evolved because they develop three axes movement of body. The movement of tetrapod limbs is less in pisces, increases gradually in amphibians and reaches its climax in mammals. The movement of organs and appendages takes place along three axes in the following pattern.

(a) Movement of body with two limbs (left hand and right leg) due to weak force and strong force respectively along X-axis,
(b) Movement of vertebra and head along Y-axis,
(c) Movement of body with two limbs (right hand and left leg) due to electromagnetic force and gravitational force respectively along Z-axis.

The time machine cannot reach infinite level and time machine cannot produce largest human beings of infinite size having age and longevity up to infinite level. The length, width and breadth of living beings vary along three axes and if it increases along one axis it reduces and compensates along rest two axes. The age and longevity of human beings and life forms never reaches infinity because its components start degenerating and decomposing at certain age level and perish finally.

The effect of will power drags more volume of breath in human being towards brain and due to higher energy value pituitary gland releases secretions which increases kinetic energy of the human body. The increase in will power increases solidification in human being and drags body towards seventh point of ionization. The sound waves emitted by animals and human beings bounce and are reflected back from ozone layer and space and effect the living beings concerned. Spoken sound waves hit back and effect all living beings, animals and human beings. The impact is observed more on close relations and blood relations due to action of electromagnetic force on body. All the human beings are inter-related to each other on account of forces acting on body along three axes and sound wave packets bounce from ozone layer and space to effect the body of living beings. The sound 'wave packets' affect and shape all living beings including human beings on planets.

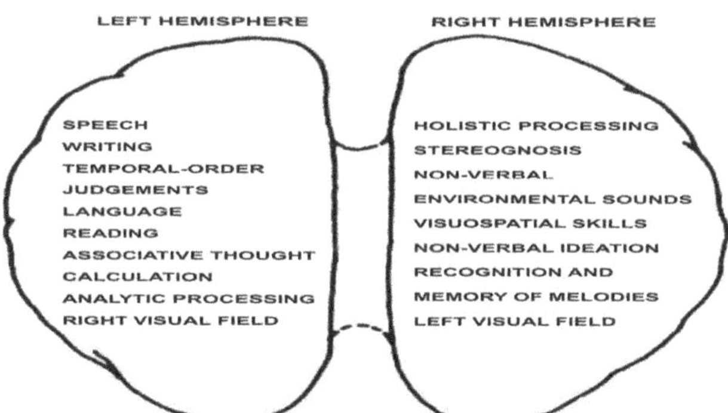

SPECIALIZATION IS OBSERVED IN BOTH CEREBRAL HEMISPHERES OF BRAIN OF HUMAN BEING. IN THE SPINAL CORD SIXTH CENTRE FROM BELOW IS KNOWN AS 'OHM' WHICH CONTAINS TWO CEREBRAL HEMISPHERES. ABOVE SIXTH CENTRE IS SEVENTH KNOT IN BRAIN WHICH IS CLOSE TO BOTH EYE BROWS AND CULMINATES IN CEREBRAL CORTEX CALLED AS *SAHASRASARA*.

Fig. 1.10

Language is the outcome of sound waves emitted from living body and emission of symbols synchronizes with development of nerves inside body parts of living body. We can write a language with discrete symbols, e.g., alphabets. Speech is generally continuous for the most part. Neither the acoustic signal (sound waves) nor the movements of speech articulators (tongue and lips) can be broken down into written symbols. For example, watch the waveform of different words. A waveform graph changes in the amplitude of the sound wave (vertical axis) against time (horizontal axis). Like this one the waveforms of most speech samples have continuous patterns, the discrete symbols of written speech are not reflected in these acoustic representations. An overlap in articulation is observed by comparing the pronunciation of the syllables, e.g., *bee, bah, bay and boo* etc. When you pronounce the letter *b*, your tongue is already in position to pronounce the following vowel. Further, the lips are already pursed when you pronounce the letter *b* in *boo* etc. A writing system with its set of linearly ordered discrete symbols is actually an idealization of the physical instantiation of speech. The concrete aspects of speech contain alphabetic representations of different languages.

'Power wave packets' containing mass of atoms of elements create languages and Sound Waves. Phonetics is concerned with how speech sounds are produced and articulated in the vocal tract as well as with the physical properties of speech of sound waves generated by the larynx and vocal tract. The term phonetics usually refers to the study of the articulatory and acoustic properties of sound whereas the term phonology is often used to refer to the abstract principles that govern the distribution of sound in a language. Speech sound shows slight variation on different latitudes and longitudes on earth.

PHYSIOLOGY OF SPEECH PRODUCTION

At the fundamental level speech signals are rapidly flowing series of noises that are produced inside throat, mouth and nasal passages and that come out from mouth and sometimes from the nose also. Learning to speak a language requires the control of a few muscles that move lips, jaw and tongue. These anatomical structures are easily observed during speech production. In reality about 100 muscles exercise directly and continuously control production of sound waves that carry speech. The sound waves are produced by a complex interaction of
- (a) an outward flow of air from the lungs,
- (b) modifications of airflow at larynx (Adam's apple or voice box in the throat) and
- (c) additional modifications of airflow by position and movement of tongue, teeth and other anatomical structures of the vocal tract.

The flow of air from lungs during speech differs in many respects from the airflow during quiet breathing. During speech. three to four times more air is exhaled compared to quiet breathing. During speech the normal breathing rhythm changes radically and inhalation is more rapid and exhalation is much more drawn out. Further, the number of breaths per unit time decreases during speech. The flow of air is unimpeded during quiet breathing whereas in speech the airflow encounters resistance from the obstructions and closures that occur in the throat and mouth.

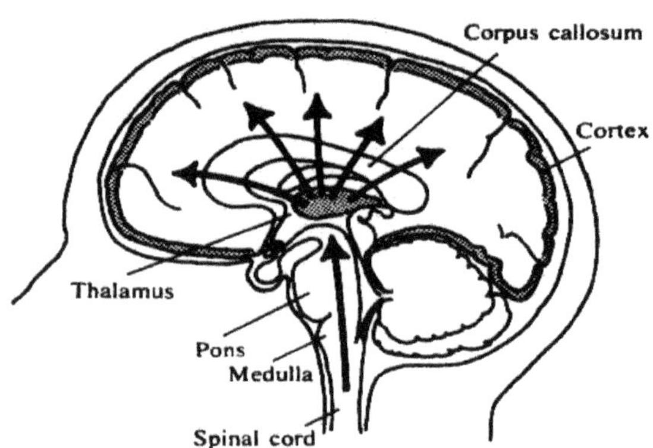

PICTURE SHOWS FIBER RADIATIONS FROM THALAMUS TO CORTEX

Fig. 1.11

One of the primary mechanisms for expanding lungs during both quiet breathing and speech is the contraction of diaphragm, a sheet of muscular tissue that separates chest cavity from the abdominal region. This contraction causes the diaphragm to lower and flatten out, leading to an increase in the size of chest cavity. The other primary mechanism for expansion of chest cavity is the set of muscles between ribs in the rib cage (*external intercostals*). Contraction of these muscles causes the ribs to lift up and because of the way that the ribs are hinged, they swing out, increasing the volume of the chest cavity. Since the lungs are attached to the walls of the chest cavity, when the chest cavity expands, either from diaphragm contraction or from rib

30

movement, the lungs being elastic, also expands. As the lungs expands, air flows up to the point when inhalation is completed. During quiet breathing the diaphragm relaxes at this point and the stretched lungs begin to shrink, allowing air to flow out quite rapidly at the beginning as with air escaping from a filled balloon. During speech, however, the muscles of the diaphragm and the rib cage continue to be active restraining the lungs from emptying too rapidly. Without this checking force, speech would be loud at first and then would become quieter as the lungs empties. Thus humans have developed special adaptation for breathing during speech. Speech is not merely added to the breathing cycle rather the breathing cycle is adapted to the needs of speech.

The languages help in changing longitude and latitude of human being and effect position of human being from place of birth. Human beings will shift in position either towards east, west, north or south from place of its birth due to impact of languages on human beings. Pronunciation of vowels and consonants by human beings changes the direction of man and makes the man sit in north direction because Ferro magnet faces towards north from earth. The changes inside animal body take place due to various factors on the planet. The electromagnetic waves in the wavelength range of Power waves, i.e., 1×10^4 - 1×10^7 meters approxiamately have frequency range of about 100 Hz to 10,000 Hz. They behave as Sound Wave Packets and produce languages equivalent to sound waves. Phonetics also depends upon longitude, latitude and altitude and emission of sound of human beings varies from place to place.

The longitude, latitude and altitude of animals are effected along three axes on any spherical planet. The growth of animals is highest at equator. The height, breadth and width of animals along three axes are effected by longitude, latitude and altitude respectively, Depending upon deposition of tissues inside the animal body, many genus of animals are produced at different places on spherical planets. Every genus of animal produces many different species at different places on spherical planet. Depending upon the longitude, altitude and latitude many new species of every genus are produced on planets and languages help in migration of human beings.

NORTH POLE

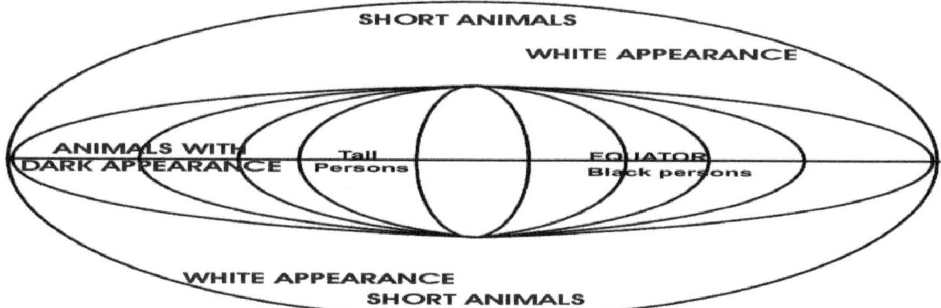

SOUTH POLE
IMPACT OF LONGITUDE, LATITUDE AND ALTITUDE
Fig. 1.12

1.3 IMPACT OF ALTITUDE

Astronauts became a few centimeters taller on moon because anti-matter force was high and atmospheric pressure was less dominant as compared to earth. Altitude will stretch the body due to high anti-matter force and less matter force. The force of gravitation was less on moon as compared to earth. So the living bodies with mass and all bodies containing mass of earth density will decrease in volume on moon and on smaller astral bodies. Thus force of gravitation as experienced on moon will be less as compared to earth by all compact living bodies having mass. Increase in altitude increases use of vowels and soft language and decreases the use of consonants by living beings. During the course of evolution intermixing and overlapping of characters is commonly seen between different groups and regions. The result is production of new species and sub-species which survive for thousands of years in any place and then become extinct during course of time. The impact of *Swaras*, i.e., Sa (Do with frequency 256 Hz), Re (Re with frequency 324.7 Hz), Ga (Mi with frequency 363.4 Hz), Ma (Fa with frequency 407.2 Hz), Pa (Sol with frequency 439.5 Hz), Dha (La with frequency 464.3 Hz) and Ni (Ti with frequency 491.5 Hz) will reduce gradually during increase of altitude and will reduce solidification inside body. The voice and tone of people near equator is harsh and rough whereas the voice becomes sweet and soft with increase in altitude. There will be increase in soft voice and use of vowels by people with increase in altitude of planet.

1.4 IMPACT OF LATITUDE

The life forms become longer, wider and taller in size when they reach near equator. The expansion is seen along three axes near equator and expansion makes the life forms hefty and compact near equator. The life forms along Poles show more expansion along one or two axis. The animals near poles tend to become round and thinner in size. The animals near both the poles become round, small and compact in size and shape. The size and shape of human being is partially affected due to change in latitude. The ecliptic contains human being of taller heights and white complexion at the latitude of Tropic of Cancer whereas ecliptic contains human being of taller heights and dark color at the latitude of Tropic of Capricorn. The human being will be darker in color near equator and hardy in stature. The impact of '*Sa* wavelength packet containing mass' (*Do*) with 256 Hz. frequency is observed more on equator and this wave helps in solidification of body. People inhabiting Tropic of Cancer are soft-spoken and their languages have emphasis on vowels whereas people inhabiting Tropic of Capricorn speak harsh with high tone languages having emphasis on consonants.

1.5 IMPACT OF LONGITUDE

The expansion of body is seen along three axes near equator and expansion makes the life forms hefty and compact near equator. The life forms along Poles show high expansion along one or two axis. The animals near equator become taller and hefty in size. The animals near both the poles become round and compact in size and shape. The metallic elements inside human being help in changing longitude whereas non-metallic elements effect position of human being from place of birth. Human beings will shift in position either towards east or west or towards north or south from place of his birth. Wearing and use of metals by human beings changes the direction and position of man. The ferro-magnet made up of $^{56}_{26}Fe$ makes the man sit in north direction because Ferro-magnet faces towards north. Wearing of Gold makes man sit in east direction due to effect of gold metal. The human being near equator will be taller, hefty and dark complexioned and these features will decrease gradually towards both the poles. Electromagnetic waves show increase of energy towards Arctic and Antarctic on earth. The voice and tone of people near equator is harsh and rough with emphasis on consonants whereas the voice becomes sweet and soft with emphasis on vowels towards both the Poles. Human being born east of prime meridian will be smaller, weaker and tender in constitution whereas persons born west of prime meridian will be hefty, taller and tough in body constitution.

The intermixing and overlapping among characters is commonly seen in animals throughout the planet. The character of different animals mix with each other during movement of planets and produces different animals depending upon the position of living beings. The longitude, latitude and altitude of the place decide the type of animal that will be produced on that planet. The characters keep changing during long interval of time period of movement of planets. There may be overlapping in the characters also and new species and sub-species with different varieties may be produced at different longitudes, latitudes and altitudes. Many species appear with time, develop different characteristics at different places, change their characteristics due to movement of planet and vanish with time.

The languages help in changing longitude and latitude of human being and effect position of human being from place of birth. Human being will shift in position either towards east or west or towards north or south from place of his birth due to impact of sound wave packets on human beings. People in northern hemisphere have soft pronunciation as compared to people of southern hemisphere on earth. Pronunciation of vowels and consonants by human beings changes the direction of man and makes the man sit in north direction because Ferro magnet faces towards north from earth. The electromagnetic waves in the wavelength range of Power waves, i.e., 1×10^4 - 1×10^7 meters have frequency range of about 100 Hz to 10,000 Hz. They behave as 'sound wave packets' and are equivalent to sound waves in their impact. It is said that

"Sat kosh par pani badale aur Choudah Kosh par Vani". The meaning

is that every seven *kosh* (fourteen miles distance), taste of water and soil texture changes and every fourteen *kosh* (twenty eight miles distance) changes the pronunciation and accent of language of people. The impact of sound waves is very powerful and effects solid human body. Impact of sound waves on living beings are perceived on every part, organ and seven systems and sound waves in the form of voice can change the body features, size and shape. The sound waves like noise, voices, thunderstorms and emission of waves at different frequencies by animals and human beings etc act along three axes.

2
INDUS CIVILIZATION

All civilizations grew near river banks where fresh water and fertile agriculture field was available to people for their livelihood. Indus civilization having egalitarian society grew near Indus and adjoining rivers of North-Western India and flourished with good agriculture, cattle and continuous supply of water. Sanskrit was the language of Indus people and script of a language is the letter or character used for writing. It is a distinct writing system based on specific elements or symbols of a language. Every language in the past developed with one or many scripts in any community. The number of letters in any language may vary from place to place and script may also show some changes with passage of time.

Indus valley civilization was a Bronze Age civilization which started in north-western region of south Asia. The civilization started in Indus valley and gradually spread and expanded covering entire western part of Indian sub-continent. The civilization is famous for urban planning, houses with baked bricks, excellent drainage system and cluster of houses and buildings. They had very good trade relations with Mesopotamia and adjoining countries. Variety of artifacts and seals alongwith jewellery speak about culture of the civilization. The cities developed in pre-planned manner and it seems that governance existed at that time whose orders were carried out by people. Standardization of high level was maintained by centralized orders of authority. However, traces of kingship, priesthood and orders of central authority are not available.

Sanskrit language which has emerged from nerves of human body was the most prominent language in Indian sub-continent. Brahmi script was one of the old scripts of the world created by Rhishabhadeva for providing knowledge about letters and numerals to Brahmi. It is an abugida which uses a system of discritical marks to associate vowels with consonant symbols. It had indigenous origin through nerves of human body and had some connection with Indus script. Some numerals found in Brahmi script are part of modern numeral system. Prakrit script was common among Indus people. Gradually Pali and Kharoshthi gained prominence in some areas. Initially the impact of all these scripts was observed on Indus script. Devanagari script without upper line on letters (*Shirorekha*) developed in Sanskrit language during Indus period of civilization. During that period many original and native scripts developed throughout Indian sub-continent as mentioned.

Brahmi script is old writing system of India and is considered as ancestor of all modern Indian scripts. Prakrit script was used for writing religious texts, literature, poem and inscriptions by ancient Indian rulers. Pali script was more cosmopolitan and was written in many scripts including Brahmi, Kharoshthi, Sinhalese, Burmese, Thai, Khmer and Roman etc. Kharoshthi script also known as *Gandhari* script was ancient writing system common in Afghanistan, North-Western India and Central Asia.

2.1 DEVANAGARI SCRIPT

Devanagari is a writing system commonly used for writing Sanskrit, Hindi and Marathi etc. During Indus period, Sanskrit letters were written without Upper line (*Shirorekha*) and *Shirorekha* was added in scripts of later Civilizations.

2.2 INDUS CIVILIZATION SCRIPT

Sanskrit was the language of Indus people and letters of Sanskrit mixed with signs of *Navagrahas, Rashis, Asterisms,* calendar days and Roman numerals was the script. 'Alphabet like structures' show letters of Sanskrit without *Shirorekha* mixed with signs of asterisms. Compound and complex words were created with vowels and consonants of Sanskrit mixed with signs of nava-grahas and rashis. 'Roman numerals' or 'Indus numerals' and 360 days of calendar were mixed with letters to convey proper meaning. Indus script is easily deciphered by study of compound words made of letters and signs. Sanskrit grammar developed later.

Civilization was very developed with excellent town planning and people had very high civic sense. Original script of Indus civilization was highly symmetrical and written on scientific lines as evidenced from seals, pottery and other artifacts. Picture of seven statues or Sapta-Rishis along with other rituals shows that people had idea about astronomy, seven stars of Ursae Minor and ceremonies. Symmetry shows that they had good idea about dimensions and pictures at different places speak about it. Dimensions increased in the order 1 : 2 : 4 in the metallic works and construction of houses and bricks etc. In the alphabets, signs of spring, double springs, O, OO and outer covering, elliptical shape of alphabets, notch, arrow and inverted signs was observed at many places. Hyphen, dash, vertical and diagonal signs were letters of Sanskrit added with asterisms. *Shirorekha* (upper line) on letters and words developed later on during late Indus period.

Seals were created to show specific place, time and date of manufacture and value of commodity during trade. We get hundreds of signs and signages on seals at different places having pictures of animals and birds. Seals with many 'scripts' and 'signs' were used as identification marks of particular tribe, clan, place, merchant, priest and group head of areas. Many seals shows resemblance with seven suras or swaras which had resemblance with lyrical voice and sound of animals. Pictures of these animals are seen at many places. Further changes were shown with arrows or dash or lines or direction basing upon calls of people, requirement of community and use of words at different places. The impact of sound wave packets or seven *Swaras* was observed in the following manner:

(a) Shadaja (SA) voice developed from rapturous sound of peacock.

(b) Rishabha (Re) voice developed from bellowing of a cow or bull.

(c) Gandhar (GA) voice developed from bleating of a goat in a flock.

(d) Madhyam (MA) voice developed from is the cry of a heron.

(e) Panchama (PA) voice developed from sound of Indian Kokila (Nightingale) in spring.

(f) Dhaivata (DHA) voice developed from neighing of a horse.

(g) Nishad (NI) is voice developed from trumpeting of an elephant.

The animals associated with seven swaras have been shown on seals at many places and people knew about seven swaras. It shows their interest in dance, music, art and peaceful social existence.

2.3 KNOWLEDGE ABOUT SAPTARISHIS AND ASTRONOMY

Seals show that Indus people had ideas about *Saptarishis*, *Navagrahas* (Nine Planets System), twelve Zodiac Stars and twenty seven Asterisms. Symbols of alphabet and signs show closeness with twelve signs of zodiac stars and show slight modification at some places. They had knowledge about months, calendar and astronomy. Formation of triangles and similar structures show that they had idea about 27 asterisms Most of the impressions were not single letter rather words or compound words with specific meaning. Sanskrit was the language of Indus people and at later stage it developed some local modifications. It contained sixteen vowels and thirty two consonants totalling forty eight letters in number. Other 'Alphabet-like' or 'Script-like structures' were trade symbols of ruling elite of Indus civilization.

The script developed on the lines of geometric progression, i.e., 2 x 3 x ....12,,,,,,24,.....,32. Script resembled Brahmi and Pali script with some modifications. In many places it was close to holographic pattern of writing. Indus civilization was wide spread and script though common to local people shows some variation at many places. The script was showing standardization of signs and signages at many places. Alphabets show solid crystalline structures, elliptical structures and circular structures. Vowels and consonants developed in geometric progression.

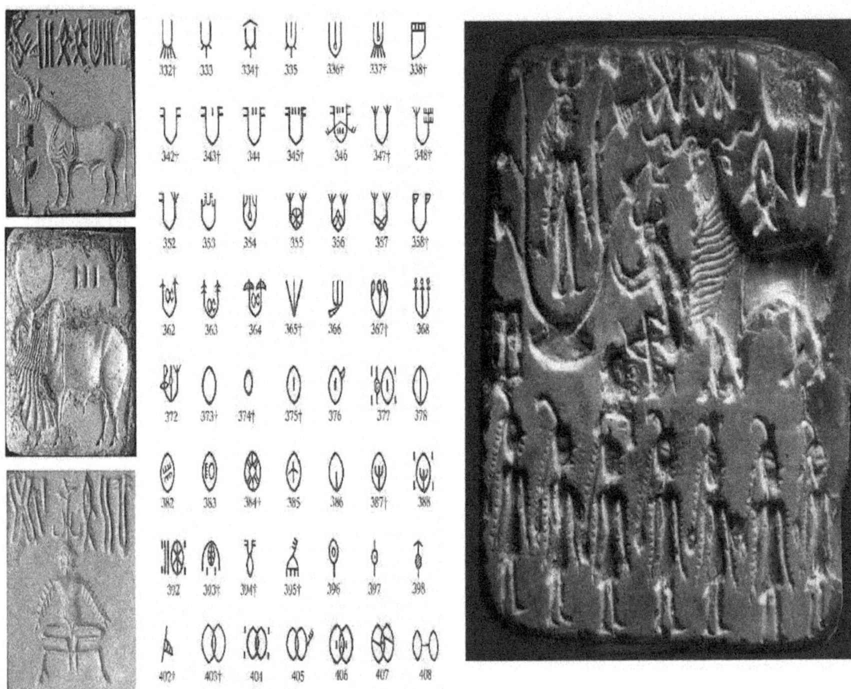

PICTURES OF SEALS SHOWING ANIMALS AND SAPTARISHIS. IN SANSKRIT, *PA, PHA, BA* AND *BHA* ARE FOUR MASCULINE LETTERS FROM WHICH WORDS LIKE PAPA, FATHER, BROTHER AND *BHAIA* ETC HAVE BEEN DERIEVED. WHEN UPPER LINE OF SANSKRIT LETTERS (*SHIROREKHA*) ARE REMOVED, THEY GIVE 'U' OR 'V'

SHAPED IMPRESSION AND MANY LETTERS OF INDUS SCRIPT WERE PREPARED
ON THAT LINE. THE LETTERS *YA, THA* AND *SA (MURDHANI SHA)* ALSO GIVE
SAME TYPE OF IMPRESSION WHEN SHIROREKHA IS REMOVED. SPHERICAL,
ROUND AND OVAL SHAPE HAVE BEEN DERIEVED FROM TWENTY SEVEN
ASTERISMS AND PHALLIC SYMBOLS ETC. ROUND AND OVAL SYMBOLS ARE
ALSO RELATED TO THIRTEENTH VOWEL OF SANSKRIT *'O'* AND FOURTEENTH
VOWEL *'AU'* FOR WRITING WITH CONSONANTS.

Fig. 2.1

Fish-like symbol of Revati Nakshatra, fish-like symbol of Mean Rashi and six spoke wheel
was considered as auspicious and used on seals mixed with some Sanskrit letters. Sanskrit
letters were mixed to express some meaning of 'word' which related to trade, commodity, time,
date and name and place of elite ruler..

Vowels - अ आ इ ई उ ऊ ऋ ॠ ऌ ॡ ऐ ऐ ओ औ अं अः

Consonants -

क ख ग घ ङ

च छ ज झ ञ

ट ठ ड ढ ण

त थ द ध न

प फ ब भ म

य र ल व

श ष स

LETTERS OF SANSKRIT WITHOUT UPPER LINE (*SHIROREKHA*) WERE USED BY

INDUS PEOPLE IN THEIR WRITING MIXED WITH NATURAL SIGNS. VOWELS LIKE *'A'*, *'AA'*, *'U'*, *'OO'* AND *'AN'* WERE MIXED WITH SIGNS OF ASTERISMS OR *NAVA-GRAHAS* FOR WRITING ON SEALS. SIMILARLY CONSONANTS LIKE *KA, GHA, JHA, PA, PHA, BA, BHA, RA, VA* AND *SHA* ETC WERE ADDED WITH THE SIGNS OF ZODIAC STARS AND WERE USED FOR WRITING AND SPEAKING. THESE LETTERS FORMED U=SHAPED, V-SHAPED AND FUNNEL-LIKE STRUCTURE AND WERE COMMONLY USED. SIMILARLY, KA, KHA, THA AND DHA ETC FORMED SPHERICAL STRUCTURES WHICH APPEAR ON SEALS. GLOBULAR AND ROUND MODIFICATIONS ARE SEEN WITH VOWELS AND SIGNS OF NAVA-GRAHAS AND RASHIS.

Fig. 2.2

Sanskrit alphabet contains 16 vowels and consonants are 32 in number starting from *Ka* and ending at *Sa*. Addition of arrow, dash, hyphen or notch like structure on left side reduced the value by 1, 2, 3 and onwards while addition on right side increased the value of number by 1, 2, 3 and onwards in alphabets. In initial six vowels, addition of dash, hyphen, arrow, notch, circle and spring like structure on the left side of letter stands for *a, aa, i, ee, u, oo*. In last six vowels, addition of dash, hyphen, arrow, notch, circle and spring like structure on the right side of letter stands for *e, ai, o, au, am* and *ah*. Four middle vowels, i.e., *Ri, Rhee,Lri* and *Lree* appear like logogrphic writing in inscriptions.

Indus script inscriptions appear on various materials found in the area. It includes seals, seal impressions, stoneware bangles,shells and bones, bronze tools, pottery, ivory paintings and copper tablets etc. Seals were used as identification marks mainly for trade purposes. The scripts feature narrative imagery and combine texts with natural signs like nava-grahas etc. Letters of Sanskrit were added with lines, Indus numerals, human or cattle sketches and important natural signs to produce meaningful 'Alphabets'.

Vowels and consonants of Sanskrit without upper line (*Shirorekha*) mixed with signs of zodiac stars, asterisms, *nava-grahas* and calendar dates formed 'Alphabet like structures'. They were not 'true words' because knowledge about Sanskrit grammar was very less during early Indus period. Sanskrit grammarians created their texts and rules late and then creation of words and sentences started. Scripts at some places show intermixing like logographic languages. Logographic language uses single character or symbol to represent a word or morpheme. Writing of vowels and consonants shows prominence of geometric pattern. Compound words of various types appear at many places but sentences are less prevalent which makes the script difficult to understand and decipher. Knowledge about geometry, trigonometry and crystal structure was very high. Knowledge about star and natural signs and mixing them with vowels and consonants during reading and writing shows that Indus people were highly scientific in their approach. It does not mean that they were religious and superstitious in their approach.

2.4 KNOWLEDGE ABOUT TWELVE ZODIAC STARS

They had fairly good idea about twelve signs viz, Aries, Taurus, Gemini, Cancer, Leo, Virgo, Libra, Scorpio, Sagittarius, Capricorn, Aquarius and Pisces in their day to day life. In the solar calendar of 30 x 12 = 360 days, Rashi was commonly used and depicted on seals with picture of animals. Twelve months of year produce letters mixed with Sanskrit vowels and consonants.

(1) Aries sign was mixed with vowel and consonant letters of Sanskrit to produce words which were energetic and courageous.

(2) Taurus sign was mixed with vowel and consonant letters of Sanskrit to produce words which gave determination.

(3) Gemini sign was mixed with vowel and consonant letters of Sanskrit to produce words which were curious and versatile.

(4) Cancer sign was mixed with vowel and consonant letters of Sanskrit to produce words which were emotional and creative.

(5) Leo sign was mixed with vowel and consonant letters of Sanskrit to produce words which were linked to loyalty and confidence.

(6) Virgo sign was mixed with vowel and consonant letters of Sanskrit to produce words for hard working and modest.

(7) Libra sign was mixed with vowel and consonant letters of Sanskrit to produce words for diplomatic and charming personality.

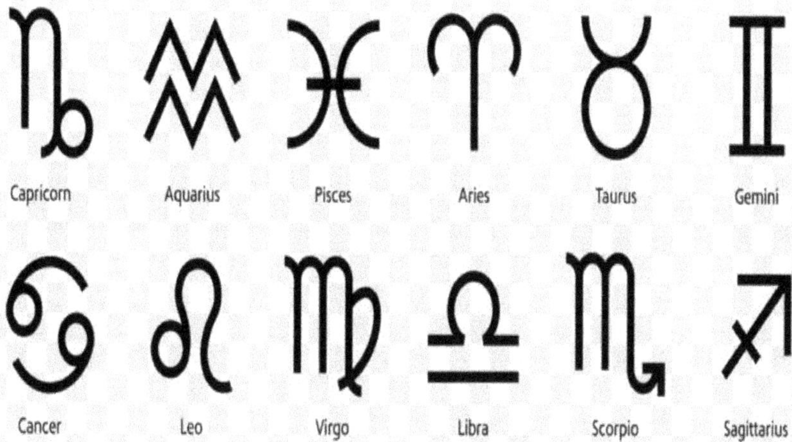

SIGNS OF TWELVE ZODIACS WAS SEEN ON SEALS AND SCRIPT. SIGNS OF SPRING, DOUBLE SPRING, O, OO WITH OUTER COVER OR ELLIPTICAL SHAPE etc., NOTCH, DOUBLE NOTCH, ARROW, DOUBLE ARROW AND INVERTED V IN THE ZODIAC SIGNS WAS OBSERVED. IT WAS DONE TO SHOW THE TIME, DATE AND PLACE OF WORK, COMMENCEMENT, VALUE OF TRADE AND NAME OF TRADER OR RULING ELITE WITH PLACE OF COMMODITY.

Fig. 2.3

(8) Scorpio sign was mixed with vowel and consonant letters of Sanskrit to produce words for devotion.

(9) Sagittarius sign was mixed with vowel and consonant letters of Sanskrit to produce words for intelligent and cheerful.

(10) Capricorn sign was mixed with vowel and consonant letters of Sanskrit to produce words for ambitious and hard working.

(11) Aquarius sign was mixed with vowel and consonant letters of Sanskrit to produce words for independent and innovative.

(12) Pisces sign was mixed with vowel and consonant letters of Sanskrit to produce words for generous and creative.

Twelve Rashis stand for twelve cranial nerves of brain of human being. Use of calendar was common and this is the reason hundreds of seals have been found at different places. Letters of Sanskrit were often used with Rashis on seals and that expressed particular meaning of the event.

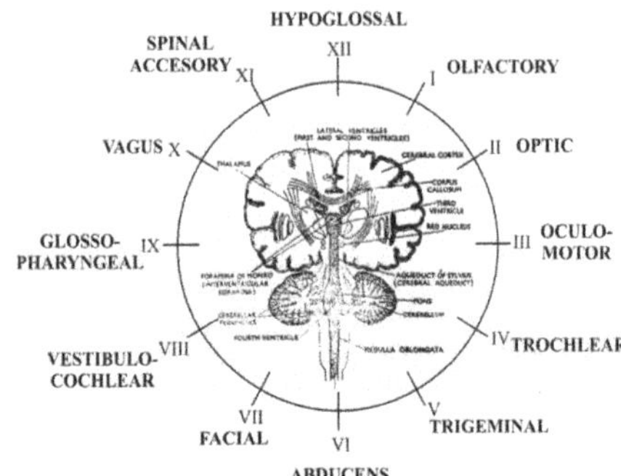

CREATION OF BODY PARTS DUE TO GRAVITATIONAL FORCE ALONG ONE AXIS INSIDE HUMAN BODY. CORONAL SECTION THROUGH CEREBRAL HEMISPHERE AND BRAIN STEM SHOWS THAT SPHERICAL BRAIN INSIDE SKULL IS CONTROLLED BY TWELVE PAIRS OF CRANIAL NERVES. TWELVE CRANIAL NERVES SHOW CHARACTERISTICS OF TWELVE ZODIAC STARS.

Fig. 2.4

Letters of Sanskrit without *Sirorekha* (upper line) mixed with natural signs were the lingua franca of Indus people. During writing on seals and other places they used Sanskrit letters joined with signs of asterisms etc. Square and rectangular structures contained letters of alphabets and gradually helped in creation of upper line above letters and words.

2.5 KNOWLEDGE OF SANSKRIT

Sanskrit was the language of Indus civilization people, Sanskrit is the eternal language of nerves of human body with 16 vowels and 32 consonants. Civilizations after Indus people added four consonants, i.e., *ha, ksha, tra, jnya* in the language gradually and increased the number to 36. Civilizations growing after Indus civilization added *Shirorekha* (upper line) above letters to give proper shape to letters. The alphabets of Indus civilization show many structures like hyphen, dash, notch, globules, rounded structures, spring and arrow etc. These structures are added with vowels and consonants and provide full meaning to letters. *A* and *Aa* was created by dash, *ee* and *i* was created with spring like structure, *u* and *oo* was created by globules, arrows created *e* and *ai*, rounded structures created *o* and *au* and dots created *Am* and *Ah*. They added spring like structure with *i* and *ee*, globules in *u* and *oo*, arrow on *e* and *ai*, notch in *o* and *au* etc. They added notch in consonant letter *bha*, hyphen in *sa* and *jha*, dash in *murdhanni Sa*, rounded structure as *tha* etc.

Seals show picture of man or saint sitting in yogic posture. It shows that people had clear idea about Kundalini Shakti and emergence of Sanskrit letters from nerves of human body.

40

Persons practising Kundalini Shakti (Serpent Power) will develop knowledge about nerves and nervous system of body. Sixteen Sanskrit vowels and thirty two consonants were mixed with asterisms while depicting the facts about civilization and hundreds of seals with notch, arrow and hyphen etc have been found.

I, II, III, IV, V, VI, VII, VIII, IX, X, L, C, D, M

अ आ इ ई उ ऊ ऋ ॠ ऌ ॡ ए ऐ ओ औ अं अः

क ख ग घ ङ	
च छ ज झ ञ	
ट ठ ड ढ ण	
त थ द ध न	
प फ ब भ म	
य र ल व	
श ष स	

क्ष त्र ज्ञ	
न द ल व	
त्त त्थ द्व भ म	
प ग ट ठ व	
च छ ज झ न	
त थ द ध न	
क ख ग घ ङ	

अ आ इ ई उ ऊ ऋ ॠ ऌ ॡ ए ऐ ओ औ अं अः

SANSKRIT WAS THE LANGUAGE OF INDUS CIVILIZATION PEOPLE. MANY LETTERS TURNED UPSIDE DOWN OR FORMED MIRROR IMAGES DURING IMPRESSION AND

WRITING ON SEALS. THE LANGUAGE AND SCRIPT INITIALLY RESEMBLES WITH BRAHMI AND PRAKRIT AND GRADUALLY MIXED WITH PALI IN LATER STAGE. DEVANAGARI SCRIPT DEVELOPED LATER ON AND *SHIROREKHA* (UPPER LINE) WAS ADDED IN THE SCRIPT OF SANSKRIT. PICTURE SHOWS SIGNS OF VOWELS OF INDUS ALPHABETS WITH SPRING, DOUBLE SPRING, O, OO WITH OUTER COVER OR ELLIPTICAL SHAPE etc. NOTCH, DOUBLE NOTCH, ARROW, DOUBLE ARROW AND INVERTED V SHOW VOWELS OF LETTERS. ROMAN OR INDUS NUMERALS WERE COMMON ON ALL SEALS. WE GET PLENTY OF SEALS SHOWING ASHWINI NAKSHATRA WITH MODIFICATIONS OF DATES, *GRAHAS* (PLANETS) AND *RASHIS* (ZODIACS). 'U' TYPE ALPHABET WAS PROBABLY DERIEVED FROM ASHWINI NAKSHATRA SYMBOL IN INDUS ALPHABETS. LETTERS OF SANSKRIT WERE ADDED IN THE SYMBOLS OF RASHI, NAVAGRAHA AND NAKSHATRAS DURING WRITING AND 'ALPHABETS' WERE CREATED.

Fig. 2.5

Development of vowels of letters took place in circular manner taken up in fixed pattern. First vowel (*A*) started from extreme left to left (*Aa*) and then gradually turned upwards to produce *i* and *ee* subsequently. Then left notch turned upwards in the vowels *u* and *Oo*. *Rhi, Rhee, Lri* and *Lree* shows sign in vertical direction. The vowels become fully vertical in *Ae, Aei, o, au* and then turned right in *Am* and finally moved to extreme right in *Ah* in circular manner. Thirty two consonant letters also were written in fixed pattern. The line of first letter (*K*) starts moving from left side to right side. All odd letters, *ka, ga, anga, chha, ..., sa (Murdhanni Sa*) follow the same pattern of writing from left to right. In even letters, i.e., *kha, gha, cha, ja,......., Sa (Danti Sa*) the line starts from right side and moves towards left side in letters. There was notch and blank space in upper space in letters like, *jha, bha, dha* and *sa*.

Compound and complex words are less in number because they had less idea about Sanskrit grammar. Good knowledge about grammar developed during late Indus period and its use was found in subsequent civilizations. Sanskrit was the common language of people but use of grammar was very less and this may be one of the reasons that complex words of Sanskrit are found in less number on seals. Complex words and long sentences were very less in number as seen on seals, pottery and other artifacts of Indus civilization and long sentences etc written on seals and leaves etc vanished due to flood, drought and migration during course of time. Traces of compound words and sentences are very less throughout the areas of civilization.

Letters and words of Sanskrit were mixed with signs of astronomy, rashis, nakshatras and navagrahas and projected on seals. Its impact was observed on scripts of other countries with which they were having trade relations. It is seen from the seals that creation of straight lines, upper lines and *shirorekha* had started above letters at some places. Square and rectangular structures contained letters of alphabet and gradually helped in creation of upper line above letters and words. During Indus period, use of *Shirorekha* was not observed and many letters gave the impression like U and V shaped pots mixed with natural signs.

Meluha, Maaluha, Maaluhaa is the name for Indus Civilizaion people who were trading partners of Sumerians in the middle Bronza age. In Mesopotamian trade this name (literally Ma, Maa or mother land, loha or louh means iron) and meluha means a land of mother with properties of iron element and availability of iron ores. Indus civilization was located near 90^0 East Longitude with prominence of electromagnetic force. Opposite to it was the land of father at 90^0 West Longitude which was known as Papa, papua, with prominence of gravitational force. Elaborate Town planning, drainage and sewerage system of Indus civilization shows that mathematical calculations were known to them and they were utilizing their skill for the same.

2.6 KNOWLEDGE OF ASTROLOGY AND NUMERALS

Indus people had good idea about Astrology, movement of stars and planets and their impact on human body. Seals, pottery and other artifacts shows that Line, dash, hyphen, circle, notch and projection etc mentioned on left side reduced the value and number whereas the same thing mentioned on right side increased the number and value of the object. BODMAS (Bracket, of, division, multiplication, addition and subtraction) was known to them and their signs with letters in different forms are available at many places. In Indus civilization, Numerals developed with lines denoting one, two and three etc. Five was written as capital V and lines written on left side reduced the value while lines written on right side increased the value of numbers. Due to trade relations with neighbouring countries, the following system of numerals was observed, i.e.,

I, II, III, IV, V, VI, VII, VIII, IX, X and onwards.

Numerals appear on almost all the seals and it appears that numerals originated in Indus civilization and spread to other communities and countries during trade and cultural exchange. 'Indus Numerals' were the precursor of all other numerals and flourished in modified forms in adjoining countries in the name of Roman numerals. The numeral system was developed by Indus people and give and take relationship and use of numerals on seals between adjoining countries indicates that trade flourished with all adjoining countries at that time. Seals were identification marks of local tribe, clan, elite ruler, merchant, place or community in Indus civilization. They were used for many purposes by civilians including trade. Square seals have been found in plenty which shows it belonged to big merchant or ruler while cylindrical and rectangular seals were less in number. Seals with alphabets and numbers have been found and number of 'alphabet like words' is very high which makes it difficult to frame a sentence and derieve clear meaning out of it.

2.7 KNOWLEDGE OF NAVAGRAHAS (NINE PLANETS SYSTEM)

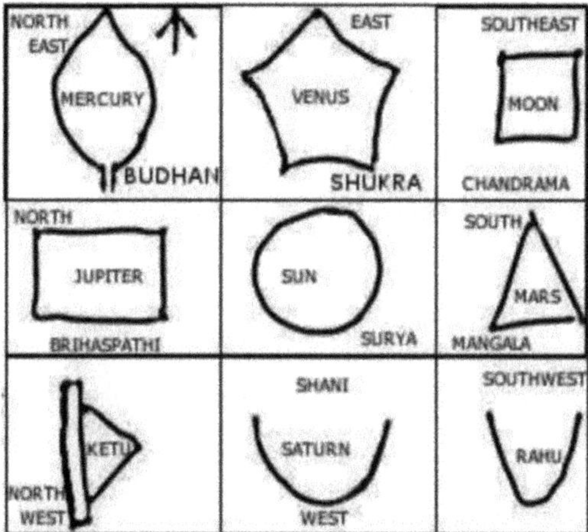

SIGNS OF NAVAGRAHAS (NINE PLANETS SYSTEM) WAS AVAILABLE ON SEALS AND SCRIPT. SMALLER SIGNS WERE ADDED IN NAVA-GRAHAS TO PROVIDE NUMERICAL VALUE TO LETTERS. SIGNS WERE GIVEN TO SHOW TIME, DATE AND PLACE OF WORK COMMENCEMENT OF

2.8 KNOWLEDGE OF 27 NAKSHATRAS (ASTERISMS)

Seals show that Indus people had ideas about nine colors cycle and their geometrical distribution. Movement of planets within twenty seven nakshatras was known to them and they started their work in particular nakshatra to get better results.

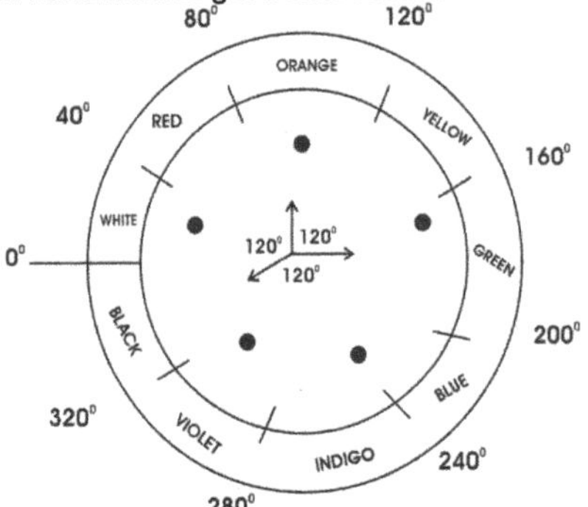

Indus people knew about twenty seven asterisms as mentioned below: Ashwini, Bharani, Krittika, Rohini, Mrigashirsha, Ardra, Punarvasu, Pushya, Ashlesha, Magha, Purva Phalguni, Uttara Phalguni, Hasta, Chitra, Swati, Vishakha, Anuradha, Jyeshtha, Moola, Purva Ashadha, Uttara Ashadha, Shravana, Dhanishta, Shatabhisha, Purva Bhadrapada, Uttara Bhaadrapada and Revati. They are spread at a distance of $13°20'$ around all stars within nine colors cycle.

Fig. 2.7

Many 'Alphabet like structures' are words created by combination of twenty seven Nakshatras with Sanskrit letters. Some U-shaped Words on seals show combination of many Sanskrit letters with particular nakshatra. Many 'Alphabets' are words created by combination of Sanskrit letters and numerals with symbol of 'O' shaped nakshatra or oval shaped nakshatra. All such words carried specific meaning for day to day life, trade, worship, date, number and agricultural practices. Twety seven asterisms produce many letters mixed with Sanskrit vowels and consonants.

(1) Ashwini Nakshatra mixed with Sanskrit letters is observed in U shape or V shape on seals. It is dynamic and resourceful.
(2) Bharani Nakshatra mixed with Sanskrit letters is observed for passionate and determined.
(3) Krittika mixed with Sanskrit letters is observed for assertive and bold.
(4) Rohini mixed with Sanskrit letters is observed for creative and artistic skill.
(5) Mrigashirsha mixed with Sanskrit letters is observed for curious and inquisitive.
(6) Ardra mixed with Sanskrit letters is observed for strong intellect.
(7) Punarvasu mixed with Sanskrit letters is observed for optimistic and intelligent.
(8) Pushya mixed with Sanskrit letters is observed for compassionate and responsible.
(9) Ashlesha mixed with Sanskrit letters is observed for sharp and emotional.
(10) Magha mixed with Sanskrit letters is observed for sense of authority and legacy.
(11) Purva Phalguni mixed with Sanskrit letters is observed romantic and artistic.
(12) Uttara Phalguni mixed with Sanskrit letters is observed for disciplined and organized.
(13) Hasta mixed with Sanskrit letters is observed for creativity and practicality.

(14) Chitra mixed with Sanskrit letters is observed for charming and dynamic.
(15) Swati mixed with Sanskrit letters is observed for independent adventurous.
(16) Vishakha mixed with Sanskrit letters is observed for intelligence and leadership.
(17) Anuradha mixed with Sanskrit letters is observed for loyal empathetic.
(18) Jyeshtha mixed with Sanskrit letters is observed for responsible leadership.
(19) Moola mixed with Sanskrit letters is observed for independent and freedom loving.
(20) Purva Ashadha mixed with Sanskrit letters is observed for determination and optimism.

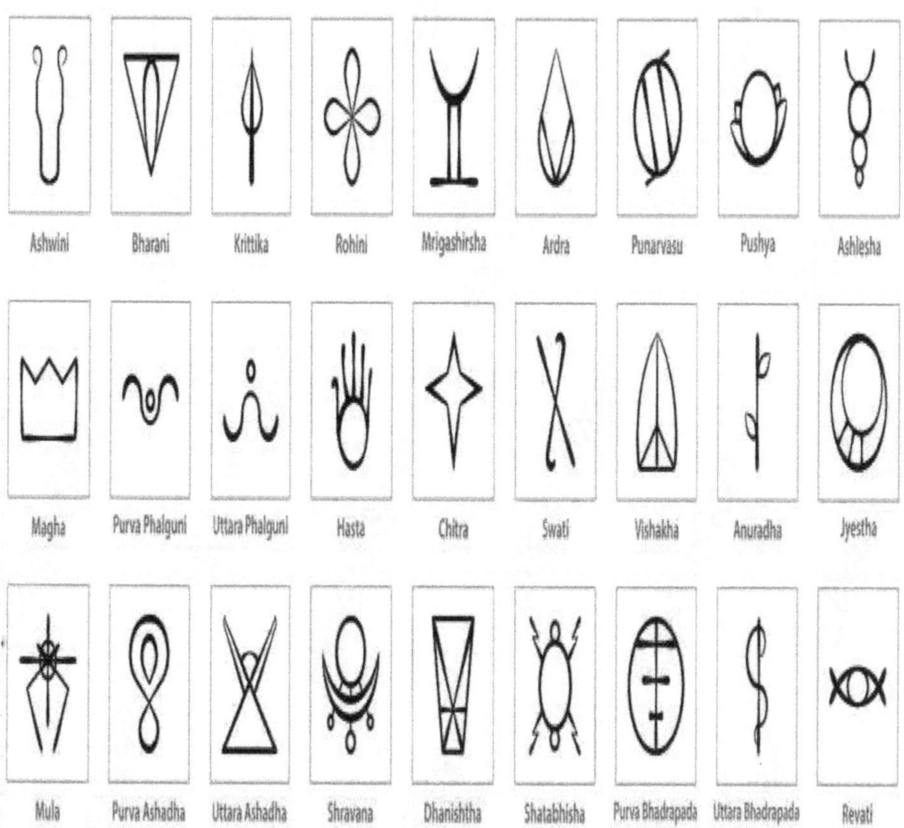

TWENTY SEVEN ASTERISMS (*NAKSHATRAS*) SIGN WAS AVAILABLE ON SEALS AND SCRIPT. SIGNS OF SPRING, DOUBLE SPRING, O, OO WITH OUTER COVER OR ELLIPTICAL SHAPE, NOTCH, DOUBLE NOTCH, ARROW, DOUBLE ARROW AND INVERTED V IN THE ZODIAC SIGNS WAS OBSERVED. IT WAS DONE TO SHOW PARTICULAR TIME, *MUHURTA*, DATE AND PLACE OF COMMENCEMENT OF TRADE WITH VALUE OF COMMODITY. ALPHABETS OF INDUS CIVILIZATION CONTAINS 16 + 32 = 48 LETTERS ONLY. VARIOUS

Fig. 2.8

(21) Uttara Ashadha mixed with Sanskrit letters is observed for ethical and dependable.
(22) Shravana mixed with Sanskrit letters is observed for good listeners and intelligent.
(23) Dhanishta mixed with Sanskrit letters is observed for artistic and social.
(24) Shatabhisha mixed with Sanskrit letters is observed for independent and innovative.
(25) Purva Bhadrapada mixed with Sanskrit letters is observed for idealistic and spiritual.
(26) Uttara Bhaadrapada mixed with Sanskrit letters is observed for open mind and wealthy.
(27) Revati mixed with Sanskrit letters is observed for spiritual and creative.

2.9 KNOWLEDGE OF LUNAR AND SOLAR CALENDAR

Indus people knew about lunar and solar calendar and seals show the pictures of *Nava-grahas* and twenty seven *Nakshatras*. People knew about 30 days lunar month and 365 days solar month. Addition of dates (*tithis*) in lunar calender and change in position of moon was depicted on 'Alphabets' as observed on seals. Every day of year was given one symbol or 'Alphabet' where addition of notch, line or globules was shown in left or right side of symbol to depict increase or decrease of date. Thus all the days of year were given a particular identity basing upon twelve *Rashis* (zodiac stars) and twenty seven asterisms in a year. It is the reason that seals show many types of 'Alphabet like' structures which are actually dates associated with signs of asterisms. People used to start their work on particular date, nakshatra and time basing on lunar and solar calendars. The seals show importance of all nakshatras with dates and numbers of tithis of calender.

In the lunar months of 29 or 30 days, they used to put lines before or after the main symbol to show decrease or increase of dates of months. In the solar months, they used to add pictures of twelve zodiac signs to mark beginning of month. Words of Sanskrit were added with dates and months to show identity of particular tribe or clan or name of elite ruler. Many 'Alphabet like structures' are created by combination of Sanskrit letters and twenty seven nakshatras. Many 'Alphabets' show numerals with one of *rashis* or *grahas* (planet) which stands for date of sale and purchase according to calendar.

The civilization subsisted primarily on agriculture supplemented by commerce. Wheat, barley, peas, cotton and mustard etc were grown. Cows, buffaloes and dogs were commonly found. Ivory was probably obtained from Indian elephants of forest areas and was used for trade. Social stratification was existing and crafts developed to high extent. Extensive trade was well regulated and provided employment to all class of people. There was uniformity in weights and measures and granaries were well controlled. Lingua franca was one and uniformity was found at every level of livelihood. Artistic activity was common in people and they produced all types of figures, e.g., seated men, animals, standing persons, dancing girls in cast-bronze figures. Toys, small chariots, carts and animal figures were commonly found. Bronze statue prepared with high technical excellence shows highly developed art of Indus people.

Tera-cota figurines contain standing females laden with jewellery and accompanying males show peaceful and happy life of society. Tradition of painting shows delicacy and devotion of people and painted pottery were common, both for local use and trade purpose. Best known artifacts were seals prepared from steatite carved in intaglio or incised with a copper burin. Animals of seven suras, e.g., bull, elephant, rhinoceros, tiger, bison etc were commonly shown on seals along with Indus numerals and signs of asterisms. Important metals used for preparation of tools and implements was bronze and copper. Implements included knives, chisel, arrowheads, spears and saws etc. People knew about casting, chiseling and hammering and produced beautiful vessels.

Statues of men, women and animals were made by lost wax process. Gold, silver and lead was also used for different purposes including bead making. Manufacture of earthenware decorated with colored glazes was common and persists even today in many parts of sub-continent. Working of shell and ivory was also common especially for trade. Cotton textiles were used and people knew about spinning, weaving and dying of textiles. Indus oeople employed systematic and regular system of weights and measures. Accuracy in architectural works was excellent and use of high quality mortar preserved the houses for longer periods. Regular give and take and trade with cities and empire of Mesopotamia was common.

Thirty two class of crystal symmetry was known to Indus people. They were knowing about seven crystal system, i.e., triclinic, monoclinic, orthorhombic, cubic, trigonal, tetragonal and hexagonal. The shape of crystals influenced formation of letters and script. Letters are created as 'Sound Wave Packets' having mass as 32 consonant letters within atmosphere of planet earth. Many 'Alphabet like structures' are words created by combination of Sanskrit letters and solid crystal forms. Words on seals show combination of letters with nakshatra and numerals showing value of articles. Many 'Alphabets' are words created by combination of Sanskrit letters and numerals stand for date of sale and purchase etc.

Seven crystal system was known to them and alphabets are projected in mostly crystalline forms. Crystals of different forms with some modification on left or right side show value of object at that place. Signs and signages developed in crystalline forms for dockyards, storage godowns, trade centres and rest rooms etc. Symbols for worship and places of congregation developed in symmetrical crystalline forms. Town planning was excellent and people loved peaceful life.

2.10 KNOWLEDGE OF DESH, KAL AND DISHA

In all scientific calculations, three things are important for consideration as mentioned below:
1. Place (Desh): It stands for longitude, latitude and altitude.
2. Time (Kaal): It stands for 24 hours rotation, 365.25 days revolution and 43.20,000 years period of precession of planets and stars.
3. Direction (Disha): It means four directions, i.e., east, west, north and south. All the objects are guided by four directions due to four forces.

Indus scripts mention about place with different marks. They have mentioned day, tithi and zodiac months with symbols on seals. Direction has been shown by arrow on seals in four directions. Bigger and raised houses were located in western side of the town and smaller houses were found in eastern part of town. Ruling elite resided in bigger houses in western part of town and their doors opened towards east direction. In the morning when they opened their doors, sunlight and sun was visible to them in east direction. It shows that they worshiped Rashis (zodiac) signs.

2.11 KNOWLEDGE OF HUMAN ANATOMY AND PHYSIOLOGY

U - shaped tube like structures show that they had good idea about spinal cord or nervous system. The spinal cord stores oxygen and becomes vibrant from bottom to top in gradual maner.

The idea about Kundalini Shakti and raising of air and breath inside spinal cord up to seventh point is observed in seals, pottery and other artifacts.

PICTURE OF SEVEN KNOT KUNDALINI SHAKTI AND YOGA WHICH WAS KNOWN TO INDUS PEOPLE. *ANAHATA* KNOT HAS BEEN SHOWN WITH A CIRCLE NEAR HEART IN ONE SEAL AND IT IS THORACIC HEART PLEXUS IN SPINAL CORD. *ANAHATA* KNOT CONTAINS TWELVE SPINAL NERVES WHICH ARE *KA, KHA, GA, GHA, ANGA, CHA, CHHA, JA, JHA, EINA, TA* AND *THA* SPREAD IN CIRCULAR FASHION INSIDE SPINAL CORD.

Fig. 2.9

One seal shows that enlightenment takes place at upper most highest point of spinal cord which shows dash, coils and round structures. Human nervous system has about 100 billion neurons, majority of the neurons occur in the brain. The contraction of neurons increases the thinking power of brain and inner energy becomes more powerful. The oxygen element devours time and stops the impact of time on human body. It is read as *"Sushumna bhakshayate Samayah"*. Oxygen inside spinal cord protects body, devours time and preserves body for long time in cold places and stops degeneration of body. Extra-oxygenation of spinal column protects body, enriches body growth increases metabolism and provides energy to body. It protects human body from decay and degeneration for long time. This science was known to them and one seal shows man practising kundalini shakti. One circle near heart shows thoracic heart plexus which contains 12 thoracic nerves in spinal cord.

48

CENTERS OF NERVES INSIDE SPINAL CORD OF HUMAN BEINGS

NUMB-ER OF KNOTS	FIXED CENTRES OR KNOTS INSIDE SPINAL CORD	NAME OF THE KNOT CENTRE FROM BOTTOM OF SPINAL CORD	NUMBER OF NERVES EMER-GING FROM KNOT	NAME OF GROUP	NUMBER OF EFFEC-TIVE NERVES DURING LIFTING UP OF AIR	TOTAL NUMBER OF NERVES ACTING INSIDE CENTRAL NERVOUS SYSTEM
7	Cerebral cortex of brain	Sahasra-sara	1024	**Vacuum**		$1024 \times 10^2 \times 10^2 \times 10^2$ $=$ 1024,000,000 Nerves
6	Thalamus Plexus Basal Ganglion (two lobes of brain)	ॐ Ohm	2	Gas	2	512×2 = 1024 Nerves
5	Throat Cervical plexus	हं Ham	16	Liquid	16	32×16 = 512
4	Heart plexus Thoracic	यं Yam	12	Solid	20 + 12 = 32	20 + 12 = 32
3	Coeliac-Axis Plexus Lumbar	रं Ram	10	Solid	10 + 10 = 20	10 + 10 = 20
2	Hypogastric Plexus Sacral	वं Bam	6	Solid	4 + 6 = 10	4 + 6 = 10
1	Basic or Pelvic plexus Coccygeal (base of spinal cord joining both respiratory tracts)	Lam लं	4	Solid	4	4

Table 2.1

The Indus civilization was highly developed and they had knowledge about quantification and computing system with designs, calculations and engineering methods for building construction and sewerage system etc. Statues, pictures of animals and idols etc of different seals and sites show qualitative advancement of the civilization and projection has been done mostly with local features. The creation of words and literature for all their excellent work is not traceable now. It can not be said that Indus people did not have elaborate writing system. During late Indus period, scholars of Sanskrit grammar came into prominence and formation of words of different types developed. Sanskrit grammarians emerged on scene during late Indus period and clear words were created late. Subsequently sentences were framed with these words in subsequent civilizations. Probably clear writing system of civilization is not traceable and was destroyed in course of time. Many seals, metallic plate inscriptions and statues showing cultural values etc have vanished in course of time and are traceable in less numbers.Sanskrit was the main language of Indus people and Prakrit and Pali languages were mixed at different places during course of time.

Intelligent persons of civilization were having good idea about nervous system and Kundalini Shakti. They knew that Sanskrit Language emerged from nerves of human body. The cervical nerves, thoracic nerves, lumbar nerves, sacral nerves and coccygeal nerves produce sixteen vowels and thirty two consonants respectively. Intellectuals of civilization had clear idea about human nervous system and Sanskrit language was given by them to posterity on earth. The vowels and consonants of Devanagari script were created by them with structures like, *shirorekha*, hyphen, dash, notch, globules, rounded structures, spring and arrow etc. They created most systematic language on scientific lines for posterity.

Indus script was close to hieroglyphic alphabets of other countries with which it had trade relations and regular give and take was taking place among adjoining countries including Egypt. Many symbols were not alphabets but 'trade symbols' for commercial purposes, e.g., parking place with anchor, storage godown, stairs and halt etc. The civilization had trading relations with many provinces, countries and communities and trade symbols were shown at many places to convey message to outside traders and ships near coastal areas. Many symbols which appear as alphabets were signs and signages of capital of place, kingdom, ladies places, gurukul or schools, bathing place, market place, ladies place, ruler's palace and godown of foodgrains etc. The places of worship and arms storage etc was not found and it seems that kingship and kingdom was not established. It may be one of the reasons for migration of civilization because command of ruler was not there and directives of ruler to common people have not been found. General people engaged themselves in agriculture, animal husbandry, trade and festivals etc and lack of polity and future direction by ruler may be one of the reasons for lack of cohesion and consequent migration by people to different places.

Devanagari script is an abugida based on ancient Prakrit and Brahmi script. The orthography of script reflects the pronunciation of language. It has strong preference for symmetrical rounded shapes within squared outlines and is recognized by a horizontal line that runs along top of full letters. It bears the name *Deva* (God) + *Na* (No or not) + *Gra, Gree, Gri* (Gurutva or self gravitation). It means language of gods that do not settle on earth. It means language of gods or Aryans or intellectuals who do not live at one place and are moving in air in floating state. It is said as *Vani Vihar* or script of a language (*Vani*) moving freely and floating (*Vihar*) in atmosphere. It developed in later period.

2.12 KNOWLEDGE OF FOURTEEN STARS CLUSTER

Script shows many signs and symbols which appear as atoms of elements placed in numerical order. They knew about fourteen stars cluster, ions and formation of elements and compounds. They knew about chemical elements, metals, melting of metals and preparation of statues and other articles from copper and bronze. It is observed from appearance of same type of symbols with slight modification in every symbol. It is evident from alphabet like structures which who show increase in complication and addition of hyphen, notches and circles in gradual manner.

The statues, metallic plates and metallic toy like structures show that people knew about chemical elements, metals and their properties. The civilization flourished in a big area and survived for quiet long time. Some letters show structures like wire mesh, dance, rituals and small factories etc. There was no downfall of civilization rather people migrated to adjoining areas due to many reasons. One possible reason of migration may be their experimentation for artificial use of fission energy with heavy elements in 'laboratory'. Somehow they came to know about fission. It seems that nuclear implosion test was carried out without any protection efforts and people gathered there to see the result. Experiment on Nuclear fission test without adopting safety measures might have led to blast and death of many persons who were present at site. This may be one of the possible reasons that many people died on spot and their bones were found at that place in plenty. This may be one reason for migration of Indus civilization people to other areas later on.

There was no outside attack on Indus civilization and no decline of civilization. If there was outside attack on people then signs of cut and attack on skull and skeleton could have been observed. Further, attack of any epidemic and flood etc will not kill so many persons at one place and at one time. Gradually people of villages migrated to adjoining areas in search of better habitations, clean water and fertile lands. They settled throughout the sub-continent spreading their knowledge with acculturation and local modifications in different geographical areas. The living pattern with pastoral life has been modified drastically at many places but life style continues to be the same in rural areas even today. They migrated to Eastern part of Indian sub-continent upto Singhbhum plateaus of old Bengal Province and in Western part upto Afghanistan Province. In Northern India they inhabited land upto Tibet and in Southern India they migrated upto Tamil Nadu State. Cultural continuity persists even today throughout the Indian sub-continent.

2.13 LANGUAGE READING

Indus people were reading Sanskrit mixed with signs of nature. Words were created with date and time of *nava-grahas*, as for example, three days before full moon or five days after new moon, this happening took place. As for example, marriage will solemnize three hours after rise of sun during this day during Purva Phalguni Nakshatra and daughter will leave house four hours after Libra sign of zodiac star. House construction will begin three days after krittika nakshatra begins. Schools will begin on first day of Uttara Phalgun nakshatra. Auspicious time begins on second day of ashwin nakshatra of lunar calendar. Vowels and consonants created words which was mixed with natural signs in the form of pictures and were spoken in regional languages. Some of the regional languages with local modifications are spoken even today.

Vowels with spring symbol, double spring, triple spring either on one side or both sides were seen with consonant letters. Notch, arrow or double arrow with consonant letters was created with some meaning and was used in daily affairs. Seals were mainly for trade purposes and signs related to money transaction, rulers identity, goods sold and value with date was mentioned on seals. Indus numerals were common on all the seals accompanied with signs of Revati nakshatra and Min rashi. Probably these two symbols were goods of trade. Consonant letters, i.e., *Pa, Pha, Ba, Bha, Gha, Jha, Tha, Dha, Sha (Murdhanni Sha)* mixed with natural signs created words which were commonly used. Letters of Sanskrit were added with solar and lunar calendar days for trade and reference. Addition of dash, hyphen, arrow, notch, circle and spring like structure on the left side of letter stands for *a, aa, i, ee, u, oo*. In last six vowels, addition of dash, hyphen, arrow, notch, circle and spring like structure on the right side of letter stands for *e, ai, o, au, am* and *ah*.

2.14 LANGUAGE WRITTING

Indus people were writting letters of Sanskrit mixed with signs of nature. Words were created in devanagari script without *sirorekha* and mixed with date and time. During writing many local features, e.g., pictures of animals, plants, flower and human being have also been added with letters. Many pictures were derieved from seven suras of sound and appeared on seals. Addition of dash, hyphen, arrow, notch, circle and spring like structure on the left side of letter stands for *a, aa, i, ee, u, oo*. In last six vowels, addition of dash, hyphen, arrow, notch, circle and spring like structure on the right side of letter stands for *e, ai, o, au, am* and *ah*. Consonant letters, i.e., *Pa, Pha, Ba, Bha, Gha, Jha, Tha, Dha, Sha* (*Murdhanni Sha*) mixed with natural signs created many words which were commonly used. Square and rectangular structures contained letters of alphabets and gradually helped in creation of upper line above letters and words. Letters of early Indus civilization period did not contain *Shirorekha* on all vowels and consonants of Sanskrit.

2.15 LANGUAGE SPEAKING

Indus people were speaking Sanskrit mixed with signs of nature. Colloquial language created with date and time by addition of dash and hyphen etc was common. Hundreds of dialects were spoken throughout the sub-continent and voice (*Vani)* varied at a distance of every fourteen *Kosh* (Twenty eight miles distance). Common dialect included Sanskrit mixed Sindhi of the region as language of people. Sindhi dialects include Ladri, Thari, Lassi, Siroh or Siraike, Bhill, Khojikl, Memoni, Vicholi, Dhatkali and kutchi etc. Vichauli was the most common language in later times..Lassi was common in western part and Thari was close to Rajasthani. It is said that '*Sat kosh par pani badale aur Choudah kosh par vani*' meaning that every seven kosh (fourteen miles) taste of water changes and voice changes every fourteen *Kosh* (Twenty eight miles distance).

2.16 DEVELOPMENT OF SANSKRIT GRAMMAR

During early Indus civilization period scripts of many types mixed with vowels and consonants of Sanskrit were noticed. They knew about Sanskrit but knowledge about grammar was less and formation of words and sentences was less prevalent. Smallest part of sound wave which cannot be divided further creates letters of Sanskrit. During late period, scholars of Sanskrit grammar became prominent and formation of words of different types developed. Scholars created grammar during late Indus period and afterwards. Use of words and sentences continued in later civilizations throughout the sub-continent.

During late Indus civilization period and afterwards Sanskrit grammar became prominent. Many grammarians came into prominence and created complex and compound words and sentences. We get traces of Sandhi or addition of vowels and consonants with the nakshatra signs on seals at many places. 'Complex word like structure or Alphabet' was created which carried some meaning to traders of Indus civilization.

The knowledge of dot above line (*Anuswar*), *Visarga* (:), *Jihwamuliyya* (X) and *Updhamaniya* (X) appears on seals. Short vowels (*Harshwa swara*), long vowels (*Dirgha swara*) and protracted vowels (*Pluta swara*) were mentioned on seals in the form of hyphen, dash, globules and spring like structures. Images on pottery depict that people knew about simple vowels and Diphthongs.

2.17 CREATION OF WORDS

Indus people were reading Sanskrit mixed with signs of nature. Words were created with date and time. On seals we get traces of arrow and lines with vowels and consonants and it shows that they had developed the idea of creation of words with natural signs. Creation of words took place during late Indus period or probably after Indus period of civilization.

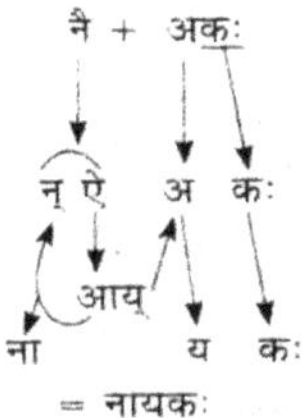

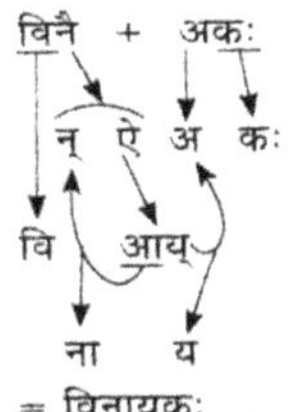

WORDS ARE CREATED AS 'SOUND WAVE PACKETS' BY INTERMIXING OF VOWELS AND CONSONANTS.
Fig. 2.10

Sixteen Sanskrit vowels and thirty two consonants were mixed to create compound words and complex words are less in number because they had less idea about Sanskrit grammar. Good knowledge about grammar developed late and its use was found in subsequent civilizations. Sanskrit was the common language of people but use of grammar was very less and this may be one of the reasons that complex words of Sanskrit are found in less number on seals. Complex words and long sentences were very less in number as seen on seals, pottery and other artifacts of Indus civilization and long sentences etc written on seals and leaves etc are not found. Use of compound words and sentences developed during subsequent civilization period later on.

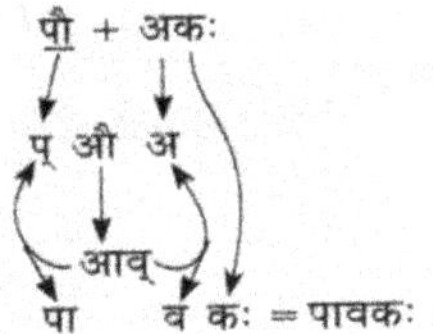

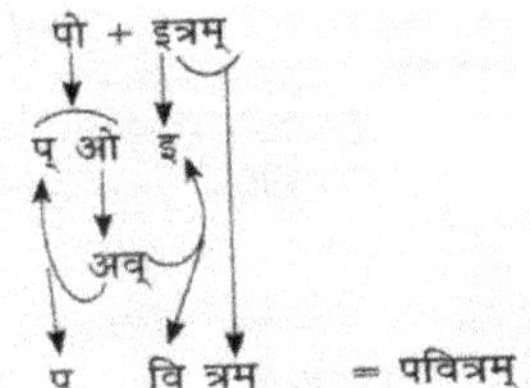

WORDS ARE CREATED AS 'SOUND WAVE PACKETS' BY INTERMIXING OF VOWELS AND CONSONANTS.
Fig. 2.11

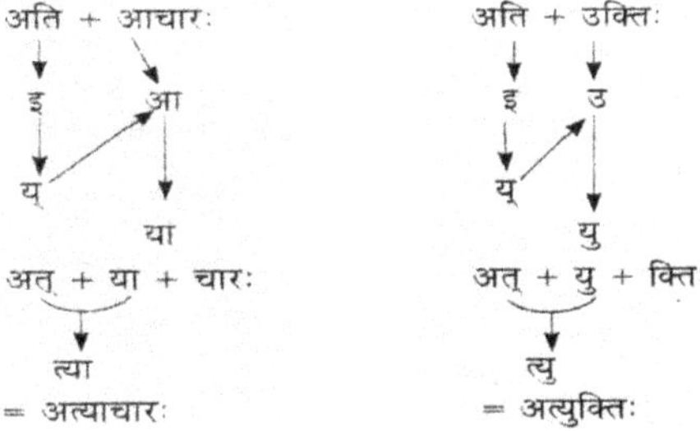

WORDS ARE CREATED BY INTERMIXING OF DIFFERENT VOWELS AND CONSONANTS.
Fig. 2.12

Sanskrit is a systematic language of nerves developed on the basis of body parts along three axes and 'jumbled words' developed in Sanskrit effect body parts of human beings.

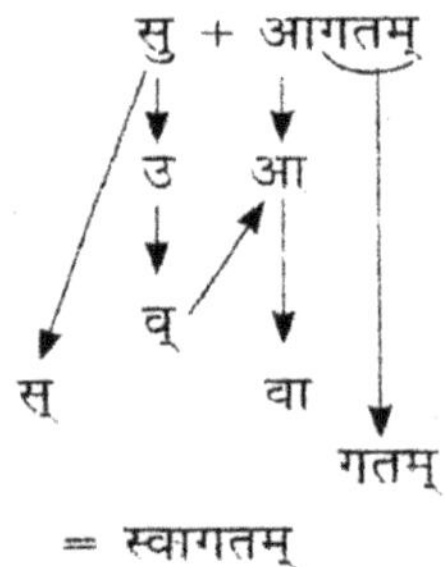
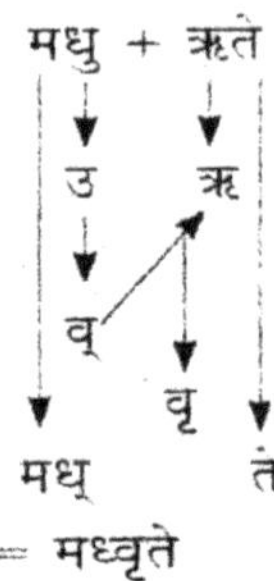

CREATION OF WORDS TAKES PLACE BY INTERMIXING OF VOWELS AND CONSONANTS
Fig. 2.13

The creation of alphabets, letters and words takes place by retention and settlement of mass in the same pattern as elements are created. The letters form words, jumbled words and combination of words makes sentences containing many letters inside it in many forms. It takes place in the similar pattern as molecules and compounds are created out of many elements.

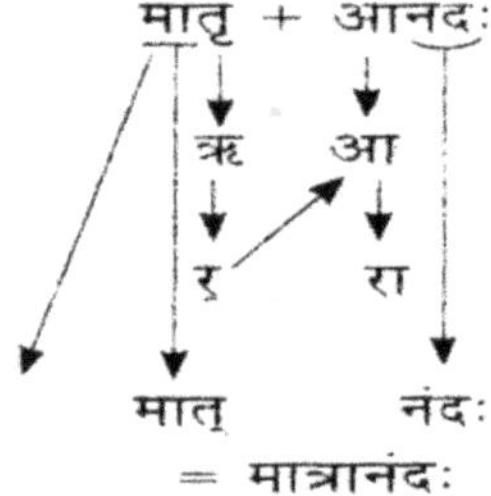
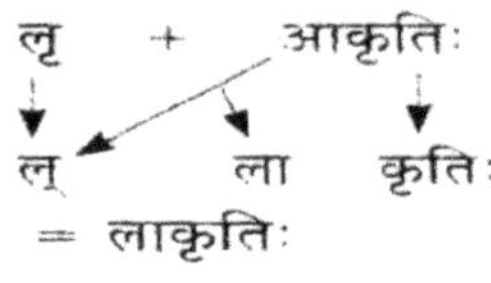

WORDS ARE CREATED AS 'SOUND WAVE PACKETS' BY INTERMIXING OF VOWELS AND CONSONANTS.
Fig. 2.14

During late Indus civilization period and subsequent civilizations, Sanskrit was the main language and Devanagari script added *Shirorekha* on words and sentences at all places.

Knowledge about twelve rashis, twenty seven asterisms, navagraha etc persisted with Indus people even after migration to distant areas. They mixed their knowledge with local skill and old knowledge persisted with them.They persued their old habits like bathing, cultivation, drainage, house construction etc meticulously in different parts of the continent. They pursued their inherent knowledge and even today we get traces of road construction and cleanliness etc. They completed their works in date and time and according to rashis and natural signs. As for example, construction of house in Ashwini Nakshatra (*U* type symbol), marriage in Revati nakshatra which is having fish like symbol, commencement of work in Aries sign in third or fourth date (*tithis*) of calender etc continues even today. Lunar and solar calenders are followed meticulously by residents of the continent. Datails of pursuance are observed in bath, drainage, worship pattern etc.

During early Indus civilization period, scripts of many types mixed with vowels and consonants of Sanskrit were noticed. They knew about Sanskrit but knowledge about grammar was less and formation of words and sentences was less prevalent. During late period, scholars of Sanskrit grammar came into prominence and formation of words of different types developed.

Sixteen Sanskrit vowels and thirty two consonants were mixed to create compound and complex words. These are less in number because they had less idea about Sanskrit grammar. Good knowledge about grammar developed late and its use was found in subsequent civilizations. Sanskrit was the common language of people but use of grammar was very less and this may be one of the reasons that complex words of Sanskrit are found in less number on seals. Complex words and long sentences were very less in number as seen on seals, pottery and other artifacts of Indus civilization and long sentences etc written on seals and leaves etc are not found. Use of compound words and sentences developed in subsequent civilizations later on.

People of early Indus phase and mature phase wrote and spoke Sanskrit mixed with asterisms and *nava-grahas* etc. Late Indus phase saw development of word and shirorekha on words. Evidence shows that they participated in vast maritime sea trade which extended from central asia to middle east. Imported raw materials included minerals from Iran and Afghanistan, jade from China and cedar wood floated down rivers from Kashmir and Himalayas. Analysis of cuboid weights suggest that they followed binary system for lower denominations - 1, 2, 4, 8, 16, 32. Decimal system was adopted for large weights.

Artistic activities provide insight into living pattern, religious and natural beliefs but people were not orthodox and coperaation among people was very high. It is evident from flourishing trade and exports. Technical excellence of the bronze articles shows highly developed art of Indus people. Seals show a high level of workmanship at all places of civilization. Thousands of mature Indus sites have been reported and some have been excavated and uniformity was found in script and language and use of natural signs with Sanskrit was observed at all places. Widespread occurrence of inscriptions indicate that lingua franca was same and there was uniformity as deciphered from seals.

3
SANSKRIT

Sanskrit or Samskrutam or Sanskritam is the language of human body. It originated from different nerves of human body and controls different parts, organs and systems of human body. Sanskrit is the adorned and perfected oldest language for which substantial documentation exists throughout the world. It was the general language of Indian Sub-continent in ancient times. Its history can be traced back to the people who spoke Aryan languages, Indo-European languages with several hundred related languages and dialects. Sanskrit manuscript on palm leaf is available at many places and it was used to write the Vedas and texts. The script of Sanskrit language was Devanagari which became common during Vedic age. Language and script are based on nerves of human body and its control over functioning of organs, systems and parts of human body along three axes.

Sanskrit is the oldest eternal language because it has emerged from different nerves of human body. Sanskrit comes from Samyak Krutam of language. It means 'whole or perfect and complete pious knowledge' with 'krutam' means work done. Sanskrit is the original language which incorporates all knowledge brought together at one forum. Its origin lies in nervous system of human body and every nerve produces one letter of vowels and consonants. All the nerves constitute nervous system and provide information to brain about the letters and words. The voice that comes out from vocal cord is the product of all nerves guided and coordinated by brain. Vedic Sanskrit was orally preserved as part of the vedic chanting traditions, predating alphabetic writings in India for several centuries. The language contained 32 consonants and 16 vowels.

Sanskrit is a secular human body language and it has no link with any caste, creed, class, community, religion and country. The language based on nerves of human beings accompanied with chanting of words of particular frequency developed in Northern snowy mountains, North Himalayas, Singhbhum, Tibet and Central Asian places called as Sanskrit with *Devanagari* script and was common among group of intelligent people. It was given different names by different communities and gradually mixing with other languages it spread to many countries. Any community may develop language and alphabets depending upon the charge and energy associated with elements, letters and words. It will help in strengthening the community, migration to better places and improvement of health of that community. Sanskrit language developed with 32 consonants and 16 vowels and gradually accommodated many letters of mixed alphabets in different countries of the world. Samskrutam often referred as Sanskrit language has developed on scientific lines of vocal cord, spinal nerves, cervical nerves, cranial nerves and seven body systems developed on seven colors system in human body.

Sanskrit has emerged and developed on scientific lines and shows links with many other branches of science. The 'sound wave packets' like power wave packets, which are emitted from the vocal cord of animals and human beings, move towards atmosphere, ozone layer and space and convert into electromagnetic waves of higher frequency and low energy. These wave packets hit back the animal body, human body and groups of different genus and species on planets and effects growth of body along three axes. The sound wave packets called letters (*Varnas*) are of different types emitted by different animals and human beings. Forty eight sound wave packets emitted from mouth of human being produce sixteen vowels and thirty two consonants as mentioned below:

(a) Gutturals (kanthaya): (*Ka - Varga* : *Ka* to *Anga*) - These letters are pronounced with the help of throat.

(b) **Palatals (talabya):**   (*Cha - Varga : Cha* to *Eina*) - These letters are pronounced with the help of jaw.

(c) **Cerebrals (murdhanya):** (*Ta – Varga : Ta* to *Na*) - These letters are pronounced with tongue hitting the roof of the mouth.

(d) **Dentals (dantya):**   (*Ta – Varga : Ta* to *Na*) - These letters are pronounced with the help of teeth.

(e) **Labials (oushthya):**   (*Pa – Varga : Pa* to *Ma*) - These letters are pronounced with the help of lips (upper and lower lips should meet each other).

(f) **Soft Consonants (Antastha):** (*Ya* to *Va*) - Four letters from *Ya* to *Va* are emitted from mouth as Soft Ungrouped Consonants.

(g) **Sibilant Consonants (Oushma):** (*Sha* to *Sa*) - Three Hard consonants from *Sha* to *Sa* are created with a hissing noise. They are known as *Aghosh Sangharshi.*

The 32 consonants of this language correspond to *ka, kha, ga, gha, anga, cha, chha, ja, jha, iena, ta, tha, da, dha, anda, ta, tha, da, dha, na, pa, pha, ba, bha, ma, ya, ra, la, va, sha, sha, sa* (32 consonants in the form of 32 crystal classes and vertical groups of elements). Four letters, i.e., *ha, ksha, tra* and *jnana* are created by mixing of different letters. In total, 32 letters from *ka* to *sa* emerge from spinal nerves in human body. The 16 vowels of this language correspond to *a, aa,, i, ee, u, oo, rhi, rhee, lri, lree, e, ai, o, au, am* and *ah*. Vowels are produced by throat or '*Kantha*' from cervical nerves called '*Kanthaya*'.

Vowels -   अ आ इ ई उ ऊ ऋ ॠ लृ लॄ ऐ ऐ ओ औ अं अः

Consonants -   क ख ग घ ङ
च छ ज झ ञ
ट ठ ड ढ ण
त थ द ध न
प फ ब भ म
य र ल व
श ष स

Sanskrit language is based on emissions from 32 pairs of spinal nerves, 12 pairs of cranial nerves and nine body systems along three axes. Man-made languages control the nerves of animal body or human body like buttons of piano or musical instruments. The language shows impact on particular and specific nerves of every body part, organ and system and can be used for cure of diseases of living body. Life forms will be the same on all planets in terms of chemical composition, building blocks, biochemistry and genes etc. The actual shape, size and mass of life forms will be decided by expansion and contraction of mass along three axes on planets. Persons born on other planets in the universe will also have same types of characteristics having three axes attachment. The size, shape and mass of persons in the universe may vary from life forms on earth but their inner and outer features will always be dictated by three axes contraction of matter and simultaneous three axes expansion of matter.

All spoken human languages have sound systems made up of consonants and vowels. The languages vary greatly in number of these sound types. All the languages function successfully as communication systems in spite of their extremely different numbers of speech sounds. Despite numerical differences the vowels found in the world's languages are often quite similar and are produced in similar portions of the mouth. A group of sounds that may be unfamiliar to speakers of English and of European and Asian languages are the so-called click sounds found in several African languages. In the production of clicks, the tongue makes a closure with the roof of the mouth not just at one point but at two points (both at the velum and at one other point farthest forward). The primary airflow is created by making the sealed-off space larger, creating a partial vacuum, usually by lowering the tongue and jaw. When the front stoppage is released and air rushes into the partial vacuum, a click sound results. Some click sounds are made by English speakers and although they are not part of the English language itself, they are still used for communication.

Thirty two pairs of spinal nerves, i.e., sixty four nerves inside human body create all vowels and consonants of alphabet. Any community may develop language and alphabets depending upon negative and positive charge associated with elements, letters, words and alphabets. It will help in strengthening the community, migration to better places and improvement of health of that community. The alphabet may contain118 vowels and consonants to the maximum and their impact will be observed on entire body of living being. Sanskrit is created basing on 12 element blocks, nine body systems and 14 matter zones which are created in group of 32 (2 + 6 + 10 + 14) as Periodic table of elements.

Sanskrit was the language of people who migrated probably from snowy hilly areas of Himalayas or Northern hills of Earth. These places are full of snow and protect life forms from decay for millions of years inside snow. The corpse remains protected inside cold snowy mountains and after getting heat becomes active and vibrant during course of time. Intellectuals or elderly people were persons who emerged from these areas and possessed knowledge about development, anatomy and physiology of body parts along three axes. Sanskrit language is based on emissions from 32 pairs of spinal nerves, 12 pairs of cranial nerves and nine body systems along three axes. Sanskrit language controls the nerves of animal body or human body like buttons of piano or musical instruments. The language shows impact on particular and specific nerves of every body organ and system and can be used for curing the diseases of living body.

Evolution of language is the gradual change in human language over a period of time on earth. It includes origin and divergence of different languages and language families and is analogous and similar to biological evolution. The words are created by vocal cord and mouth parts of every animal under the guidance of nervous system and all body parts of animal and human being. The words are expression of a particular cause or sentiment with specific meaning for every animal and human being. The words emitted by vocal cord and mouth of animal and human being effect the body parts and organs of every living body. The words are made up of wave packets of sound waves and show definite impact on body of every living being through energy of electromagnetic waves. The sound waves inherent in languages create words as 'wave packets' at particular frequency which acts as electromagnetic waves of low frequency effecting the body of living beings. It is said that *'Raghukul rit sada chali aai, pran jaye par*

vachan na jahin'. It means that 'sound wave packets' or words emitted from mouth through vocal cords of human beings are more powerful than energy of seven color electromagnetic waves that creates human body and body parts.

अ	आ	इ	ई	उ	ऊ	ए	ऐ	ओ	औ	अं	अः
क	का	कि	की	कु	कू	के	कै	को	कौ	कं	कः
ख	खा	खि	खी	खु	खू	खे	खै	खो	खौ	खं	खः
ग	गा	गि	गी	गु	गू	गे	गै	गो	गौ	गं	गः
घ	घा	घि	घी	घु	घू	घे	घै	घो	घौ	घं	घः
च	चा	चि	ची	चु	चू	चे	चै	चो	चौ	चं	चः
छ	छा	छि	छी	छु	छू	छे	छै	छो	छौ	छं	छः
ज	जा	जि	जी	जु	जू	जे	जै	जो	जौ	जं	जः
झ	झा	झि	झी	झु	झू	झे	झै	झो	झौ	झं	झः
ट	टा	टि	टी	टु	टू	टे	टै	टो	टौ	टं	टः
ठ	ठा	ठि	ठी	ठु	ठू	ठे	ठै	ठो	ठौ	ठं	ठः
ड	डा	डि	डी	डु	डू	डे	डै	डो	डौ	डं	डः
ढ	ढा	ढि	ढी	ढु	ढू	ढे	ढै	ढो	ढौ	ढं	ढः
ण	णा	णि	णी	णु	णू	णे	णै	णो	णौ	णं	णः
त	ता	ति	ती	तु	तू	ते	तै	तो	तौ	तं	तः
थ	था	थि	थी	थु	थू	थे	थै	थो	थौ	थं	थः
द	दा	दि	दी	दु	दू	दे	दै	दो	दौ	दं	दः
ध	धा	धि	धी	धु	धू	धे	धै	धो	धौ	धं	धः
न	ना	नि	नी	नु	नू	ने	नै	नो	नौ	नं	नः
प	पा	पि	पी	पु	पू	पे	पै	पो	पौ	पं	पः
फ	फा	फि	फी	फु	फू	फे	फै	फो	फौ	फं	फः
ब	बा	बि	बी	बु	बू	बे	बै	बो	बौ	बं	बः
भ	भा	भि	भी	भु	भू	भे	भै	भो	भौ	भं	भः
म	मा	मि	मी	मु	मू	मे	मै	मो	मौ	मं	मः
य	या	यि	यी	यु	यू	ये	यै	यो	यौ	यं	यः
र	रा	रि	री	रु	रू	रे	रै	रो	रौ	रं	रः
ल	ला	लि	ली	लु	लू	ले	लै	लो	लौ	लं	लः
व	वा	वि	वी	वु	वू	वे	वै	वो	वौ	वं	वः
श	शा	शि	शी	शु	शू	शे	शै	शो	शौ	शं	शः
ष	षा	षि	षी	षु	षू	षे	षै	षो	षौ	षं	षः
स	सा	सि	सी	सु	सू	से	सै	सो	सौ	सं	सः

THIRTY TWO CONSONANTS IN ASSOCIATION WITH SIXTEEN VOWELS CREATE 512 LETTERS WHICH ARE EMITTED BY VOCAL CORD OF HUMAN BEINGS. LETTERS INTERMINGLE WITH EACH OTHER AND CREATE WORDS WHICH EFFECT PARTS, ORGANS AND SYSTEMS OF HUMAN BODY ALONG THREE AXES. THIRTY TWO CONSONANT LETTERS OF DEVANAGARI SCRIPT IN COMBINATION WITH TWELVE VOWELS ARE SHOWN ABOVE IN THE TABLE.

Table 3.1

Life with present level of science and intelligence existed on earth 43,20,000 years ago and has emerged for second time. Aryan race and intellectuals knew about anatomy and physiology of human body and developed and spoke Sanskrit language which was based on physiology of human body. Evolution of languages depend upon pressure due to gravity, temperature and atmospheric volume of individual planet. The development of living body along three axes decides the type of language which will be emitted by vocal cord of that living body. Since time immemorial, human beings have developed '*Mantras*' or cluster of jumbled words from Sanskrit alphabets which effect different parts of body and systems and help in curing the diseases. Sanskrit is the product of intellectual race who spread knowledge among local people about vocal cord, sound waves and emission and reception of language by human body. The combination of vowels with consonants produces sixteen types of letters like, as for example, *ka, kaa, ki, kee, ku, koo, kri, kree, klri, klree, ke, kai, ko, kau, kam* and *kah*.

The instruction of nervous system produces Voices, letters, alphabets and Language under impact of Spinal nerves and Cervical nerves through vocal cords inside Life forms. Vowels are produced under impact of cervical nerves whereas consonants are produced under impact of spinal nerves of nervous system. Infants of human beings at the time of birth cry and make sound like '*K...A..N....AH*', '*K...A.....AH*', '*K...A....H.....AH*', '*K...A..N... A.... AH....AH*'. The child emits first letter of sound wave packet, i.e., *Ka* from first Thoracic nerve near 8th Cervical nerve of spinal cord. It continues from ka, to kha, ...to last vowels of the cervical nerve, i.e., '*An,.....Ah*' of spinal cord of human body. It reaches its climax at 16th vowel *Ah* of cervical nerve of human body. The crying of infant at the time of birth confirms that formation of spinal nerves and cervical nerves in the infant is normal and perfect. The infant begins emission of sound from mouth from first consonant of spinal nerves, i.e., *Ka* and stretches up to last vowel, i.e., *Ah* of cervical nerves.

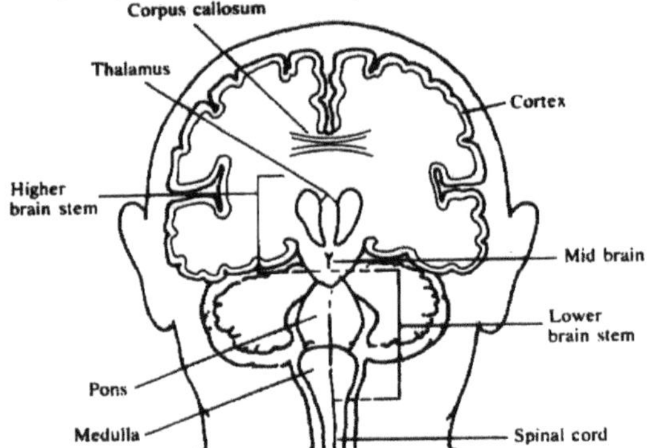

**SECTION SHOWING THE HIERARCHICAL ARRANGEMENT OF CENTRAL NERVOUS SYSTEM.
NERVES DEVELOP COORDINATION BETWEEN LANGUAGES SPOKEN AND HEARING IN HUMAN BODY.
THE NERVES IGNITE VOCAL CORD TO PRODUCE LETTERS AND WORDS THROUGH MOUTH.**

Fig. 3.1

It has been observed that left cerebral area shows speech dominance and planum temporale has been found to be larger even in fetal brains which suggests readiness of the left hemisphere for language dominance. The central and peripheral nervous systems form an intricate communication network through which the behavior of body is governed. The brain and spinal cord constitute central nervous system and are linked to peripheral nervous system by bundles of nerve fibers that extend to all parts of the body. Impulses received from peripheral receptors are sorted, interpreted and responded by the CNS. The basic cellular unit of nervous system is neuron which are about 12 billion in number in human body. Each neuron is structurally distinct and composed of (a) a cell body, (b) receptors known as dendrites and (c) a conductive mechanism or axon. Letters are produced from seven places in the human body.

(a)	*Kantha* (Throat)
(b)	*Talu*
(c)	*Moordha*
(d)	*Dantya*
(e)	*Oushtha*
(f)	*Nasika*
(g)	*Jihwa mool* (Root of Tongue)

Sanskrit is the most scientific original language created through nerves and emitted from vocal cords of human body. It is emitted by human body in Sanskrit language and often it is referred to as "Immortal Language". Its impact persists for generations and effects all human beings on earth through electromagnetic waves emitted from mouth. Sound waves are protected and proliferate inside atmospheric covering around planet. 'Sound Wave Packets' are produced like lightning in the atmosphere which exists for few seconds, shows its impact on all materials around it within atmosphere and vanishes. Its impact is visible afterwards and its existence is observed everywhere afterwards. Basing on the place of origin of pronunciation of letters, following types of letters are produced by human being:

(1) कण्ट्य वर्ण (अकुहविसर्जनीयानां कण्ठः) : अ, आ, कवर्ग, ह और विसर्ग कण्ठ से उच्चरित होने के कारण 'कण्ट्य वर्ण' कहलाते हैं ।

(2) तालव्य वर्ण (इचुयशानां तालु) : इ, ई, चवर्ग, य और श तालु से उच्चरित होते हैं इसलिए ये 'तालव्य वर्ण' हैं ।

(3) मूर्धन्य वर्ण (ऋटुरषाणां मूर्धा) : ऋ, ॠ, टवर्ग, र और ष-मूर्धन्य वर्ण हैं; क्योंकि इनका उच्चारण-स्थान मूर्धा है ।

(4) दन्त्य वर्ण (लृतुलसानां दन्ताः) : लृ, तवर्ग, ल और स—'दन्त्य वर्ण' हैं; क्योंकि इनका उच्चारण-स्थान दाँत है ।

(5) ओष्ट्य वर्ण (उपूपध्मानीयानामोष्ठी) : उ, ऊ, पवर्ग और उपध्मानीय वर्ण ओष्ठ से बोले जाने के कारण 'ओष्ट्य वर्ण' कहलाते हैं ।

(6) नासिक्य वर्ण (अमङणनानां नासिका च/ नासिकानुस्वारस्य) : ङ, ञ, ण, न, म और अनुस्वार नाक से उच्चरित होने के कारण 'नासिक्य वर्ण' कहलाते हैं ।

(7) कण्ठतालव्य वर्ण (एदैतोः कण्ठतालु) : ए और ऐ का उच्चारण कंठ और तालु दोनों से होने के कारण ये 'कण्ठतालव्य वर्ण' हैं ।

(8) कण्ठोष्ट्य वर्ण (ओदौतोः कण्ठोष्ठम्) : ओ और औ का उच्चारण-स्थान कण्ठ एवं ओष्ठ दोनों हैं । इसलिए ये दोनों वर्ण 'कण्ठोष्ट्य' हैं ।

(9) दन्तोष्ट्य वर्ण (वकारस्य दन्तोष्ठम्) : 'व' का उच्चारण-स्थान दाँत और ओष्ठ है ।

(10) जिह्वामूलीय वर्ण (जिह्वामूलीयस्य जिह्वामूलम्) : जिह्वामूलीय का उच्चारण-स्थान जिह्वामूल है ।

The central nervous system is hierarchically organized, higher structures are more complex than the lower ones. The cerebral hemisphere emerges from the higher brain stem and are covered with a convoluted sheath of gray matter called the cortex. In outward appearance the two cerebral hemispheres are roughly similar being composed of convolutions called gyri and depressions or fissures known as sulci. Within each hemisphere there are areas which serve specific functions. In front of and running parallel to the central sulcus is a strip of cortex known as the precentral gyrus which controls fine, highly skilled and voluntary motor movements. This area is also referred to as the primary motor area or primary motor cortex. Sections of primary motor area are related to voluntary movements in particular parts of the body; for example the facial and laryngeal muscles are represented in the lower end in close proximity to Broca's area.

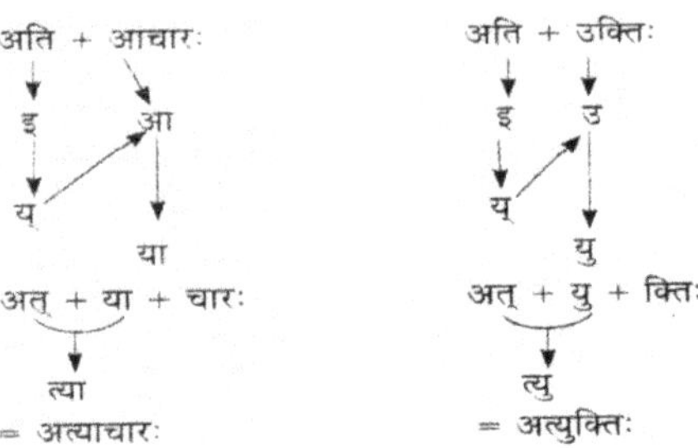

WORDS ARE CREATED BY INTERMIXING OF DIFFERENT VOWELS AND CONSONANTS OF SANSKRIT AND IN SIMILAR MANNER ATOMS AND MOLECULES OF ELEMENTS CREATE DIFFERENT COMPOUNDS.

Fig. 3.2

Sanskrit is a systematic language of nerves developed on the basis of body parts along three axes and 'jumbled words' developed in Sanskrit effect body parts of human beings. The language is a system of vocal symbols by which a social group is created and controlled in any community.

CENTERS OF NERVES

NUMBER OF KNOTS OR GROUPS	FIXED CENTRES OR KNOTS INSIDE SPINAL CORD	NUMBER OF NERVES EMERGING	NAME OF GROUP	NUMBER OF EFFECTIVE NERVES DURING LIFTING UP OF AIR INSIDE SPINAL CORD	TOTAL NUMBER OF NERVES ACTING INSIDE CENTRAL NERVOUS SYSTEM
7	Cerebral cortex of brain	1,024,000	Top of body	1024 nerves x 1000 =1,024,000 nerves	Billions of nerves
6	Thalamus Plexus Basal Ganglion (two lobes of brain)	2	Gas	512 x 2 = 1024 nerves	512 x 2 = 1024 nerves
5	Throat Cervical plexus	16	Liquid	32 x 16	32 x 16 = 512
4	Heart plexus Thoracic	12	Solid	20 +12 = 32	20 + 12 = 32
3	Coeliac-Axis Plexus Lumbar	10	Solid	10 + 10	10 + 10 = 20
2	Hypogastric Plexus Sacral	6	Solid	4 + 6	4 + 6 = 10
1	Basic or Pelvic plexus Coccygeal (base of spinal cord joining both respiratory tracts)	4	Bottom of body	4	4

Table 3.2

Sixteen vowels and thirty two consonants of Sanskrlt are basically emissions from spinal nerves of human body. The emission of one letter from vocal cord through mouth is like pressing one button of piano or harmonium. It effects the nerves of that particular organ and transmits impulse to brain. Sixteen Cervical nerves effect vocal cord and at the time of emission of voice of letters, the cervical nerves modify consonant letters with either of the sixteen vowels and produce particular sound as voice.

Sound waves are longitudinal waves and particles of the medium are pushed and pulled along the direction of propagation of sound. If the disturbance produced as wave passes along the direction of wave propagation, the wave is called longitudinal wave. All the waves cannot be characterized as either longitudinal or transverse. A very common example of wave that is neither longitudinal nor transverse is wave on the surface of water. On water surface the waves are produced because the water particles move in elliptic or circular path as the wave passes through them. The elliptic motion has two components, i.e., both along and perpendicular to the direction of propagation of wave.

Thirty two pairs of spinal nerves, i.e., sixty four nerves inside human body in total create all consonants of alphabet of Sanskrit. The sound waves require medium for propagation and they are also called elastic or mechanical waves. These waves travel in the medium of matter waves through vibration of the medium particles about their mean positions. If the vibration of medium particles is along the direction of propagation of wave, they form compression and rarefaction in the medium and the wave is called longitudinal wave, e.g., sound waves in air, solid and inside liquid. The longitudinal waves can travel in solid, liquid as well as in gas. On the other hand if the medium particles vibrate normal to the direction of propagation, forming crests and troughs, the wave is called transverse wave, e.g., solid waves in solid medium and in matter zones. Transverse waves are formed only in those media which possess rigidity. They can travel only in solids and in matter zones.

Language production is both physical and mental work and both act together to produce languages. The proper action of vocal cords and human ear are equally responsible for production and hearing of languages. The human being have developed wonderful and delicate aural system which connects human brain with all systems, organs and body parts. The human nervous system helps in understanding human language and speech. Animals respond to various noise and various voice tones but programmed way of language production is common feature of human beings. Human beings and animals have links between thought of brain, hearing capacity, speech and production of sound from mouth which is unique feature.

In the human brain, adjoining to Wernicke's area in the temporal lobe is the superior temporal gyrus known as the primary auditory cortex. When auditory impulses arrive at the superior temporal gyrus a noise is perceived but meaningful interpretation must be made by the adjacent auditory association area (Wernicke's area). This pattern of cortical organization consisting of interpretive regions of the cortex lying adjacent to sensory receiving areas is repeated in the visual cortical system and in the system receiving sensation from the body. Much progress has been made with regard to understanding how language is stored and processed by the brain. PET scans and MRI have greatly increased our ability to look inside the working of brain. ERP research offers a new and exciting approach to the study of electrical activity of the brain and data from which can be linked to specific structural and meaningful properties of human languages. White matter and Grey matter link brain with spinal cord and play significant role in transmission of information from one end to another. One of the guiding principles for research is to expand our knowledge about collection, storage and processing of information and knowledge by the brain of human beings. The speech in human beings results from an integrated cortical and sub-cortical system.

Alphabets are created according to the impact of different forces on living beings. The alphabets are created in the multiples of 9 x 12 x 14 inside any living being. The alphabets tend to develop in the multiples of nine color energy cycle. The creation of alphabets is totally dependent upon movement of spherical astral bodies in space and according to movement of astral bodies the living beings develop many parts and organs and alphabets. As higher and bigger will be the size of living being so higher and bigger will be the number of alphabets of animal concerned.

The sound waves behave as mechanical waves caused due to vibrations produced in any object placed in an elastic medium. Human being can hear vibrations of certain frequencies range only, i.e., 20 Hz to 20,000 Hz. This is called audible frequency range. The sound waves having frequency more than 20,000 Hz are called ultrasonic and waves having frequency less than 20 Hz are called infrasonic. The sound waves are further divided into two categories, (i) longitudinal waves and (ii) transverse waves. In the propagation of a longitudinal wave medium particles vibrate about their mean position in the direction of motion of the wave. When these medium particles come very close to each other it is called compression and when these particles move away it is called rarefaction. The impact of sound waves is observed as power waves but it cannot produce animals of gigantic size on any planet because all the life forms on any planet are bound by three axes attachment like electromagnet.

A longitudinal wave can travel in all three medium, i.e., solids, liquids and gases. Speed of a longitudinal wave in a medium is given by, $V = \sqrt{E/d}$, where E is elasticity of the medium and d is its density. On the other hand in the propagation of transverse waves, medium particles vibrate about their mean position perpendicular to the direction of motion of the wave. These waves can travel in solids and on liquid surface. The gas molecules are relatively free from each other and transverse waves are not possible in gases. The voice box in the mouth of human beings is one of the prominent sources of sound. It can produce sound waves having frequency range 100-1100 Hz. Different animals can also produce sound but of different frequency range. For example the mew of cat has frequency range 150-750 Hz and chirping of bird has frequency range, 2000-13000 Hz.

The sound is produced in a material medium by vibrating source. As the vibrating source moves forward, it compresses the medium past it, increasing the density locally. This part of the medium compresses the layer next to it by collisions. The compression travels in the medium at a speed which depends on elastic and inertia properties of the medium. As the source moves back, it drags the medium and produces a rarefaction in the layer. The layer next to it is dragged back and thus the rarefaction pulse passes forward. In this way, compression and rarefaction pulses are produced which travel in the medium. Sound waves constitute alternate compression and rarefaction pulses travelling in the medium. The sound is audible only if the frequency of alteration of pressure is between 20 Hz to 20,000 Hz in case of animals and human beings. The waves with frequency below audible range are called infrasonic waves and the waves with frequency above audible range are called ultrasonic waves. The compression and rarefaction in a sound wave is caused due to the back and forth motion of particles of the medium. This motion is along the direction of propagation of sound and hence sound waves are longitudinal. The impact of infrasonic waves can be observed in space.

The sound produced at some point by a vibrating source travels in all directions in the medium if the medium is extended. The sound wave packets are, in general, three dimensional wave packets. For a small source, we have spherical layers of medium on which the pressure at various elements have the same phase at a given instant. The appearance of sound to human ear is characterized by three parameters, i.e., pitch, loudness and quality. All the three are subjective description of sound though they are related to objectively defined quantities. Pitch is related to frequency, loudness is related to intensity and quality is related to waveform of sound waves.

The sound waves emitted by animals and human beings can form 'electromagnetic wave packets'. The sound waves can convert into electromagnetic waves in any medium in space. They show their impact on visible spectra (4000Å to 7500Å) of electromagnetic waves. The sound waves effect growth and development of body parts in living animals. The electromagnetic waves having frequency between 256 Hz to 512 Hz effect body organs of living animals. The electromagnetic waves in the range 4000Å to 7500Å effect body organs of all living beings. The voice box in the mouth of human beings is one of the prominent sources of sound. It can produce sound waves having frequency range 100-1100 Hz which is equivalent to power waves. Different animals produce sound waves in different frequency range. The mew of cat has frequency range between 150-750 Hz and chirping of bird has frequency range between 2000-13000 Hz. The sound waves emitted by different animals effect the entire gamut of life forms on planets in different frequency ranges because sound wave packets convert into electromagnetic waves. The sound waves emitted by animals effect the growth and development of all animals within visible spectra (4000Å to 7500Å) of electromagnetic waves on all planets in the universe.

In electromagnetic waves the charge and magnetic component work together and it is effective up to 7500Å. Above 7500Å, i.e., in microwave, radio wave and power wave regions the iron element melts and electromagnetic waves act as electric waves only. The charge accompanied with waves become equivalent to power waves and acts as sound wave packets. In the universe, in space and on planets, the sound waves act as power waves and their impact is experienced in similar manner. The frequency range of human voice ranges between 100 Hz to 1100 Hz and its impact in space becomes equivalent to power waves. The impact of sound waves is more powerful than electromagnetic waves in visible spectra range on animal body. The action and impact of sound wave packets supersedes the impact of electromagnetic waves in the range 400nm to 750nm which create human body and body parts on planets.

3.1 TYPES OF LETTERS (*VARNAS*)

The smallest part of sound wave which cannot be divided further is called Letter or *Varna*. The 'sound wave packets' are created by friction between two particles. In animals and human beings rubbing of two solid organs inside body creates sound waves. In clouds hitting of cloud particles with charges creates sound waves and collision among particles also creates sound waves. The letters created with prominence of fusion energy behave as vowels whereas letter created with prominence of fission energy behave as consonants. The number of vowels will be five as minimum on account of five electronegative non-metallic peaks. The number of vowels will be sixteen to the maximum on account of creation of elements due to colors on earth. Vowels are created and controlled by sixteen Cervical nerves in human beings. Consonants are created and controlled by thirty two pairs of spinal nerves inside human body. *Varnas* or letters emerge from nerves of nervous system of human body in the multiples of eight in geometric progression.

Phonetics (Dhwani-Shashtra) and Phonemics (Dhwani Vijnan) are two terms commonly used for speaking and listening of sound waves by human beings. It relates to production of 'sound wave packets', characteristics, musical instruments, classification of sound waves, listening and interpretation of sound wave packets by human beings. It teaches about proper and correct pronunciation of letters and words. Correct pronunciation of words and sentences effect nerves of human body. Pronunciation relates to emission of sound from proper place of vocal cord and precision in pronunciation produces correct words and sentences with justified meaning. If pronunciation is not correct than the effect will not be seen on required nerves of body. Due to improper pronunciation, the words change their form and meaning, e.g., *satya* becomes *sach*, *ghrit* becomes *ghee*, *sandhya* becomes *sanjh* and *gram* becomes *gaon* etc. Study of pronunciation informs us about changes and evolution in languages throughout the world, e.g., *Tri* - three, *Pitra* - Father, *Matri* - Mother etc.

Human being exhale carbon dioxide, nitrogen, water vapour and dust particles and along with that 'sound wave packets' of letters, words and sentences come out. The air coming out passes through mouth, nasal passage and through both and controls production of sound waves. All related parts, e.g., tongue, cord, palate, teeth, lips and uvula etc. play significant role in production of letters, words and sentences. The sound wave packets move by compression and rarefaction of waves from one place to another. Letters or *Aksharas* are created in geometric progression by different nerves of human body.

3.1.1 VOWELS (*SWARA*): Vowel is a syllabic speech sound pronounced without

any stricture from vocal cord. It gives open and clear sound without friction. Vowels act as 'unwinding force' and try to release mass from the clutches of crystals of elements on any planet. Vowels act as a balancing force as the elements settle on earth as settlement element. Different languages have got different numbers of vowels and consonants in them. The number of vowels will vary from five to sixteen in animals and human beings. The number of vowels may be different for other animals on other planets. It is fixed as sixteen for human beings. Vowels try to take matter upwards and release mass particles from atoms of elements.

A vowel is a sound for whose production the oral passage is unobstructed so that air current can flow from lungs to lips and beyond without being disturbed, without squeezing through a narrow constriction, without being deflected from the median line of its channel and without causing any supraglottal organs to vibrate. Vowels are created by rare medium zone and their impact is perceived on sixteen (eight pairs) nerves of cervical vertebrae. Vowels are sixteen in number in human beings and they effect growth and development of the human body. Vowels (*Swaras*) are short vowels (*hraswa swaras*) and long vowels (*deergha swaras*).

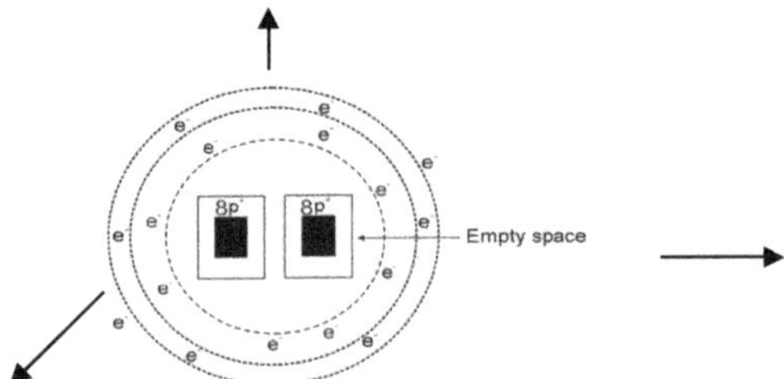

IN OXYGEN MOLECULE THE SOLID NUCLEUS PLACED TOGETHER AND SURROUNDED BY MASS OF ELECTRONS PROVIDE WAVY NON-METALLIC FORM TO OXYGEN MOLECULE. THREE AXES ATTACHMENT OF ANIMAL AND HUMAN BODY EMPOWERS VOCAL CORDS TO PRODUCE 'SOUND WAVE PACKETS MADE UP OF POWER WAVES' WHICH EFFECTS HUMAN BODY WITHIN ATMOSPHERIC COVERING OF PLANET.

Fig. 3.3

The celestial sphere can be divided in degrees starting from 1^0 to 360^0. Time is spherical in shape and divisions can be made in geometrical progression. The division in geometrical progression creates many constellations by contraction and expansion in the multiples of 2 x 2 x 3 x 3 x.........in space. It is compulsory for every solar system to contain nine planets system along axis of rotation at the time of creation in space. In the nine planets system, nine colors, e.g., white, seven colors and black play dominant role in maintaining the sequence. Vowels are created and controlled by colors cycle. Vowels are created and controlled by sixteen Cervical nerves in human beings.

66

By the process of intermixing of waves of different sizes, particles and elements, human bodies are created. The living beings with their voice release waves at different frequencies. The waves of different wave lengths create solid particles by intermixing which falls on our body and effects body with words. Different wave lengths create different words which are observed as phonetics. The permutation and combination of letters of sound create different words which have specific effect on human body. The multiplication of letters in different proportions creates different combination of words which show specific impact on human body. The increased number of alphabets increases size of body and makes body fatty and hefty.

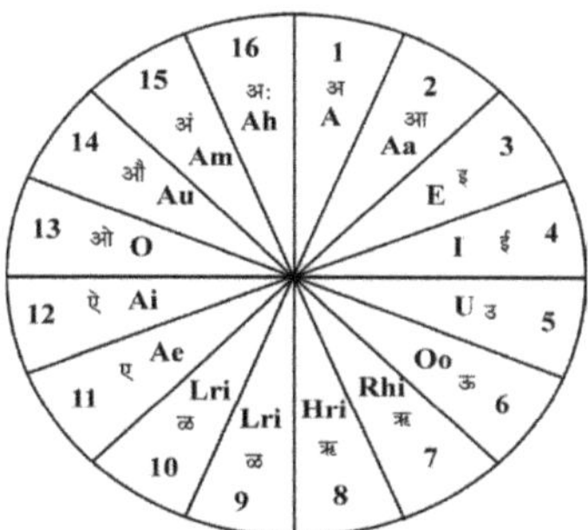

DIVISION OF CELESTIAL SPHERE IN SIXTEEN PARTS CREATES 1 + 7 + 7 + 1 = 16 ZONES OF NINE COLORS WHICH SUBSEQUENTLY CREATE NINE PLANETS SYSTEM IN GEOMETRIC PROGRESSION. NINE PLANETS SYSTEM ARE CREATED AROUND EVERY STAR ALONG AXIS OF ROTATION IN SPACE. CREATION OF SIXTEEN VOWELS TAKES PLACE IN THROAT CERVICAL PLEXUS DUE TO IMPACT OF ELECTROMAGNETIC FORCE IN GEOMETRIC PROGRESSION IN CIRCULAR ORBITS.

Fig. 3.4

Oxygen element shows peripheral crystallization of mass inside animals, human body and other life forms mainly by compounds of oxygen element. The audible range of sound waves will be different for different animals on different planets. The sound waves are equivalent to their corresponding electromagnetic waves, i.e., power waves. So the sound waves of human beings are more powerful than electromagnetic waves of seven colors (4000Å - 7500Å) that constitute the human body and create human body parts. The sound waves effect human body like power waves and sound waves can last longer like power waves in the atmosphere. The sound waves will not perish and on the patterns of power waves it will affect human body with impact on future growth. The sound waves of animal body effect present time and will affect the body in future also because power waves last longer in the atmosphere. It is the reason that 'sound wave packets' are considered to be more powerful than electromagnetic waves in visible range which shapes and constitutes human body.

Most of the languages show independent origin and maintain their individuality at many isolated places and pockets on earth. Many languages originated basing on their religious practices. Many languages having independent and isolated origin gradually mixed with other languages due to inter-marriages between different tribes, groups, clans and races. Many isolated and tribal languages having independent and isolated origin gradually mixed with other languages due to migration of people of different tribes, groups, clans and races. In flat lands and civilizations developing near major rivers the languages having independent and isolated origin gradually mixed with other languages due to acculturation between different tribes, groups, clans and races. The languages having independent origin but spoken by majority of the groups gradually mixed with other languages due to cultural integration between different tribes, groups, clans, communities and races.

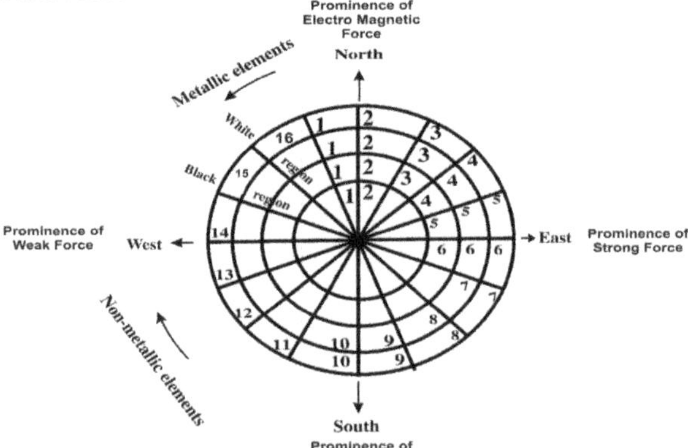

CELESTIAL SPHERE CAN BE DIVIDED INTO SIXTEEN PARTS OF 22.5⁰ EACH. ACCUMULATION OF NEGATIVELY CHARGED AND POSITIVELY CHARGED PARTICLES TAKES PLACE IN SIXTEEN MATTER ZONES IN SPACE. IT CONSISTS OF ONE WHITE ZONE + SEVEN COLOR NON-METALLIC ZONES + SEVEN COLOR METALLIC ZONES + ONE BLACK ZONE. SIXTEEN PARTS OF ANY SPHERE HELP DEVELOP ONE WHITE REGION + SEVEN COLORS REGION + BLACK REGION UNDER NINE COLORS CYCLE. FIFTEENTH (WHITE) AND SIXTEENTH (BLACK) ZONES ACT AS TRANSITION ZONES IN SPACE. CELESTIAL SPHERE IS DIVIDED INTO SIXTEEN EQUAL PARTS UNDER THE IMPACT OF FOUR FORCES. IMPACT OF ELECTROMAGNETIC FORCE IS OBSERVED IN THE MULTIPLES OF TWO, STRONG FORCE IS OBSERVED IN THE MULTIPLES OF SIX, GRAVITATIONAL FORCE IS OBSERVED IN THE MULTIPLES OF TEN AND WEAK FORCE IN THE MULTIPLES OF FOURTEEN. ACCUMULATION OF ELEMENTS TAKES PLACE IN FOURTEEN MATTER ZONES INSIDE PLANETS AND STARS. PLANETS AND STARS CONSIST OF WHITE PERIPHERAL ATMOSPHERIC ZONE + SEVEN COLOR NON-METALLIC ZONES + SEVEN COLOR METALLIC ZONES + ONE BLACK ZONE IN THE CORE. IN THE SIMILAR MANNER, HUMAN BODY CONTAINS SIXTEEN CERVICAL NERVES WHICH CONTROLS VOCAL CORD AND PRODUCES SIXTEEN VOWELS.

Fig. 3.5

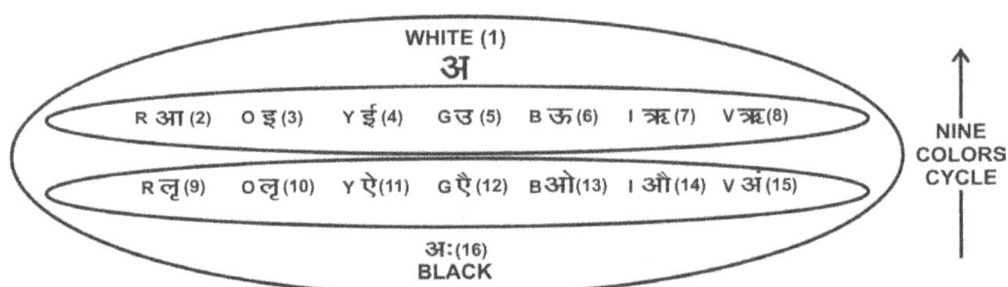

THROAT CERVICAL PLEXUS PRODUCES SIXTEEN VOWELS. EIGHT PAIRS OF CERVICAL NERVES DEVELOP SIXTEEN VOWELS EMITTED THROUGH HUMAN VOCAL CORD. IT DEVELOPS ON THE PATTERN OF SEVEN COLORS CYCLE WITH WHITE AT THE TOP AND BLACK AT THE BOTTOM. SEVEN 'SVARAS' MADE UP OF SOUND WAVES OF HUMAN BEINGS DEVELOP ON THE PATTERN OF SEVEN COLORS CYCLE ON PLANET EARTH.

Fig. 3.6

The vowels oscillate either as long vowels or short vowels from guttural, palatal, retroflex and dental to labial. Vowels are shaped by different parts of mouth in which tongue plays definite role in articulation. The front, middle and rear portion of tongue help in pronunciation. The part of tongue used for emission of letters and words depends upon the opening of mouth cavity. Partial opening, half opening and full opening decides the type of vowel emitted by mouth. Size and position of lips also varies and it may be fully rounded, partially rounded and un-rounded. Rounded lips produce the sound *U* and *Oo* whereas partially rounded and unrounded lips produce other vowels. Depending upon the time of pronunciation of letters, vowels have been divided into Small (*Harshwa Matra*) and Large (*Dirgha Matra*). *Harshwa Swaras* include *A, I, U, Rhi,* and *Lri. Dirgha Swaras* include *Aa, Ee, Oo, Rhee, Lree, Ee, Ae, O, Au.* During respiration *Hrshwa Swaras* relate to Left side breath (*Ida*) whereas *Dirgha Swaras* relate to Right side breath (*Pingala*).

3.1.2 CONSONANTS (*VYANJAN*): Thirty two classes of crystal symmetry
create thirty consonant letters of Sanskrit. Matter settles with trough of wave and creates thirty two consonant letters. The crest portion of wave creates vowels.For every settlement of two troughs of wave, one crest with one vowel letter is created. Thus creation of 32 consonant letters is related to creation of 16 vowel letters of Sanskrit. The letters are created by friction and their sound is a bit harsh. The number of consonants may vary from one to 118 in different animals and human beings. Consonants act as binding agents with high binding force and try to squeeze and retain mass in elements and in 'sound wave packets' on any planet. Consonants try to contract matter inside atoms of elements and keep mass particles bound along three axes inside human body. A consonant is the type of sound for whose production air current is completely stopped by an occlusion of the larynx or oral passage or is forced to squeeze through a narrow constriction or is deflected from the median line of its channel through a lateral opening or causes one of the supraglottal organs to vibrate.

The clockwise motion shows impact on contraction of mass in geometrical shape due to flattening of axial ratios and gradual reduction of axial angles in mass particles. The reduction of axial angles takes place in this manner: $360^0 \rightarrow 360^0 / 2 \rightarrow 180^0 / 2 \rightarrow 90^0 / 2 \rightarrow 45^0 / 3 \rightarrow 15^0 / 3 \rightarrow 5^0$. Thus contraction of waves in the multiples of 2 x 2 x 2 x 3 x 3 x 5 degrees produces mass particles of different sizes and shape and creates seven crystal systems. However, contraction of waves takes place in pairs and it will contract waves in the multiples of 2 x 2 x 2 x 2 x 3 x 3 x 5 x 5 = 3600 parts = 360^0 x 10 parts of mass particles of different sizes and shapes and creates seven crystal systems. These seven crystalline forms produce seven types of solid nucleus of atoms of elements during rotation of earth in 24 hours time period of day. The rotation of earth under seven colors cycle makes the elements cycle move in seven days week and store mass particles within seven colors cycle.

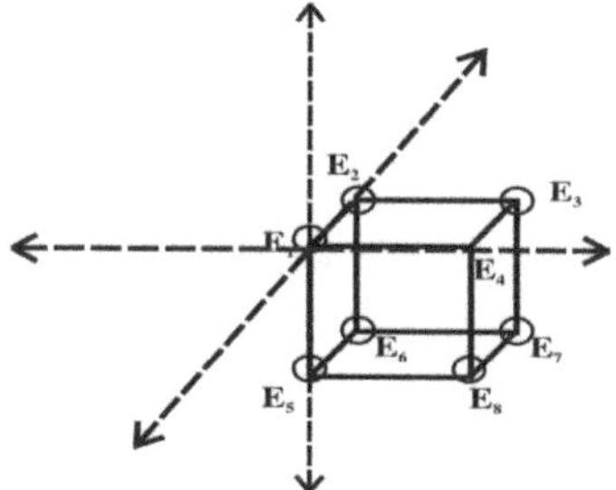

FORCES ACTING ALONG 3 AXIS

CONTRACTION OF MASS WITH THE HELP OF AXIAL RATIOS AND AXIAL ANGLES TAKES PLACE IN GEOMETRICAL PROGRESSION INSIDE PLANETS AND STARS. CONCENTRATION OF FORCES ON 24

Fig. 3.7

The contraction of mass takes place inside all the particles of elements and contraction up to $^7\sqrt{10}$ mass units shows value of 1.01815 mass units after seventh root of contraction. The contraction of mass inside crystals and compaction of individual crystals by outside crystals takes place in all the seven types of crystal system but highest quantity of mass is compacted in case of cubic crystals. The contraction of mass takes place along three axes in the ratio $10^{-84} \times 10^{-84} \times 10^{-84}$ grams or 10^{-252} units of mass and it is achieved in core of planets and stars where speed of light or 'C' becomes equal to zero. The sub-atomic particles inside atom become motionless and store energy of electromagnetic waves below 4000 Angstroms.

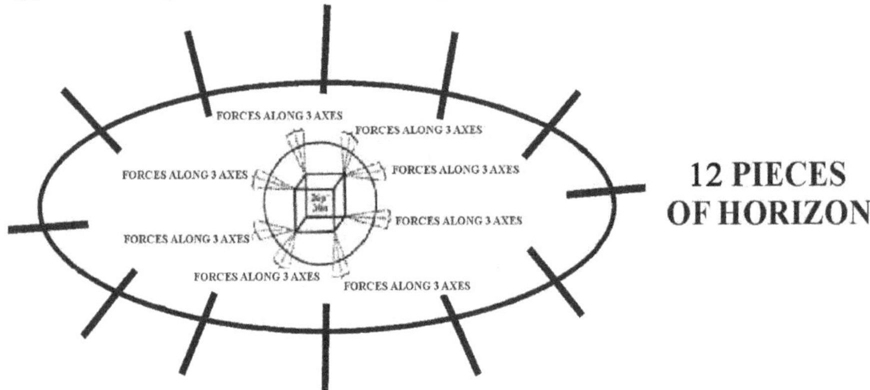

Fig. 3.8

On any planet, the atoms, compounds and minerals contain central crystal compacted by outside crystals from all around and highest level of compaction is observed due to compaction by six crystals to fourteen crystals. Full compaction of any crystal is observed by six surrounding crystals and compaction increases gradually to seven, eight, nine, ten, eleven, twelve, thirteen and fourteen surrounding crystals. Thus nine types of compactions are created from 6 to 14 inside every planet. In the ladder of evolution, it leads to formation of nine planets system due to compaction of crystals inside planets of solar system. This results in formation of nine planets system along axis of rotation of planets in solar system.

CRYSTAL SYSTEM	POSITIVELY CHARGED PARTICLES SHAPE AXIAL RATIOS	NEGATIVELY CHARGED PARTICLES SHAPE AXIAL ANGLES
Cubic	$a = b = c$	$\alpha = \beta = \gamma = 90^0$
Tetragonal	$a = b \neq c$	$\alpha = \beta = \gamma = 90^0$
Orthorhombic or Rhombic	$a \neq b \neq c$	$\alpha = \beta = \gamma = 90^0$

Monoclinic	$a \neq b \neq c$	$\alpha = \beta = 90^0, \gamma \neq 90^0$
Rhombohedral or Trigonal	$a = b = c$	$\alpha = \beta = \gamma \neq 90^0$
Triclinic	$a \neq b \neq c$	$\alpha \neq \beta \neq \gamma \neq 90^0$
Hexagonal	$a = b \neq c$	$\alpha = \beta = 90^0, \gamma = 120^0$

ELECTROMAGNETIC WAVES ARE CARRIERS OF ENERGY WHICH MOVE IN SPACE AS WHITE LIGHT. ENERGY OF ELECTROMAGNETIC WAVES BREAKS INTO POSITIVE CHARGE AND NEGATIVE CHARGE. BOTH THE CHARGES ARE EQUAL AND OPPOSITE OF EACH OTHER IN SPACE. CHARGES CANNOT REMAIN ALONE IN SPACE AND THEY CREATE POSITIVELY CHARGED PARTICLES AND NEGATIVELY CHARGED PARTICLES. POSITIVE CHARGE OF PARTICLE SHAPES AXIAL RATIOS WHILE NEGATIVE CHARGE OF PARTICLE SHAPES AXIAL ANGLES OF CRYSTALS. DURING FORMATION OF CRYSTALS, BOTH THE CHARGES JOIN HANDS AND CREATE THREE-DIMENSIONAL STRUCTURES IN GEOMETRICAL PROGRESSION INSIDE ALL ASTRAL BODIES, PLANETS AND STARS IN SPACE. ELECTRONS AND PROTONS ARE NOT EMBEDED ON ATOMS RATHER THEIR MASS DISPERSES ALONG EDGES AND DIAGONALS AND FORMS LAYER AROUND SOLID NUCLEUS OF ATOMS OF ELEMENTS. MAXIMUM CONTRACTION IS OBSERVED BETWEEN 90⁰ TO 120⁰ = SPAN OF 30⁰ WHERE SEVEN CRYSTAL SYSTEMS ARE CREATED. 7 CRYSTAL SYSTEMS X 12 PARTS OF ECLIPTIC = 84 CRYSTAL SYSTEMS ARE CREATED DURING EVERY REVOLUTION OF PLANETS AND STARS IN SPACE.

Table 3.3

Contraction of mass in geometric progression produces seven crystals system and stores matter inside planets and stars. Crystals tend to aggregate mass in the multiples of $1^3 : 2^3 : 4^3$ along three axes through axial ratios inside all life forms. Contraction of mass through axial angles in the range 90^0 to 120^0 produces seven crystals system. Seven crystals system move in twelve blocks and produce $7 \times 12 = 84$ types of crystals during every revolution of planets along one axis.

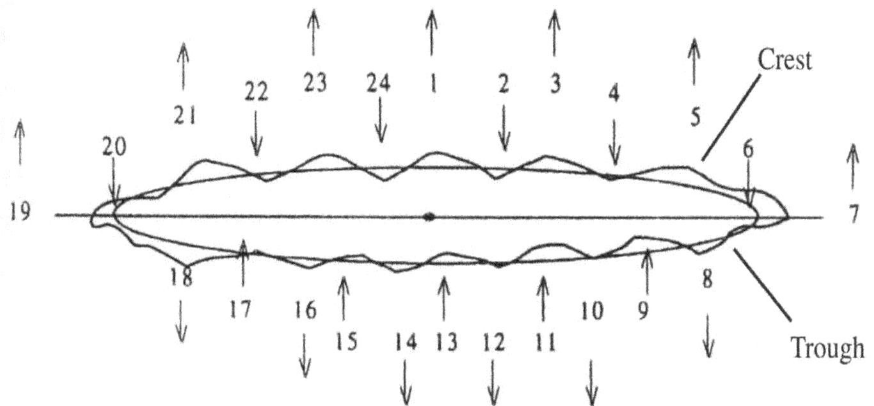

CONTRACTION OF MASS IN GEOMETRIC PROGRESSION PRODUCES CRYSTALS OF HIGHEST SYMMETRY WITHIN TWELVE CRESTS AND TWELVE TROUGHS. STAGE OF EQUILIBRIUM SHOWS CONTRACTION OF MASS DUE TO GRAVITATIONAL FORCE INSIDE SPHERICAL ASTRAL BODIES. STAGE OF EQUILIBRIUM SHOWS THAT IMPACT OF GRAVITATIONAL FORCE IS HIGHEST AT TWENTY FOUR POINTS INSIDE ASTRAL BODIES, PLANETS AND STARS.

Fig. 3.9

Every day time period of movement can be divided into $24 \times 360^0 \times 10 = 24 \times 60 \times 60$ seconds in quantitative terms for settlement of mass particles inside elements. The settlement of mass particles takes place in pairs and settlement of mass along with time takes place in the

71

multiples of 2 x 2 x 2 x 2 x 3 x 3 x 5 x 5 = 3600 particles. The time periods of movement in ideal conditions and in actual practice are different. The inclination of earth during movement shows different values along three axes.

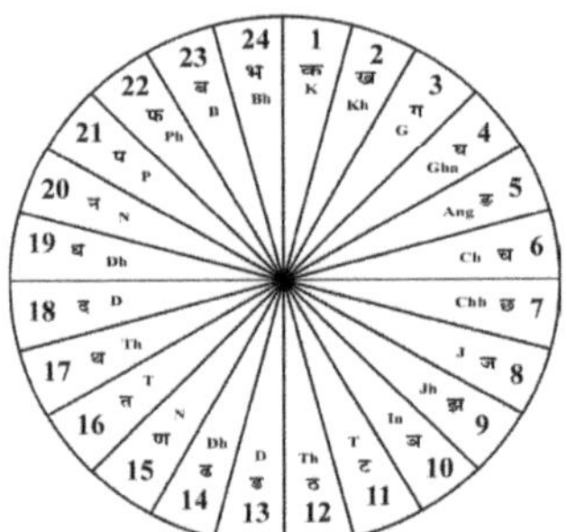

DIVISION OF CELESTIAL SPHERE IN TWELVE PARTS IN GEOMETRIC PROGRESSION CREATES TWELVE STARS CONSTELLATION AROUND EVERY STAR IN STAR DYNASTY. CREATION OF TWENTY FOUR LETTERS TAKES PLACE IN CIRCULAR ORBITS DUE TO IMPACT OF GRAVITATIONAL FORCE IN GEOMETRIC PROGRESSION. NEUTRAL MASS PARTICLES MOVE IN CIRCULAR ORBITS.

Fig. 3.10

TIME PROGRESSES AND PLANETS AND STARS MOVE AND FLOAT IN SPACE IN THE MULTIPLES OF 25 AND ABOVE PIECES.

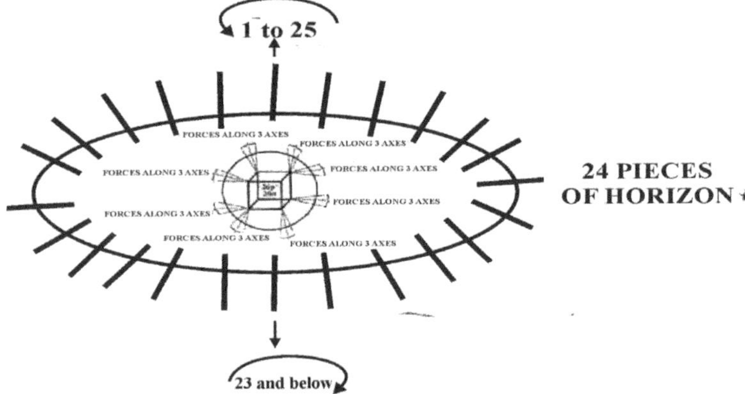

TIME RETROGRESSES AND SETTLES MASS INSIDE PLANETS AND STARS IN THE MULTIPLES OF ONE TO 23 PIECES OF HORIZON.

CONCENTRATION OF FORCES ON 24 POINTS SHOW HIGHEST LEVEL OF ATTRACTION AND EQUILIBRIUM IN LIFE FORMS, SPHERICAL ASTRAL BODIES, PLANETS AND STARS IN SPACE. EDGES AND DIAGONALS OF CUBIC CRYSTALS CONTAIN FOUR PROTONS EACH AND 56 PROTONS IN TOTAL. ELEMENT CREATED WITH ATOMIC NUMBER 56 IS VERY STRONG ON ANY ASTRAL BODY. CRYSTALS UPTO 56 POINTS RETAIN HIGHEST QUANTUM OF ENERGY AND BEYOND THAT EMISSION BECOMES PROMINENT.

Fig. 3.11

Contraction in geometric progression tries to make orbit of movement circular whereas movement in arithmetic progression makes the orbit of movement elliptical due to charges of atoms of elements. Round time frame is the greatest arbiter and as much movement expands at any point of time so much mass contracts within the atom of element and within letter or *Akshara*.

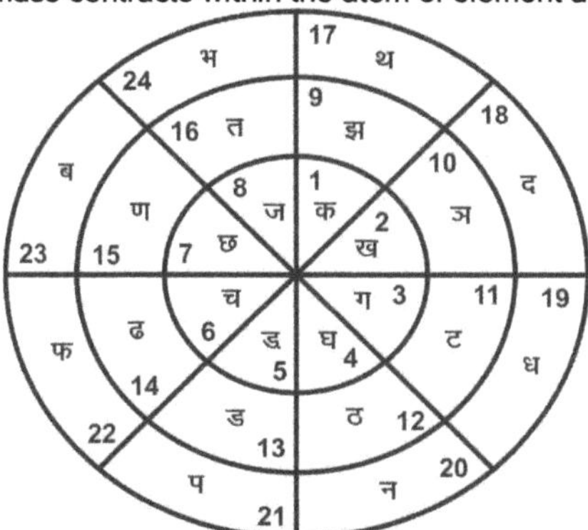

DIVISION OF ECLIPTIC IN TWENTY FOUR PARTS DUE TO IMPACT OF GRAVITATIONAL FORCE IN GEOMETRIC PROGRESSION RETAINS 15 X 12 NEUTRAL MASS PARTICLES IN EVERY ROUND OF ELEMENT CYCLE. CREATION OF LETTERS TAKES PLACE IN THE CYCLE OF THREE HOURS MULTIPLIED BY EIGHT *PRAHARS (PAHARS)* IN TWENTY FOUR HOURS EVERY DAY.

Fig. 3.12

Mass particles encircled by time frame create body of life forms and produce seven systems inside body. The nervous origin of language was known to people in every part of earth and that is the reason many words are common for many things, e.g, father and mother etc. Creation of consonants begins with *Ka* having lowest energy and goes up to *Pa, Pha, Ba* and *Bha* (24th consonant) having highest energy. Letters from one to twenty four show movement of energy in 24 parts of the sphere froming crystals with attachment along three axes. From twenty fifth letter onwards up to thirty two letters, crystal symmetry weakens and produces crystals with lesser symmetry. From 25th letter, *Ma* onwards, energy goes down and produces feminine sound and electronegative energy. From *Ma* onwards up to *Sa* the consonant letters show prominence of negative energy. Masculine representations and male figures are emitted by *Pa, Pha, Ba* and *Bha* in all the languages throughout the world. Similarly, feminine representations and female figures with female sound are emitted by *Ma* onwards up to *Sa* in all the languages of the world. It shows that nervous origin of letters was known to people in all the parts of the world and Sanskrit was accepted as language in some form or other in every part of the world.

Consonants are created due to contraction of mass particles into 32 vertical groups of elements on the pattern of 32 crystal classes. The sound waves in living beings and human beings tend to convert waves into particles and produce strong, solidified and symmetrical bodies. The elements showing non-metallic behavior start showing metallic behavior due to impact of sound waves and tend to convert sub-atomic particles into mass particles of elements. The electrons change their wavy character, convert into discrete mass particles and create molecules, compounds and body parts of human beings. In the universe letters create words and assimilation of words creates animals, human bodies and planets. The letters created out of sound waves behave like elements nucleosynthesized during evolution of human beings. The assimilation of sound waves in space and energy associated with sound waves creates 16 vowel letters and 32 consonant letters as creation of non-metallic elements and metallic elements respectively. 32

classes of crystal symmetry create 32 consonant letters as crystals and 32 teeth inside mouth of human beings. Similarly 16 vowel letters create sixteen mass zones inside human beings. Consonants are created and controlled by thirty two pairs of spinal nerves inside human body.

The elements are created in fixed numerical order and in the same manner words are created in numerical order. The words contain waves of particular wavelength and have impact like astral bodies. The elements are created as integers or whole numbers in numerical order. In the similar manner letters are also created in every living being in fixed numerical order. Phonetics depends upon longitude, latitude and altitude and sound of human beings varies from place to place. The impact of words affects the size, shape and built of human beings due to frequency and wavelength of sound waves. The sound waves are more powerful than solid living body. The impact of sound waves is perceived on living beings and shape and size of human beings is shaped by energy associated with sound waves. The sound waves like names, voices, thunderstorms and emission of longitudinal waves at different frequencies by animals etc. act along three axes. The particles show their impact along three axes and jumbled words produced by animals show their impact along three axes. The jumbled words are created in numerical order along three axes. Human Body language derivation and other animals body language depends upon sound waves and synthesis of words with 32 letters to the maximum. The words are created in seven shells of human body and effect body parts in totality.

Alphabets in 1st shell = 5 x 16 vowels = 80 nerves in first shell.
Alphabets in 2nd shell = 5 x 16 vowels = 80 nerves in second shell.
Alphabets in 3rd shell = 5 x 16 vowels = 80 nerves in third shell.
Alphabets in 4th shell = 5 x 16 vowels = 80 nerves in fourth shell.
Alphabets in 5th shell = 5 x 16 vowels = 80 nerves in fifth shell.
Alphabets in 6th shell = 4 x 16 vowels = 64 nerves in sixth shell.
Alphabets in 7th shell = 3 x 16 vowels = 48 nerves in seventh shell.

Total consonants   = 32   Total nerves = 512

Two lobes of human brain contain 512 x 2 = 1024 nerves. The permutation and combination of vowels and consonants produces many words on planets. During course of evolution the planets are created, produced in equilibrium and annihilated in space like 1024 words combinations. Thirty two letters are produced as consonants by 32 pairs of spinal nerves. *Ka* to *Ma* are called Grouped Consonants (*Vargiya Vyanjana*). *Ya* to *Sa* are called Un-grouped Consonants (*Avargiya Vyanjana*). The Grouped Consonants (*Vargiya Vyanjana*) are divided into (a) *Alpa-Prana* - the 1st and 3rd alphabet of each Group (Varga), (b) *Maha-Prana* - the 2nd and 4th alphabet of each group (Varga) and (c) *Anunaasika* - Nasal Consonants, the 5th alphabet of each Group (Varga).

Depending upon emergence of 32 nerves from vertebral column the human body shows attachment with different waves by 32 nerves and they are observed as 32 consonant letters spoken by human beings. These 32 consonant letters are controlled by 16 cervical nerves which relate to 16 vowel letters. The vowels create sound and produce 16 types of sound waves in human beings. Thus vowels and consonants in total create 32 x 16 = 512 x 2 = 1024 types of sound wave packets. The sound waves are more powerful than solid body. Impact of sound waves on living beings are perceived on every part, organ and seven systems of body and sound waves in the form of voice can change the body features. Sixteen vowels are produced by cervical region which tends to mix with consonants to create different words.

The energy of 32 consonants multiplied with energy of 16 vowels creates 512 words which stores energy in the form of human bodies on planet. Thus 512 negatively charged particles control left side of human body whereas 512 positively charged particles control right side of human body. In total, 1024 solid particles controlled by sound waves effect human body. The

74

prominence of negatively charged particles produce left side organs of human body whereas prominence of positively charged particles produces right side organs of human body. The energy associated with sound waves in space is the precursor which creates all solid three-dimensional bodies in space. Every planet, star and human being in the universe is created at certain "frequency equilibrium" under 1024 types of solid bodies.

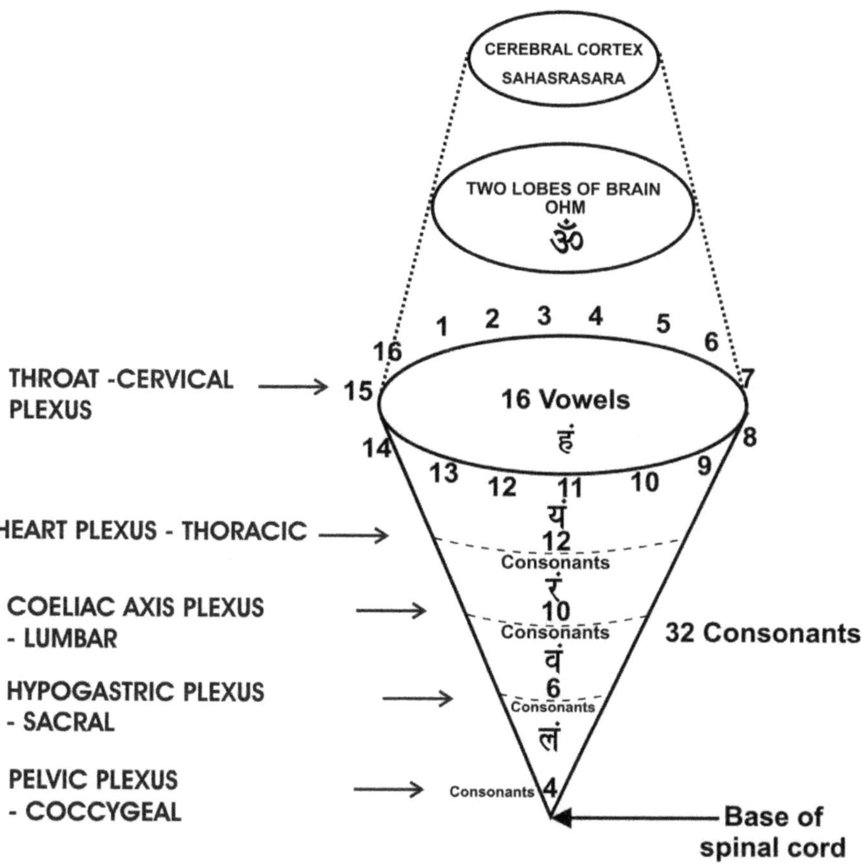

GRADUAL EVOLUTION OF CONSONANTS AND VOWELS TAKES PLACE DUE TO SOUND WAVES INSIDE HUMAN BODY. SOUND WAVES EMERGE FROM SPINAL CORD AND CREATE 32 CONSONANTS AND 16 VOWELS. IN HUMAN BEINGS IMPACT OF 32 CONSONANTS AND 16 VOWELS IS OBSERVED AS DEPICTED IN SANSKRIT LANGUAGE. PHONETICS AND IMPACT OF WORDS IS OBSERVED ON HUMAN BEINGS DUE TO FREQUENCY AND WAVELENGTH OF SOUND WAVES.

Fig. 3.13

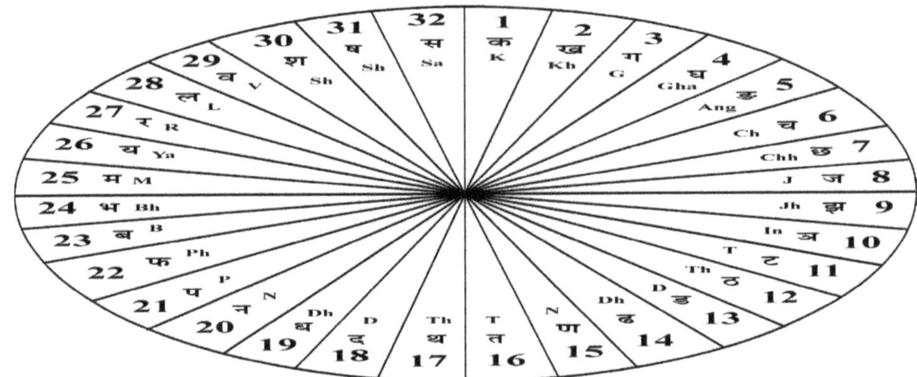

ELLIPTICITY OF ORBIT DEVELOPS DUE TO FORMATION OF ANIONS (Y⁻, Y²⁻, Y³⁻, Y⁴⁻, Y⁵⁻, Y⁶⁻, Y⁷⁻) AND CATIONS (X⁺, X²⁺, X³⁺, X⁴⁺, X⁵⁺, X⁶⁺, X⁷⁺) IN THE ATOMS OF ELEMENTS IN ARITHMETIC PROGRESSION. CREATION OF THIRTY TWO LETTERS TAKES PLACE IN ELLIPTICAL ORBITS DUE TO IMPACT OF STRONG FORCE AND WEAK FORCE IN ARITHMETIC PROGRESSION.

Fig. 3.14

The living beings develop and exist as close thermodynamic systems on planets. Layer by layer deposition of elements, cells, soft tissues and hard tissues increases the size of living body along three axes on planets. In this process complex and bigger living body is produced and as big and tough is the body so long is the age of that life form. The growth and development of body may be different along three axes depending upon position of life form on planet. The impact of pressure, volume and temperature decides the size and shape of individual living being on planet. Every living being maintains individual thermodynamic equilibrium on planets. The thermodynamic equilibrium of living body depends upon four forces and combined action of pressure (p), volume (v) and temperature along three axes on living body.

Basing on points of places of articulation, Consonants can be divided into following types:

(a) Glottal or Laryngeal (*Swarayantramukhi*): This sound wave emerges from Glottis. Example is *Ah, Haa* (*Visarga*) etc.

(b) Pharyngeal (*Upalijihwiya*): This sound wave emerges in pharynx near uvula.

(c) Uvular (*Jihwamuliya or Alijihwya*): It emerges from back of tongue or root of tongue.

(d) Guttural or Soft Palatal (*Kanthaya*): This sound wave is produced when back portion of tongue touches soft palate.

(e) Cerebral (*Murdhanya*): This sound wave is produced when tongue bends and touches cerebrum.

(f) Palatal (*Talabya*): They are pronounced from hard palate.

(g) Alveolar (*Vartasya*): The tip of tongue when touches alveolus produces these sounds.

(h) Dental (*Dantya*): The tip or front portion of tongue touches teeth and produces these sounds.

(i) Labio-dental (*Dantoshthya*): The sound produced by combination of upper teeth and lower lips.

(j) Bilabial (*Dwayoshthya*): The sound wave produced with the help of both lips.

76

Basing on efforts to release the air from mouth, it can be divided into five types:

(a) Stops or Plosive (*Sparsh*): The sound which comes out from mouth cavity after crossing obstruction.

(b) Spirants (*Sangharshi or Oushma*): The sound which comes out from narrow aperture or slit after facing friction during emission.

(c) Laterals (*Parshvik*): The sound comes out from one or both sides of tongue.

(d) Trills (*Lunthis or Kampit*): The sound causes sudden tremor in tongue during emission.

(e) Nasals (*Nasik*): The sound wave produced with the help of nasal passage.

Every animal has its own alphabet. The words and alphabets are created by body of the animals which is shaped by seven-crystal system, twelve pairs of nerves, spinal nerves and nine colors cycle. The smaller animals having less and simplified organs have few letters in their alphabets. The mammals have highest number of letters in their alphabets because organs of mammals are created by nerves, seven holes in skull and seven physiological systems.

Human spinal cord is segmented through segments which are not visible from outside. The part of spinal cord to which a pair of spinal nerves (right and left) are attached is called spinal segment. The number of spinal segments relates to number of vertebrae in thoracic, lumbar and sacral regions. In cervical region one segment is more than number of vertebrae and in coccygeal region there are two segments for four coccygeal vertebrae. The spinal cord contains 32 (8 + 24) spinal segments:

(1) Cervical - 8,

(2) Thoracic - 12,

(3) Lumbar - 5, (Nerves develop in pairs and fuse at the lower end.)

(4) Sacral - 5, (Nerves develop in pairs and fuse at the lower end.)

(5) Coccygeal - 1 (Nerves develop in pairs and fuse at the lower end giving appearance of one nerve. Coccygeal contains two nerves which are fused and appear as one.)

The nerves are produced in even numbers and their number is highest in cervical plexus and thoracic plexus. It decreases gradually from 16 ⋯⋯▶ 12 ⋯⋯▶ 10 ⋯⋯▶ 8 ⋯⋯▶ 6 4 ⋯⋯▶ 4 ⋯⋯▶ 2 in the lower spine. In the lowest area of spinal cord the nerves appear in horse tail form and generally fuse to create nerves in even numbers.

3.2 CREATION OF LETTERS FROM NERVES

Due to complexity of organs the number of letters in human beings increases and as increases size and complexity so increases the number of alphabets and complex words emitted by human beings. The creation of letters and words inside human body takes place exactly on the same pattern as creation of elements and compounds during evolution of astral bodies. Eight pair of cervical nerves effect production of sixteen vowel letters as follows:

1. Cervical Nerve 1 (Left) produces letter 'अ' (*A*). It effects and controls emission and production of vowel letter 'अ'. This is first letter and it combines with other vowels and consonants to create words, e.g., *Achal, Amar* (अचर, अमर) etc.

2. Cervical Nerve 1 Right produces letter आ (AA). It effects emission and production of vowel letter 'आ'. This letter combines with other vowels and consonants to create words, e.g., *aastha, aajivan* (आस्था, आजीवन) etc.

3. Cervical Nerve 2 Left produces letter इ ('I'). It effects emission and production of vowel letter 'इ'. This letter combines with other vowels and consonants to create words, e.g., *Eikha, Eidam* (इख, इदम) etc.

4. Cervical Nerve 2 Right produces letter ई (Ee). It effects emission and production of vowel letter 'ई'. This letter combines with other vowels and consonants to create words, e.g., *Eeshwar* (ईश्वर) etc.

5. Cervical Nerve 3 Left produces letter उ ('U'). It effects emission and production of vowel letter 'उ'. This letter combines with other vowels and consonants to create words, e.g., Umra, *Upar* (उम्र, उपर) etc.

6. Cervical Nerve 3 Right produces letter ऊ ('Oo'). It effects emission and production of vowel letter 'ऊ'. This letter combines with other vowels and consonants to create words, e.g., Oodyam, *Swayambhoo* (ऊद्यम, स्वयंभू) etc.

7. Cervical Nerve 4 Left produces letter ऋ ('Ri'). It effects emission and production of vowel letter 'ऋ'. This letter combines with other vowels and consonants to create words, e.g., *rich* (ऋच) etc.

8. Cervical Nerve 4 Right produces letter ॠ ('Hree'). It effects emission and production of vowel letter 'ॠ'. This letter combines with other vowels and consonants to create words, e.g., *Hrishi* (ॠषि) etc.

9. Cervical Nerve 5 Left produces letter ऌ ('Lri'). It effects emission and production of vowel letter 'ऌ'. This letter combines with other vowels and consonants to create words, e.g., *Rhilrika* (ऋलृक) etc.

10. Cervical Nerve 5 Right produces letter ॡ ('Lree'). It effects emission and production of vowel letter 'ॡ'. This letter combines with other vowels and consonants to create words, e.g., *Lritulsanan* (लृतुलसानां) etc.

11. Cervical Nerve 6 Left produces letter ए ('Ae'). It effects emission and production of vowel letter 'ऐ'. This letter combines with other vowels and consonants to create words, e.g., *Aeravat* (ऐरावत) etc.

12. Cervical Nerve 6 Right produces letter ऐ ('Aei'). It effects emission and production of vowel letter 'ऐ'. This letter combines with other vowels and consonants to create words, e.g., *Aeinak* (ऐनक) etc.

13. Cervical Nerve 7 Left produces letter ओ ('O'). It effects emission and production of vowel letter 'ओ'. This letter combines with other vowels and consonants to create words, e.g., *Okhali* (ओखली) etc.

14. Cervical Nerve 7 Right produces letter औ ('Au'). It effects emission and production of vowel letter 'औ'. This letter combines with other vowels and consonants to create words, e.g., *Aurat* (औरत) etc.

15. Cervical Nerve 8 Left produces letter अं ('Am'). It effects emission and production of vowel letter 'अं'. This letter combines with other vowels and consonants to create words, e.g., *Amgur* (अंगूर) etc.

16. Cervical Nerve 8 Right produces letter अः ('Ah'). It effects emission and production of vowel letter 'अः'. This letter combines with other vowels and consonants to create words, e.g., *Aha* (अहा) etc.

Consonant letter are produced by Thoracic nerves and nerves below that. They produce solidified, symmetrical and solid body like "sound wave packets". The letters created like 'sound wave packets' behave like elements nucleosynthesized during evolution of human beings. The assimilation of sound waves in space and energy associated with sound waves creates 16 vowel letters and 32 consonant letters as creation of non-metallic elements and metallic elements respectively. 32 classes of crystal symmetry create 32 consonant letters as crystals inside human beings.

1. Thoracic Nerve 1 produces letter क ('Ka'). It controls emission and production of consonant letter 'क'. This letter combines with other vowels and consonants to create words, e.g., *Kalam, Kamal, Kashtha, kriya* (कलम, कमल) etc.

2. Thoracic Nerve 2 produces letter ख ('Kha'). It controls emission and production of consonant letter 'ख'. This letter combines with other vowels and consonants to create words, e.g., *Kharbuj* (खरबूज) etc.

3. Thoracic Nerve 3 produces letter ग ('Ga'). It controls emission and production of consonant letter 'ग'. This letter combines with other vowels and consonants to create word, e.g., *Gamla* (गमला) etc.

4. Thoracic Nerve 4 produces letter घ ('Gha'). It controls emission and production of consonant letter 'घ'. This letter combines with other vowels and consonants to create words, e.g., *Ghar* (घर) etc.

5. Thoracic Nerve 5 produces letter ङ ('Anga'). It controls emission and production of consonant letter 'ङ'. This letter combines with other vowels and consonants and creates words.

6. Thoracic Nerve 6 produces letter च ('Cha'). It controls emission and production of consonant letter 'च'. This letter combines with other vowels and consonants to create word, e.g., *Charan* (चरण) etc.

7. Thoracic Nerve 7 produces letter छ ('Chha'). It controls emission and production of consonant letter 'छ'. This letter combines with other vowels and consonants to create words, e.g., *Chhata* (छाता) etc.

8. Thoracic Nerve 8 produces letter ज ('Ja'). It controls emission and production of consonant letter 'ज'. This letter combines with other vowels and consonants to create words, e.g., *Jahaj* (जहाज) etc.

9. Thoracic Nerve 9 produces letter झ (Jha'). It controls emission and production of consonant letter 'झ'. This letter combines with other vowels and consonants to create words, e.g. Jharna (झरना) etc.

10. Thoracic Nerve 10 produces letter ञ ('Eina'). It controls emission and production of consonant letter 'ञ'. This letter combines with other vowels and consonants to create words.

11. Thoracic Nerve 11 produces letter ट ('Ta'). It controls emission and production of consonant letter 'ट'. This letter combines with other vowels and consonants to create words, e.g., Tamatar, Tanga (टमाटर) etc.

12. Thoracic Nerve 12 produces letter ठ ('Tha'). It controls emission and production of consonant letter 'ठ'. This letter combines with other vowels and consonants to create words, e.g., *thathera* (ठठेरा) etc.

13. Lumbar Nerve 1 Left (five pairs in total) produces letter ड ('Da'). It controls emission and production of consonant letter 'ड'. This letter combines with other vowels and consonants to create words, e.g. Damru (डमरू) etc. Lumbar nerves are ten in total produced in pair of five nerves.

14. Lumbar Nerve 1 Right (Five Pairs in Total) produces letter ढ ('Dha'). It controls emission and production of consonant letter 'ढ'. This letter combines with other vowels and consonants to create words, e.g., *Dhakkan* (ढक्कन) etc.

15. Lumbar Nerve 2 Left produces letter ण ('Na'). It controls emission and production of consonant letter 'ण'. This letter combines with other vowels and consonants to create words, e.g., *Pani* (पाणि) etc.

16. Lumbar Nerve 2 Right produces letter त ('Ta'). It controls emission and production of consonant letter 'त'. This letter combines with other vowels and consonants to create words, e.g., *Tarbuj* (तरबूज) etc.

17. Lumbar Nerve 3 Left produces letter थ ('Tha'). It controls emission and production of consonant letter 'थ'. This letter combines with other vowels and consonants to create words, e.g., *Than* (थन) etc.

18. Lumbar Nerve 3 Right produces letter द ('Da'). It controls emission and production of consonant letter 'द'. This letter combines with other vowels and consonants to create words, e.g., *Dan, Dakshina* (दान) etc.

19. Lumbar Nerve 4 Left produces letter ध ('Dha'). It controls emission and production of consonant letter 'ध'. This letter combines with other vowels and consonants to create words, e.g., *Dhan* (धन) etc.

20. Lumbar Nerve 4 Right produces letter न ('Na'). It controls emission and production of consonant letter 'न'. This letter combines with other vowels and consonants to create words, e.g., *Nadi* (नदी) etc.

21. Lumbar Nerve 5 Left produces letter प ('Pa'). It controls emission and production of consonant letter 'प'. This letter combines with other vowels and consonants to create words, e.g., *Pani* (पानी) etc.

22. Lumbar Nerve 5 Right (In five pairs) 10 produces letter फ ('Pha'). It controls emission and production of consonant letter 'फ'. This letter combines with other vowels and consonants to create words, e.g., *Phatinga* (फतिंगा) etc.

23. Sacral Nerve 1 produces letter ब ('Ba'). It controls emission and production of consonant letter 'ब'. This letter combines with other vowels and consonants to create words, e.g., *Ber* (बेर) etc. Sacral nerves are six in number and one nerve appears to be fused with other nerve.

24. Sacral Nerve 2 produces letter भ ('Bha'). It controls emission and production of consonant letter 'भ'. This letter combines with other vowels and consonants to create words, e.g., *Bharat* (भारत) etc.

25. Sacral Nerve 3 produces letter म ('Ma'). It controls emission and production of consonant letter 'म'. This letter combines with other vowels and consonants to create words, e.g., *Matasya* (मतस्य) etc.

26. Sacral Nerve 4 produces letter य ('Ya'). It controls emission and production of consonant letter 'य'. This letter combines with other vowels and consonants to create words, e.g., *Yamraj, kriya* (यमराज) etc.

27. Sacral Nerve 5 Left produces letter र ('Ra'). It controls emission and production of consonant letter 'र'. This letter combines with other vowels and consonants to create words, e.g., *Ram* (राम) etc.

28. Sacral Nerve 5 Right (one nerve appears to be fused with Nerve 5) produces letter ल ('La'). It controls emission and production of consonant letter 'ल'. This letter combines with other vowels and consonants to create words, e.g., *Lattu* (लट्टू) etc.

29 - Coccygeal Nerve 1 Left produces letter व ('Va'). It controls emission and production of consonant letter 'व'. This letter combines with other vowels and consonants to create words, e.g., *Van* (वन) etc. Coccygeal nerves are four in total and it appears they are fused at the bottom.

30. Coccygeal Nerve 1 Right produces letter श ('Sha'). It controls emission and production of consonant letter 'श' (Talavya Sha). This letter combines with other vowels and consonants to create words, e.g., *Shani* (शनि) etc.

31. Coccygeal Nerve 2 Left produces letter ष ('Sa'). It controls emission and production of consonant letter 'ष' (Murdhanya Sa). This letter combines with other vowels and consonants to create words, e.g., *Shatkon* (षट्कोण) etc.

32. Coccygeal Nerve 2 Right produces letter स ('Sa'). It controls emission and production of consonant letter 'स' (Dantya Sa). This letter combines with other vowels and consonants to create words, e.g., *Sita* (सीता) etc. All the Coccygeal nerves appear to be fused and joined at the base of spinal cord.

Spinal segment is the area where a pair of spinal nerves is attached to spinal cord. Each spinal nerve passes out of the vertebral canal through its inter-vertebral foramen. The spinal cord ends at much higherlevel because of its slower growth relative to the vertebral column. The lower spinal segments do not correspond in level with vertebrae. The upper spinal nerves pass out transversely to their exits at the inter-vertebral foramina but the lower nerves pass obliquely downwards to get out of their respective foramina. Spinal nerves develop in pairs and decreases gradually in numbers from 8 ⋯⋯▶12 ⋯⋯▶10 ⋯⋯▶ 8 6 ⋯⋯▶ 4 ⋯⋯▶ 2 in lower portion. In the lowest area the nerves appear in the form of bottle brush and generally fuse to create nerves in even numbers.

It is observed that L - 1 and L - 2 spinal segments lie at the level of 10th thoracic vertebra. L - 3 and L - 4 spinal segments lie at the level of 11th thoracic vertebra. L - 5 spinal segments lie at the level of 12th thoracic vertebra. Sacral and coccygeal segments lie at the level of 1st Lumbar vertebra. Cauda Equina is the bunch of joint lower spinal nerves (Lumbar, Sacral and Coccygeal) below the termination of spinal cord. These nerves surround the Conus Medullaris and Filum terminale and give appearance of a Horse's tail and that is why it has been called Cauda Equina. This appearance is due to obliquity and vertical direction of lower spinal nerves as they pass down to their respective inter-vertebral foramina. Human body shows thirty one pair of spinal nerves from outside. In fact, many spinal nerves are fused and show one nerve. It shows degenerating trend in human body along one axis towards lower side. Along other two axes, i.e., twelve pairs of cranial nerves and nine body systems, the body does not show any degeneration. For all practical purposes, Cervical nerves are eight pairs (sixteen nerves) and lower Spinal nerves (thoracic, lumbar, sacral and coccygeal) are 32 pairs in spinal cord. The nerves appear to be fused at the lower level in spinal cord.

The coccyx commonly called as tailbone is a small triangular bone resembling small tail located at the bottom of spine. It is composed of four coccygeal vertebra or spinal bones. These four fused vertebrae act as base of spinal cord for human being. A coccygeal vertebra contains BNCT that involves medullary cavity and extends through cortex into soft tissues by displacing the periosteum. The number of spinal nerves decreases gradually towards lower spinal cord due to narrowing down of spinal cord.

The coccyx commonly called as tailbone is a small triangular bone resembling small tail located at the bottom of spine. It is composed of four coccygeal vertebra or spinal bones. These four fused vertebrae act as base of spinal cord for human being. A coccygeal vertebra contains BNCT that involves medullary cavity and extends through cortex into soft tissues by displacing the periosteum. The number of spinal nerves decreases gradually towards lower spinal cord due to narrowing down of spinal cord.

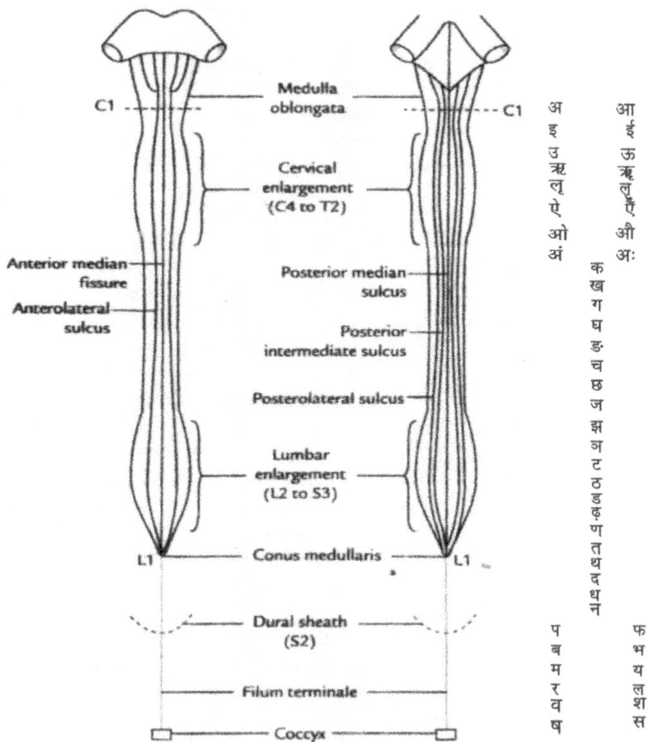

THROAT CERVICAL PLEXUS PRODUCES SIXTEEN VOWELS AND SPINAL NERVES PRODUCE THIRTY TWO CONSONANTS FROM SPINAL CORD OF HUMAN BEINGS. SPINAL NERVES IN THE LOWER PORTION OF CORD ARE FUSED IN LUMBAR, SACRAL AND COCCYGEAL REGIONS. WE LEARN FROM PURANAS AND SERPENT POWER (*KUNDALINI SHAKTI*) AND FROM VERTEBRA WE GET TRACES OF EXISTENCE OF 4 + 6 + 10 + 12 = 32 SPINAL NERVES WHICH PRODUCE CONSONANTS.

Fig. 3.16

The elements are created as integers or whole numbers in numerical order. In the similar manner letters are also created in every living being in fixed numerical order. The sound waves affect electromagnetic waves and frequency of sound waves effects the growth of animals. The particles show their impact along three axes and jumbled words produced by animals show their impact along three axes. The jumbled words are created in numerical order along three axes. Human body language derivation shows that Sanskrit is the most advanced body language dependent upon three axes attachment of body with planets and stars in universe. Other animals' body language differs from the body language of human being. Human body language derivation and other animals body language depends upon sound waves and synthesis of words with 32 + 16 letters to the maximum.

Words are created by combination of many letters. Words contain vowels and consonants and become meaningful words when they exist like planets in the universe. The application of magnetic force on human body will tend to make the body straight like ferromagnetic polar rod, reduce fats of body along second axis and reduce the expansion and bulging of body parts along third axis. The application of magnetic forces make the body tall, erect in posture, slim, shed fats of belly and other parts of body and try to maintain breadth, width and length in the ratio $1^3 : 2^3 : 4^3$ or 1 : 8 : 64. Words shape human body in three dimensions.

The longitudinal waves expand and create non-metallic octets along with sound waves. Speed of sound is the highest in granite having metallic octets and lowest in non-metallic octets. The permutation and combination of letters of sound create different words which have specific effect on human body. The transverse waves are absorbed and accumulated in metallic octet and inside human body, e.g., electric waves.

CENTERS OF NERVES INSIDE SPINAL CORD OF HUMAN BEINGS

NUMBER OF NERVES	LETTERS OR AKSHARAS	NAME OF THE KNOT CENTRE FROM BOTTOM OF SPINAL CORD	NUMBER OF NERVES EMERGING FROM KNOT	NUMBER OF EFFEC-TIVE NERVES DURING LIFTING UP OF AIR	TOTAL NUMBER OF NERVES ACTING INSIDE CENTRAL NERVOUS SYSTEM
1 to 16	अ आ इ ई उ ऊ ऋ ॠ ळ लृ ए ऐ ओ औ अं अः	Ham हं	Cervical -1 to Cervical-16	16	32x16=512
21 - 32	क ख ग घ ङ च छ ज झ ञ ट ठ	Yam यं	TH–1 to TH–12	20+12=32	20+12=32
11 - 20	ड ढ ण त थ द ध न प फ	Ram रं	L–1 to L–10	10+10=20	10+10=20
5 -10	ब भ म य र ल	Bam वं	S – 1 to S – 6	4+6=10	4+6=10
1 2 3 4	व श ष स	Lam लं	C – 1 C – 2 C – 3 C – 4	4	4

INFANTS IN HUMAN BEINGS AT THE TIME OF BIRTH CRY VIGOROUSLY AND EMIT SOUND LIKE "K......A.......R.....A......N....A...........N.....A......H". OR "K......A.......H......A". OR "K.....A.......H......N......AH". OR "K......A.....R....A.....N......AH". THE EMISSION OF FIRST LETTER OF SOUND WAVE PACKET, i.e., *KA* TAKES PLACE FROM THORACIC NERVE. IT MIXES WITH VOWELS, FIRST VOWEL A........AA... AND ENDS AT 16TH POSITION OF CERVICAL

NERVE, i.e., *AN..... AH* IN CERVICAL NERVES OF HUMAN BODY. THE INFANT BEGINS UTTERING OF LANGUAGE FROM FIRST CONSONANT OF SPINAL NERVES (*'KA'*) AND ENDS AT LAST VOWEL (*'AH'*) OF CERVICAL NERVES NEAR THROAT AND UTTERING IS SAME EVERYWHERE THROUGHOUT THE WORLD. VOCAL CORD BEGINS PRODUCTION OF VOICE OF VOWELS AND CONSONANTS STARTING FROM KA.....KAA.....KI.....KEE.....KU.....KOO.....KRI.....KREE.....KLRI.....KLREE.....KE.....KAI.....KO.....KAU.....KAM.....KAH IN HUMAN BEINGS. SIMILAR PATTERN OF EMISSION IS OBSERVED IN ALL 32 CONSONANT LETTERS.

Table 3.4

The multiplication of letters in different proportions creates different combination of words which show specific impact on different parts of human body. The sound waves effect the growth and development of human body. Two lobes of human brain contain 512 x 2 = 1024 nerves in the multiples of thousands. The permutation and combination of vowels and consonants produces many words and on similar pattern planets are produced in the universe.

AKSHARA DHAAM
(SANSKRIT LETTERS UDYAAN)

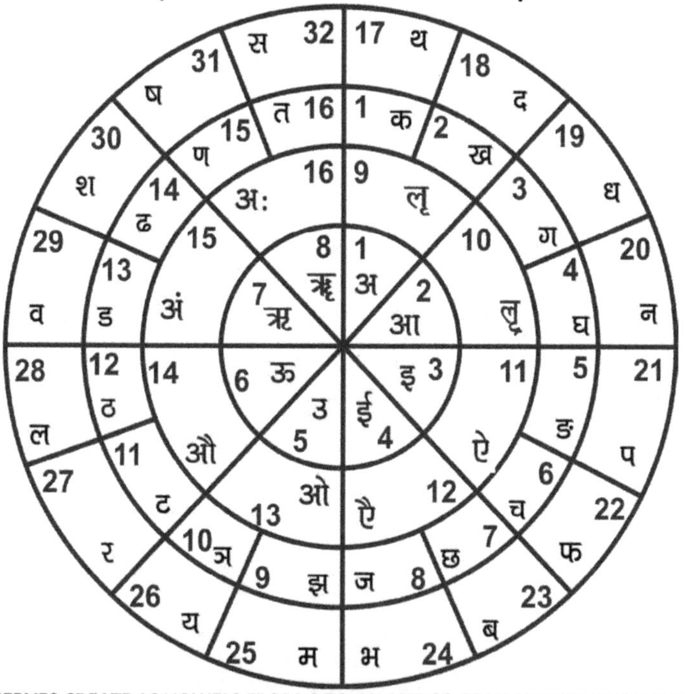

SPINAL NERVES CREATE 16 VOWELS FROM *A* TO *AH* AND 32 CONSONANTS FROM *KA* TO *SA* IN HUMAN BEINGS. THESE LETTERS OR *AKSHARAS* CREATE WORDS OR *SHABDAS* AND FINALLY *PADAS* AND SENTENCES. SOUND WAVE PACKETS MOVE BY COMPRESSION AND RAREFACTION OF WAVES FROM ONE PLACE TO ANOTHER. LETTERS OR *AKSHARAS* ARE CREATED IN GEOMETRIC PROGRESSION BY DIFFERENT NERVES OF HUMAN BODY.

Fig. 3.17

In human body there exists a network of neurobiological structure which helps in production of distinct human language. The interacting brain helps in emergence of neurobiological model of language. Production of language is more than word processing and much information is given in the acoustic or orthographic sounds that enter sensory cortices. It needs involvement of networks of functionally overlapping body parts, organs and systems.

Different animals produce sound waves in different frequency range. The mew of cat has frequency range between 150-750 Hz and chirping of bird has frequency range between 2000-13000 Hz. The sound waves emitted by different animals effect the entire gamut of life forms on planets in different frequency ranges because sound waves convert into electromagnetic waves of visible spectra. The sound waves emitted by animals affect the growth and development of all animals within visible spectra (4000Å to 7500Å) of electromagnetic waves on all planets of universe. A musical scale is a sequence of frequencies which have a particularly pleasing effect on human ear. A widely used musical scale is a sequence of frequencies which have a particularly pleasing effect on human growth. A widely used musical scale, called diatonic scale, has eight frequencies covering an octave. Each frequency is called a note.

Development of letters and words of Sanskrit are based on 12 blocks, 16 (1 + 7 + 7 + 1) cervical nerves and 32 (2 + 6 + 10 + 14) crystal class groups as periodic table of elements. Sanskrit is a systematic language of nerves developed on the basis of body parts along three axes and 'jumbled words' developed in Sanskrit effect body parts of human beings

Development of Sanskrit language is based on:

32 Consonants or nerves (expansion of periodic table of elements in periods on 32 classes of crystal symmetry from '*Ka*' to '*Sa*')

x 16 Vowels emitted through throat – Cervical Plexus from '*A*' to '*Ah*' (1 + 7 + 7 + 1)

x 12 Times contraction of Mass in Geometrical Progression

x 7 Crystal Systems

= 32 classes of crystal symmetry x 9 colors cycle x 12 times contraction of mass

x 7 crystal systems = 24,192 Nerves and its multiples.

Any community may develop any type of language and alphabets depending upon the positive charge and negative charge associated with elements, their words and alphabets. It will help in strengthening the community, migration to better places and improvement of health of that community. Languages can play positive role in giving proper shape and size to human body and maintaining health of human body in particular and community in general.

Sanskrit language is based on emissions of 32 pairs of spinal nerves, 12 pairs of cranial nerves and nine body systems along three axes. Sanskrit language controls the nerves of animal body or human body like buttons of harmonium or musical instruments. The language shows impact on particular and specific nerves of every body organ and system and can be used for curing the diseases of living body. Its impact is observed on all animals and human bodies along three axes.

The creation of alphabets, letter and words takes place by retention and settlement of mass in the same pattern as elements are created. The letters form words, jumbled words and combination of words makes sentences containing many letters inside it in many forms. It takes place in the similar pattern as molecules and compounds are created out of many elements. The jumbled words and bigger words in the sentences have capability to make independent existence in the similar manner as compounds and molecules make independent existence. Creation of words takes place with waves of different colors. Intermixing among colors and creation of jumbled words is seen on the pattern of creation of molecules and compounds. The words are created under seven crystals system, nine colors cycle and combined effect of four forces producing 32 classes of crystal symmetry.

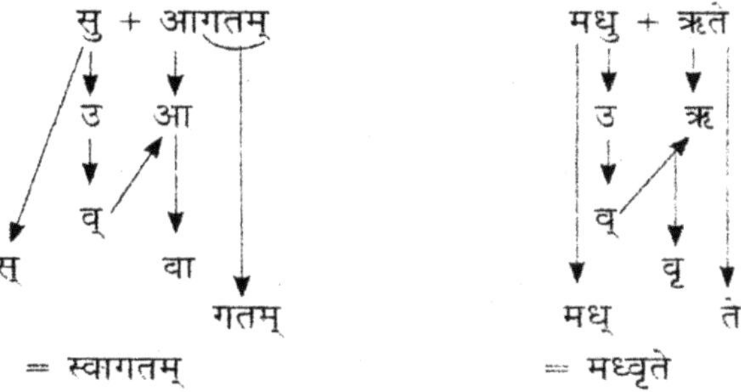

CREATION OF WORDS TAKES PLACE BY INTERMIXING OF VOWELS AND CONSONANTS
Fig. 3.18

During late Indus civilization period, Sanskrit grammar became prominent. Many grammarians came into prominence and created complex and compound words and sentences. Sanskrit Grammar was elaborate and contained many branches for formation of words and sentences. Some of them are given below:

1. *Sandhi* (Enphony), संधि
2. *Subant Prakaran,* सुबन्त प्रकरण
3. *Tiangant Prakaran,* तिड़न्त प्रकरण
4. *Niajant Prakaran,* णिजन्त प्रकरण
5. *Upasarga Prakaran,* उपसर्ग प्रकरण
6. *Pratyaya Prakaran,* प्रत्यय प्रकरण
7. *Avyaya Prakaran,* अव्यय प्रकरण
8. *Samochcharit Shabda,* सोमच्चरीत शब्द
9. *Paryayavachi Shabda,* पर्यायवाची शब्द
10. *Vilomarthi Shabda,* विलोमार्थी शब्द
11. *Kriya Suchi,* क्रिया सूची
12. *Karak Prakaran,* कारक प्रकरण
13. *Samas Prakaran,* समास प्रकरण
14. *Vachya Prakaran.* वाच्य प्रकरण

The electromagnetic waves from 4000Å to 7500Å behave as building blocks and make the perceptible world of color waves which create 118 atoms of elements. In this range mass particles move in the form of floating energy with waves and behave as building blocks. The sound waves emitted by animals and human beings form electromagnetic wave packets in the atmosphere. The sound waves can convert into electromagnetic waves in any medium in space. They show their impact on visible spectra (4000Å to 7500Å) of electromagnetic waves. The sound waves effect the growth and development of body parts in living animals and human beings. The electromagnetic waves in the wavelength range $1 \times 10^4 - 1 \times 10^7$ having frequency between 256 Hz to 512 Hz effect body organs of living human beings. The electromagnetic waves in the range 4000Å to 7500Å create body organs of all living beings. The voice box in the mouth of human beings is one of the prominent sources of sound. It can produce sound waves having frequency range between 100–1100 Hz.

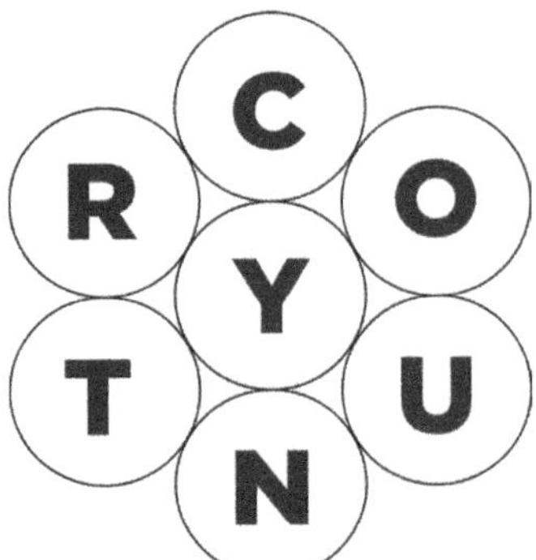

"SOUND WAVE PACKETS" ARE CREATED DUE TO INTERMINGLING OF SEVEN TYPES OF AUDIBLE SOUND WAVES OR 'SWARAS'. SOUND WAVE PACKETS ARE CREATED AND EMITTED FROM MOUTH IN THE PATTERN OF WORDS CREATED FROM LETTERS AND CHEMICAL COMPOUNDS CREATED FROM ATOMS OF ELEMENTS. SOUND WAVE PACKETS ARE EFFECTED BY PRESSURE, VOLUME AND TEMPERTURE ALONG THREE AXES.

Fig. 3.19

The electromagnetic waves in the wavelength range of power waves, i.e., 1×10^4 - 1×10^7 have frequency range of about 100 to 10,000 Hz. The electromagnetic waves in the range of power waves can convert into audible sound waves of human beings and animals because the impact of $^{56}_{26}Fe$ ceases in power wave region. The impact of $^{56}_{26}Fe$ is observed in electromagnetic waves up to 7500 Å in space. The sound waves in the range 100 Hz to 10000 Hz can convert into equivalent power waves of electromagnetic waves and effect the growth and development of animals, human beings and life forms on planets in the universe. The sound waves in the equivalent range of power waves of electromagnetic waves affect the life forms, animals and human beings. The aggregation of atoms, molecules and compounds inside animal body in the power waves range of 1×10^4 - 1×10^7 meters is effected by sound waves on earth. This frequency range may vary on different planets but growth pattern along three axes will remain the same on all planets in the universe. The binding energy among elements reaches highest point at atomic number 26 and then starts decreasing gradually in elements of later rounds. Languages with more number of alphabets, i.e., 27 and onwards contain less quantum of force during expression.

Language is always effected by social, political, cultural and economic impact on inhabitant human beings of society. Dialectology and tonetics show that dialects and tones vary in geographically separated societies and communities. This paves the way for formation of new languages in different parts of the world. Sanskrit is an independent body language which has consistency of letters, economy of use of letters with nerves and exhaustiveness of letters and words. Sanskrit has developed on scientific lines and it can shape, mould and cure diseases of human body in scientific manner. A Sentence or potentially complete utterance is the longest spoken structure which gives full grammatical meaning. Sanskrit utterances provide full meaningful stretches with impact on human body. Broadly it can be said that Language science has four wings:

a. Phonology: It deals with sound (*Dhwani)*. It deals with production of 'sound wave packets' by mouth of human being. Sound wave packets are produced by vowels or consonants or combination of both.

b. Morphology: *Pad or Shabda* (Form) which is created by letters and words.

c. Syntax: *Vakya* formation or sentence formation takes place due to combination of words.

d. Semantics: Meaning or *Artha Vijnan* deals with creation of meaningful words and sentences which provide strength and stability to human body. Historical and geographical features of the inhabitants effect phonetics and intermixing of languages. Sentence is the significant unit which makes meaning of words clear and effective.

Vocal cord and musical instruments produce sound which stops at some places, faces friction at some places and passes smoothly at some places. In musical instrument air enters from one side, stops at different places and produces different types of voice (Suras). In human beings the outgoing gases from trachea carry sound waves which passes through trachea. The degree of opening and closing of vocal cord decides the type of letters emitted by human being. Vocal cord generally remains open during inhalation. During exhalation the vocal cord becomes slightly narrow and voice coming out is 'voiceless'. During emission of sound waves, air faces friction and produces letters. The friction decides volume of sound, intensity and pitch. Partial opening and partial closure of vocal cord produces 'whispering' and 'murmuring'.

Glottis is the open space of vocal cord and helps in inhaling and exhaling of air. Below the root of tongue, one epiglottis is available which moves forward and backward and helps in pronunciation of letters. Above glottis is the open area which is called pharynx. The pharyngeal cavity can be narrowed down for control of pronunciation sound which comes out either through mouth or through nasal passage. At this juncture is found uvula. Soft palate and uvula in combined form produce different types of sound waves. In normal conditions the uvula rests with soft palate and produces sound like *Hun, Haan, Hin* etc. In active state, Uvula obstructs nasal passage and common vowels and consonants are produced. When uvula remains in the middle, it effects out coming air and nasal consonants are produced.

Upper portion of Mouth cavity contains teeth, alveolar ridge, hard palate, palate and soft palate. During pronunciation of vowels and *ka, kha, ga* etc, soft palate moves up and closes nasal passage. During pronunciation of nasal sound, soft palate comes down and closes mouth cavity. During sleep, soft palate vibrates and produces snoring sound in human being. Teeth are thirty two in number and upper two teeth are very important in emission of sound.

Tongue is very important for emission of sound and during speaking it comes in contact with different places of mouth cavity. Depending upon structure, it is divided into following parts: (a) Tip of Tongue, (b) Blade of the Tongue, (c) Front of Tongue, (d) Back of tongue, Dorsum and Root of Tongue. (a) Tip or Apex of tongue is the front portion which is most active. It helps in emission of many vowels, consonants and words. (b) the outermost part of tongue which generally comes out from mouth is the blade. It helps in emission of letter, e.g., *sa*. (c) Front of tongue is located below hard palate. It helps in production of *Talabya* sound waves. It stops air flow and produces tenth consonant,e.g., *Eina*. The change in position of front of tongue produces different types of letters. It produces palatal (*Talabya*) and front (*Agrya*) sound. The sound produced from front, middle and back portion of palate is called Pre-palatal, Mid-palatal and Post-palatal. (d) Back and root of the tongue produces many types of vowels and consonants. The sound produced is called as *Kanthaya* and can be divided into Pre-velar, Mid-velar and Post-velar.

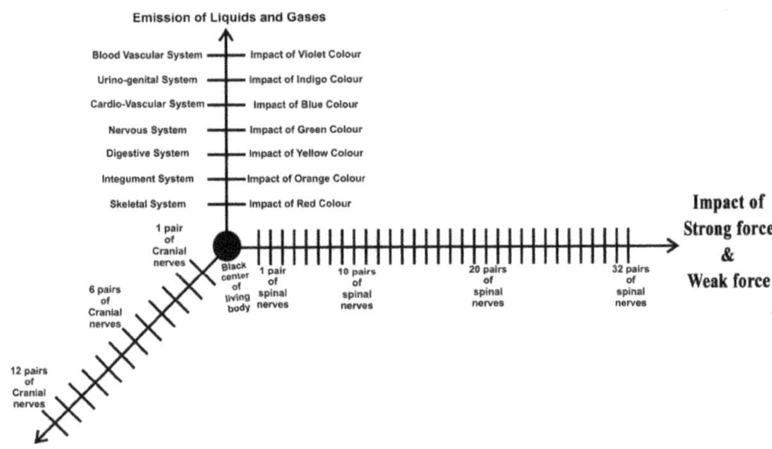

DEPOSITION OF BLACK MATTER OF Fe IN THE CENTRE OF LIVING BODY IS THE GREATEST ARBITER THAT DECIDES DEVELOPMENT AND EVOLUTION OF PARTS ALONG THREE AXES INSIDE LIVING ANIMALS AND HUMAN BEINGS. EVOLUTION OF CHARACTERS ALONG THREE AXES PRODUCES DIFFERENT TYPES OF ANIMALS ON PLANETS AND THERE IS GRADUAL INCREASE IN COMPLEXITY OF VOCAL CORDS INSIDE ANIMALS AND HUMAN BEINGS. DIFFERENT ANIMALS DEVELOP DIFFERENT TYPES OF LANGUAGES DEPENDING UPON EVOLUTION OF THEIR BODY PARTS. DIFFERENT NERVES ESTABLISH RELATIONSHIP BETWEEN SPEECH AND HEARING. IN SPACE AND IN VACUUM, SOUND WAVES EMITTED BY VOCAL CORD OF ANIMALS OR HUMAN BEINGS WILL BE INEFFECTIVE AND INAUDIBLE IN THE ABSENCE OF ATMOSPHERE OF PLANET. THREE AXES ATTACHMENT OF ANIMAL AND HUMAN BODY EMPOWERS VIBRATIONS AND VOCAL CORD TO PRODUCE 'SOUND WAVE PACKETS MADE UP OF POWER WAVES' WHICH EFFECTS HUMAN BODY WITHIN ATMOSPHERIC COVERING. ATMOSPHERE OF PLANET HELPS IN CONVERSION OF POWER WAVES INTO AUDIBLE RANGE OF SOUND WAVES ALONG THREE AXES. IT ACTS AS ELECTROMAGNETIC WAVE ALONG THREE AXES ON PLANET AND BECOMES AUDIBLE BY HUMAN BEINGS.

Fig. 3.20

The outer most part of mouth are lips. The lower lip is more active than upper lip. Combination of both the lips and their position produces different types of sound of letters and words. It produces *Oushthya* sound and it is of two types: Bilabial (*Dwayoshthya*) produced by combination of both upper and lower lip and Labio-dental (*Dantoshthya*) produced by combination of upper teeth and lower lip. The shape and size of lips changes position and looks like: (a) Normal lip producing normal sound, (b) Round lips producing whistle sound and (c) Expanded lips producing *Dirgha* sound. Diphthong is the combined form of two vowels where both become one *Swara* and come out from mouth as one vowel. Examples are *Ae, Aei, O* and *Au.* Sanskrit language, which is based on nervers of human body, should be declared as one of the UNESCO World Heritage Languages of Earth. Sanskrit is the eternal body language of animal body and human body linked with rotation, revolution and precession of planets and star of the solar system.

The human body science tallies with language science, number of nerves, impact of nerves on different parts of body and creation of 118 elements of periodic table in the universe. Nothing has developed in isolation in the universe and emission of 'sound wave packets' is guided by pressure, volume and temperature along three axes within atmosphere of planet earth. The ideas of Sanskrit language are generally accepted because it tallies with other parallel sciences of the universe.

Sanskrit is a scientific language. Its systematic structure is exceptional. Its grammatical structure is well defined and precisely laid out by Maharshi Panini. It is self contained language and new vocabulary or structure can be generated within language itself. Many scientific discoveries and literature are available in Sanskrit. It can create endless number of words. It is not an object specific language. There are many words for a single object. Sanskrit learner uses words specific to the object describing many properties of that object. So for example many words used for water describe particular property of the water in different forms at different places and time. We can create any number of words required for our use in Sanskrit.

In Sanskrit, vowels and consonants are arranged in sepate groups in logical fashion. Each sound has impact on our vocal cord and nervous system. Each sound wave strikes a different chord inside the human body. Sanskrit letters are created in geometric progression and help in improving nervous system, concentration, memory and perception.The Sanskrit alphabet with its orderly and scientific arrangement provides a simple means of understanding the production of phonemes and memorizing them. Sanskrit's versatility of expressions, its amazing power to create new words, its ability to meet the challenges and needs of future, its incredible flexibility and its utility for future is remarkable. The stop consonants in Sanskrit are arranged in an alternating fashion. The first and third sounds of each group are articulated with minimal breath release while the second and fourth are articulated with maximal breath release.

Sound wave packets are produced by human beings on the pattern of creation of 118 elements in periodic table of elements along three axes. During creation 118 elements are created in different rounds, groups and periods and position of elements varies from one animal body to another animal body due to rotation, revolution and precession movement of planets and stars. The impact of four forces decides the position of individual elements inside human body. The sedimentation of elements and compounds takes place layer by layer on human body due to rotation, revolution and precession. From the above analysis, discussion and interpretation, it is proved that Sanskrit is the Fundamental Language of Human body and Solar System. It has emerged on scientific lines from spinal nerves of Human body. Sanskrit may be declared as UNESCO World Heritage Language of the Planet.

VOWELS AND CONSONANTS OF SANSKRIT ARE PRODUCED BY SPINAL NERVES OF HUMAN BODY. SANSKRIT IS LANGUAGE OF SPINAL NERVES OF HUMAN BODY

CERVICAL -1 RIGHT (आ)
CERV - 2 RIGHT (ई)
CERV - 3 RIGHT (ऊ)
CERV - 4 RIGHT (ॠ)
CERV - 5 RIGHT (ॡ)
CERV - 6 RIGHT (ऐ)
CERV - 7 RIGHT (औ)
CERV - 8 RIGHT (अः)
THORACIC NERVE (क)
THOR – 2 (ख)
THOR – 3 (ग)
THOR – 4 (घ)
THOR – 5 (ङ)
THOR – 6 (च)
THOR – 7 (छ)
THOR – 8 (ज)
THOR – 9 (झ)
THOR – 10 (ञ)
THOR – 11 (ट)
THOR – 12 (ठ)
LUMBAR – 1 RIGHT (ढ)
LUMBAR – 2 RIGHT (त)
LUMBAR – 3 RIGHT (द)
LUMBAR – 4 RIGHT (न)
LUMBAR – 5 RIGHT (फ)
SACRAL 5 (ल)
COCCYGEAL RIGHT 1 (श)
COCCYGEAL RIGHT 2 (स)
CERVICAL-1 LEFT (अ)
CERV - 2 LEFT (इ)
CERV - 3 LEFT (उ)
CERV - 4 LEFT (ऋ)
CERV - 5 LEFT (ऌ)
CERV - 6 LEFT (ए)
CERV - 7 LEFT (ओ)
CERV - 8 LEFT (अं)
THORACIC NERVE 1
LUMBAR – 1 LEFT (ड)
LUMBAR – 2 LEFT (ण)
LUMBAR – 3 LEFT (थ)
LUMBAR – 4 LEFT (घ)
LUMBAR – 5 LEFT (प)
SACRAL 1 (ब)
SACRAL 2 (भ)
SACRAL 3 (म)
SACRAL 4 (य)
SACRAL 5 (र)
COCCYGEAL LEFT 1 (व)
COCCYGEAL LEFT 2 (ष)

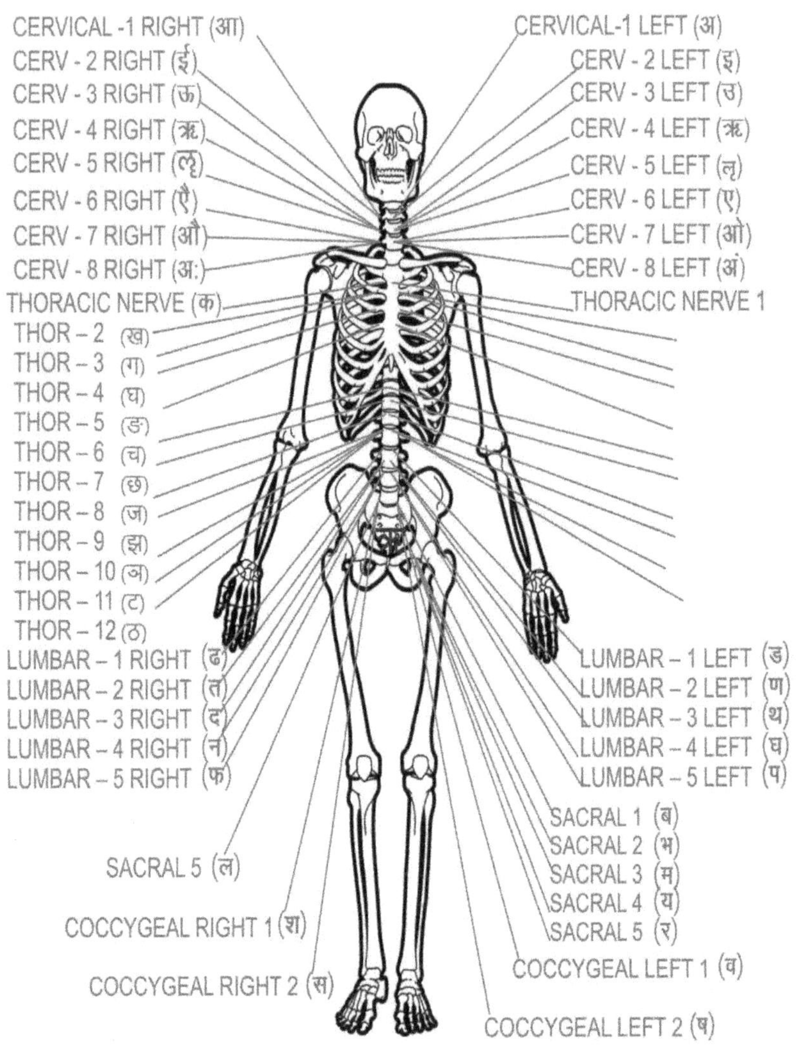

Fig. 3.21

4

HUMAN NERVOUS SYSTEM

The entire nervous system is derived from ectoderm except its blood vessels and some neuroglial elements. The specific cells of early ectoderm which gives rise to entire nervous system and special sense organs is called as neural ectoderm. Neural ectoderm differentiates into three parts, e.g., neural tube, neural crest cells and ectodermal placodes. The neural tube produces central nervous system, neural crest cells form peripheral nervous system and ectodermal placodes help in creation of cranial sensory ganglia, hypophysis and inner ear.

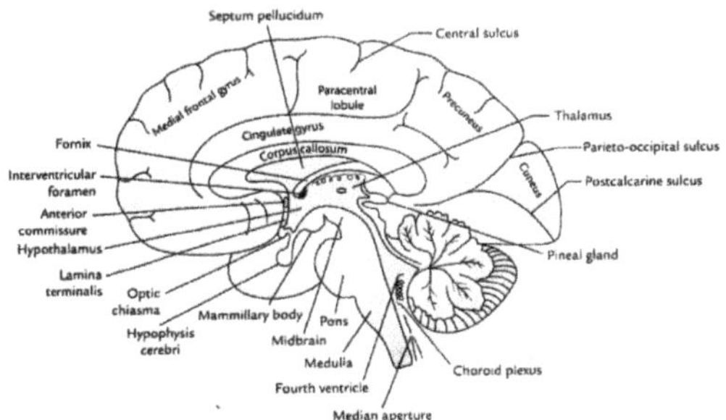

SAGITTAL SECTION OF HUMAN BRAIN

Fig. 4.1

Main functions of nervous system is reception of sensory stimuli from internal and external sources, integration of all information and control and coordination of involuntary and voluntary actions. The nervous system contains three functional types of neurons: sensory, motor and interneurons. Sensory neurons detect stimuli and motor neurons transmit command to effector organs. The interneurons analyze and store all information. The sensory stimuli (afferent impulses) received from body are coordinated within nervous system and then motor response (motor impulses) is sent to effector organs, muscles and glands.

The nervous system can be divided into two parts, central nervous system and peripheral nervous system. Central nervous system consists of brain and spinal cord. Brain is located inside cranial cavity and spinal cord is located inside vertebral canal. The CNS processes and coordinates sensory data and sends appropriate motor commands. Peripheral nervous system contains all neural tissues outside the CNS such as cranial nerves, cervical nerves and spinal nerves. The PNS provides sensory information to CNS and transmits its motor commands to peripheral tissues and body systems. Functionally nervous system can be divided into two parts, i.e., afferent and efferent divisions. The afferent division transmits sensory information to CNS. The efferent division transmits motor commands to muscles and glands.

Spinal cord is the lower elongated part of central nervous system. It is cylindrical in shape and occupies upper three-fourth part of vertebral canal. It measures about 45 cms in adult male and 42 cms in adult female and weighs about 30 grams. It extends from the level of upper border of Atlas (1st Cervical Vertebra) to the level of lower border of 2nd Lumbar Vertebra. It shows slight variation in different human beings. It extends downwards from medulla oblongata starting from upper border of the posterior arch of first cervical vertebra to approximate lower border of sacral vertebra. Its lowest tapering extremity is called conus medullaris. The tip of conus medullaris continues downwards as thin filament called filum terminale. Filum terminale is very delicate thread like structure extending from tip of conus medullaris to first coccygeal vertebra. It is about 22 cms long and is composed of non-nervous fibrous tissue (pia). It contains 1st, 2nd, 3rd and 4th coccygeal nerves embedded in it which appear to be fused.

Spinal cord provides attachment to all spinal nerves which connect it to the tissues of trunk, girdles, limbs and viscera. Spinal cord contains large number of ascending and descending pathways which work as conduits for nervous information passing to and fro from different parts of body and the brain. Functions of the spinal cord are execution of reflexes and transmission of impulses to and from brain. Spinal cord is surrounded by three protective membranes called spinal meninges. From outside these are dura mater, arachnoid mater and pia mater. (a) Spinal dura mater extends from foramen magnum to lower border of second sacral vertebra. The space between spinal dura mater and vertebral canal is termed epidural space which contains loose areolar tissues, semi-liquid fat and internal vertebral venous plexus. The space between dura mater and arachnoid mater is termed sub-dural space and it contains capillary layer of fluids. (b) Arachnoid mater is thin avascular membrane which invests spinal cord. Above this layer is found arachnoid mater of brain and below this layer it extends up to sacral vertebra. (c) Pia mater is vascular membrane that invests spinal cord and continues with it like a thread type prolongation called filum terminale. The sub-arachnoid space between pia mater and arachnoid mater is filled up with cerebrospinal fluid.

The anterior portion of spinal cord present anterior median fissure and two anterolateral sulci while the posterior portion presents posteromedian sulcus, two posterolateral and two posterointermediate sulci. Spinal nerves emerge from the sides of cord. Every spinal nerve is attached to the cord by two roots, anterior motor root and posterior sensory root. The posterior root has a ganglion consisting of pseudounipolar cells. Both the roots are made up of number of rootlets that arise from spinal cord up to some length.

The spinal cord is segmented like vertebral column but the segments are not visible from outside. The part of spinal cord to which a pair of spinal nerves, both left and right, are attached is known as spinal segment. The length of spinal cord (45 cms) is smaller as compared to length of vertebral column (65 cms). Spinal segments are short and crowded in the lower part of cord. The spinal and vertebral segments do not lie at the same plane. The spinal segments always lie above their numerically corresponding vertebral spines. In lower part of spinal cord they lie above their corresponding vertebrae. In sacral and coccygeal regions they appear to be fused and mixed with each other.

The spinal cord is cylindrical in shape with an average diameter of 1.3 cms. Spinal cord is shorter in length than the vertebral column and length and obliquity of spinal nerve roots increases progressively from above to downwards. The nerve roots of lumbar, sacral and coccygeal nerves from caudal part of the cord (conus medullaris) takes a vertical course and forms a bunch of nerve fibers around filum terminale called cauda equina. The spinal cord is made up of inner core of grey matter and peripheral area of white matter.

Grey matter is present as H-shaped (butterfly shaped) fluted column extending throughout the length of cord. It is divided into symmetrical right and left comma-shaped matter which is connected across the midline by a transverse grey commissure. The central canal of spinal cord passes through centre of grey commissure. The central canal is surrounded by substantia gelatinosa centralis. The comma-shaped mass of grey matter is again divided by a transverse grey commissure into narrow elongated posterior horn and broad anterior horn. The posterior horns are connected to outer surface through gelatinous substance called substantia gelatinosa. The quantity and shape of horns of grey matter varies from white matter at different levels inside cord. The quantity of grey matter available at particular level is related to the mass of tissue it connects and supplies. It is maximum in cervical and lumbar enlargement region which connects

94

the limbs and associated girdles. The horns are biggest in cervical and lumbar enlargement areas.

The quantity of white matter inside spinal cord shows progressive increase from below upwards. It is observed that progressively more number of ascending fibers are added to the cord from below upwards. At the same time, the number of descending fibers decreases inside spinal cord from above downwards because some of them terminate in every spinal segment. The quantity of white matter is more in cervical segments and less in sacral segments of spinal cord. White matter of the spinal cord surrounds central H-shaped mass of grey matter and mainly contains nerve fibers. The nerve fibers are myelinated and give it white appearance. The fibers in white matter inside spinal cord are divided into three types:
  (a) Sensory fibers: It includes central processes of sensory neurons of posterior root ganglia which enters the spinal cord and ascends or descends inside it.
  (b) Motor fibers: It includes descending fibers from higher centers to the spinal cord.
  (c) Association fibers: It originates and ends inside spinal cord.

White matter inside spinal cord can be divided into three parts called funiculi or white columns. The anterior white columns are joined together through white commissure. Every white column consists of tracts which are either ascending (sensory), descending (motor) or inter-segmental (associated). Spinal cord contains cerebrospinal fluid which occupies the ventricular system within the CNS and in subarachnoid space surrounding the CNS. It circulates in external and internal surfaces of the brain and spinal cord and provides protective cushion between the CNS and surrounding bones of CNS. Cerebrospinal fluid is about 150 ml in adult male out of which 30 ml is available in ventricular system and rest occupies subarachnoid space. CSF is colorless and slightly alkaline fluid having specific gravity of 1005 - 1008. CSF contains inorganic salts with some quantity of glucose and proteins. The per day production of CSF in adults is about 500-600 ml. About 85 percent of the CSF is produced by the choroid plexuses within lateral ventricles and the rest is produced by choroid plexuses in the third and fourth ventricles.

CSF is produced mainly in the lateral ventricles from where the fluid passes through inter-ventricular foramina into the third ventricle. The fluid passes further via cerebral aqueduct into the fourth ventricle. Then it moves via median aperture and lateral apertures in the roof of lateral ventricle. The fluid further moves in subarachnoid space over brain and spinal cord. Most of the CSF moves upwards through the gap in tentorium cerebelli and then enters laterally over the inferior surface of the cerebrum. It further ascends on the superolateral aspect of each cerebral hemisphere to reach arachnoid villi and granulations penetrate into the superior sagittal sinus. The CSF flows into blood stream of sinus through the mesothelial cell lining of these villi and granulations. Small quantity of CSF flows inferiorly to the subarachnoid space around spinal cord and cauda equina. The movement of CSF is facilitated by pulsation of cerebral and spinal arteries present in the subarachnoid space and by the movements of head and spine.

CSF serves as cushion between CNS and surrounding bodies. It acts as shock absorber of CNS and supports the brain and spinal cord. It nourishes brain and maintains uniform pressure on CNS. It removes the metabolites and waste products and serves as pathway for pineal secretions to reach pituitary gland. Evolution of languages depends upon pressure due to gravity, temperature and atmospheric volume of individual planet. The development of living body along three axes decides the type of language which will be emitted by vocal cord of that living body. Since time immemorial, human beings have developed '*Mantras*' or cluster of jumbled words from Sanskrit alphabets which effect different parts of body and systems and help in curing the diseases.

It is said that "*Susumna bhakshayate Samayah*" which means that spinal cord devours and kills time in human beings. The cerebrospinal fluid absorbs oxygen gas taken through nostrils (ida and pingala) which keeps this liquid, cord and brain fresh and alive for very longer period. In ancient times, the saints used to store and retain oxygen gas inside spinal cord and used to survive in cold places or snowy mountains for lakhs of years.

Ancient intellectual race knew about anatomy and physiology of human body and developed and spoke Sanskrit language which was based on nerves and physiology of human body. The development of life forms will be the same on all planets in terms of chemical composition, building blocks, biochemistry and genes etc. The actual shape, size and mass of life forms will be decided by expansion and contraction of mass along three axes on planets. Nerves emerge in group of nerves from spinal cord and look like knots of nerves at six points on spinal cord.

SANSKRIT BHASHA UDYAAN

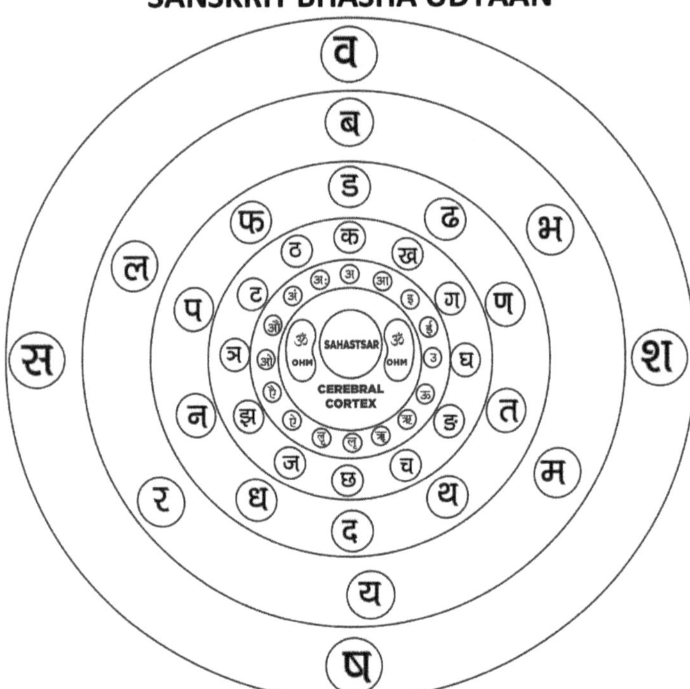

16 VOWELS AND 32 CONSONANTS OF SANSKRIT ARE EMITTED AND CONTROLLED BY NERVES IN SEVEN TIERS IN HUMAN NERVOUS SYSTEM. SAHASRASAR (BRAIN)AND THEN CEREBRAL CORTEX LIES AT THE CENTRE AND TOP OF HEAD. PRODUCTION OF VOWELS TAKES PLACE FROM CERVICAL NERVES. THEN CONSONANTS ARE PRODUCED BY SPINAL NERVES WHICH REACH THE PERIPHERAL PORTION OF HUMAN BODY. LETTERS LIKE 'SOUND WAVE PACKETS' ARE MADE UP OF POWER WAVES IN THE FREQUENCY RANGE Of 256 Hz TO 512 Hz. PRODUCTION OF 32 CONSONANTS ARE BASED ON THIRTY TWO CLASSES OF CRYSTAL SYMMETRY. NERVES EMERGE IN THE MULTIPLES OF EIGHT IN GEOMETRIC PROGRESSION FROM NERVOUS SYSTEM OF HUMAN BODY.

Fig. 4.2

The audible range of sound waves will be different for different animals on different planets. The sound waves are equivalent to their corresponding electromagnetic waves, i.e., power waves in space. So the sound waves of animals and human beings are more powerful than electromagnetic waves of seven colors (4000Å -7500Å) that constitute and make animal and human body. The sound waves effect animal body like power waves and sound waves can last longer like power waves in the space. The sound waves will not perish and on the patterns of power waves it will affect animal body with impact on future growth and development. The sound waves of animal body effect the present time and will affect the body in future also because power waves last longer in the space. The sound waves of animals and human beings form a circular outer covering around their planets like power waves range in space. The black element melts in radio wave and power wave region and sound waves become more powerful than the visible spectra range that creates 118 elements and forms astral bodies, planets, stars, animal bodies and human beings. Depending upon emergence of 32 nerves from vertebral column the human body shows attachment with different waves by 32 nerves and they are observed as 32 consonant letters spoken by human beings. These 32 consonant letters are controlled by 16 cervical nerves which relate to 16 vowel letters. The vowels create sound and produce 16 types of sound waves in human beings. Thus vowels and consonants in total create 32 x 16 = 512 x 2 = 1024 types of sound waves.

During the course of evolution of life forms the inner characters and outer features of body show different types of development depending upon movement of planets along three axes. The inner features of body of life forms show same types of evolution and development and exhibit creation of characters along three axes. The life forms tend to develop seven body systems due to seven colors cycle along one axis, twelve body parts in geometrical progression along second axes and fourteen layers of development along third axis inside body. The outer features of life forms may look different. The outer appendages, features, color and stature may look different depending upon position of life forms at different longitude, latitude and altitude on planet. As for example, chimpanzee, gorilla, apes, monkey, man and many similar extinct forms show different outer features but their inner development along three axes during evolution was the same.

The biggest human being shall contain mass up to atomic number 118 under impact of four forces. The Au element with 79 protons and 120 neutrons shall be the highest limit of mass that a human being can retain inside it. The strong force equilibrium becomes less powerful from atomic number 80 and elements from atomic number 80 and onwards develop and produce crystals of less symmetry, liquids and gases of elements. The size of human body increases during stage of creation up to 26 years, attains equilibrium from 26 years to 79 years and starts decaying and tends to lose three axes attachment gradually from 80 to 118 years.

Layer by layer deposition of elements, cells, soft tissues and hard tissues increases the size of living body along three axes on planets. In this process complex and bigger living body is produced and as big and tough is the body so long is the age of that life form. The growth and development of body may be different along three axes depending upon position of life form on planet. The impact of pressure, volume and temperature decides the size and shape of individual living being on planet. Every living being maintains individual thermodynamic equilibrium on planets. The sound waves in the low frequency range become equivalent to power waves and act as power waves. Eight pair of cervical nerves effect sixteen parts, organs and body systems as follows on left and right side of the body:

1. Cervical Nerve 1 (Left) guides and controls human body parts and organs. It cures the diseases concerned with following body parts. It acts on left side of the body. Cervical nerve 1 is a spinal nerve of cervical segment. Cervical 1 carries mostly motor fibres but also meningeal branch that supplies sensation to parts of the dura around foramen magnum. This nerve gives rise to nerves

of the geniohyoid which moves hyoid bone upwards and expands the airway and thyrohyoid which depresses the hyoid bone and elevates larynx.

2. Cervical Nerve 1 (Right) guides and controls human body parts and organs. It cures the diseases concerned with body parts and acts on right side of body. Cervical nerve 1 is a spinal nerve of cervical segment. Cervical 1 carries mostly motor fibres but also meningeal branch that supplies sensation to parts of the dura around foramen magnum. This nerve gives rise to nerves of geniohyoid which moves the hyoid bone upwards and expands the airway and thyrohyoid which depresses the hyoid bone and elevates larynx. It covers neck and head portion.

3. Cervical Nerve 2 (Left) guides and controls human body parts and organs. It cures the diseases concerned with body parts. The cervical 2 dermatome handles cause sensation for upper part of the head.

4. Cervical Nerve 2 (Right) guides and controls human body parts and organs. It cures the diseases concerned with body parts. The cervical 2 dermatome handles sensation for upper part of the head.

5. Cervical Nerve 3 (Left) guides and controls human body parts and organs. It cures the diseases concerned with body parts. It helps control the head and neck including movements forward, backward and to the sides.

6. Cervical Nerve 3 (Right) guides and controls human body parts and organs. It cures the diseases concerned with body parts. It helps control the head and neck including movements forward, backward and to the sides.

7. Cervical Nerve 4 (Left) guides and controls human body parts and organs. It cures the diseases concerned with body parts. Cervical 4 controls upward shoulder movements. It also helps the diaphragm and sheet of muscles that stretch to the bottom of rib cage for breathing. The dermatome covers parts of the neck, shoulders and upper parts of arms. It contributes nerve fibres to the phrenic nerve, the motor nerve to the thoraco-abdominal diaphragm. It contributes some sensory fibres to supraclavicular nerves responsible for sensation from the skin above clavicle.

8. Cervical Nerve 4 (Right) guides and controls human body parts and organs. It cures the diseases concerned with body parts. Cervical 4 controls upward shoulder movements. It helps the diaphragm and sheet of muscles that stretch to the bottom of rib cage for breathing. The dermatome covers parts of the neck, shoulders and upper parts of arms. It contributes nerve fibres to the phrenic nerve, the motor nerve to thoraco-abdominal diaphragm. It contributes some sensory fibres to supraclavicular nerves responsible for sensation from skin above the clavicle.

9. Cervical Nerve 5 (Left) guides and controls human body parts and organs on both sides of the body. It cures the diseases concerned with body parts. Cervical 5 helps control the deltoids which form rounded contours of the shoulders and biceps which allow bending of elbow and rotation of fore arm. The dermatome covers outer part of the upper arm down to near elbow. It contributes to the phrenic nerve, long thoracic nerve and dorsal scapular nerve before joining cervical spinal nerve 6 to form upper trunk, a trunk of the brachial plexus which then forms lateral cord and finally musculo-cutaneous nerve.

10. Cervical Nerve 5 (Right) guides and controls human body parts and organs. It cures the diseases concerned with following body parts. Cervical 5 helps control the deltoids which form rounded contours of shoulders and the biceps which allow bending of elbow and rotation of fore arm. The dermatome covers outer part of the upper arm down to near elbow portion. It contributes to the phrenic nerve, long thoracic nerve and dorsal scapular nerve before joining cervical spinal nerve 6 to form upper trunk, a trunk of the brachial plexus which then forms the lateral cord and finally musculo-cutaneous nerve.

11. Cervical Nerve 6 (Left) guides and controls human body parts and organs. It cures the diseases concerned with body parts. The location of cervical 6 vertebra allow them to support both neck and head and allows range of motions. It provides blood flow to the brain. It shares common branch from cervical 5 and has a role in innervating many muscles of the rotator cuff and distal arm.

12. Cervical Nerve 6 (Right) guides and controls human body parts and organs. It cures the diseases concerned with body parts. The location of cervical 6 vertebra allow them to support both neck and head and allows range of motions. It provides blood flow to the brain. It shares common branch from cervical 5 and has a role in innervating many muscles of the rotator cuff and distal arm.

13. Cervical Nerve 7 (Left) guides and controls human body parts and organs. It cures the diseases concerned with body parts. The cervical myotome is a group of muscles controlled by C7 nerve. These muscles include works involved in straightening elbow, lifting of wrist, elongating the fingers to stretch hands and triceps muscles in upper arm.

14. Cervical Nerve 7 (Right) guides and controls human body parts and organs. It cures the diseases concerned with body parts. The cervical myotome is a group of muscles controlled by Cervical 7 nerve. These muscles include works involved in straightening the elbow, lifting of wrist, elongating fingers to stretch hands and triceps muscles in upper arm.

15. Cervical Nerve 8 (Left) guides and controls human body parts and organs. It cures the diseases concerned with body parts. Cervical 8 nerve forms part of the radial and ulnar nerves via brachial plexus and has motor and sensory functions in the upper limb. It receives sensory afferents from C8 dermatome. This consists of all the skin on little finger and continuing up slightly past the wrist on the palmar and dorsal aspects of the hand and forearm. It contributes to the motor intervention of many of muscles in the trunk and upper limb. Its primary function is the flexion of fingers.

16. Cervical Nerve 8 (Right) guides and controls human body parts and organs. It cures the diseases concerned with body parts. One pair of nerve serves both left side and right side of body. Cervical 8 nerve forms part of the radial and ulnar nerves via brachial plexus and has motor and sensory functions in the upper limb. It receives sensory afferents from C8 dermatome. This consists of all the skin on little finger and continuing up slightly past the wrist on palmar and dorsal aspects of the hand and forearm. It contributes to motor intervention of many muscles in the trunk and upper limb. Its primary function is flexion of fingers. Cervical nerves are eight in pairs and their impact is observed on sixteen vowels.

The letters created out of sound waves behave like elements nucleosynthesized during evolution of human beings. The assimilation of sound waves within atmosphere and energy associated with sound waves creates 16 vowel letters and 32 consonant letters as creation of non-metallic elements and metallic elements respectively. 32 classes of crystal symmetry create 32 consonant letters as 'crystal packets' in human beings. Similarly 16 vowel letters create 'sixteen mass packets' in human beings. Consonant letter are produced by Thoracic nerves and nerves below that. They produce solidified, symmetrical and solid body like "sound wave packets".

1. Thoracic Nerve 1 guides and controls human body parts and organs. It cures the diseases concerned with body parts. It feeds into nerves that go to the top of chest and into the arms and hand.

2. Thoracic Nerve 2 guides and controls human body parts and organs. It cures the diseases concerned with body parts. This nerve goes to the top of chest and into arms and hands. This nerve consists of different nerves moving along the spinal column. The nerves control sensory and motor signals from spinal column to body enabling body to react to the movement of spine.

3. Thoracic Nerve 3 guides and controls human body parts and organs. It cures the diseases concerned with body parts. Each nerve is named for the vertebra above it. Thoracic 3 nerve roots run between T3 vertebra and T4 vertebra. They control motor and sensory signals mainly of upper chest portion.

4. Thoracic Nerve 4 guides and controls human body parts and organs. It cures the diseases concerned with body parts. The nerve fibres transmit information between spinal cord and parts of body. Its nerves control the gall bladder and common duct and affects lungs and bronchial tubes. Its symptoms of pain can show themselves through gall bladder problem, gall stones and jaundice.

5. Thoracic Nerve 5 guides and controls human body parts and organs. It cures the diseases concerned with body parts. It affects muscles of upper chest, mid-back and abdominal muscles. They control the rib cage, lungs, diaphragm and muscles that help in breathing. It protects the nerves of liver and nerve bundles that affect release of hormones, metabolism, glucose production and insulin.

6. Thoracic Nerve 6 guides and controls human body parts and organs. It cures the diseases concerned with body parts. Thoracic spinal nerve 6 is a spinal nerve of thoracic segment. It controls motor and sensory signals of upper back, chest and abdomen.

7. Thoracic Nerve 7 guides and controls human body parts and organs. It cures the diseases concerned with body parts. Thoracic nerve 7 can feed chest and abdomen portions. It controls motor and sensory signals of upper back, chest and abdomen.

8. Thoracic Nerve 8 guides and controls human body parts and organs. It cures the diseases concerned with body parts. The nerves and muscles help control rib cage, lungs, diaphragm and muscles which helps in breathing. It is important for balance and posture and help in expelling foreign particles.

9. Thoracic Nerve 9 guides and controls human body parts and organs. It cures the diseases concerned with body parts. Thoracic nerve fibers transmit information between spinal cord and various parts of the body.

10. Thoracic Nerve 10 guides and controls human body parts and organs. It cures the diseases concerned with body parts. These nerves help rib cage, lungs and adjoining muscles in breathing. It is important for balance and straight posture.

11. Thoracic Nerve 11 guides and controls human body parts and organs. It cures the diseases concerned with body parts. The vertebrae and nerves are important for control of kidneys, ureters, colon, small intestine, lymph circulation and hip muscles. The ventral ramus becomes an intercostals nerve which travels along the same path as the ribs.

12. Thoracic Nerve 12 guides and controls human body parts and organs. It cures the diseases concerned with body parts. The nerves control motor and sensory signals mostly for the upper back, chest and abdomen of human body.

13. Lumbar Nerve 1 (Left) (five pairs in total fuse within vertebra and appear as five nerves) guides and controls human body parts and organs. It cures the diseases concerned with body parts. This spinal nerve provides sensation to the genital regions and helps in movement of hip muscles. It provides sensation to the front part of thigh and inner part of lower leg. They control movements of hip and knee muscles. It innervates abdominal internal obliques through ilioinguinal nerve. It effects left side of the body.

14. Lumbar Nerve 1 (Right) guides and controls human body parts and organs. It cures the diseases concerned with body parts. This spinal nerve provides sensation to the genital regions and helps in movement of hip muscles. It provides sensation to the front part of thigh and inner part of lower leg. They control movement of hip and knee muscles. It innervates abdominal internal obliques through ilioinguinal nerve. One side of pair effects right side of the body.

15. Lumbar Nerve 2 (Left) guides and controls human body parts and organs. It cures the diseases concerned with body parts. It supplies many muscles which may be innervated with L2 as single origin or be innervated by other spinal nerves. The muscles are quadratus lumborum. It provides sensation and control to front part of thigh and inner side of lower leg. One side of pair effects left side of the body.

16. Lumbar Nerve 2 (Right) guides and controls human body parts and organs. It cures the diseases concerned with body parts. It supplies many muscles which may be innervated with L2 as single origin or be innervated by other spinal nerves. The muscles are quadratus lumborum. It provides sensation and control to front part of thigh and inner side of lower leg. One side of pair effects right side of the body.

17. Lumbar Nerve 3 (Left) guides and controls human body parts and organs. It cures the diseases concerned with body parts. It provides support to front part of thigh and inner side of lower leg. It is positioned in the middle of lumbar spine and plays important role in supporting the weight of torso and protecting the cauda equina.

18. Lumbar Nerve 3 (Right) guides and controls human body parts and organs. It cures the diseases concerned with body parts. It provides support to front part of thigh and inner side of lower leg. It is positioned in the middle of lumbar spine and plays important role in supporting the weight of torso and protecting the cauda equina.

19. Lumbar Nerve 4 (Left) guides and controls human body parts and organs. It cures the diseases concerned with body parts. This nerve originates from spinal column below the lumbar vertebra. It is innervated with L4 along with other nerves. It is an area of skin that receives sensations through L4 spinal nerve and includes parts of thigh, knee, leg and foot. It is group of muscles controlled by L4 spinal nerve and includes parts of many muscles in pelvis, thigh, leg and foot.

20. Lumbar Nerve 4 (Right) guides and controls human body parts and organs. It cures the diseases concerned with body parts. This nerve originates from spinal column below the lumbar vertebra. It is innervated with L4 along with other nerves. It is an area of skin that receives sensations through L4 spinal nerve and includes parts of thigh, knee, leg and foot. It is group of muscles controlled by L4 spinal nerve and includes parts of many muscles in pelvis, thigh, leg and foot.

21. Lumbar Nerve 5 (Left) guides and controls human body parts and organs. It cures the diseases concerned with body parts. The nerves innervate lower limbs of human body. Compression and inflammation of the nerve root may cause radiculopathy symptoms or sciatica. It causes pain and numbness in buttock, thigh, leg and feet. Lumbar nerve is found in pairs and both sides effect left and right side of the body.

22. Lumbar Nerve 5 (Right) (in total five pairs) guides and controls human body parts and organs. It cures the diseases concerned with body parts. The nerves innervate lower limbs of human body. Compression and inflammation of the nerve root may cause radiculopathy symptoms or sciatica. It causes pain and numbness in buttock, thigh, leg and feet. Lumbar nerve is found in pairs and both sides effect left and right side of the body.

23. Sacral Nerve 1 guides and controls human body parts and organs. It cures the diseases concerned with body parts. The sacral plexus is a network of nerves emerging from lower parts of the spine. The nerves provide motor control and receive sensory information from most of the pelvis and leg. This nerve root supplies innervations for the ankle jerk and a loss of this reflex indicates S1 impingement. Sacral nerves are six in number and they are fused and appear to be five in number,

24. Sacral Nerve 2 guides and controls human body parts and organs. It cures the diseases concerned with body parts. Sacral nerve supplies to many muscles either directly or through nerves originating from S2. They are innervated with S2 and partly by other spinal nerves. They govern the toes. Damage to the nerve affects back of thighs.

25. Sacral Nerve 3 guides and controls human body parts and organs. It cures the diseases concerned with body parts. Sacral plexus is a nerve plexus which provides motor and sensory nerves for the posterior portion of thigh, lower leg and foot and part of the pelvis. The muscles are iliococcygeus.

26. Sacral Nerve 4 guides and controls human body parts and organs. It cures the diseases concerned with body parts. S4 supplies many muscles originating from S4. They are innervated with S4 and partly by other spinal nerves. The muscles are Sphincter aniexternus muscle.

27. Sacral Nerve 5 (Left) guides and controls human body parts and organs. It cures the diseases concerned with body parts. It appears to be fused with sixth sacral nerve. They provide

motor control to and receive sensory information from most of the pelvis and leg. Sacral 5 roots and coccygeal nerves leave sacral canal through sacral hiatus. These nerves provide sensory and motor innervations to their respective dermatomes and myotomes. They provide partial innervation to many pelvic organs including the uterus, fallopian tubes, bladder and prostate.

28. Sacral Nerve 5 (Right) (fused with Nerve 5) guides and controls human body parts and organs. It cures the diseases concerned with body parts. They provide motor control to and receive sensory information from most of the pelvis and leg. Sacral 5 roots and coccygeal nerves leave sacral canal through sacral hiatus. These nerves provide sensory and motor innervations to their respective dermatomes and myotomes. They provide partial innervation to many pelvic organs including the uterus, fallopian tubes, bladder and prostate.

29. Coccygeal Nerve 1 (Left) guides and controls human body parts and organs. It cures the diseases concerned with body parts. All the coccygeal nerves appear to be fused at base. The sacral roots and coccygeal nerves leave sacral canal through sacral hiatus. They provide sensory and motor innervation to their respective dermatomes and myotomes. They also provide partial innervations to pelvic organs, uterus, fallopian tubes, bladder and prostate. It innervates the skin in the coccygeal region around tailbone.

30. Coccygeal Nerve 1 (Right) guides and controls human body parts and organs. It cures the diseases concerned with body parts. It emits Sanskrit letter '*Talavya Sha*'. All the coccygeal nerves appear to be fused at base. The sacral roots and coccygeal nerves leave sacral canal through sacral hiatus. They provide sensory and motor innervation to their respective dermatomes and myotomes. They also provide partial innervations to pelvic organs, uterus, fallopian tubes, bladder and prostate. It innervates the skin in the coccygeal region around tailbone.

31. Coccygeal Nerve 2 (Left) guides and controls human body parts and organs. It cures the diseases concerned with body parts. It emits Sanskrit letter '*Murdhanya Sa*'. All the coccygeal nerves appear to be fused at base. The sacral roots and coccygeal nerves leave sacral canal through sacral hiatus. They provide sensory and motor innervation to their respective dermatomes and myotomes. They also provide partial innervations to pelvic organs, uterus, fallopian tubes, bladder and prostate. It innervates the skin in the coccygeal region around tailbone. The tiny nerve which is composed of axons from spinal nerves. It innervates the coccygeus and skin over the coccyx.

32. Coccygeal Nerve 2 (Right) guides and controls human body parts and organs. It cures the diseases concerned with body parts. It emits Sanskrit letter '*Dantya Sa*'. Coccygeal plexus originates from S4, S5 and Co 1 spinal nerves. It is interconnected with lower part of the sacral plexus. The only nerve in this plexus is the anococcygeal nerve, which serves sensory innervations of the skin in the coccygeal region. Four coccygeal nerves are fused at the bottom within vertebra and appear as one nerve.

Spinal segment is place where a pair of spinal nerves is attached to spinal cord. Each spinal nerve passes out of the vertebral canal through its inter-vertebral foramen. The spinal cord ends at much higher level because of its slower growth relative to the vertebral column. The lower spinal segments do not correspond in level with vertebrae. The upper spinal nerves pass out transversely to their exits at the inter-vertebral foramina but the lower nerves pass obliquely downwards to get out of their respective foramina. It is observed that L - 1 and L - 2 spinal segments lie at the level of 10th thoracic vertebra. L - 3 and L - 4 spinal segments lie at the level of 11th thoracic vertebra. L - 5 spinal segments lies at the level of 12th thoracic vertebra. Sacral and coccygeal segments lie at the level of 1st Lumbar vertebra. Cauda Equina is the bunch of joint lower spinal nerves (Lumbar, Sacral and Coccygeal) below the termination of spinal cord. These nerves surround the Conus Medullaris and Filum terminale and give appearance of a Horse's tail and that is why it has been called Cauda Equina. This appearance is due to obliquity and vertical direction of lower spinal nerves as they pass down to their respective inter-vertebral foramina.

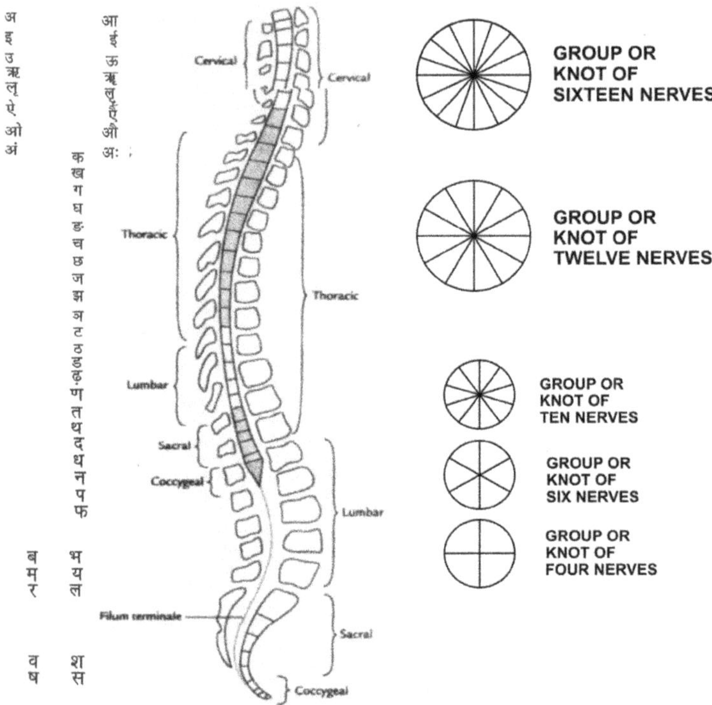

VOCAL CORD BEGINS PRODUCTION OF VOICE OF VOWELS AND CONSONANTS STARTING FROM KA.....KAA.....KI.....KEE.....KU.....KOO.....KRI.....KREE.....KLRI.....KLREE.....KE.....KAI.....KO.....KAU.....KAM.....KAH IN HUMAN BEINGS. IMPACT OF VOWELS AND CONSONANTS ON CERVICAL AND SPINAL NERVES OF HUMAN BODY. NERVES CREATE GROUPS OR KNOTS AT FIVE PLACES INSIDE SPINAL CORD AND SHOW IMPACT IN GROUPS. COCCYX COMMONLY CALLED AS TAILBONE IS SMALL BONE RESEMBLING SMALL TAIL AND IS LOCATED AT THE BOTTOM OF SPINE. IT IS MADE UP OF FOUR COCCYGEAL VERTEBRA OR SPINAL BONES. THESE FOUR VERTEBRAE ACT AS BASE OF SPINAL CORD FOR HUMAN BODY AND CONTAIN NERVES IN FUSED FORM. A COCCYGEAL VERTEBRA CONTAINS BNCT THAT INVOLVES MEDULLARY CAVITY AND EXTENDS THROUGH CORTEX INTO SOFT TISSUES BY DISPLACING THE PERIOSTEUM. FOUR FUSED VERTEBRAE ACT AS BASE OF SPINAL CORD IN HUMAN BEINGS AND CONTAIN FOUR COCCYGEAL NERVES IN FUSED FORM. CRY OF INFANTS BORN IN AFRICA AND CRY OF INFANTS BORN IN AUSTRALIA AT THE TIME OF BIRTH HAVE SAME TONE OF UTTERING, i.e.,.... KA..... KHA......AR......AN......AH......AH....KEHAN....

Fig. 4.3

104

Human body shows thirty one pair of spinal nerves from outside. In fact, many spinal nerves are fused and show one nerve. It shows degenerating trend in human body along one axis towards lower side. Along other two axes, i.e., twelve pairs of cranial nerves and nine body systems the body does not show any degeneration. For all practical purposes, Cervical nerves are eight pairs (sixteen nerves) and lower Spinal nerves (Thoracic, Lumbar, Sacral and Coccygeal) are 32 pairs in spinal cord. The nerves appear to be fused at the lower level in spinal cord. Human spinal cord is segmented through segments which are not visible from outside. The part of spinal cord to which a pair of spinal nerves (right and left) are attached is called spinal segment. The number of spinal segments relates to number of vertebrae in thoracic, lumbar and sacral regions. In cervical region one segment is more than number of vertebrae and in coccygeal region there are two segments for four coccygeal vertebrae. The spinal cord contains 32 (8 + 24) spinal segments:

(1) Cervical - 8,
(2) Thoracic - 12,
(3) Lumbar - 5,
(4) Sacral - 5,
(5) Coccygeal - 2 (fused).

The nerves are produced in even numbers and their number is highest in cervical plexus and thoracic plexus. It decreases gradually from 16 ⋯⋯►12 ⋯⋯►10 ⋯⋯►8 ⋯⋯► 6 4 ⋯⋯► 4 ⋯⋯►2 in the lower spine. In the lowest area of spinal cord the nerves appear in horse tail form and generally fuse to create nerves in even numbers. On Earth the growth pattern having fixed thermodynamic equilibrium is effective at particular pressure, volume and temperature of $18^{0}C$. The pressure, volume and temperature may vary on other planets and other planets may produce different types of life forms depending upon their growth pattern along three axes. The highest evolved animals will show development of seven systems along one axis, twelve body parts along second axis and 32 teeth and spinal nerves (2 + 6 + 10 + 14) along third axis. The nerves of spinal cord ignite vocal cord to emit and produce letters and words through mouth. Thirty two pairs of spinal nerves, i.e., sixty four nerves inside human body in total create all vowels and consonants of alphabet of Sanskrit.

The life forms develop as close thermodynamic systems on planets. The continuity of above conditions along with outer covering layer of oxygen on planets creates different life forms during evolution. The impact of pressure, volume and temperature may vary on other planets depending upon stage of evolution of life forms on that planet. The human body having highest momentum will have highest time component stored with it. Similarly, solid body having lowest momentum will store lowest time component inside it. The momentum of every human body along every axis is different and that makes relative motion of every human body different along every axis. In the human body many spinal nerves are fused with each other and show one nerve. It shows degenerating trend in human body along one axis. Along other two axes, i.e., twelve pairs of cranial nerves and nine body systems the body does not show any degeneration.

The speed of compression of sound wave in solids is determined by the medium's compressibility, shear modulus and density. In fluid dynamics, the speed of sound in a fluid medium (gas or liquid) is used as a relative measure for the speed of an object moving through the medium. The ratio of speed of an object to the speed of sound in the fluid is called the object's Mach Number. Objects moving at speeds greater than Mach 1 are said to be travelling at supersonic speeds. Sound waves emitted from vocal cords of animals and sound emitted due to movement of wings of animals are limited within seven types of waves. These sound waves are effective within atmosphere of any planet. Power waves in the frequency range 256-512 Hertz are not audible in space because they are not responded by nerves of animals and human beings. The audible nerves of animals and human beings can recognise waves in the frequency range

256-512 Hertz of power waves within atmosphere of planets. Central nervous system is effective within three axes attachment of animals and human body inside atmospheric covering of planet which is bound by pressure, temperature and volume of body along three axes. Movement of arrows and missiles above speed of sound affect growth of animals and human beings and will deplete ozone layer around earth. Ancient people knew about this fact and did not allow any body to fire above speed of sound. Control over society was exercised by Saints or *Gurus* who asked *Aeklabya* to cut down his thumb so that he cannot fire any arrow above speed of sound in future and Earth could be saved.

Radio waves and power waves having very less frequency are absorbed inside planets and stars and they behave as radio wave towers. Human beings having less frequency sound wave act as radio wave towers and transmit and respond to waves in the frequency range 256 Hz to 512 Hz. In flat lands of earth and in civilizations developing near major rivers the languages having independent and isolated origin gradually mixed with other languages due to acculturation between different tribes, groups, clans and races. The languages having independent origin but spoken by majority of the groups gradually mixed with other languages due to integration between different tribes, groups, clans and race.

The distinction between languages is observed between conditioning through learning by imitation and learning by rules applied through incoming signals of nervous system. The vocal cords of animals and especially human beings are like genetic gifts. Preganglionic fibers arise from the spinal cord and pass through ventral roots of spinal nerves and first three lumber spinal nerves and then go to the chain ganglia. Some preganglionic fibers pass through the sympathetic chain of each side and go to the head to communicate with some cranial nerves. Some preganglionic fibers and post-ganglionic fibers go to visceral organs under the involuntary control of nose, eye muscles, salivary glands, heart, larynx, trachea, bronchi, lungs, alimentary canal, liver, pancreas, adrenal glands, kidneys, bladder and gonads. The secretions of post-ganglionic fibers of the sympathetic system stimulates organs, e.g., the fibers dilate pupils and bronchi, increase heart beat, decrease secretion of saliva and digestive juices, temporarily reduce peristalsis, contract hair muscles causing hairs to stand up and cause sweat glands to secrete. All these reactions are usually associated with fear, anger, pain and they cause expenditure of energy due to emission of sound waves through words.

The external appearance, size, shape, body features and weight of life forms along three axes depends upon pressure, volume and temperature of every planet. The pattern of internal evolution of life forms along three axes will always be similar to creation of elements in the periodic table. The elements are created along three axes in periodic table and in similar manner cells, tissues, parts, organs and systems will be created as internal structures inside life forms on planets. Due to power waves the big size stars act like microwave or power wave towers which effect and control human body that is made up of electromagnetic waves of visible spectra. It is the reason that sound waves are considered to be more powerful than electromagnetic waves that shapes and constitutes human body.

Cervical Plexus in throat portion emits 16 vowels and emission of voice of female is more closer to vowels than to consonants of alphabets. Male folk emit more consonants than vowels and their voice is harsh as compared to females. Due to harsh voice, male folk can pull and drag more breath inside spinal cord and exercise higher will power than females. The power wave packets possessing mass of atoms of elements create different types of Sound Waves in human beings. Grey matter and white matter pass from brain to spinal cord and transmit the messages from brain to spinal nerves and from spinal nerves to brain.

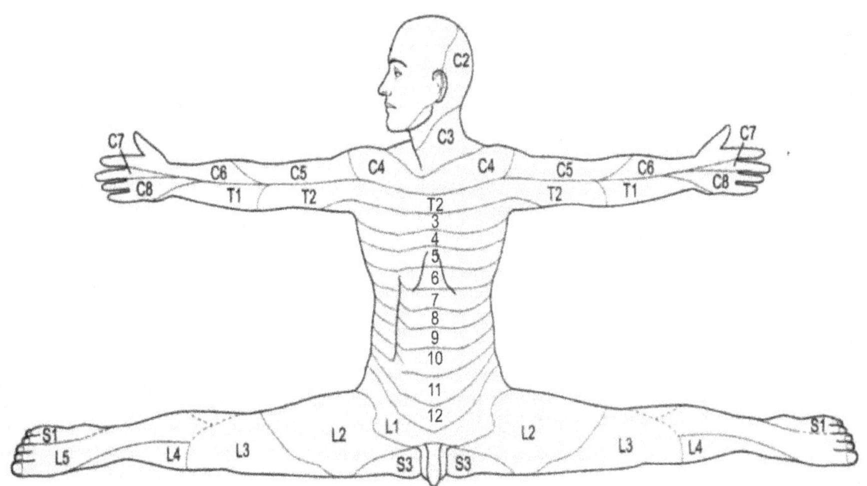

OXYGEN GAS STORED INSIDE SPINAL CORD INCREASES ITS STRENGTH AND MAKES IT LAST LONGER. IT HAS THE CAPACITY TO KILL TIME. *"SUSHUMNA BHAKSHYATE SAMAYAH"* MEANS AIR INSIDE SPINAL CORD MOVING WITH CEREBRO-SPINAL FLUID ABSORBS TIME AND KILLS (DEVOURS) TIME. IT INCREASES LONGEVITY AND AGE OF SPINAL CORD, NERVOUS SYSTEM AND HUMAN BODY LASTS LONGER.

Fig. 4.4

Speed of sound is the distance travelled per unit time by a sound wave as it propagates through an elastic medium. Speed of sound at sea level is 340.29 meters per second. In dry air at 20^0C (68^0F), the speed of sound is 343.21 meters per second or one kilometer in 2.914 second. The speed of sound in an ideal gas depends only on its temperature and composition. The speed has weak dependence on frequency and pressure in ordinary air, deviating slightly from ideal behavior. In common everyday speech, speed of sound refers to the speed of sound waves in air. However, the speed of sound varies from substance to substance : sound travels very slowly in gases; it travels faster in liquids; and faster still in solids. For example, sound travels at 343.21 meter per second in air, it travels at 1484 meters per second in water and at 5,120 meters per second in iron. In an exceptionally hard material such as diamond, sound travels at 12,000 meters per second, which is around the maximum speed that sound will travel under normal conditions. Sound waves in solids are composed of compression waves (as in gases and liquids), but there is also a different type of sound wave called a shear wave, which occurs only in solids. These different types of waves in solids usually travel at different speeds, as observed in seismology.

Human nervous system has about 100 billion neurons, majority of the neurons occur in the brain. The contraction of neurons increases the thinking power of brain and soul can become more powerful. Soul can be transferred from one living body to other body and it depends upon will power of the living body.

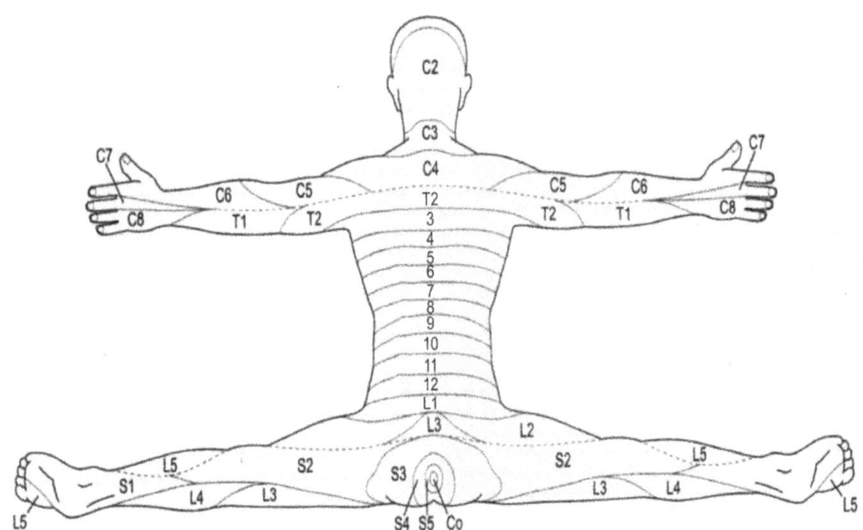

'SOUND WAVE PACKETS' EMERGE AS VIBRATIONS OR ECHOES AND EFFECT BODY PARTS ON PLANETS.
THE ECHOES CAN PROLIFERATE UP TO SEVEN POINTS OF BODY ON THE PATTERN OF IONIZATION OF ATOMS
OF ELEMENTS. THE LETTERS ARE CREATED ON THE PATTERN OF ATOMS OF ELEMENTS AND WORDS
ARE CREATED LIKE COMPOUNDS HAVING JUMBLED CONFIGURATIONS.

Fig. 4.5

The body of movable life forms retains more breath inside spinal cord in the form of air inside the tissues. The ventral air with the help of left side nostril and right side nostril takes the air of circulation and retains air component inside spinal cord in the body. Both the breath of two nostrils instead of entering lungs of the human body and animals enter the spinal cord and refresh the spinal cord and central nervous system. The air inside the spinal cord strengthens body and makes peripheral nervous system weak temporarily. But at the same time retention of air inside spinal cord makes the central nervous system fresh, aerated and long lasting. It provides additional life to nervous cells of central nervous system and makes the life of animal and human body longer in age.

The atoms of Oxygen (Z=8) have the capacity to capture and store energy and transform the same inside living body by changing form from gas state to liquid and then to solid state. During circulation of blood inside living body the energy is released during respiratory process and oxygen is converted into carbon dioxide which is released from living body. The oxygen gas has capability to store energy in liquid form and solid form inside living being. When the respiration stops in living beings owing to death the flow of oxygen inside body stops, gaseous form of oxygen fails to convert into liquid form and release of energy by respiration is stopped. Living matter is made up of biochemical materials and genetic material are also biochemical in nature.

The chanting of words, emission of words and sound from mouth of human body depends upon nerves of nervous system and every letter and word effects particular nerve and organ of human body. The impact of sound waves can cure and affect body parts and systems and can

108

affect whole body. The combination of letters and words effect body parts and have the capacity to improve or harm body parts. The audible range of sound waves will be different for different animals on different planets. The sound waves are equivalent to their corresponding electromagnetic waves, i.e., power waves. So the sound waves of human beings are more powerful than electromagnetic waves of seven colours (4000Å -7500Å) that constitute the human body and create human body parts. The sound waves effect human body like power waves and sound waves can last longer like power waves in space. The sound waves will not perish and on the patterns of power waves it will affect human body with impact on future growth and development. The sound waves of animal body effect the present time and will affect the body in future also because power waves last longer in atmosphere.

The speech of a person transmits from one speaker to listener through sound waves and air inside the atmosphere. Both ears receive the signal and they contain three important parts, i.e., external ear, middle ear and internal ear or labyrinth. External ear collects sound waves and transmits through external auditory meatus to tympanum and then to malleus. Middle ear contains three bones through which it acts for impedance matching and controls for pressure regulation of sound waves. Internal ear controls auditory nerves.

The internal parts, organs and systems of life forms develop along three axes on the patterns of creation of elements in the periodic table. The external features of life forms depend upon pressure and gravity prevailing on planet and its atmosphere. It also depends upon volume and temperature of planet. The external features of life forms may show prominence along three axes during development or may show dominance of round time frame in outer covering or may show prominence of four forces in development of body parts of life forms. During evolution of life forms on planets, different characteristics are produced along three axes that shapes different types of life forms. Depending upon pressure, volume and temperature, characteristics of life forms vary and change in size and shape along three axes. Life forms with 30 pairs of spinal nerves, 11 pairs of cranial nerves, 10 body parts and 6 systems will be different and similarly life forms with 32 pairs of spinal nerves, 9 pairs of cranial nerves, 6 body parts and 5 systems will be different on planets. The life forms having 32 pairs of spinal nerves, 12 pairs of cranial nerves and nine (one black + seven colored + one white) systems will be the most advanced and closer to human beings in characteristics.

Vocal organs of human body start from lungs which emits gases and along with gases comes out the 'sound wave packets'. Trachea or wind pipe transmits air in and out and helps in transmission of sound waves. Larynx controls inhaling, exhaling and emission of letters and words in human beings. The open area between vocal cord is called Glottis and it emits Glottal sound waves. Above glottis is Uvula which serves for opening or obstruction of nasal passage. Mouth cavity can broadly be divided into teeth, alveolar ridge, hard palate, cerebrum and soft palate. Lips play an important role in emission of language and its size produces different vowels. It produces two types of sound, bilabial (combination of both lips) and labiodental (combination of upper teeth and lower lip). Movement of tongue plays definite role in production of speech and basing on its structure, tongues can be classified into (a) tip of tongue, (b) blade of tongue, (c) front of tongue, (d) back of tongue and (e) root of tongue.

The impact of emission of letters is observed on all nerves throughout the body. It effects body parts, systems, organs and all activities of body. Impact of alphabets on nerves makes body free flowing and stream lined. The transmission of energy of alphabets through nerves and its impact of different parts of body makes Sanskrit specialized language and great. The electromagnetic energy connects nerves of one human body with nerves of other human body and in this manner connects all human bodies of entire society. Connectivity with nerves makes the language a unifying force for entire community at large irrespective of their differences on the grounds of caste, creed and physical barriers etc.

The central nervous system consists of cerebrum, cerebellum, brain stem and spinal cord. The ventricles in cerebrum, brain stem and central canal of the spinal cord contain cerebro-spinal fluid. There are twelve pairs of cranial nerves and 32 pairs of spinal nerves. The last pair of spinal nerve is fused and is not visible. The central nervous system is mainly concerned with higher intellectual properties, maintains muscle tone and regulates posture and equilibrium. The autonomic nervous system consists of sympathetic and parasympathetic nerves. They control secreting glands and involuntary muscles etc. Hypothalamus is the high centre for autonomic nervous system. Besides other functions, hypothalamus plays an important role in regulation of body temperature and controls the functions of different endocrine glands.

The sense organs mainly consist of taste, smell, vision and hearing. It comprises of brain, spinal cord, cranial and spinal nerves and autonomic nervous system. This system controls and coordinates different activities of various body parts. It includes sense organs such as eyes, ears, nose, tongue and skin. The organs of this system receive senses and convey the same to nervous system. It is formed of ductless gland whose secretions are known as hormones, which influence various metabolic processes of the body. Hormones act as chemical messengers. The power of imagination and change in circumference and diameter ratio of waves connected with neurons helps in contraction of mass inside human body.

The nervous tissue in general develops from ectoderm of the embryo, but the microgliocytes arise from mesoderm of the embryo. The special properties of cells of the nervous tissue are excitability and conductivity. Excitability is the ability to initiate nerve impulse in response to stimuli (changes outside and inside the body). Conductivity means the ability to transmit a nerve impulse (potential change in membrane of a nerve cell). The reaction is called response. The response may be sensation, such as pain or some activity such as muscle contraction or glandular secretion. A neuron is a structural and functional unit of the nervous tissue and hence the nervous system. Certain neurons may almost equal the length of body itself. Thus neurons with longer processes (projections) are the longest cells in the body. Human nervous system has about 100 billion neurons, majority of the neurons occur in the brain. Fully formed neurons never divide and remain in interphase throughout life. Shortly after birth, new neurons do not develop. Certain neurons have flask shaped cytons and are called Purkinje cells, which occur in cerebellum of the brain.

Depending upon emergence of 32 pairs of nerves from vertebral column the human body shows attachment with different waves by 32 nerves and they are observed as 32 consonant letters spoken by human beings. These 32 consonant letters are controlled by 16 cervical nerves which relate to 16 vowel letters. The vowels create sound and produce 16 types of sound waves in human beings. Thus vowels and consonants in total create 32 x 16 = 512 types of sound waves.

The central nervous system receives impulses from sensory receptors and afferent nerves (the afferent system). Some of the impulses enter consciousness or produce awareness of the world around us and also position and state of our own body. Many of them do not enter consciousness but still play an important role in maintaining or regulating many processes like action of heart and digestion which are constantly going on in the centers. The destination of these efferent impulses is called the effectors organ and usually they are muscles and the glands. They are thrown into action and this represents the response by the center to meet the particular voluntary movements. The CNS is made up of a somatic or the voluntary system and the autonomic or involuntary system, the former controlling voluntary activities and the latter regulating involuntary functions.

The central nervous system is a modified tube consisting of brain which gives rise to twelve pairs of cranial nerves and the spinal cord from which thirty two pairs of spinal nerves emerge. The hollow portions of the tube are modified to form the ventricle cord and they contain cerebrospinal fluid. The brain stem comprises medulla, pons and midbrain. The spinal cord is downward continuation of the medulla. The cerebral cortex is concerned with the highest functions of association, memory and intelligence. The brain and spinal cord being delicate viral structures are well protected by their location in bony cavities, the skull and the vertebral column. They are covered by three membranes or meninges (i) outer fibrous dura mater (ii) middle arachnoid mater and (iii) inner vascular pia mater. The space between arachnoid and pia maters (sub-arachnis space) contains the cerebrospinal fluid (CSF) which is also present in the ventricles of brain and central core of the spinal cord. The nervous system is ectodermal in origin.

The nervous system develops from primitive layer of cells, ectoderm and also develops from the neural plate or medullary plate which on further differentiation gives rise to median neural groove limited on each side by neural folds fusing with each other into neural tube. The central nervous system contains gray matter and white matter. The gray matter contains nerve cells (cell bodies) and unmediated nerve fibres as well as neuroglia cells and fibers. The white matter contains myelinated nerve fibers, but no cell bodies; it also contains neuroglia cells and fibers. The nervous system is created by seven crystal systems inside human body. The crystals belonging to any one system may differ in shape, size, form, elements of symmetry etc but their axial angles and axial ratios will always remain fixed.

The spinal cord being surrounded by its covering lies loosely within the vertebral column and is extended from the foramen magnum as far down as the inter-space between the 12th thoracic segment and the lower border of the 1st lumbar vertebra. Due to disproportionate development of the cord and the vertebral column, the spinal cord, being anchored to the medulla oblongata, is pulled upward in the spinal canal and causing its caudal end to reach the lower border of the first lumbar spines in the adult. The spinal cord is cylindrical in shape and is flattened antero-posteriorly. It has got five swelling or knots, one each in cervical, thoracic, lumbar, sacral and coccygeal region of the spinal cord.

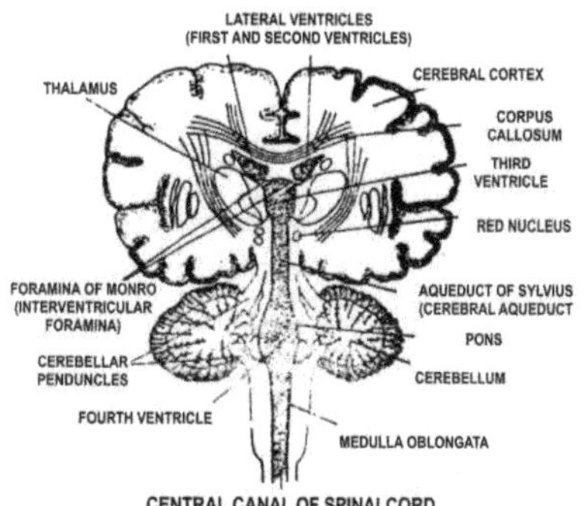

PICTORIAL REPRESENTATION OF THE CORONAL SECTION THROUGH CEREBRAL HEMISPHERE, BRAIN STEM AND SPINAL CORD.

Fig. 4.6

The central or somatic nervous system is symmetrically arranged into two lateral halves, one half being the mirror image of other half. It consists broadly of spinal cord inside vertebral column and brain inside the cranial cavity. The foramen magnum is the limiting line. Physiologically, the spinal cord is regarded as made up of a series of superimposed segments, from each of which a pair of nerve roots arise. Intrinsically the spinal cord is a continuous and un-segmented structure with 32 pairs of nerves emerging from it. Each segment of the spinal cord gives rise to dorsal and

111

ventral root filaments. Dorsal and ventral roots together form a single pair of nerves. 32 segments of the spinal cord correspond to 8 pairs of cervical and 12 pairs of thoracic, 5 pairs of lumbar and 5 pairs of sacral and two pairs of coccygeal nerves. Five lumbar nerves, one sacral nerve and three coccygeal nerves are fused and not visible clearly. As the cord ends at the level of lower border of 1st lumbar vertebra, spinal segments evidently do not correspond numerically with the vertebrae overlying them.

During early development, each segment of the spinal cord corresponds closely with the respective embryonic vertebrae. The spinal nerves also pass lateral to their intervertebral foramina. During development the vertebral column develops more rapidly than spinal cord and segments of the latter do not correspond the respective vertebra. For this reason the interval between spinal origin of the nerve and existence of its vertebra is different from segment to segment. Hence the lumbar and sacral nerves have long roots. Spinal cord from its upper limit to tip of the conus medullaris is about 45 cms in male and 42 cms in female. The weight of spinal cord is about 30 gms. The following broad facts about arrangement and working processes of nervous system help in study about aerobic practices and storage of oxygen inside spinal cord.

1. Division of nervous system: The central or somatic nervous system is responsible for consciousness and voluntary control. The autonomic nervous system regulates the activities of viscera.

2. Symmetrical arrangement: The nervous system is arranged symmetrically into two lateral halves. Consequently all the centers, tracts and nerves etc are bilateral.

3. Neuron doctrine: The neurons are structural and functional units.

Varieties of nerve impulses: Two types of nerve impulses are described, i.e., afferent and efferent.

(1) Afferent: These are sensory, centripetal or incoming impulses. They may be either conscious or unconscious. They are sub-divided into three groups:

(i) Exteroceptive - the impulses set up by stimuli coming from outside, viz., cutaneous senses like touch, pain, temperature etc and by special senses like vision, hearing, taste and smell.

(ii) Proprioceptive - the kinaesthetic impulses, i.e., those coming from the muscles, tendons, ligaments, joints etc. The labyrinthine impulses (vestibular) belong to this group. Proprioceptive impulses give information regarding the position of head and other parts of body.

(iii) Enteroceptive - the impulses arising from the viscera. They mostly belong to the autonomic system.

(2) Efferent: These are outgoing, centrifugal or motor. They are sub-divided into two types:

(a) reflex (involuntary) and (b) voluntary (motor unit).

ARRANGEMENT OF GRAY AND WHITE MATTER IN SPINAL CORD

The spinal cord is primary centre of reflex action for the trunk and limbs and consists of main conducting paths to and from higher centres in the spinal cord and brain. The cord may be considered as consisting of more or less autonomous segments. Each segment is related by afferent and efferent nerve fibres to its own specific segmental area of the body as well as to the segments above and below. It is obvious from the large amount of spinal cord space devoted to ascending and descending tracts that the brain exerts an important controlling influence over the segments. Spinal cord is symmetrically divided into two lateral halves, dorsally by a septum known as posterior median septum and ventrally by a fissure known as anterior median fissure. The brief histological details are as follows:

1. Central canal: It is centrally located lined by cubical ciliated epithelium, the ependyma and cerebrospinal fluid circulates through this canal. The central canal actually pierces through the

isthmus (commissure) of the two symmetrical lateral halves of gray matter. Parts of the gray matter in front of the central canal is known as anterior (ventral) gray commissure and the same behind central canal is known as posterior (dorsal) gray commissure.

2. Gray matter: In the form of a rough crescent one on each side. Each crescent has three parts-anterior horn, lateral horn and posterior horn. Gray matter is chiefly composed of three elements:

   (a) Nerve cells: There are three important collections of nerve cells:

      (i) Anterior horn cells (motor) - The cells are multipolar and are arranged in different groups. a- and y- motoneurones are present. a-motoneurons innervate the intrafusal fibers of the muscle spindle. Renshaw cells, a group of interneurons, are present in the antero-medial part of the anterior horn cells. These cells send antidromic inhibitory impulses to the motoneurones. The anterior nerve root takes origin from these cells.

      (ii) Posterior horn cells (sensory) - Relay station for posterior nerve root. At the base of the posterior horn there are specialized cells known as clarke's column or dorsal nucleus. It is found only in the lower cervical, thoracic and upper lumbar regions (C.7-L.3). They are the relay stations for spinocerebellar fibers. At the tip of the posterior horn there are closely packed cells called substantia gelatinosa of Rolando. At the medial part of the posterior horn there are large round or oval nerve cells.

      (iii) Lateral horn cells (autonomic) - Relay station for autonomic nerves. It is found only in the thoracic and upper lumbar regions. The cells are smaller than those of anterior horn cells. They are also known as intermedio-lateral cell groups. They give preganglionic sympathetic fibers and come out through the anterior spinal root.

   (b) Neuroglia: There are two important collections, viz.,

      (i) Substantia gelatinosa centralis around the central canal.

      (ii) Substantia gelatinosa of Rolando at the tip of posterior horn.

   (c) Nerve fibers, dendrites or axons which are mostly unmyelinated fibers supported by a group of neuroglial cells.

3. White matter: White matters of the spinal cord surround gray matter and consist of myelinated and unmyelinated fibers. Myelinated fibers are predominating. It has been described that the white matter is incompletely divided into two symmetrical lateral halves. The lateral half of white matter on each side is divided into three compartments, e.g., anterior white column (funiculus), lateral white column (funiculus) and posterior white column (funiculus) by the fibers of ventral and dorsal spinal roots. White matter in front of the gray commissure is known as anterior (ventral) white commissure and the same behind the gray commissure is known as posterior (dorsal) white commissure. Ascending and descending tracts and transverse fibers are passing through white matter to occupy their respective positions.

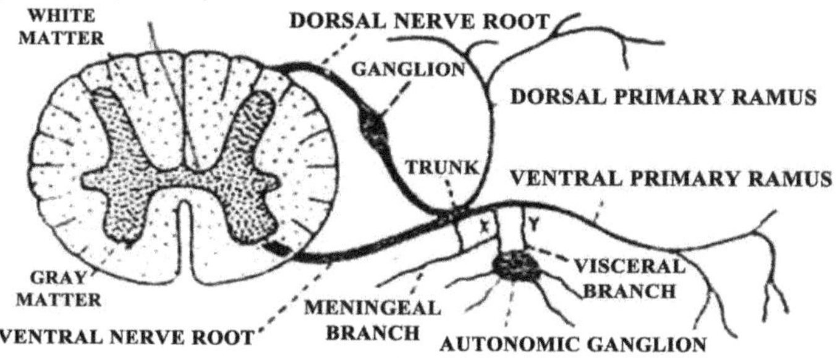

DIAGRAMMATIC REPRESENTATION OF BRANCHES OF A TYPICAL THORACIC SPINAL NERVE.

Fig. 4.7

There are 32 pairs of spinal nerves in total. The last pair of coccygeal nerves at bottom (32nd pair) is fused with 31st and not visible easily. The first cervical nerve originates from the medulla oblongata and leaves the spinal canal between the occipital bone and atlas. Other cervical spinal nerves arise from the spinal cord and each leaves the spinal canal through an inter-vertebral foramen above the vertebra whose number it bears. The eighth spinal nerve emerges from the vertebral column below the seventh cervical vertebra. All the other spinal nerves emerge from the spinal cord below the vertebra whose number it bears. The coccygeal nerves pass from the lower extremity of the spinal canal. Spinal nerves consist primarily of medullated nerve fibers and are named mixed nerves due to contents of motor and sensory fibers. Each spinal nerve is formed by the union of anterior and posterior roots.

(a) Anterior spinal root: It is composed entirely of motor fibres. They are (i) the axons of anterior horn cells (somatic) and (ii) axons of the lateral horn cells (autonomic) in the thoracic and upper lumbar regions only. The autonomic fibers represent the preganglionic fibers of sympathetic nerve (pupil dilator, pilomotor, vasomotor, cardiac accelerator, etc)

(b) Posterior spinal root: It consists of afferent fibers only. The posterior root is composed of the axons of posterior root ganglion and contains both somatic and autonomic fibers. The somatic afferents come from the skin and deep somatic structures. Autonomic afferents come from the viscera. All have their cell stationed in the posterior root ganglia. The nerve fibers of posterior root are 40 percent non-modulated and 60 percent modulated. Nerve fibers have been broadly classified into three: A, B and C. The A fibers are thickest and come from the touch and kinaesthetic endings. The B fibers are medium and carry thermal sensations and probably localized pain. The C fibers are thinnest and carry diffuse skin pain, ischemic muscle pain etc.

Distribution of terminal branches of spinal nerves

After leaving the spinal column, each spinal nerve mainly divides into: (a) the recurrent branch which is distributed to the meninges, (b) the ventral branch which supplies the extremities and parts of the body wall in front of spine and (c) the dorsal branch which supplies the muscles and skin of the back of head, neck and trunk. Another one is the visceral branch which is supplied by the nerves from T 1 to L 3. All these connect with the sympathetic ganglia by means of white and gray rami fibers which pass from the nerve to the ganglia and vice versa. From sympathetic ganglia to their final distribution the autonomic nerves are formed. These nerves form cardiac, coeliac or solar, hypo gastric, pelvic and enteric nerves. A quite number of nerve fibers from the sympathetic ganglia return to and are distributed with the spinal nerve to innervate sweat glands, arrector pili muscles and smooth muscles of all blood vessels.

After emerging from the cord, spinal nerves form cervical, brachial, lumbar and sacral plexuses from which the peripheral nerves are formed. In the thoracic region there is no plexus but the fibers pass as inter-costal nerves out into the inter-costal spaces to innervate inter-costal muscles, upper abdominal muscles and the skin of abdomen and chest. The ventral rami of four upper cervical nerves (C.1 - C.4) form cervical plexus. The 2nd, 3rd and 4th nerves divide into a lower and upper branch, these in turn unite to form three loops from which the peripheral nerves are distributed. These cervical nerves communicate with the hypoglossal, vagus and accessory cranial nerves to muscular system of head and neck.

CORTICOBULBAR (CORTICO-NUCLEAR) TRACTS

These tracts originated from cells in the inferior portion of the precentral gyrus and caudal part of the interior frontal gyri pass through the internal capsule and are largely distributed bilaterally to the intercalated neurons in the reticular formation. These intercalated neurons then in turn project abundantly into the motor cranial nerve nuclei. Golgi studies of the intrinsic organization of the reticular formation have indicated presence of such connection between the intercalated neurons and the cranial nerve nuclei. It is indicated that in man some corticofugal fibers pass directly to the motor trigeminal, facial and hypoglossal and also supraspinal nuclei. The corticobulbar tracts are essentially meant for volitional control of the muscles of larynx, pharynx, palate, upper and lower face, jaw, eye etc. Pseudobulbar palsy is a condition, resulting in paralysis or weakness of the muscles which control swallowing, talking and movements of the tongue and lips due to bilateral lesions of the corticobulbar tracts.

EXTRAPYRAMIDAL TRACTS

Extrapyramidal tracts are those motor pathways which may act as the alternative route for volitional impulses and which form the platform on which the pyramidal system works skillfully. With this conception of the extrapyramidal system, it is expected that all tracts belonging to this system must be connected, directly or indirectly, with the corpus striatum or cerebrum or both. It is integrated at various levels all the ways from the cerebral cortex to the spinal cord. When the neural pathway is interrupted, the integrated activities below bladder and rectum are increased and these activities are under the control of parasympathetic system. Crying is under the control of parasympathetic nerves. In emotional speech and outburst, there are often changes in respiration and also profound vasodilatation. Cardiac abnormality leading to death may be associated with emotional stress. These all effects are precipitated due to autonomic imbalance.

CEREBROSPINAL FLUID (CSF)

It is a modified tissue fluid present in the cerebral ventricles, spinal canal and subarachnoid spaces thus bathing the entire nervous system. The central nervous system is devoid of lymphatics. Cerebrospinal fluid replaces lymph here. It is a clear, colorless, transparent fluid, does not coagulate on standing, reaction alkaline and contains about 5 lymphocytes per cu. mm, Sp.gr.-1.004-1.006. Volume - about 150 ml in adults. Pressure-110-130 mm H_2O. Pressure rises on standing, coughing, squeezing, crying, etc. Compression of internal jugular veins increases pressure. It resembles colloid-free plasma with certain variations of crystalloid content. It is formed by choroid plexuses in the ventricles, especially the lateral ventricles. The endothelial cells of the capillaries are not flat as elsewhere but are granular and cubical with mitochondria and vacuoles. This arrangement indicates active metabolic processes in the cells.

During circulation the fluid passes from the lateral ventricles (first and second) then fluid goes through the foramina of Monro (right and left inter-ventricular foramina) to the III ventricle, thence through the midbrain as aqueduct of sylvius (cerebral aqueduct) to the IV ventricle in the medulla. From the IV ventricle it also passes into the central canal of the spinal cord. The ciliary movements of the ependymal cells help in the circulation of the cerebrospinal fluid. Different Sanskrit grammar scholars have given their opinion regarding number of vowels and consonants and their link with nerves.

A certain preganglionic fiber synapses with the postganglionic neurons supplying one effector system only, a dissociation of sympathetic actions, e.g., vasomotor and pseudomotor activities, can take place. While the actions of the sympathetic and parasympathetic system are generally antagonistic on the viscera they supply, in the case of the urinary bladder, for example, the normal emptying and filling of the viscous are controlled only by the parasympathetic system, the sympathetic system being concerned with blood supply of the organ. Some of afferent sympathetic fibers mediate pain impulses. On the other hand, afferent parasympathetic fibers are concerned with visceral reflexes which operate under normal conditions of life. In most cases afferent sympathetic fibers are probably concerned with unusual or pathological reflexes.

The autonomic ganglia are cellular aggregations of varying size and shape, each surrounded by a connective tissue capsule. Trabeculae extending from the capsule constitute an internal framework which contains numerous, often pigmented cells, between which are irregular plexuses of myelinated and unmyelinated fibres. Besides these ganglia, there are the isolated autonomic cells or non-encapsulated aggregations of such cells widely distributed throughout the viscera. The autonomic cells are typically multipolar in shape and have a clear spherical or ovoid nucleus, delicate neurofibrils, and fine chromophilic bodies. Binucleated or even multinucleated cells are also found. Most of the cells are surrounded by cellular capsules similar to those surrounding the spinal ganglion cells.

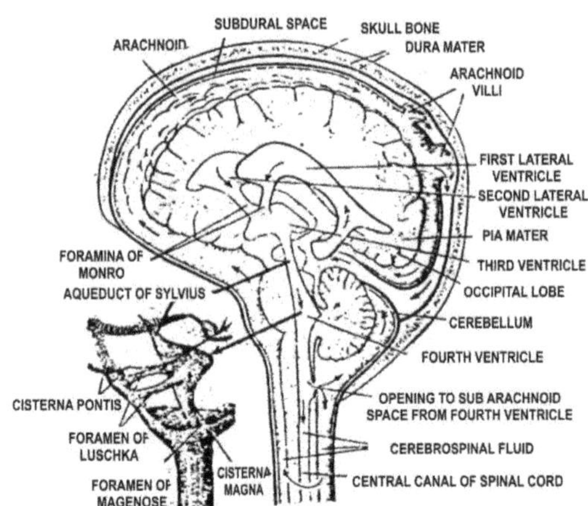

THERE IS VERY GOOD COORDINATION BETWEEN SPEECH AND HEARING BEING CONTROLLED THROUGH BRAIN. FIGURE SHOWS VENTRICLES OF THE BRAIN AND CENTRAL CANAL OF THE SPINAL CORD (LATERAL VIEW) THROUGH WHICH THE CEREBROSPINAL FLUID CIRCULATES.

Fig. 4.8

In the autonomic ganglia of man, some of the cells commonly have short dendrites which ramify within the capsules. Others have long, slender dendrites which pierce the capsule and run for varying distances in the intercellular plexuses. Some cells have both short and long processes. The intra-capsular dendrites may arborise symmetrically on all sides of the cell or they may form glomerular structures on one side. These glomeruli are generally formed by the interlocking dendritic processes of two or more cells, and all the cells so interlocked are enclosed within a single capsule. Such cells presumably receive common terminal arborisations of preganglionic fibers. The extra capsular dendrites terminate in similar and arborisations at varying distances from the cell body. Numerous preganglionic fibers end in synaptic relation with the bodies and dendrites of the postganglionic cells. They branch repeatedly within the ganglion and form pericellular arborisations, the terminal fibrils ending by neuro-fibrillar rings or loops on the cell body.

The coccyx called as tailbone in human beings is a small triangular bone resembling small tail located at the bottom of spine. It is composed of four coccygeal vertebra or spinal bones. These four vertebrae contain four coccygeal nerves which are fused at the base of spinal cord in human beings. A coccygeal vertebra contains BNCT that involves medullary cavity and extends through cortex into soft tissues by displacing the periosteum. The sympathetic outflow takes place from the thoracic and lumbar regions. The connector cells lie in the lateral horn cells situated only in the thoracic and upper three lumbar segments. In the cat, dog and monkey

116

sympathetic fibers are also found in the anterior root of the lumbar segment 4. Since the effector neurons lie outside the central nervous system, the axons of lateral horn cells of the spinal cord (intermediate lateral tract) pass out through the anterior root and enter anterior divisions of the mixed spinal nerve. These fibers are thinly medullated and white. They leave the nerve in the form of a branch called the white ramius communicans and enter the sympathetic ganglion. It may end in this ganglion or may simply pass through it to other ganglia up or down the sympathetic chain or even to other distant ganglia.

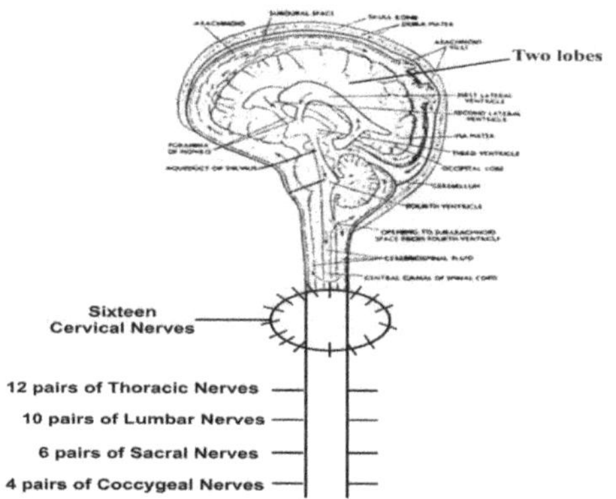

LONGITUDINAL SECTION PASSING THROUGH SPINAL CORD OF HUMAN BEING SHOWS NUMBER OF NERVES AROUND THE SPINAL CORD. VOWELS INSIDE HUMAN BODY ARE CREATED BY SIXTEEN CERVICAL NERVES OF THROAT PORTION. THE NERVES BELOW CERVICAL NERVES ARE DOUBLE IN NUMBER, i.e., THIRTY TWO AND THEY CREATE CONSONANTS INSIDE HUMAN BODY. INCREASE IN OXYGENATION OF SPINAL CORD INCREASES ENERGY AND METABOLISM OF LIVING HUMAN BODY. HIGH CONTENT OF OXYGEN MAKES HUMAN BODY LAST LONGER AND INCREASES LIFE SPAN OF ALL LIVING BEINGS. IF OXYGEN SUPPLY INSIDE SPINAL CORD IS INCREASED ARTIFICIALLY THE HUMAN BODY WILL HAVE HIGHER ENERGY AND LONGER LIFE PERIOD OF SURVIVAL.

Fig. 4.9

The nerve roots of lumbar, sacral and coccygeal nerves from the caudal part of cord (conus medullaris) takes vertical course and form a bunch or leash of nerve fibers around filum terminale called cauda equina. The cauda equina consists of roots of lower lumbar, sacral and coccygeal nerves in fused form. The actual number of lumbar nerves is ten pairs, sacral six pairs and coccygeal four pairs in spinal cord. Number of spinal nerves decreases gradually towards lower end of the spinal cord due to squeezing of nerves. The best medicine which emerges from Sanskrit Language is through Nerves in the form of *Slokas,* or *Mantras* or *Chantings.* The chantings or mantras cure many diseases just like plants, medicinal plants etc on human body. The letters, i.e., 16 vowels and 32 consonants emitted from mouth are outcome of nerves of nervous system and they effect human body just like medicinal plants or medicines. Sanskrit letters emitted from mouth effect seven human body systems of human being. They cure diseases acting like medicines.

5
EVOLUTION OF VOCAL CORDS

The vocal cords of animals and human beings produce sound waves as 'wave packets' or letters or '*Aksharas*'. The frequency of wave packets emitted by different animals varies from one animal to other and constitutes building blocks of different languages. Most of the languages show independent origin and maintain their individuality at many isolated places and pockets on earth. The frequency of sound waves are equivalent to power waves. The sound waves having low frequency range become equivalent to power waves and act as power waves in atmosphere. Lower animals move their wings and body parts in such a manner that vibration of low frequency is produced which appears as sound waves. All the higher animals develop vocal cords in different forms. The vocal cords are undeveloped in early invertebrates and insects develop and emit sound waves in many forms. Their sound waves are having higher frequency and low wavelength.

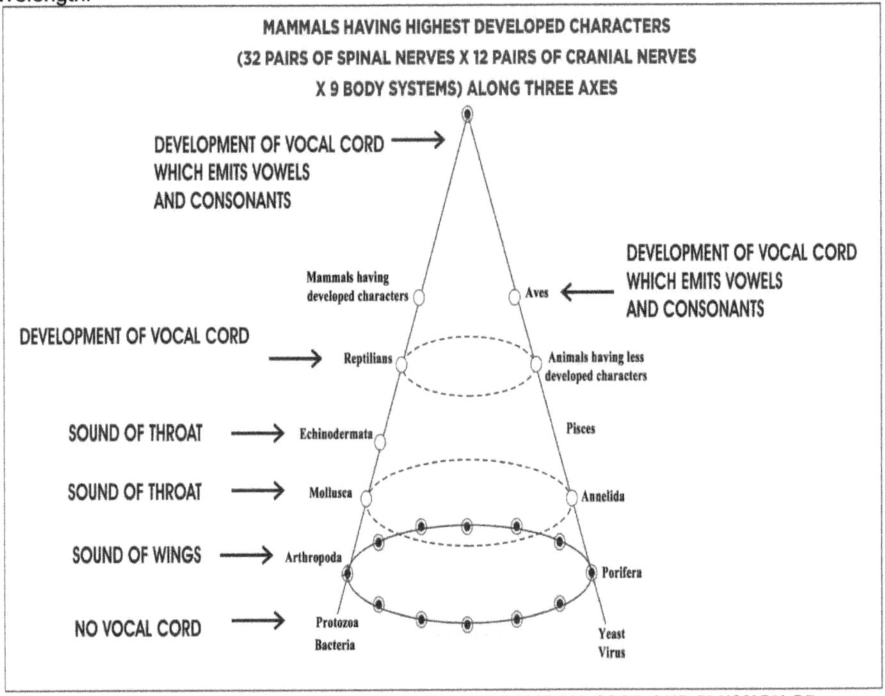

GRADUAL DEVELOPMENT AND IMPROVEMENT OF VOCAL CORD AND EMISSION OF VARIOUS SOUND WAVES BY DIFFERENT ANIMALS AND HUMAN BEINGS.

Fig. 5.1

The animals can communicate but not in the positive and scientific manner by reading the mind or intentions of communicator. Most animal cries and tribal languages relate to distress belonging to the pack, mating approaches or antagonism. As regards the origin of language, linguistics first made attempts to link human language with animal communication but could not get positive results. The chattering and ape-folk sounds transformed the 'need motivated languages' and habits into the phonological complexity which gradually developed different sets of languages throughout the world.

Voices, letters, alphabets and Language is produced under the impact of Spinal nerves and Cervical nerves by vocal cords inside Life forms. Vowels are produced by impact of cervical nerves whereas consonants are produced by impact of spinal nerves of nervous system. The complexity in the vocal cord increases gradually from lower invertebrates to insects, molluscs and then to vertebrates. In the vertebrates vocal cords of Pisces are less developed and uttering of sound waves becomes clear in amphibians. From amphibians onwards the vocal cords develop clear connection with nerves of nervous system along three axes and develop different types of letters in their utterances. The letters also become distinct in the form of vowels and consonants.

(a) **Protozoa : No vocal cord available.**

(b) **Porifera : No vocal cord available.**

(c) **Coelenterata : No vocal cord available.**

(d) **Annelida : No vocal cord available.**

(e) **Arthropoda : Very less developed voices due to movement of wings and body parts.**

(f) **Mollusca : Very less developed voices due to movement of body parts. The vocal folds are located at the top of trachea. They open during inhalation and come together to close during swallowing and phonation.**

(g) **Echinodermata : Very less developed voices due to movement of body parts.**

(h) **Pisces : Very less developed vocal cord and voices. Fishes produce drumming sounds like thumps, purrs, pulses and knocks etc. Their vocal folds are two bands of smooth muscle tissue found in the voice box. They produce sound by oscillating or vibrating their swim bladder or by rubbing the bones where fins attach with the body.**

(i) **Amphibian : Less developed vocal cord and voices. All amphibians have a larynx voice box at the top of throat that protects airways. They contain vocal sacs as projections of floor of mouth or buccal cavity as seen in frogs and toads. Clicking and hissing are common in amphibians.**

(j) **Reptilia : Developed voices with less developed vocal cords having connection with spinal nerves and cervical nerves. Reptiles have a larynx and multi-layered membranes known as vocal folds. It regulates air flow during vibration. Reptilians produce sound like chirps, clicks and squeaks etc.**

(k) **Mammalia : The mammalians contain various types of vocal cords depending upon their stages of evolution. The most developed vocal cord is found in human beings which contain well developed organs and nerves for emission of sound waves of different frequencies. In**

119

mammals the cranial nerves, cervical nerves, spinal nerves and seven color systems shape nerves which are associated with vocal cords of different animals.

(I)   Aves : Birds develop voices and chirping with less developed vocal cords. The number of spinal nerves and cervical nerves are different and level of evolution varies. Syrinx is the vocal box of birds located at the base of wind pipe or trachea. At the point where wind pipe divides is located birds syrinx or voice box.

Lower animals develop false vocal folds known as vestibular folds or ventricular folds etc. They play less role in normal phonation and can produce deep sonorous tones, screams and growls. The most intelligent and evolved animal and human being will have twelve pairs of cranial nerves inside brain, 16 cervical nerves, 32 pairs of spinal nerves in spinal cord and seven body systems with developed organs. The organs and parts of living body must show movement along three axes during their movement. The animals and human beings containing above characteristics will be the highest evolved and most advanced on any planet in any solar system on any star dynasty in the universe. The mammalians contain various types of vocal cords depending upon their stages of evolution. The most developed vocal cord is found in human beings which contain well developed organs and nerves for emission of sound waves of different frequencies. In mammals the cranial nerves, cervical nerves, spinal nerves and seven color systems shape nerves associated with vocal cords of different animals and developed hearing system of body maintain coordination with central nervous system..

In highest evolved mammals, e.g., human beings (*Homo sapiens*) twelve cranial nerves, thirty two pairs of spinal nerves and nine colors system develop prominently and develop well pronounced vocal organs. In case of human beings and higher mammals two separate processes are involved in vocalization:

     (a)   Phonation
     (b)   Articulation

The whole process of sound production and vocalization is dominated and coordinated by speech centre in the cerebral cortex. Phonation is due to vibration of vocal cords which are folds of muscles stretched along the lateral wall of the larynx between thyroid and arytenoid cartilages. The whole process of emission of sound waves is dominated and coordinated by speech centre in the cerebral cortex inside brain. This should not be disturbed otherwise it will lead to permanent aphasia.

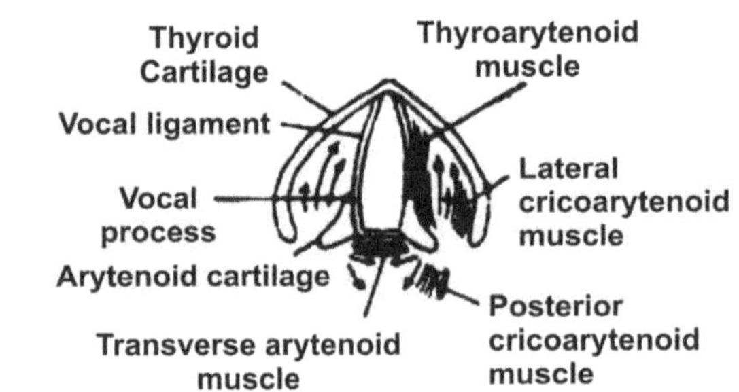

CROSS SECTION OF VOCAL CORD OF HUMAN BEING
Fig. 5.2

Phonation is due to vibration of vocal cords which are folds stretched along the lateral wall of the larynx between thyroid and arytenoid cartilages. These are positioned close to each other and their tension is regulated by intrinsic muscles of the larynx. The concerned intrinsic muscles and their mode of action are given below:

1. Thyroarytenoid muscle is made of many small slips of muscles fibres controlled separately by different nerve fibres. The contraction of these muscle fibres independent of each other are responsible for control of shape of vocal cord, thick or thin or with sharp and blunt edge during phonation of different types of letters.

2. Posterior crico-arytenoid muscle pulls the arytenoid cartilages away from thyroid cartilage and thereby stretches the vocal cords increasing their tension.

3. The transverse arytenoid muscle pulls the arytenoid cartilages together and thus draws the vocal cords towards each other.

4. The lateral crico-arytenoid muscle pulls the arytenoid cartilages forwards and increases the gap between vocal cords to allow easy respiration.

The vocal cords vibrate laterally because pressure of air from below pushes the vocal cords apart. The rapid flow of air between their margin creates a negative pressure which approximates the cords towards each other. The cycle is then repeated again and again. The changes in frequency of vibration of vocal cords are effected by

    1. Alteration in tension of the cords and
    2. Alteration in thickness of the vibrating edge.

Tension of the vocal cords is regulated by intrinsic laryngeal muscles described above, e.g., posterior crico-arytenoid and transverse arytenoid muscles which increase tension and lateral crico-arytenoid muscles which decrease tension of the vocal cords. The thickness of the vibrating edge is regulated by the muscle fibers of the thyro-arytenoid muscles. It has been mentioned that groups of muscle fibers in this muscle may contract independent of each other, i.e., one group producing thin edge and other group producing thick edge of the vocal cord. Extrinsic muscles of the larynx also has got a role to play. Elevation of the larynx increases tension and depression of the larynx decreases tension of the vocal cords. Articulation and resonance takes place through three major organs in human beings for articulation which are given below:

    (a) Lips,
    (b) Tongue and
    (c) Soft palate

The buccal cavity, nose, nasal sinuses, pharynx and chest cavity etc act as resonators and determine the quality of voice. Thus if the nose is blocked due to cold then the quality of voice is appreciably changed. The sound waves coming out from the vocal cord of human beings are like smaller 'wave packets' made up of power waves. These 'wave packets' with lower wavelengths and higher energy act as electromagnetic waves and their energy effects and shapes the human body. It is the reason it is said that sound wave packets made up of smaller pieces of power waves are more powerful than energy of seven color electromagnetic waves on planets. The words are created by vocal cord and mouth parts of every animal under the guidance of nervous system and all body parts of animal and human being. The words are expression of a particular cause or sentiment with specific meaning for every animal. The words emitted by vocal cord and mouth of animal and human being effect the body parts and organs of every living body. The words are made up of wave packets of sound waves and show definite impact on body of every living being through energy of electromagnetic waves. The sound waves inherent in language create words or 'wave packets' at particular frequency which acts as electromagnetic waves of low frequency effecting the body of living beings.

The sound waves are mechanical waves caused due to vibrations produced in any object placed in any elastic medium. Human being can hear vibrations of certain frequencies range only, i.e., 20 Hz to 20,000 Hz. This is called audible frequency range. The sound waves having frequency more than 20,000 Hz are called ultrasonic and waves having frequency less than 20 Hz are called infrasonic. In the propagation of a longitudinal wave medium, particles vibrate about their mean position in the direction of motion of wave. When these medium particles come very close to each other it is called compression and when these particles move away it is called rarefaction. Power wave packets containing mass of atoms of elements create 'Sound Wave Packets'.

The central nervous system consists of cerebrum, cerebellum, brain stem and spinal cord. The ventricles in the cerebrum, brain stem and central canal of the spinal cord contain cerebro-spinal fluid. There are twelve pairs of cranial nerves and thirty two pairs of spinal nerves. Some of the last pair of lumbar, sacral and coccygeal nerves are fused but it is not visible. The central nervous system is mainly concerned with higher intellectual properties, maintains muscle tone and regulates posture and equilibrium. The autonomic nervous system consists of sympathetic and parasympathetic nerves. They control secreting glands and involuntary muscles etc. Hypothalamus is the high centre for autonomic nervous system. Besides other functions, hypothalamus plays an important role in regulation of body temperature and controls the functions of different endocrine glands. The contraction of nerve cells gives extra powers to human brain to perceive and visualize things and imagination can reach better depths in vacuum medium. In human beings, testosterone secreted by the gonads causes major change in the cartilages and musculature of larynx when it is available in sufficient quantity. It is seen generally during an adolescent boy's puberty. The thyroid becomes prominent and vocal folds enlarge and become rounded. Epithelium thickens and formation of three distinct layers takes place.

Vacuum medium connects every individual with another individual through contraction and expansion of nerve cells of brain. The nerve cells can contract in diameter from 11 to 5.5 in solid forms. The contraction of circumference upon diameter ratio from 22/11 to 22/5.5 tends to change the wavy character of nerve cells to tough nerve cells. The nerve cells transmit the message from human brain to body parts. Regular contraction and expansion of nerve cells inside human brain connects the central nervous system with vacuum, astral bodies, planets and stars in space. The sense organs mainly consist of taste, smell, vision and hearing. It comprises of brain, spinal cord, cranial and spinal nerves and autonomic nervous system. This system controls and coordinates different activities of various body parts. It includes sense organs such as eyes, ears, nose, tongue and skin. The organs of this system receive senses and convey the same to nervous system. It is formed of ductless gland whose secretions are known as hormones, which influence various metabolic processes of the body.

The fibers carrying different sensations enter spinal cord through the posterior roots. Inside the cord, a rearrangement takes place. Fibers carrying one kind of impulse tend to collect into a bundle. Such bundles are called sensory tracts. Motor tracts are also formed on similar lines. A tract may be defined as a bundle of fibers carrying one or a group of motor or sensory impulses in the central nervous system. Functionally nerve tracts (fasciculi) may be grouped in each column (funiculus) into ascending (sensory), descending (motor) and inter-segmental fibers.

I. Ascending tracts (Sensory tracts):

1. Tract of Goll (Fasciculus gracilis).
2. Tract of Burdach (Fasciculus cuneatus).
3. Comma tract of Schultze (Tractus interfascicularis).
4. Dorsal spinothalamic tract (Lateral spinothalamic tract)
5. Spinotectal tract.
6. Dorsal spinocerebellar tract (Flechsig's tract)
7. Ventral spinocerebellar tract (Gower's tract).

8.   Spino-olivary tract.
9.   Spinoreticular tract.
10. Spinovestibular tract.
11. Spinopontine tract
12. Spinocortical tract
13. Ventral (anterior) spinothalamic tract.

II. Descending tracts (Motor tracts):

1.   Pyramidal tracts:
(a) Crossed pyramidal tract (Large lateral corticospinal tract)
(b) Direct pyramidal tract (Uncrossed anterior corticospinal tract)
(c) Uncrossed small lateral pyramidal (corticospinal) tract.
2.   Corticobulbar tract.
3.   Extrapyramidal tracts :
(a) Rubrospinal tract
(b) Tectospinal tract and Tectobulbar tract
(c) Reticulospinal tract
(d) Dorsal vestibulospinal tract.
(e) Ventral vestibulospinal tract.
(f) Olivospinal tract (Bulbospinal tract)
(g) Descending medial longitudinal fasciculus.

III. Intersegmental fibres (both ascending and descending):

1.   Ground bundle of anterior column or funiculus (Anterior intersegmental or sulcomarginal fasciculus)
2.   Ground bundle of lateral column or funiculus (Lateral intersegmental fasciculus).

Functions of the pyramidal tracts:

1.   The pyramidal tracts convey motor impulses to the spinal cord for controlling the voluntary movement especially the movement of fingers and hand.
2.   They also form a part of the pathways for superficial reflexes like the cremasteric, abdominal and planar reflexes.

Effects of section of the pyramidal tracts:

At the lower level of the medulla oblongata or in the lateral column of the spinal cord following effects are observed:

(a) Voluntary movement: Disturbance of voluntary movements especially of the opposite arm and leg. The discrete movements of fingers, walking, grasping, scratching, etc, cannot be properly performed.
(b) Muscle tone: Diminution of muscle tone especially of the limbs is encountered. Increased muscle tone and exaggerated reflexes occur after section of both pyramidal and extra-pyramidal tracts.
(c) Reflexes. Abolition of superficial reflexes namely abdominal etc and slowing of the deep reflexes.

The nervous tissue in general develops from ectoderm of the embryo, but microgliocytes arise from mesoderm of the embryo. The special properties of the cells of nervous tissue are excitability and conductivity. Excitability is the ability to initiate nerve impulse in response to stimuli (changes outside and inside the body). Conductivity means the ability to transmit a nerve impulse (potential change in membrane of a nerve cell). The reaction is called response. The response may be sensation, such as pain or some activity such as muscle contraction or glandular secretion. A neuron is a structural and functional unit of the nervous tissue and hence the nervous system. Certain neurons may almost equal the length of body itself. Thus neurons with longer processes (projections) are the longest cells in the body. Human nervous system has about 100 billion neurons, majority of the neurons occur in the brain. Language is the expression of human communication by which knowledge, belief and behavior are expressed, experienced, explained and shared. It is based on systematic conventionally used signs, sounds, gestures or marks that convey desired meaning within a group, community, society, region or country.

DEVELOPMENT OF NERVES INSIDE SPINAL CORD AND PRODUCTION OF SPINAL NERVES WHICH PRODUCE 32 CONSONANTS INSIDE HUMAN BODY. 32 PAIRS OF SPINAL NERVES PRODUCE 32 CONSONANTS OF DEVANAGARI SCRIPT IN SANSKRIT LANGUAGE.

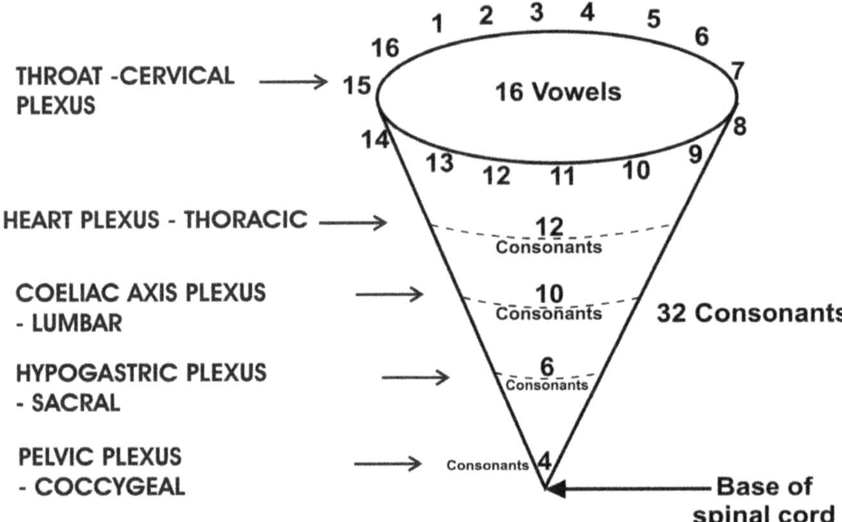

GRADUAL EVOLUTION OF CONSONANTS AND VOWELS TAKES PLACE DUE TO SOUND WAVES INSIDE HUMAN BODY. SOUND WAVES EMERGE FROM BASE OF SPINAL CORD AND CREATE 32 CONSONANTS AND 16 VOWELS. THE UPPER MOST PART OF SPINAL CORD HAVING THROAT-CERVICAL PLEXUS PRODUCES 16 VOWELS IN HUMAN BEINGS.

Fig. 5.3

Depending upon emergence of 32 nerves from vertebral column, human body shows attachment with different waves by 32 nerves and they are observed as 32 consonant letters spoken by human beings. These 32 consonant letters are controlled by 16 cervical nerves which relate to 16 vowel letters. The vowels create sound and produce 16 types of sound waves in human beings. Thus vowels and consonants in total create 32 x 16 = 512 types of sound waves under any atmospheric condition. There should be continuity of mean temperature of 18 degrees centigrade on planets in different ages so that continuity of genus and species is maintained. The first learning of language is a mixture of genetic evolution of human being and social development. The people learn to communicate and react differently to voices and languages in societies.

The chanting of words, emission of words and sound from mouth of human body depends upon spinal nerves and cervical nerves of nervous system and every letter and word effects particular nerve and organ of human body. The impact of sound waves can cure and affect body parts and systems and can affect whole body. The combination of letters and words effect body parts and have the capacity to improve or harm body parts. The audible range of sound waves will be different for different animals on different planets. The sound waves are equivalent to their corresponding electromagnetic waves, i.e., power waves. So the sound waves of animals and human beings are more powerful than electromagnetic waves of seven colors (4000 Å -7500 Å) that constitute and make animal and human body. The sound waves effect animal body like power waves and sound waves can last longer like power waves in the atmosphere. The sound waves will not perish and on the patterns of power waves it will affect animal body with impact on future growth and development. The sound waves of animal body effect the present time and will affect the body in future also because power waves last longer.

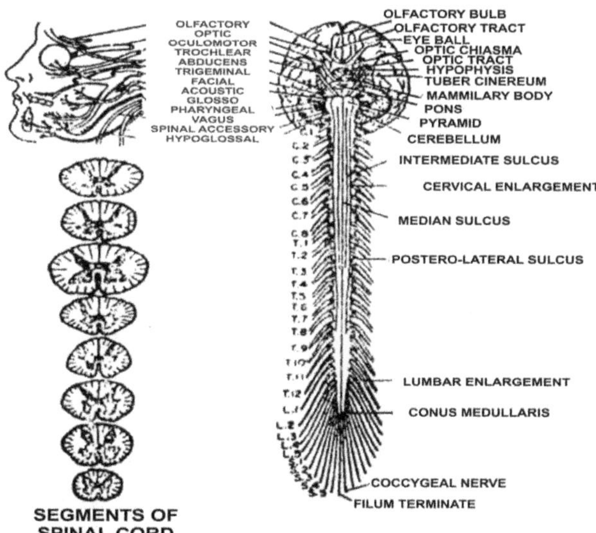

REPRESENTATION OF BRAIN STEM WITH 12 PAIRS OF CRANIAL NERVES. SPINAL CORD WITH 8 PAIRS OF CERVICAL NERVES, 12 PAIRS OF THORACIC NERVES, 10 LUMBAR NERVES, 6 PAIRS OF SACRAL NERVES, FOUR COCCYGEAL NERVES SQUEEZED AT BASE.

Fig. 5.4

The letters are created by every living being in fixed numerical order. The sound waves affect electromagnetic waves and frequency of sound waves effects the growth of animals. The particles show their impact along three axes and jumbled words produced by animals show their impact along three axes. The jumbled words are created in numerical order along three axes. Human body language derivation shows that it is most advanced body language dependent upon three axes attachment like planets and stars in universe. Other animals body language differs from the body language of human beings. Voices, letters, alphabets and Language are produced due to impact of Spinal nerves and Cervical nerves through vocal cord inside life forms. Vowels are produced by impact of cervical nerves whereas consonants are produced by spinal nerves of nervous system.

Mammals are distinct anatomically, physiologically and pharmacologically. The sympathetic system arises from the thoraco-lumbar region of the central nervous system, the parasympathetic

125

from cranio-sacral region. Typically, each visceral organ receives both sympathetic and parasympathetic fibers; one is excitatory, while the other is inhibitory. The contraction of neurons increases the thinking power of brain and soul can become more powerful. Nerves establish coordination between audible power of ears and languages spoken by the individuals.. Due to power waves the big size planets act like microwave or power wave towers which effect and control human body that is made up of electromagnetic waves of visible spectra. It is the reason that sound waves are considered to be more powerful than electromagnetic waves of seven colors range which shapes and constitutes human body. The 'Sound Wave Packets' act like water waves or free flowing waves within the atmosphere of Planet.

In animals the sound wave packets or alphabets are produced by vocal cords or frequency of body parts. The sound waves require medium for propagation and they are also called elastic or mechanical waves. These waves travel in the medium of matter waves through vibration of the medium particles about their mean positions. If the vibration of medium particles is along the direction of propagation of the wave, they form compressions and rarefactions in the medium and the wave is called longitudinal wave, e.g., sound waves in air, solid and inside liquid. The longitudinal waves can travel in solid, liquid as well as in gas. On the other hand if the medium particles vibrate normal to the direction of propagation, forming crests and troughs, the wave is called transverse wave, e.g., solid waves in solid medium and in matter zones. Transverse waves are formed only in those media which possess rigidity. The evolution of animals shows that there is no connection with animal communication and language of human being because it is species specific creation and has originated in humanity through genetic changes. The evolution of languages from apes to human beings shows that the extent of human language is unique creation based on genetic evolution.

Lower animals move their wings and body parts in such a manner that vibration of low frequency is produced which appears as sound waves. Alphabets are created according to the impact of different forces on higher living animals. The alphabets are created in the multiples of 9 x 12 x 14 inside any living being. The alphabets tend to develop in the multiples of nine in energy cycle. The alphabets tend to develop in the multiples of 12 on the lines of compaction of mass from outside. The alphabets also tend to develop in living beings according to compaction of mass particles by 14 outside particles in the ladder of evolution. The creation of alphabets is totally dependent upon movement of spherical astral bodies along three axes in space and according to movement of astral bodies the living beings develop many parts, organs and alphabets. As higher and bigger will be the size of living being so higher and bigger will be the number of alphabets of animal concerned. In case we compare astral bodies with living beings than we find that animals behave like planets, which absorbs all the electromagnetic radiations coming from space and do not emit any radiation from itself.

5.1 ROLE OF LARYNX

The first point where airflow from the lungs encounters a controlled resistance is at larynx, which is a structure of muscle and cartilage located at the upper end of trachea. The resistance can be controlled by different positions and tensions in the vocal cords. During quiet breathing the cords are relaxed and spread apart to allow free flow of air to and from the lungs. During swallowing the cords are drawn tightly together to keep foreign material from entering the lungs. For speech the most important feature of the vocal cords is that they can be made to vibrate if airflow between them is sufficiently rapid and if they have proper tension and proximity to each other. This rapid vibration is called voicing or phonation. The frequency of vibration determines the perceived pitch. The vocal cords of adult males are larger in size, their frequency of vibration is relatively lower than the frequency of vibration in female and children. The pitch of adult male voices is thus lower than that of female and children.

Voicing is the extra noise, the buzz that accompanies the production of z-sound version of the plural morpheme. We say that z-sound is voiced whereas s-sound is voiceless. The lack of voicing in s is due to the fact that vocal cords are more spread apart and tenser than during the production of z, thus creating conditions that inhibit vocal cord vibrations. Other speech sounds found in human languages also require other types of vocal cord configurations and movements. Speakers have high degree of control over the sounds that vocal cords can produce. 'Sound Wave Packets' emitted from mouth are made up of air and gas which carry letters and words in wavy form that spreads within atmosphere of earth. The human body exhales carbon dioxide and nitrogen gas along with other dust particles and water vapour etc. The 'sound wave packets' come out with gases from mouth of body in the atmosphere and are transmitted to different places.

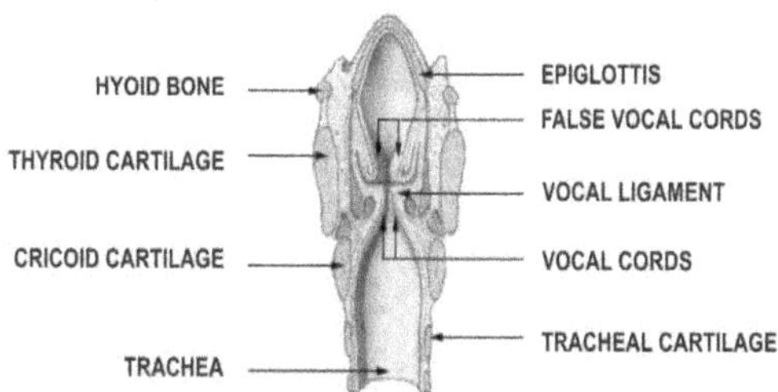

CROSS SECTION OF LARYNX

Fig. 5.5

The ability to sing a melody depends on being able to change the vocal cord positions and tensions rapidly and accurately to hit the right notes. Although the ability to sing well is subject to much individual variations, the ability to control the vocal cord positions and tensions necessary for speech is well within the ability of all normal speakers. Further the space between vocal cords is called glottis and linguists frequently refer to sounds that involve a constriction or closure of this space between vocal cords as glottal sounds. The vocal tract, the region above the vocal cords that includes the oral pharynx portion, the oral cavity and the nasal cavity, is the space within which speech sounds of human languages are produced. The anatomical features of the vocal cords show how consonants and vowels are formed.

The sound waves are longitudinal waves found roaming in space and in inter planetary medium. The light waves are transverse waves and they tend to make the orbit of astral bodies elliptical due to both charges being concentrated at two opposite polar points. The Sound Wave Packets are not observed in protozoans etc and increases gradually in invertebrates and reaches its climax in vertebrates. The mammals possess highly developed alphabets with sixteen vowels and 32 consonants which are emitted in the form of sound wave packets.

A longitudinal wave can travel in all three medium, i.e., solids, liquids and gases. Speed of a longitudinal wave in a medium is given by, $V = \sqrt{E/d}$, where E is elasticity of the medium and d is its density. On the other hand in the propagation of transverse wave medium particles vibrate about their mean position perpendicular to the direction of motion of the wave. These waves can travel in solids and on liquid surface. Since gas molecules are relatively free from each other transverse waves are not possible in gases. The voice box in the mouth of human beings is one of the prominent sources of sound. It can produce sound waves having frequency range 100 - 1100 Hz. Different animals can also produce sound but of different frequency range. For example the mew of cat has frequency range 750 - 150 Hz and chirping of bird has frequency range, 2000 - 13000 Hz.

The sound is produced in a material medium by vibrating source. As the vibrating source moves forward, it compresses the medium past it, increasing the density locally. This part of the

127

medium compresses the layer next to it by collisions. The compression travels in the medium at a speed which depends on elastic and inertia properties of the medium. As the source moves back, it drags the medium and produces a rarefaction in the layer. The layer next to it is dragged back and thus the rarefaction pulse passes forward. In this way, compression and rarefaction pulses are produced which travel in the medium. Sound waves constitute alternate compression and rarefaction pulses travelling in the medium. The sound is audible only if the frequency of alteration of pressure is between 20 Hz to 20,000 Hz in case of human beings. The waves with frequency below audible range are called infrasonic waves and the waves with frequency above audible range are called ultrasonic waves. The compression and rarefaction in a sound wave is caused due to the back and forth motion of particles of the medium. This motion is along the direction of propagation of sound and hence sound waves are longitudinal.

Vocal cords of animals and human beings are apparatus that create sound waves with low frequency power waves. Different animals have the capacity to produce different types of radio and power waves depending upon stage of evolution of animals. The sound produced at some point by a vibrating source travels in all directions in the medium if the medium is extended. The sound waves are in general three dimensional waves. For a small source, we have spherical layers of medium on which the pressure at various elements have the same phase at a given instant. The appearance of sound to human ear is characterized by three parameters, (a) pitch, (b) loudness and (c) quality. All the three are subjective description of sound though they are related to objectively defined quantities. Pitch is related to frequency, loudness is related to intensity and quality is related to waveform of sound waves. A musical scale is a sequence of frequencies which have a particularly pleasing effect on human ear. A widely used musical scale is a sequence of frequencies which have a particularly pleasing effect on human ear. A widely used musical scale, called diatonic scale, has eight frequencies covering an octave. Each frequency is called a note.

The sound waves emitted by animals and human beings can form electromagnetic waves. The sound waves can convert into electromagnetic waves in any medium in space. They show their impact on visible spectra (4000 Å to 7500 Å) of electromagnetic waves. The sound waves effect the growth and development of body parts in living animals. The electromagnetic waves having frequency between 256 Hz to 512 Hz effect body organs of living animals. The electromagnetic waves in the range 4000Å to 7500Å effect body organs of all living beings. The voice box in the mouth of human beings is one of the prominent sources of sound. It can produce sound waves having frequency range 100-1100 Hz. Different animals produce sound waves in different frequency range. The mew of cat has frequency range between 150-750 Hz and chirping of bird has frequency range between 2000-13000 Hz. The sound waves emitted by different animals effect the entire gamut of life forms on planets in different frequency ranges because sound waves convert into electromagnetic waves.

Languages, which are well structured, compact and diverse are distinctly gift by God to all human beings. Language is important topics of neuroscience and emission of sound wave packets from mouth of human beings. The early approach to study of language was to treat it as a separate module or organ within both cerebellum of brain. The structure of spinal nerves, cervical nerves, cerebellum, brain and vocal cord have demonstrated that language is integrated with entire body organs and systems with an incredibly broad range of neural processes. The electromagnetic waves of seven colors create all living beings and attach each and every living being with other living beings. In sound producing animals the sound waves act as check and balance over animals' growth, movement and migrations.

The sound waves of animals and human beings form a circular outer covering around their planets like power waves range in the atmosphere. The sound wave packets are often associated with religion, religious chanting and religious uttering. The sound waves when repeated at fixed wavelength with particular purpose become vow and being repeated time and again effect the body parts of human body. Vocal range is a measure of difference of pitches that human voice can phonate. Its common application is within singing skill where it is used as defining characteristic for classification of voices into groups called voice types. It has been explored by linguists, phonetics experts and speech and language pathology in relation to study of tonal languages and vocal disorders.

5.2 CREATION OF 'SOUND WAVE PACKETS' BY ANIMALS

The sound waves are created by friction between two particles. In animals and human beings rubbing of two solid organs creates sound waves. In clouds, hitting of cloud particles creates sound waves and collision among particles also creates sound waves. The contraction of waves leads to production of particles of smaller size and its gradual culmination into black region. Particles appear out of waves by "Self Gravitation" process due to change in density of the medium at different places in space. The energy associated with nine colors transforms particles into elements within nine colors cycle. The water waves vibrate up and down as it move along and in the similar manner electromagnetic energy of sound waves propagates within atmosphere of planet.

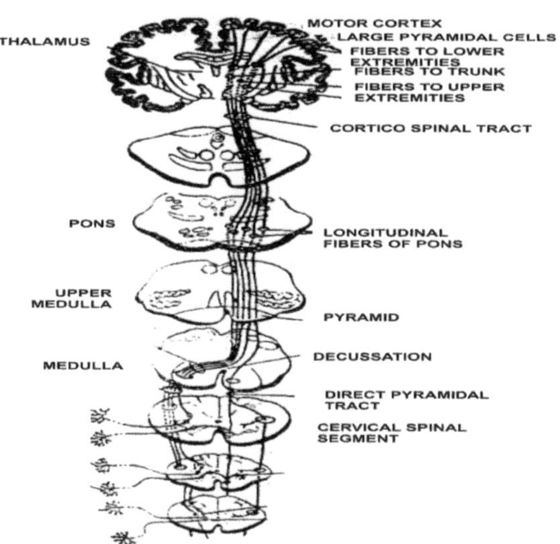

PICTURE SHOWS CROSSED PYRAMIDAL TRACT, DIRECT PYRAMIDAL TRACT AND UN-CROSSED SMALL LATERAL PYRAMIDAL TRACT.

Fig. 5.6

The nerve cells show highest capacity of contraction and expansion of cells and contraction can reach vacuum level of space. The circumference of nerve cell contracts and expands to highest level making the circumference highly elliptical. As increases the ellipticity of circumference of nerve cell so increases the power of imagination of animals because it becomes closer to vacuum state of matter. The power of imagination is less in lower animals and increases gradually in higher animals, e.g., elephant and man etc. The power of imagination can reach Pole star or other star dynasties in a fraction of second and can travel with speed more than light due

129

to high power of contraction and expansion of nerve cells. The impact of green colour creates and strengthens nervous system and cures diseases and abnormalities related to nerves. The development of nervous system in invertebrates is less and gradual increase in formation of neurons and nervous parts takes place. In vertebrates the nervous system develops systematically and forms a network inside main body. The system consists of central or somatic nervous system, autonomic nervous system and special senses.

Different animals produce sound waves in different frequency range. The mew of cat has frequency range between 150-750 Hz and chirping of bird has frequency range between 2000-13000 Hz. Electromagnetic energy may be described as a stream of waves, which are squeezed into particles, photons, each of which is a little packet or "quantum" of energy in fixed numerical order at particular atomic number. In the animals letters develop as integers and atoms of elements. In the human beings vowels are sixteen in number and consonants are 32 in number. The development of consonants is observed in the multiples of five and sound waves progress and accumulate mass inside body. The increase in number of consonants increases in the multiples of 5 + 5 + 5 + 5 + 5 + 4 + 3 = 32 consonants in human beings. These consonants create words and store energy in the form of sound waves. It varies from one animal to another.

The creation of letters and words takes place exactly on the same pattern as creation of elements and compounds. The letters created with prominence of fusion energy behave as vowels whereas letters created with prominence of fission energy behave as consonants. The number of vowels will be five as minimum on account of five electronegative non-metallic peaks. The number of vowels will be sixteen to the maximum on account of creation of fusion dominated elements on earth. Vowels act as 'unwinding force' and try to release mass from the clutches of crystals of elements on any planet. Vowels act as a balancing force for the elements settled on earth as settlements element. Different languages have got different numbers of vowels and consonants in them. The number of vowels will vary from five to sixteen on earth. In case of human beings the number of vowels is sixteen and it is emitted by eight pairs of cervical nerves of vocal cord. Consonants may vary from one to 118 on any planet. Consonants act as binding force and try to squeeze and retain mass in crystallized form in elements inside all living animals. The number of consonants in human beings is 32 and it is emitted by 32 pairs of spinal nerves.

5.2.1 CREATION OF 'SOUND WAVE PACKETS' IN HIGH FREQUENCY RANGE

The number of vowels are less in smaller organisms and their number increases gradually in higher animals and in mammals. Vowels are created due to impact of anti-matter zones and their impact is perceived on sixteen nerves of cervical vertebrae of human beings. Different animals and birds produce sound waves in different frequency range. The chirping of bird has frequency range between 2000-13000 Hz.

5.2.2 CREATION OF 'SOUND WAVE PACKETS' IN LOW FREQUENCY RANGE

The number of consonants are less in smaller organisms and their number increases gradually in bigger animals especially in mammals. Consonants are created due to sedimentation of mass particles in 32 vertical groups of elements on the pattern of 32 crystal classes. Its impact is observed on 32 pairs of spinal nerves in human beings. Different animals produce sound waves in different frequency range. The mew of cat has frequency range between 150-750 Hz.

The sound waves in living beings and human beings tend to convert waves into particles and produce strong, solidified and symmetrical bodies. The elements showing non-metallic behavior and elements showing metallic behavior tend to increase inside body due to impact of sound waves. The electrons change their wavy character, convert into discrete mass particles and create molecules, compounds and body parts of human beings. The weak force equilibrium is observed at five points and vowel letters create words and assimilation of words creates sentences on planets. The letters created out of sound waves behave like elements nucleosynthesized during evolution of human beings. The assimilation of sound waves on planet and energy associated with sound waves creates 16 vowel letters and 32 consonant letters as creation of non-metallic elements and metallic elements respectively. 32 classes of crystal symmetry create 32 consonant letters as crystals inside human beings. Similarly 16 vowel letters create nine color zones inside human beings.

The energy of 32 consonants multiplying with energy of 16 vowels creates 512 words which store energy in the form of astral bodies in space. Thus 512 negatively charged particles control left side of human body whereas 512 positively charged particles control right side of human body. In total, 1024 compounds of elements created from solid particles controlled by sound waves effect human body. The prominence of negatively charged particles produce left organs of human body whereas prominence of positively charged particles produces right organs of human body. The energy associated with sound waves in atmosphere is the precursor which creates solid three-dimensional bodies.

The square value is perceived in the form of velocity and momentum of human body and as high is the velocity so high is the angular momentum of human body. Speed of sound is the highest in granite having metallic octets and lowest in non-metallic octets. The permutation and combination of letters of sound create different words which have specific effect on human body. The multiplication of letters in different proportions create different combination of words which show specific impact on human body. The sound waves effect growth and development of human body.

Every animal has its own alphabet. The words and alphabets are created by body of the animals which is shaped by seven-crystal system, pairs of spinal and cervical nerves and nine color cycle. The smaller animals having less and simplified organs have few letter in their alphabets. The mammals have highest number of letters in their alphabets because organs of mammals are created by nerves, seven holes in skull and seven physiological systems. Due to complexity of organs the number of letters in mammals increases and as increases size and complexity so increase the number of alphabets and complex words emitted by animals.

The creation of alphabets, letters and words takes place by retention and settlement of mass in the same pattern as elements are created. The letters create words, jumbled words and combination of words containing many letters inside it creates sentences or *padas* in many forms. It takes in the similar pattern as molecules and compounds are created out of many elements. The jumbled words and bigger words have capability to make independent existence in the similar manner as compounds and molecules make independent existence. Intermixing among colors and creation of jumbled words is seen on the pattern of creation of molecules and compounds. Cubic crystal is the hardest and strongest among all the crystals. In the cubic crystal charge is concentrated at eight equidistant points and it show highest quantum of attraction. The words are also created under seven crystals system and nine colors cycle under octet effect.

During evolution, intermixing of different size organs, parts and systems; different size animal bodies are created on planet. The living being with their voice release waves at different frequencies within atmosphere of planet. The waves of different wave lengths create solid particles by intermixing which makes room in animals voice on earth as words. Different wave lengths create different words which are observed as phonetics. The permutation and combination of letters of sound create different words which have specific effect on human body. The multiplication of letters in different proportions creates different combination of words which show specific impact on animal body. Words are created by combination of many letters. Words contain vowels and consonants and become meaningful words when they exist with animals in atmosphere outlined along three axes by temperature constant, pressure constant and volume limit within ozone layer of planets in the universe.

The impact of words affects the size, shape and built of human beings due to frequency and wavelength of sound waves. The sound waves are more powerful than solid body. The impact of sound waves is perceived on living beings and shape and size of human beings is shaped by energy associated with sound waves. The particles show their impact along three axes and jumbled words produced by animals and human beings show their impact along three axes. The sound waves like noise, voices, thunderstorms are emissions like longitudinal waves at different frequencies by animals and act along three axes.

Among all the animal forms, vertebrates are highly advanced and among all the vertebrates, mammals are the most advanced. Among mammals, the animals possessing seven body systems along one axis, 32 pairs of spinal nerves along second axis and 12 pairs of cranial nerves along third axis are highest evolved. It includes man, monkey, gorilla, apes, chimpanzee and many similar extinct forms which have developed and evolved in different parts of earth. These animal forms may show different height, weight, color, features, skin texture etc but inner development of characters along three axes will be similar and common. The electromagnetic waves in the wavelength range of power waves, i.e., 1×10^4 - 1×10^7 have frequency range of about 100 to 10,000 Hz. The electromagnetic waves in the range of power waves can convert into audible sound waves of human beings and animals. The sound waves in the range 100 Hz to 10000 Hz can convert into equivalent power waves of electromagnetic waves and effect the growth and development of animals, human beings and life forms on planets in the universe. The sound waves in the equivalent range of power waves of electromagnetic waves affect the life forms, animals and human beings. The aggregation of atoms, molecules and compounds inside animal body in the power waves range of 1×10^4 - 1×10^7 meters is effected by sound waves on earth. This frequency range will vary on different planets in our solar system.

The audible range of sound waves will be different for different animals on different planets. The sound waves are equivalent to their corresponding electromagnetic waves, i.e., power waves. So the sound waves of animals and human beings are more powerful than electromagnetic waves of seven colors (4000Å - 7500Å) that constitute and make animal and human body. The sound waves effect animal body like power waves and sound waves can last longer like power waves. The sound waves will not perish and on the patterns of power waves it will affect animal body with impact on future growth and development. The sound waves of animal body effect the present time and will affect the body in future also because power waves last longer in atmosphere. The languages of animals and human beings form a circular outer covering or packet like structure within atmosphere of planet.

Languages are produced on the pattern of creation of 118 elements in periodic table of elements along three axes by human beings. The impact of time tries to grab matter inside human beings in the shape of bones and muscles and make the human body hefty, strong and stout. The impact of gravitational forces, revolution of earth around sun and accumulation of matter is observed on longitudes. The latitudinal effect near equator is similar to that of longitude but its impact changes towards poles. It produces smaller animals with spherical outline near poles. The size and height of human beings reduces near Arctic and Antarctic poles. The impact of altitude reduces the height, weight and heftiness of human body and tries to make the body light. The human body experiences weightlessness and reduces in strength with increase in altitudes and produces soft alphabets.

IND-IAN NAME	WEST-ERN NAME	FREQUENCY OF SOUND (in Hz.)	FREQUENCYO F ANIMAL SOUND (in Hz.)	TYPES OF WAVE	WAVE LENGTH OF EQUIVALENT POWER WAVES (in Meters)	EQUIVALENT ELECTRO -MAGNETIC WAVES EFFECTING LIVING BODY
(1)	(2)	(3)	(4)	(5)	(6)	(7)
		10-20	10 - 20	Power wave	$1 \times 10^7 - 10^{20}$	
			20 Hz	- do -		
Sa	Do	256	Vocal cord of Human Beings	Sound wave	- do -	Red (7500 Å - 6560 Å)
Re	Re	324.7 Hz	- Do -	Sound wave	- do -	Orange (6560 Å - 6030 Å)
Ga	Mi	363.4 Hz	- Do -	Sound wave	- do -	Yellow (6030 Å - 5430 Å)
Ma	Fa	407.2 Hz	- Do -	Sound wave	- do -	Green (5430 Å - 4990 Å)
Pa	Sol	439.5 Hz	- Do -	Sound wave	- do -	Blue (4990 Å - 4650 Å)
Dha	La	464.3 Hz	- Do -	Sound wave	- do -	Indigo (4650 Å - 4280 Å)
Ni	Ti	491.5	- Do -	Sound wave	- do -	Violet (4280 Å - 4000 Å)
Sa	Do	512	- Do -	Sound wave		
			1100 Vocal cord of Animals	- do -		
		$3 \times 10^4 - 3 \times 10^8$	Vocal cord of Birds	Radio wave	$1 - 10^4$	
			20000	- do -	$1 - 10^{-1}$	
		$3 \times 10^8 - 3 \times 10^9$	Voice of Insects	Micro wave	$3 \times 10^{-1} - 3 \times 10^{-5}$	
		$3 \times 10^9 - 4 \times 10^{14}$	Wing motion of Insects	Infra red	$1 \times 10^{-4} - 1 \times 10^{-7}$	

CHANTING OF WORDS CREATED FROM LETTERS EFFECTS ALL THE NERVES AND BODY PARTS OF LIVING BODY. PROPER CREATION AND APPLICATION OF WORDS MAY CURE DISEASES AND BRING PROFOUND CHANGES INSIDE LIVING BODY. THE SOUND WAVES SHOW DEFINITE CORRELATIONS WITH COLOR WAVES OF DIFFERENT WAVELENGTHS.

Table 5.1

The size and shape of human being reduces with every increase in altitude on earth. The size and shape may reduce to very low level and organs may start decreasing in size when the human being crosses ozone layer. The size and shape can remain intact in case human being is using artificial measures of protection from outside body. The impact of Sa (Do with frequency 256 Hz), Re (Re with frequency 324.7 Hz), Ga (Mi with frequency 363.4 Hz), Ma (Fa with frequency 407.2 Hz), Pa (Sol with frequency 439.5 Hz), Dha (La with frequency 464.3 Hz) and Ni (Ti with frequency 491.5 - 512 Hz) is observed gradually on change of altitude and these waves help in gradual reduction of solidification. These waves increase energy towards surface of earth. The voice and tone of people near surface of earth is harsh and rough whereas the voice becomes sweet and soft at higher altitudes.

As high is the contraction of crystals inside animal body and compaction of crystal by adjoining crystals inside the animal body so high becomes the size and roundness of animal body. The animals show difference in length, width and breadth along three axes. The compaction of crystals in the multiples of 1 : 8 : 64 inside ferromagnetic rod gives shape to living beings along three axes. In the similar manner nucleosynthesis of elements in fourteen matter zones inside

133

planets and stars allows highest accumulation of elements inside animal body. The electromagnetic waves in fourteen colors (7+7) zone control storage of elements as matter inside animals and impose restriction on infinite expansion or infinite contraction of mass inside any animal or human being on planets.

Speed of compression of sound wave in solids is determined by the medium's compressibility, shear modulus and density. In fluid dynamics, the speed of sound in a fluid medium (gas or liquid) is used as a relative measure for the speed of an object moving through the medium. The ratio of speed of an object to the speed of sound in the fluid is called the object's Mach Number. Objects moving at speeds greater than Mach 1 are said to be travelling at supersonic speeds. Sound waves emitted from vocal cords of animals and sound emitted due to movement of wings of animals are limited within seven types of waves. These sound waves are effective within atmosphere of any planet. Power waves in the frequency range 256-512 Hertz are not audible in space because they are not responded by nerves of animals and human beings. The audible nerves of animals and human beings can recognise waves in the frequency range 256-512 Hertz of power waves within atmosphere of planets. Central Nervous System is effective within three axes attachment of animals and human body inside atmospheric covering of planet which is bound by pressure, temperature and volume of body along three axes. The objects moving with speed greater than Mach 1 or objects moving with supersonic speeds should be banned because it is harmful to living beings on earth. It will cause damage to atmospheric ozone covering and it will allow harmful radiation to enter the atmosphere of earth. The velocity of objects moving with higher velocity above Mach 1 needs to be regulated on earth.

During evolution of life forms segmentation increases gradually in higher life forms. The segmentation increases on the patterns of cyclic (spiral) movement of elements in fourteen rounds and its multiples. The segmentation takes place in inner as well as outer organs of the human body. The outer segmentation of the body is effected by pressure, volume and temperature of the life form on planets whereas inner segmentation is effected by seven colors that create seven body systems. The outer segmentation of body is shaped by three axes movement of human body. The inner segmentation of body is shaped by seven colors cycle. The segmentation of body produces different organs and body parts and it is clearly visible in human body. Languages or Sound wave packets emitted by vocal cords of animals and human beings are 'low frequency radio waves' of space. Emission of sound waves makes living body light and disease free by reducing black iron matter content from different body parts.

Black Region	Violet	Indigo	Blue	Green	Yellow	Orange	Red	White Region
Zero$^\circ$ C temperature of living being	5° C	10° C	18° C	25° C	30° C	35° C	50° C	High temperature of living being

Table 5.2

Life forms develop on planets which maintain a outer covering of atmosphere between the temperature range zero degree to 100°C. The life forms exist on blue planets, i.e. towards low wavelength of spectra. Language is the outcome of individuals in any community, their faith, concentration and practices. The impact of sound wave *Sa* (Do with frequency 256 Hz) effects skeletal system and bones under impact of red color. Similarly, the impact of sound wave Re (Re with frequency 324.7 Hz), effects integument system under impact of orange color. The impact of sound wave Ga (Mi with frequency 363.4 Hz) effects digestive system under impact of yellow color. The impact of sound wave *Ma* (Fa with frequency 407.2 Hz), effects nervous system under

134

impact of green color. The impact of sound wave *Pa* (Sol with frequency 439.5 Hz), effects cardio-vascular system under impact of blue color. The impact of sound wave *Dha* (La with frequency 464.3 Hz) effects urino-genital system under impact of indigo color. The impact of sound wave *Ni* (Ti with frequency 491.5 - 512 Hz) effects blood circulatory system under impact of violet color.

Solid crystals form solid skeleton and bones in the multiples of seven, e.g., seven types of vertebrae. Seven holes in skull are created by seven color energy and seven systems remain in muscular, liquid and gas forms. Heavy animals, e.g., elephants contain more black mass towards center of animal body. Light animals contain comparatively less quantity of black mass and generally develop hollowness in bones and body parts, e.g., birds.

Lower animals move their wings and body parts in such a manner that vibration of low frequency is produced which appears as sound waves. Animal forms maintain seven metallic matter zones towards center and seven non-metallic matter zones towards periphery. Three types of nerves are distinguished, i.e., sensory, motor and mixed. The dorsal roots carry both sensory and motor fibers, their motor fibers supply non-motor muscles of the head. Ventral roots have only motor fibers and supply initial muscles and their derivatives.

The total number of nerves like petals corresponds with the number of letters of alphabet and the number of petals of any specific center is determined by disposition of the subtle nerves around it. These nerves bear specific power of sound and every nerve has got its specific sound power. Every alphabet has got its own language and that sound power is linked to one nerve of the body. In the life forms and inside body right side represents the electropositive form and stands for father figure (+Ve). The left side of the body represents electronegative form and stands for mother figure (-Ve), i.e., electronegative charge of the elements.

Excess of impact of electromagnetic waves of red color (*Sa* wave) improves the heart conditions and reduces brain power and intelligence. The impact of electromagnetic waves of blue color (*Pa* wave) improves brain power and intelligence but makes the heart weak. The vertebrates develop skull with seven holes which contain seven types of nerves. These seven types of nerves develop due to seven colors and control seven systems inside animal body. The innermost organs of the life forms become black and occupy interior position, e.g. navel and liver in animals. Seven colors create seven systems in living beings.

Inner structure and inner organs of living creatures contain seven systems, which develop in animals gradually from lower animals to higher animals and gradually their complexity also increases. Creation of characters are the outcome of inter-twining and intermixing of tissues, fibres and muscles of seven different colors which takes place due to gradual evolution of characters. The number of nerve centres and nerves coming out from every centre of the spinal column are 4, 6, 10, 12, 16, 2 and 1,024,000 and its multiples. The centres of the nerves are located inside the spinal column at six points and the seventh point is above the spinal cord inside brain as cerebral cortex. Every nerve and ganglia produces one type of animal. So in total 1,024,000 types of animals and life forms are produced due to sound wave packets on earth. Every complicacy and every addition of new nerve or ganglion or organ or system will produce new life forms and new types of organism.

The total number of nerves corresponds with the number of letter of alphabet and the number of nerves emerging like petals of any specific center is determined by the disposition of the subtle nerves around it. These nerves bear 'specific sound power' and every nerve of body has its specific sound power. Every alphabet has got its own sound power and that sound power is linked to one nerve of the body. In the life forms and inside the body, right side represents +Ve, i.e., the masculine form and stands for father figure. The left side of body represents the feminine form and stands for mother (-Ve), i.e., electronegative charge in the animals. Excess of impact of electromagnetic waves of red color improves the heart conditions and reduces brain power and intelligence. The impact of electromagnetic waves of dark color improves brain power and intelligence but makes the heart weak. The impact of energy of electromagnetic waves is observed on development of different organs and systems.

Speech, voice, letters, alphabets and Language is produced due to impact of Spinal nerves and Cervical nerves by vocal cords inside Life forms. Vowels are produced by impact of cervical nerves whereas consonants are produced by spinal nerves of nervous system. The movable life forms, e.g., animals show development of all the nine system inside them and behave as astral bodies i.e., planets. Every animal is specific and peculiar creation in itself.

The tallest and biggest animals in size, e.g., giraffe, elephants, whale etc. are found near equator and their growth will attain maximum size and volume near equator due to prominence of strong force and less prominent weak force near equator. The small and short animals in size, e.g., seals, penguins, etc. will be found near both the poles of earth and their growth will be small in size and less in volume near poles due to prominence of weak force and electromagnetic force near poles. The electrons effect and help in development of endoderm. Protons effect and help in development of mesoderm. Neutrons help in development of endoderm.

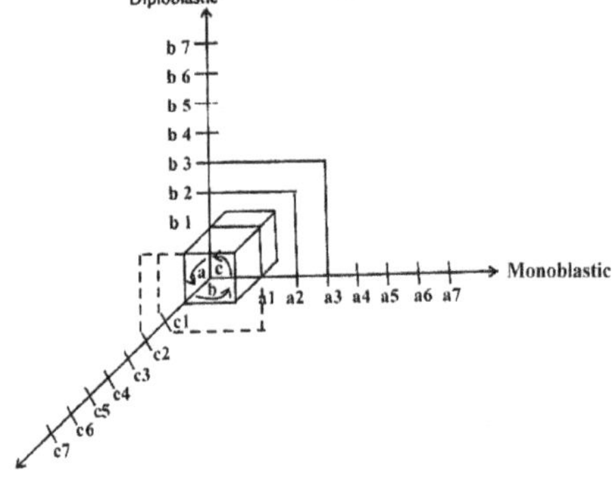

CREATION OF CELLS AND TISSUES IN SEVEN COLOR LAYERS TAKES PLACE ALONG THREE AXES. 'POWER WAVE PACKETS' ARE CREATED DUE TO IMPACT OF ELECTRONS, PROTONS AND NEUTRONS ALONG THREE AXES INSIDE ATMOSPHERE OF PLANETS. 'POWER WAVE PACKETS' ARE EMITTED BY LIVING ANIMALS AND HUMAN BEINGS AND THEY ARE CAPABLE TO AFFECT HUMAN BODY BECAUSE THEY ARE MADE UP OF ENERGY OF ELECTROMAGNETIC WAVES. POWER WAVES CONTAIN WAVES OF HIGHER WAVELENGTH WHEREAS ELECTROMAGNETIC WAVES CREATING BODY CONTAIN WAVES IN THE RANGE 4000 ANGSTROMS TO 7500 ANGSTROMS. ELECTROMAGNETIC WAVES IN THE RANGE 4000 ANGSTROMS TO 7500 ANGSTROMS CREATE BODY OF ALL LIVING BEINGS. POWER WAVES HAVING HIGHER WAVELENGTH ARE MORE POWERFUL THAN ELECTROMAGNETIC WAVES IN THE RANGE 4000 ANGSTROMS TO 7500 ANGSTROMS WHICH CREATE BODY OF LIVING BEINGS.

Fig. 5.7

The impact of seven colors and energy associated with colors are instrumental in developing holes and perforations in animal body. The skull develops seven holes, body systems develop invaginations and perforations, skin develops pores and slits through which liquids and gases come out. The negatively charged particles, electrons help in development of ectoderm and seven non-metallic zones. The positively charged particles, protons help in development of mesoderm and seven metallic zones development. The neutral mass particles, i.e., neutrons help in development of endoderm and store mass in black region. The prominence of either of the forces on animals leads to creation of animals with different characteristics. The frequency of sound waves are equivalent to power waves.

136

The prominence of strong force is higher at equator and it helps in bulging of earth at equator. The animals at equator contain and accumulate more black matter and tend to gain solid crystalline structure. The animals at poles contain less quantity of black matter and tend to gain spherical outer covering and spherical shape. The body parts, organs and structure of living animals develop under the impact of above factors. Development of life forms takes place with five states of matters.

1. Vacuum state develops mind cells of brain,
2. Gas state develops oxygen and other gases,
3. Liquid state of develops red blood, white discharge, soft tissue etc.,
4. Solid state develops bones,
5. Dense black metallic octet state develops black heart, liver and dark colored organs and parts in center and hub of body.

The body of movable life form retains more breath (air) inside the tissues. The ventral air with the help of left nostril and right nostril keeps the blood and air in circulation and retains air component inside the tissues in the body. The impact of 'opposite breath' exercised by body of the living being has the tendency to retain air in spinal cord and leave the solid body with mass as corpse. Since oxygen remains inside the spinal cord the body remains in the sleeping alive form for quite longer period. Seven color show impact on development of outer organs, limbs, body systems and inner parts. Solid crystals form solid bony portion. The jelly like cells are dominated by liquid and gas state. Heart and naval portion is dominated by black solid crystals and seven body systems are dominated by colored solid crystals.

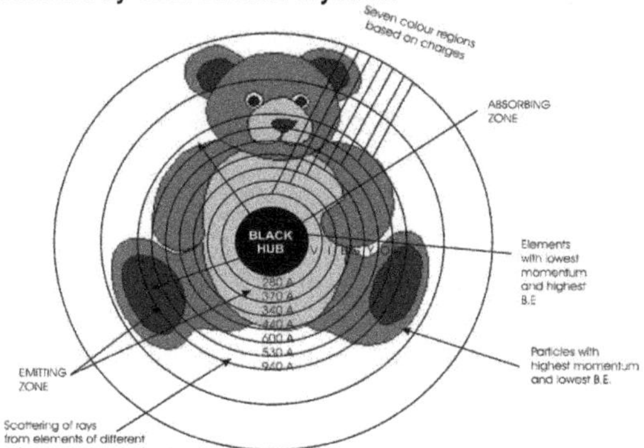

ABSORPTION AND EMISSION OF ENERGY OF SEVEN COLOR ELECTROMAGNETIC WAVES INSIDE ANIMAL BODY

Fig. 5.8

The impact of pressure, volume and temperature along three axes shapes the internal and external parts of body of all life forms. The number of glands, exocrine or endocrine, brain, nerves, size of pineal body, ears, eyes, nose, mouth, tongue, teeth, secretion of acids inside body, male sex organs, female sex organs, hands, legs, toes, nails, composition of blood, lungs, alveoli, bones, cartilages, skin, hairs, heart, kidney, liver, all body parts, size and shape of body are shaped by pressure, volume and temperature prevailing on planet. The decrease in temperature of planet increases volume of body of life forms and in similar manner increase in temperature of planet decreases the volume and size of body of life forms. Increase in pressure and gravity of planet increases volume and size of living body and in similar manner decrease in gravity of planet decreases the size of living body.

Sound wave packets emitted by vocal cords of animals and human beings are 'low frequency power waves'moving in atmosphere. Emission of high quantum of sound waves increases radio waves, microwaves and seven color component of electromagnetic waves inside body. Impact of sound waves reduces three axes attachment of human beings due to melting of iron compounds. Emission of more and more sound waves from vocal cords of animals and human beings will reduce black matter content inside body. Emission of sound waves makes living body light and disease free by reducing black iron matter content from different body parts. The ratio of expansion of length, breadth and width may take a maximum value of $1^3 : 2^3 : 4^3$ or 1 : 8 : 64 to the maximum in animals. However due to movement of astral bodies, the animal bodies tend to gain round outer covering as far as possible.

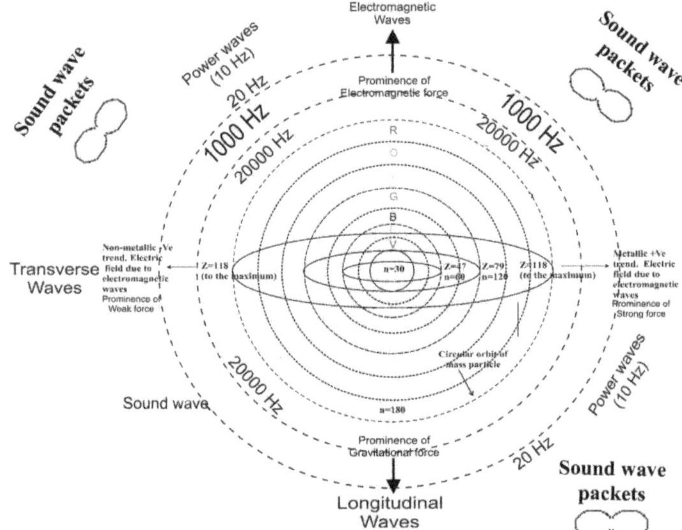

CROSS SECTION OF ANIMAL BODY SHOWING IMPACT OF SOUND WAVES. THESE POWER WAVE PACKETS ARE EMITTED BY VOCAL CORDS OF ANIMALS AND HUMAN BEINGS AND INSTRUMENTS OF HUMAN BEINGS ON PLANET. THEY WILL FAIL TO EXIST ON PLANETS AND STARS HAVING NO ATMOSPHERE. SOUND WAVES CAN CONVERT INTO ELECTROMAGNETIC WAVES AND SHOW IMPACT ON ANIMAL BODIES. MAXIMUM EXPANSION OF PARTICLES CAN TAKE PLACE UPTO 7500Å INSIDE ELEMENTS AND CREATE DIFFERENT PARTS, ORGANS AND SYSTEMS. THREE AXES ATTACHMENT OF ANIMAL AND HUMAN BODY EMPOWERS VIBRATIONS AND VOCAL CORD TO PRODUCE SOUND WAVE PACKETS MADE UP OF POWER WAVES WHICH EFFECTS HUMAN BODY WITHIN ATMOSPHERIC COVERING. POWER WAVES IN THE FREQUENCY RANGE 256 Hz TO 512 Hz CREATE SOUND WAVE PACKETS OR LETTERS OR 'AKSHARS' LIKE ATOMS OF ELEMENTS WITHIN ATMOSPHERE OF PLANET EARTH. THE ENERGY OF ELECTROMAGNETIC WAVES OF FUNDAMENTAL SUB-ATOMIC PARTICLES, i.e., ELECTRONS, PROTONS AND NEUTRAL NEUTRONS CREATES ATOMS OF ELEMENTS OR LETTERS OR 'AKSHARS'.

Fig. 5.9

Theories of evolution of languages were discussed from linguistic point of view by many scientists. Evolution of language is generic and linguists deciphered it in course of time. Some link has been found between animal and human communications. The creative and miraculous atoms of elements are involved in production of languages and develop important features in the understanding of linguistic processes.

5.3 IMPACT OF 'SOUND WAVE PACKETS' ALONG THREE AXES

The growth and development of animals and human body is controlled along three axes within atmosphere. The increase in speed of sound will have harmful effect on body and will reduce the growth of body. Any device, machine, ammunition and supersonic appliances emitting sound waves above Mach 1 needs to be banned within atmosphere of earth. Movement of appliances above speed of sound will affect growth of animals and human beings and will deplete ozone layer around earth. Power waves at this level affect ozone covering around earth and will be detrimental for growth of animal and human body. Sound waves are effective within atmosphere of any planet. Power waves in the frequency range 256-512 Hertz are audible in atmosphere because they are responded by nerves of animals and human beings. The audible nerves of animals and human beings can recognise waves in the frequency range 256-512 Hertz of power waves within atmosphere of planets. Central nervous system is effective within three axes attachment of animals and human body inside atmospheric covering of planet which is bound by pressure, temperature and volume of body along three axes.

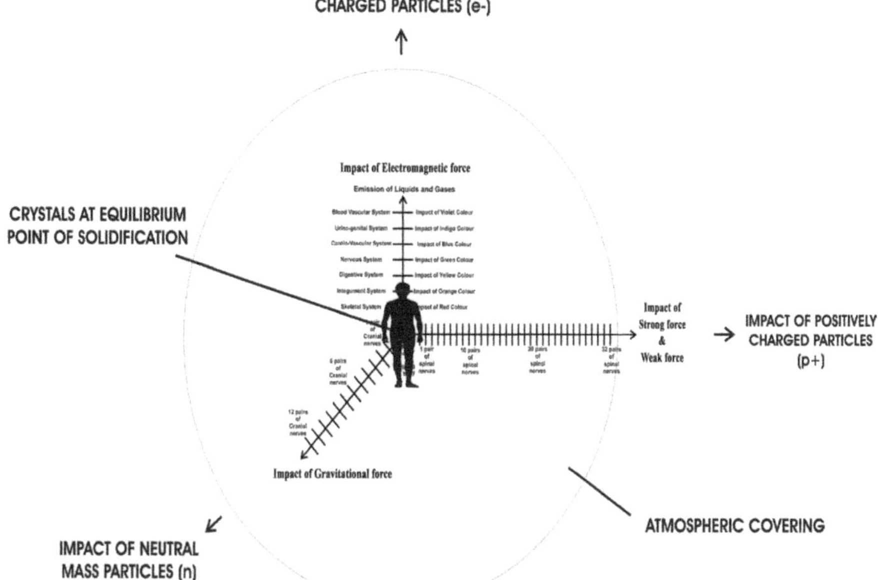

IMPACT OF 'SOUND WAVE PACKETS' IS OBSERVED ON BODY ALONG THREE AXES WHICH SHAPES GROWTH AND DEVELOPMENT OF BODY INSIDE ROUND TIME FRAME. PRESSURE INCREASES INSIDE BODY IN THE MULTIPLES OF TWELVE, TEMPERATURE IN THE MULTIPLES OF NINE AND VOLUME IN THE MULTIPLES OF 32 (2+6+10+14). ROUND OUTER COVERING OF BODY MAINTAINS THERMODYNAMIC EQUILIBRIUM ALONG THREE AXES. NEGATIVELY CHARGED PARTICLES (e-), POSITIVELY CHARGED PARTICLES (p+) AND NEUTRAL MASS PARTICLES (n) DEVELOP EQUILIBRIUM ALONG THREE AXES INSIDE ANIMAL AND HUMAN BODY.

Fig. 5.10

As increase the size and weight of animals so increase the complexity and division of mass into systems, parts and organs. The impact of colors on body organs, tissues, fibers and muscles is observed in different manner on different animals. The time stands for round and spherical shape. Any mass particle when becomes round in shape becomes synonymous to time. The time is round and impact of time tries to make outer covering of every object containing mass as round. Following are the tissues, organs and organ systems that are formed from three germ layers due to impact of electromagnetic waves.

1. Ectoderm: The development of ectoderm takes place due to impact of electron particles (e⁻) and first wave '*Sa*' of Swara of sound waves.

    (a) Epidermis of skin, epidermal derivatives like epidermal glands, hairs etc.,

    (b) Chromatophores (pigment cells of the skin),

    (c) Nervous system,

    (d) Conjunctive cornea and lens of eyes,

    (e) Iris and ciliary muscles of eyes,

    (f) Nasal and olfactory epithelia,

    (g) Outer layer of tympanic membrane,

    (h) Internal ears,

    (i) Enamel of teeth,

    (j) Epithelium of stomodaeum (fore gut) and proctodaeum (hind gut),

    (k) Some glands, e.g., sweat gland, sebaceous gland, mammary gland, lachrymal gland, salivary gland, pituitary gland, pineal gland and medulla of adrenal glands.

2. Mesoderm: The development of mesoderm takes place due to impact of proton particles (p⁺) and fourth wave '*Ma*' of Swara of sound waves.

    (a) Dermis of skin,

    (b) Muscles except iris and ciliary muscles,

    (c) Connective tissue,

    (d) Dentine of teeth,

    (e) Heart and blood vessels,

    (f) Blood and lymph,

    (g) Spleen,

    (h) Pericardium of heart and pleura of lungs,

    (i) Sclera and choroids of eyes,

    (j) Connective tissue base of tympanic membranes,

    (k) Cortex of adrenal glands,

    (l) Notochord,

    (m) Coelomic epithelia,

    (n) Mesenteries,

    (o) Most of skeleton,

    (p) Excretory system with excretion of urinary bladder and urethra,

    (q) Reproductive system with excretion.

3. Endoderm: The development of endoderm takes place due to impact of neutron particles (n) and seventh wave '*Ni*' of Swara of sound waves.

    (a) Mucosa (mucus membrane) of the gut (alimentary canal) with the exception of those portions already mentioned in the ectoderm,

    (b) Some glands - pancreas, liver, glands in the wall of gastro-intestinal tract (gastric prostate),

    (c) Inner layer of tympanic membrane,

    (d) The epithelial lining of eustachian tube and tympanic cavity,

    (e) Trachea, bronchi and lungs,

(f) Urinary bladder,
(g) Urethra etc.

The overlapping of characters, evolution, migration, adoption, determinism and mutation etc are very often noticed in all animals on planets. The longitude and latitude affect the growth and development of animals and every living organism is the product of specific longitude and latitude and overlaps different characters in course of time. Thus old species vanish and new ones are produced in course of time. The combination of vowels and consonants of a language create words with specific meaning for body due to nerves.

The intermixing of '*Sa, Ma and Ni*' sound waves creates three layers in total which form seven systems inside human body. The ectoderm, mesoderm and endoderm gradually transform and create seven systems under the impact of sound waves inside human body. The life forms are produced in 84 blocks of 7 systems x 12 organs cycle. The longitude has its impact on creation of life forms in the order of 0^0 to 360^0 on equator. Similarly the latitude also has its impact on height and length of human beings. The poles produce smallest human beings whereas the equator produces tallest and heaviest, i.e., hefty structures. The human being are found everywhere on every part on earth because of their migratory habit and migration to every part on earth. Ozone layer limits the atmosphere and keeps a check over it. The sound wave letters and '*Akshars*' cannot exist beyond atmosphere of Earth.

Every living animal emits words made up of vowels and consonants with definite grammatical arrangement. The impact of body parts, systems and organs along three axes of any living animal creates many words with different combinations. In cold places, human being feel difficult to open mouth completely and voice becomes feeble showing prominence of vowels. In hotter places comparatively the pronunciation is clear and speech shows prominence of consonants. In the highest animals and human beings, delicate vocal cord develops containing parts as mentioned below:

1. Wind Pipe: Wind pipe or trachea brings sound wave packets alongwith exhaled air outside the body.
2. Larynx and vocal cord: In the upper part of trachea, larynx is located which is the main part for sound emission. Trachea is about 15 cms long and contains cartiledge rings at intervals which keeps it open. Flaps of vocal cord are very soft and move with high velocity. Opening and closing takes place during pronunciation. For every speech production it opens and closes. During inhalation vocal cord is fully open. During exhalation vocal cord remains slightly less open. Whispering sound is produced when vocal cord is open but its posterior portion is slightly closed. Murmuring sound is produced when vocal cord oscillates slowly producing half-voice sound.
3. Glottis and epiglottis: They help in transmission of sound waves through vocal cord.
4. Uvula: Uvula is attached to soft palate and its movement up and down helps in pronunciation of letters.
5. Nasal cavity: It helps in production of nasal sound.
6. Soft palate: Soft palate is fleshy portion inside mouth whose up and down movement helps in production of sound wave packets.
7. Hard palate: It extends in the upper part of mouth and helps in production of *Talabya* sound waves.
8. Alveolus: Alveolus helps in production of sound with the help of tongue.
9. Teeth: Teeth help in production of *Dantya* sound wave packets.

10. Lips: Position of both lips produces different types of sound waves called *Ousthya.*
11. Tongue: Change in position of entire tongue produces different vowels and consonants.

Simultaneous to development of vocal organs of speech and listening, reception by ear is equally important because speech is deciphered at the same frequency. The sound wave packets of speaker propagate through air in atmosphere and reach the ear of listeners. Human beings contain two ear on both the sides of skull. The important parts of ear are:

1. External ear: It contains pinna and external auditory meatus. External auditory meatus is thin and tubular structure which narrows down to meet tympanum. Tympanum or tympanic membrane receives sound wave packets from pinna and transmits the waves to hammer like structure called malleus.

2. Middle ear: It contains three smaller bones which are arranged like snail. They are called hammer, anvil and stirrup. The bones of middle ear serve the purpose of reduction of dimensioin of vibration, impedance matching of balance between outer and inner ear and centralize the vibration to smaller area of inner ear. As a result the pressure of sound waves on middle ear becomes higher and it acts like step up transformer for ear.

3. Internal ear or labyrinth: The structure of internal ear is complicated and contains three parts, viz, ring like apparatus, elliptical outlet and cochlea. It is full of fluid and auditory nerves after coming out from brain enter this fluid and break into many smaller nerves. Cochlea is full of fluid and helps in transmission of sound waves in the form of electric waves to brain.

4. Auditory sensory nerves and Sensory nerves: External ear collects sound wave packets and transmits them to tympanum. Three bones help in transmission of vibration to proper place and Eustachian tube maintains pressure. Behind the tympanum, tympanic cavity full of air exists which contains hammer, anvil and stirrup. In the wall of middle ear, there appear two hole like structure in cochlea.

5. Cochlea: Cochlea is divided into two parts basing on membrane. The inner core of membrane contains 3500 sensory cells like hairs. The outer core also contains 12,000 to 1,20,000 hair like cells. Cochlea serves like auditory sensory centre for transmission of information to brain. Sound wave packets are produced due to vibration and ear is capable to perceive vibrations.

Capacity of ear, listening power and perception by nervous system of individual varies from person to person. The planet is a stage where many genus and species appear with different characteristics, play their role and finally produce different characteristics. The movement of planet is instrumental in producing various genus and species with different characteristics. Archaeopteryx, Dinosaurs and Ichthyosaurs etc. are examples of intermixing and overlapping of characters in the past. Due to equatorial bulging of earth, the animal forms on equator are biggest and largest in size and shape. The Arctic and Antarctic area contain comparatively smaller animals. Equator contains animals of biggest size e.g., hefty mammals having highest length, highest breath and highest width on account of prominence of strong force. Languages evolve from letters and words spoken by animals and human beings and mutual intelligibility varies from place to place depending upon longitude, latitude and altitude of planet. It depends upon speakers and listeners capability of hearing and understanding.

6

FORMATION OF 'SOUND WAVE PACKETS'

Arya or *Aryans* were tall, white complexioned people with sharp features and curly hair and their language was Sanskrit. They were intellectual race which migrated from one place to other and spread knowledge and wisdom to local people of different parts of the world. Sanskrit language is purely secular in approach and has capacity to cure diseases of human body. Ancient people used to cure their diseases through *Yog, Mantras* and used to conduct *Havanas* (camp fire and community fire) for elimination of ghosts, ugly souls and spirits. They passed their knowledge from one generation to another through *Shrutis* and *Smritis.* Gradually their culture was assimilated in many civilizations throughout the world and so changed their language and life styles.

After mass extinction, isolated cultures and civilizations grew in many parts of the worlds and they mixed their language with Sanskrit and acculturation started. Finally it led to integration of knowledge in many forms in different communities. They used to chant 'Ohm" which is created from thirteenth vowel letter 'O'. The pronunciation of letter 'O' is observed in many parts of world in different forms, e.g., O, Oh as nodding voice. Sanskrit was the language of intellectuals and Aryans who migrated probably from Himalayas and Northern hills of Earth. These places are full of snow and protect life forms for millions of years inside snow. The corpse remains protected inside cold snowy mountains and after getting heat becomes active and vibrant. Aryans were people who emerged from these areas and who contained knowledge about development of body parts along three axes.

Ancient people had full knowledge about anatomy of human body and protection of body and soul. In human beings, upward breath taken through spinal cord and its tri-junction point makes the air enter spinal cord and takes the nervous impulse out from the body. The spinal cord retains air inside it and time stops for that period. The air inside spinal cord makes the body vital, fresh and increases the air holding capacity of the human body. The human body can stop disease, retain vitality and maintain the body alive for a longer period by retaining air inside the spinal cord. The spinal cord retains air inside it and has the capacity to stop time till the air remains inside the spinal cord. The time is stored with oxygen in cerebrospinal fluid inside the spinal cord and brain and it allows human being to survive and remain alive for quite long time.

The human body can survive for millions of years buried inside snow. The human body survives on snow for quite long time and when snow melts in snowy areas of mountains corpses become alive and start utilizing their skill and knowledge. The oxygen element devours time and stops the impact of time on spinal cord and finally on human body. It is read as *"Sushumna bhakshayate Samayah".* Oxygen inside spinal cord protects body, devours time and preserves body for long time and stops degeneration of body. Extra-oxygenation of spinal column protects body, enriches body growth increases metabolism and provides energy. For protecting human body for longer period, we may provide artificial oxygenation of spinal cord. It will protect human body from decay and degeneration for quite long time.

'Sound Wave Packets' emitted from mouth are made up of air bubbles which carry letters, words and sentences in gas form and are active within atmosphere of planet earth. The human body inhales oxygen and releases carbon dioxide through breathing. The body exhales carbon dioxide, some quantity of nitrogen gas and water vapour along with other dust particles etc. The 'sound wave packets' act like *'Vani-Vihar'* and come out with gases from mouth of body in the atmosphere and are transmitted to different places. The air in gaseous form is limited and controlled by spherical time frame. The circumference and diameter are two parameters which control time in the multiples of 22/7 and create gas bubbles with mass particles. Spherical time frame is the greatest arbiter for contraction of mass and expansion of orbit of movement of all gas bubbles. The smallest unit of contraction of time takes place in solid crystallized form, i.e., e-, e+ and neutron particles. The evolution and transformation of waves and particles takes place in following manner:

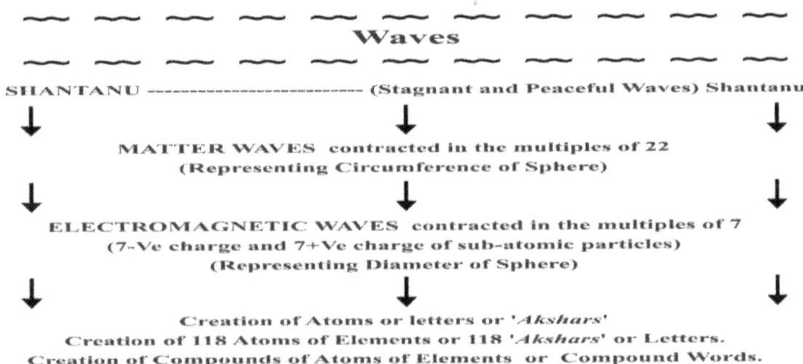

POWER WAVES IN THE FREQUENCY RANGE 256 Hz TO 512 Hz CREATE SOUND WAVE PACKETS OR LETTERS OR 'AKSHARS' LIKE ATOMS OF ELEMENTS WITHIN ATMOSPHERE OF PLANET EARTH. THE ENERGY OF ELECTROMAGNETIC WAVES OF THREE FUNDAMENTAL SUB-ATOMIC PARTICLES, i.e., ELECTRONS, PROTONS AND NEUTRONS CREATES ATOMS OF ELEMENTS OR LETTERS OR 'AKSHARS'. THE IMPACT OF FUNDAMENTAL PARTICLES TAKES PLACE ALONG THREE AXES DUE TO PRESSURE, TEMPERATURE AND VOLUME EFFECT OF ATMOSPHERE. PROTONS EFFECT PRESSURE, NEUTRONS EFFECT TEMPERATURE AND ELECTRONS CONTROL VOLUME OF LETTERS OR 'AKSHARS' WITHIN ATMOSPHERE OF PLANET. CREATION OF LETTERS LIKE ATOMS OF ELEMENTS ARE CONTROLLED BY TEMPERATURE, VOLUME AND PRESSURE ALONG THREE AXES ON PLANETS HAVING ATMOSPHERE. THESE POWER WAVE PACKETS ARE EMITTED BY VOCAL CORDS OF ANIMALS AND HUMAN BEINGS AND INSTRUMENTS OF HUMAN BEINGS ON PLANET BUT THEY WILL FAIL TO EXIST ON PLANETS AND STARS HAVING NO ATMOSPHERE.

Fig. 5.10

Sound wave packet is a short burst or envelope or capsule of localized wave action that travels as unit. A packet can be synthesized from an infinite set of component sinusoidal waves of different wave numbers with phases and amplitudes so that they interfere constructively over a small region of space or atmosphere. Each component of wave function or packet is solution of a wave equation. Depending on sound wave equation the wave packets' profile remains constant. Power waves in the frequency range 256Hz to 512Hz create sound wave packets or letters or 'Akshars' like atoms of elements within atmosphere of Earth. Sound wave packets are created like atoms of elements from mouth during speaking. Three fundamental particles create atoms of elements and in similar manner create sound waves on planets. Creation and existence of sound waves can be explained on the basis of atomic theory and creation of jumbled words takes place as formation of compounds of atoms of elements. Wave motion is a mechanism by which the energy is transmitted from one point to other.

ENERGY OF ELECTROMAGNETIC WAVES STORED INSIDE PARTICLES AND ELEMENTS IN COLORED, WHITE AND BLACK MATTER ZONES IN THE UNIVERSE

NAME OF ELECTRO-	FREQ -	WAVE LENGTH	ENERGY STORED	PROCE -SSES	STORAGE OF ENERGY	MATTER ZONES

MAGNETIC WAVES	UENCY RANGE (Hz.)	RANGE (m)	IN PHOTONS		INSIDE PARTICLES AND ELEMENTS	OF THE UNIVERSE
WHITE LIGHT	Very Less	Highest	Lowest	Movement of waves	Particles containing lowest energy	White
Power Frequencies	60 - 50	5×10^6 - 6×10^6	Lowest	Movement of waves	- do -	Matter
Radio Frequencies	3×10^7 - 3×10^4	10 - 10^4	Lower	- do -	- do -	Zone (50
Very High Radio Frequencies	3×10^8 - 3×10^7	1 - 10	Low	- do -	- do -	per cent
Ultra High Radio Frequencies	3×10^9 - 3×10^8	10^{-1} - 1	Low	- do -	Emission of energy and particles by fission	white
Micro-waves	3×10^{11} - 10^9	10^{-3} - 3×10^{-1}	Low	Nucleus of Fe melts. Sub-atomic particles are liberated. 3-D character is lost	Electromagnetic energy stored in elements inside stars increases and $^{56}_{26}Fe$ starts melting due to decrease in binding energy of element. 3-D character is lost.	White
Heat Radiation	3×10^{13} - 3×10^9	10^{-5} - 10^{-3}	Low	- do -	- do -	Light)
Infra-Red rays (IR)	4×10^{14} - 10^{13}	7.5×10^{-7} - 3×10^{-5}	Low	- do -	High energy stored in Elements	
R	4×10^{14}	7.5×10^{-7}	49.7×10^{-20}	Move	Highest energy is	Seven
O				- ment of	stored in 118	
Y					elements	Colors
G				Valence	by fusion	
B					Under Seven	
I					colour - crystals	
V	- 8×10^{14}	- 4×10^{-7}	-25.1 x	Electrons	Cycle	Zone
Ultra-Violet rays (UV)	10^{16} - $8 \times$	3×10^{-8} - $4 \times 10^{-}$	High	- do -	- do -	

	10^{14}	7				Black Matter Zone (50 per cent dark energy)
X- rays	3×10^{19} - 10^{16}	1×10^{-10} - 3×10^{-8}	Higher	Movement of dark matter and smaller particles	High energy stored inside sub-atomic particles	
γ -rays			Highest		Highest energy of electromagnetic waves stored inside dark matter particles in space	
Cosmic Rays	5×10^{20} - 3×10^{19}	6×10^{-13} - 10^{-10}	Highest	- do - - do -	- do -	

Table 5.3

'Sound Wave Packets" are created by vocal cord and after passing through teeth and tongue it is emitted by mouth of human being. Sound Wave Packets make their existence within atmosphere of planet bound along three axes and affect all living and non-living things of earth. The extent of atmosphere of planet is controlled by pressure, temperature and volume along three axes. Ozone layer limits the atmosphere and keeps a check over it. The sound wave letters and 'Akshars' cannot exist beyond atmosphere of Earth. When a particle moves through space, it carries kinetic energy with itself. Wherever the particle goes the energy is transported through it.

In the musical instruments, there is loss of energy due to air viscosity and due to lack of flexibility of string in instrument. In practice energy is lost by several processes and the loss increases as the amplitude of vibration increases. Finally a balance is reached when the rate of energy received from any source equals the rate of energy lost due to various damping processes. In steady state, waves of constant amplitude are present on the string from left to right as well as from right to left. The waves propagating in opposite directions, produce standing waves on the string. Nodes and antinodes are formed and the amplitude of vibration are large at antinodes. The phase difference with new waves depends on the number of reflections experienced by the original wave and depends on time. In a string at certain time instants the amplitude is enhanced and at some other time instants the amplitude is decreased. The average amplitude of string does not increase by interference and the vibrations are small. The string absorbs only a small amount of energy from the source.

146

VACUUM AND ANTI-MATTER ZONES IN SPACE. PERIODIC MOTION OF MATTER WAVES GIVES BIRTH TO CIRCULAR MOTION OF PARTICLES AND SELF GRAVITATION OF PARTICLES TAKES PLACE IN SPACE.

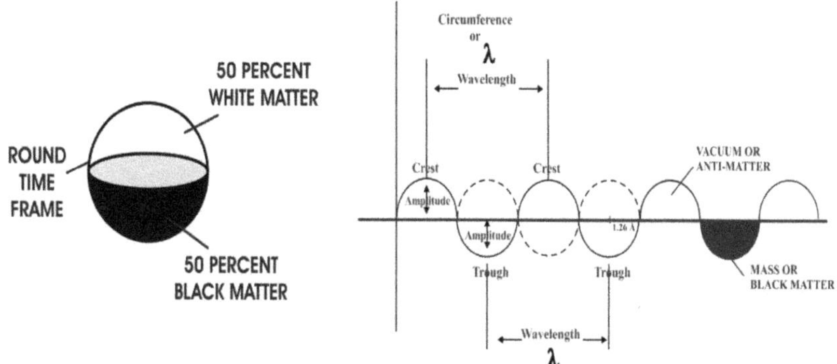

CREST PORTION OF MATTER WAVE CREATES VACUUM OR ANTI-MATTER ZONES. TROUGH PORTION OF MATTER WAVE CREATES MASS PARTICLES OR MATTER OR MATTER ZONES DURING CREATION INSIDE ATOMS OF ELEMENTS. WAVELENGTH OF ONE WAVE BECOMES EQUAL TO CIRCUMFERENCE OF ROUND SPHERE. SELF GRAVITATION OF MASS IN SPACE CREATES THREE-DIMENSIONAL STRUCTURES AND CONVERTS MASS INTO MATTER INSIDE PLANETS AND STARS. SPHERICAL TIME FRAME ENCLOSES VACUUM AND MASS AND TIME EMERGES IN VACUUM MEDIUM WITH MATTER WAVES. CREST PORTION OF WAVE CREATES WHITE MATTER AND VOWELS WHEREAS TROUGH PORTION OF WAVE CREATES BLACK MASS AND CONSONANTS. CREST PORTION CREATES VACUUM AND ANTI-MATTER. TROUGH PORTION CREATES MASS OR BLACK MATTER AND MATTER ZONES. WAVELENGTH OF ONE WAVE PIECE WHICH INCLUDES CREST AND TROUGH IS EQUIVALENT TO CIRCUMFERENCE OF ROUND WAVE IN SPACE. BRAIN CELLS OF ANIMALS AND HUMAN BEINGS HAS THE CAPACITY TO CONTRACT AND EXPAND WAVES TO THE DESIRED EXTENT DEPENDING UPON NERVES OF LIVING BODY. PARTICLES IN HUMAN BRAIN AND VOCAL CORD OF ANIMALS AND HUMAN BEINGS HAVE THE CAPACITY TO CONTRACT AND EXPAND WAVES TO THE DESIRED EXTENT OF ELECTROMAGNETIC WAVES DEPENDING UPON NERVES OF LIVING BODY. SOUND WAVE PACKETS EMITTED FROM MOUTH CONTAIN LETTERS AND WORDS IN WAVY FORMS. THE HUMAN BODY EXHALES CARBON DIOXIDE, NITROGEN GAS OF ATMOSPHERE, DUST PARTICLES AND WATER VAPOUR. 'SOUND WAVE PACKETS' COME OUT WITH GASES FROM MOUTH OF BODY IN THE ATMOSPHERE AND PROPAGATE EVERYWHERE. CREST PORTION CREATES SIXTEEN VOWELS AND TROUGH PORTION CREATES THIRTY TWO CONSONANT LETTERS. CONSONANTS SETTLE DOUBLE THE MASS OF VOWELS DURING FORMATION OF LETTERS.

Fig. 5.11

The contraction and expansion of any object can be measured with the help of two parameters, i.e., circumference and diameter of the object which can squeeze mass from eleven dimensions to three dimensions in space. The human brain has capability to contract the diameter of elliptical cell from 11 to 7 and then to 5.5 units inside circumference of cell of 22 units. The contraction of cells of neurons helps human brain to pass through vacuum medium and thought process of human brain with the help of neuron cells can perceive the movement pattern of planets and stars. The human brain with the help of neuron cells can perceive cyclic movement of energy in the universe. The planets generally develop a protective covering with liquid and gas states around them. In case of earth ozone layer forms an outer covering and retains mass in gas and liquid form in atmosphere.

147

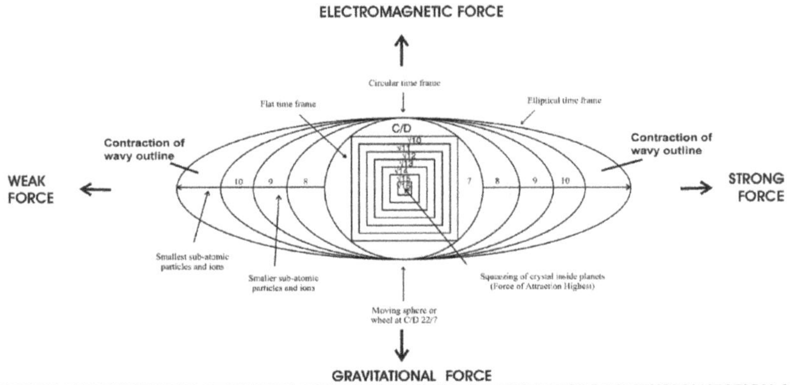

CONTRACTION AND EXPANSION OF MATTER WAVES IN VACUUM MEDIUM LEADS TO CRYSTALLIZATION AND FORMATION OF THREE-DIMENSIONAL PARTICLES IN SPACE. TWO PARAMETERS OF ANY OBJECT, i. e., CIRCUMFERENCE AND DIAMETER DECIDE THE SHAPE AND SIZE OF EVERY OBJECT WITH MASS IN THE UNIVERSE. CONTRACTION AND EXPANSION OF NERVE CELLS INSIDE BRAIN CAN CHANGE FROM ELEVEN DIMENSIONS TO THREE DIMENSIONS AND CREATE VACUUM MEDIUM WHICH INCREASES THE POWER OF IMAGINATION OF BRAIN OF HUMAN BEINGS. CONTRACTION AND EXPANSION OF NERVE CELLS INSIDE HUMAN BRAIN IMPROVES THE IMAGINATION AND PERCEPTION OF HUMAN BRAIN AND CONNECTS HUMAN BODY WITH VACUUM MEDIUM IN SPACE. CONTRACTION AND CONVERSION OF WAVES INTO MASS PARTICLES AND STORAGE OF MATTER INSIDE BRAIN CELLS SHOWS THAT HUMAN NERVOUS SYSTEM IS CONNECTED WITH VACUUM MEDIUM, ASTRAL BODY, PLANETS AND STARS IN SPACE. CONTRACTION AND CONVERSION OF WAVES INTO MASS PARTICLES TAKES PLACE DUE TO SQUEEZING OF DIAMETER OF WAVES ALONG THREE AXES. IMAGINATION OF HIGHER ANIMALS AND HUMAN BEINGS DUE TO CONTRACTION AND EXPANSION OF NEURONS CAN REACH DISTANT PARTS OF STAR DYNASTIES WITHIN FRACTION OF SECONDS.

Fig. 5.12

When a disturbance is localized only to a small part of the space at a time, we say that a wave pulse is passing through that part of the space. If the source is active for some extended time repeating its motion several times, we get a wave train or a wave packet. The velocity of a wave travelling on a string depends on the elastic and the inertia properties of the string. When a part of the string gets disturbed it exerts an extra force on the neighboring part because of the elastic property. The neighboring part responds to this force and the response depends on the inertia property. The elastic force in the string is measured by its tension and the inertia by its mass per unit length. When two or more waves pass through the same region simultaneously we say that the waves interfere or interference of waves takes place. The principle of superposition says that the phenomenon of wave interference is remarkably simple. Each wave makes its own contribution to the disturbance no matter what other waves are doing.

The universe is composed of two types of waves, i.e., electromagnetic waves and matter waves. The energy of electromagnetic waves breaks into two charged particles, -Ve charged particles and +Ve charged particles which combine to form seven crystal systems. The mass component inherent in the particles is instrumental in transferring the energy from one point to other. As much will be the stretch of diameter component in the wave and as much will be the value of diameter, so high and quick will be the transmission of energy in the medium from one point to other point. Thus, waves with highest circumference are better transmitters of energy as compared to the waves with smaller circumference.

The waves can be produced on wire by vibrating a tuning fork (by holding its stem and gently hitting a prong on a rubber pad) and pressing its stem on the platform of sound box of the sonometer. The simple harmonic disturbance is transmitted to the wire through the bridges. The frequency of vibration is same as that of tuning fork. If this frequency happens to be equal to one of the natural frequencies of wire, standing waves with large amplitudes are set up on it. The tuning fork is then said to be in resonance or in unison with the wire. If the disturbance produced is along a fixed direction, it is said that the wave is linearly polarized in that direction. If particle of string moves in small circle as wave passes through it the wave is called circularly polarized. If particle moves and goes in ellipse the wave is called elliptically polarized. If particles are randomly displaced in the plane perpendicular to the direction of propagation of wave it is called un-polarized.

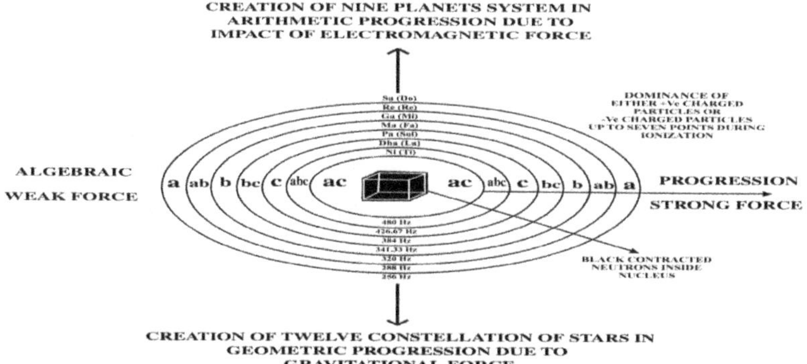

DEVELOPMENT OF NON-METALLIC AND METALLIC IONS TAKES PLACE IN SEVEN COLOR REGIONS IN FOURTEEN MATTER ZONES INSIDE PLANETS AND STARS IN ARITHMETIC AND ALGEBRAIC PROGRESSION. SOUND WAVES CAN PROLIFERATE WITHIN ATMOSPHERIC COVERING OF PLANETS ONLY. SOUND WAVES ACT AS SEVEN 'WAVE PACKETS' INSIDE PLANETS ATMOSPHERE BOUND BY THREE AXES ATTACHMENT. SOUND WAVES ACT AS THUD OUTSIDE ATMOSPHERIC COVERING OF PLANET IN SPACE. SEVEN FREQUENCIES OF SOUND WAVES ARE ACTIVE WITHIN ATMOSPHERIC COVERING OF PLANETS ONLY. CREATION OF IONS, i.e., ANIONS AND CATIONS HELP IN FORMATION OF DIFFERENT TYPES OF TISSUES, ORGANS AND PARTS INSIDE ANIMAL BODY DUE TO IMPACT OF SEVEN COLORS. ATOMS OF ELEMENTS ARE CREATED WITHIN SEVEN COLORS CYCLE. ANIONS AND CATIONS ARE CREATED DUE TO IMPACT OF ENERGY OF ELECTROMAGNETIC WAVES WITHIN SEVEN COLORS. ENERGY OF ELECTROMAGNETIC WAVES IN THE RANGE OF SEVEN COLORS, i.e., 4000 Å TO 7500 Å CONVERTS INTO ELECTRIC ENERGY DUE TO ELECTROMAGNETIC EFFECT WHICH PRODUCES SEVEN ANIONS AND SEVEN CATIONS.

Fig. 5.13

The energy of electromagnetic waves is squeezed and stored inside charged sub-atomic particles of different elements in conch shell manner in fourteen matter zones within colors cycle. The intermixing of electromagnetic waves in the range 4000 Å to 7500 Å produces many color waves which store energy inside elements. The emission and absorption spectra of different elements show lines and bands which are produced by energy of their electromagnetic waves. A stationary electric charge produces a static electric field around it. A steady current implies the uniform flow of electric charges. Since, a steady electric current produces a steady magnetic field around it, it follows that an electric charge in uniform motion produces a steady or stationary electric field. An accelerated charge should produce a magnetic field, which varies with time and depends on space. An electromagnetic wave is associated with a magnetic field, which is dependent on time and space, it follows that an accelerated charge is the source of electromagnetic wave. The most common way of possessing accelerated motion is to possess simple harmonic motion.

A charge oscillating harmonically with a frequency v produces electric and magnetic fields at that point, which vary sinusoidally with the frequency v and then produce electromagnetic waves of same frequency. The variations in electric and magnetic fields in an electromagnetic wave are perpendicular to each other and to the direction of propagation of the wave. The electromagnetic waves do not require any material medium and they can propagate in free space with the velocity of light. The orderly distribution of electromagnetic waves (according to wavelength or frequency) in the form of distinct groups having widely differing properties is called electromagnetic spectrum. Power waves have very high wavelength range varying between 5×10^6 - 6×10^6 meters. The frequency of power waves varies from a few Hz to 10^3 Hz and it contains particles of lowest energy. Sound waves belong to the category of power waves.

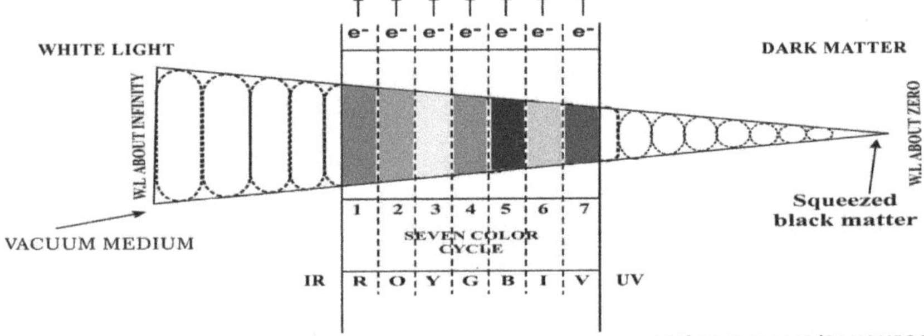

INNER MASS OF PARTICLES OF DIFFERENT CIRCUMFERENCES IS LOCKED INTO 360° TIME FRAME (24 HOURS FIXED TIME PERIOD OF DAY IN SEVEN DAYS WEEK). SEVEN SYSTEMS DEVELOP AROUND CENTRAL BLACK HARD TISSUES INSIDE ANIMAL BODY. VIOLET COLOR DEVELOPS CONDUCTING TISSUES WHICH HELP TRANSPORT MINERALS THROUGHOUT ANIMAL BODY. INDIGO COLOR HELPS DEVELOP URINO-GENITAL SYSTEM INSIDE ANIMAL BODY. BLUE COLOR DEVELOPS CARDIO-VASCULAR SYSTEM WHICH HELP TRANSPORT LIQUIDS THROUGHOUT THE ANIMAL BODY. GREEN COLOR HELPS DEVELOP ENTIRE NERVOUS SYSTEM INSIDE ANIMAL BODY. YELLOW COLOR IMPROVES DIGESTION, METABOLISM AND ENERGY SYNTHESIS WITHIN ANIMAL BODY. ORANGE COLOR HELPS IN GROWH OF SOFT TISSUES, EPIDERMIS AND PORES THROUGHOUT THE ANIMAL BODY. RED COLOR DEVELOPS HARD TISSUES WHICH PROVIDE SOLIDITY, STRENGTH AND HELP IN VERTICAL GROWTH OF ANIMAL BODY. CREATION OF IONS, i.e., ANIONS AND CATIONS HELP IN FORMATION OF DIFFERENT TYPES OF TISSUES, ORGANS AND PARTS INSIDE ANIMAL BODY DUE TO IMPACT OF SEVEN COLORS. IN THIS PROCESS ELECTROMAGNETIC ENERGY IS CONVERTED INTO ELECTRIC ENERGY. POSITIVELY CHARGED PARTICLES SHAPE AXIAL RATIOS AND NEGATIVELY CHARGED PARTICLES SHAPE AXIAL ANGLES IN CRYSTALS OF ATOMS OF ELEMENTS. DURING THIS PROCESS ELECTRIC ENERGY OF PARTICLES IS CONVERTED INTO CHEMICAL ENERGY STORED INSIDE ATOMS.

Fig. 5.14

Sound waves are emitted by collision of planets and stars in space. It is produced by thunderstorm during lightning in sky and waves in the range of power waves are produced on planets and stars. Collision of meteorites and asteroids also produces sound waves on planets and stars. The electromagnetic waves are classified according to type of excitation. Overlapping in certain parts of the spectrum means that corresponding wavelengths can be produced by two methods. For example, 10^{-4}m waves can be produced both with the help of an artificial oscillator and in the process of thermal radiation. It may be pointed out that the physical properties of electromagnetic waves are determined by the wavelength and not by the method of their excitation.

During process of nucleosynthesis, intermixing of different energy levels (colors) is observed. Energy levels show gradual contraction and absorption of maximum waves per cm towards black and dark color region of spectra. The energy of electromagnetic waves breaks into two charged particles, -Ve charged particles and +Ve charged particles which combine to form seven crystal systems. Electromagnetic waves are produced by accelerated charges. Electromagnetic waves do not require any material medium for their propagation. The electromagnetic waves obey the principle of superposition. The energy in electromagnetic waves is divided equally between the electric and magnetic field vectors. The electric current is shaped by negatively charged particles and positively charged particles. While light is polychromatic light and has all the seven wave bands present in it.

'AKSHARA' IS CREATED BY THREE LETTERS 'A' + 'KSHA' + 'RA'.

'KSHARA' MEANS MASS PARTICLES THAT ARE PERISHABLE AND 'A' MEANS SOMETHING THAT IS NOT PERISHABLE. SO, 'AKSHARA' MEANS ATOM OF ELEMENT HAVING MASS PARTICLES WHICH ARE NOT PERISHABLE. EXAMPLES ARE A, AA, I, KA, KHA, GA AND SA ETC. POWER WAVES IN THE FREQUENCY RANGE 256 Hz TO 512 Hz CREATE "SOUND WAVE PACKETS WITH MASS PARTICLES' OR LETTERS OR 'AKSHARS' LIKE ATOMS OF ELEMENTS WITHIN ATMOSPHERE OF PLANET EARTH. THE ENERGY OF ELECTROMAGNETIC WAVES OF THREE FUNDAMENTAL SUB-ATOMIC PARTICLES, i.e., ELECTRONS, PROTONS AND NEUTRONS CREATE ATOMS OF ELEMENTS OR LETTERS OR 'AKSHARS'. THE IMPACT OF FUNDAMENTAL PARTICLES TAKES PLACE ALONG THREE AXES DUE TO PRESSURE, TEMPERATURE AND VOLUME EFFECT OF ATMOSPHERE. PROTONS EFFECT PRESSURE, NEUTRONS EFFECT TEMPERATURE AND ELECTRONS CONTROL VOLUME OF LETTERS OR 'AKSHARS' WITHIN ATMOSPHERE OF PLANET. CREATION OF LETTERS LIKE ATOMS OF ELEMENTS ARE CONTROLLED BY TEMPERATURE, VOLUME AND PRESSURE ALONG THREE AXES ON PLANETS HAVING ATMOSPHERE. POWER WAVE PACKETS ARE EMITTED BY VOCAL CORDS OF ANIMALS AND HUMAN BEINGS AND INSTRUMENTS OF HUMAN BEINGS ON PLANET BUT THEY WILL FAIL TO EXIST ON PLANETS AND STARS WHICH HAVE NO ATMOSPHERE.

5.3 ATOMIC THEORY OF 'SOUND WAVE PACKETS'

A 'wave packet' refers to the case where two or more waves exist together. The length of electromagnetic waves varies from below zero angstrom to about infinite angstrom. The electromagnetic waves in the range 4000 angstrom to 7500 angstrom make this perceptible world of solid particles, atoms and elements. The electromagnetic waves of higher wavelengths having low energy content move in space and vacuum whereas electromagnetic waves of lower wavelengths having high-energy contents are absorbed in the dark core of astral bodies. The electromagnetic waves below 4000 Angstrom and above 7500 Angstrom are either absorbed or radiated or re-radiated by spherical astral bodies and planets.

Power wave packets containing mass of atoms create different types of Sound Waves. The sound produced at some point by a vibrating source travels in all directions in the medium if medium is extended. The sound wave packets act as three dimensional waves and effect life forms along three axes as three dimensional astral bodies. For a small source we get spherical layers of the medium on which the pressure at various elements have the same phase at a given instant. The surface through the points having same phase of disturbance is called a wave front. For a homogeneous and isotropic medium the wave fronts are normal to the direction of propagation. For a point source placed in a homogeneous and isotropic medium the wave fronts are spherical and the wave is called a spherical wave. If sound is produced by vibrating a large plane sheet, the disturbance produced in front of the sheet will have the same phase on a plane parallel to the sheet. The wave fronts are then planes (neglecting the end effects) and the direction of propagation is perpendicular to these planes. Such waves are called plane waves. The wave front can have several other shapes. A longitudinal wave in a fluid can be described either in terms of longitudinal displacement suffered by the particles of the medium or in terms of the excess pressure generated due to compression or rarefaction.

THREE AXES ATTACHMENT OF THREE FUNDAMENTAL PARTICLES INSIDE WAVES IS INSTRUMENTAL IN CREATING 'SOUND WAVE PACKETS' IN THE ATMOSPHERE OF PLANETS.

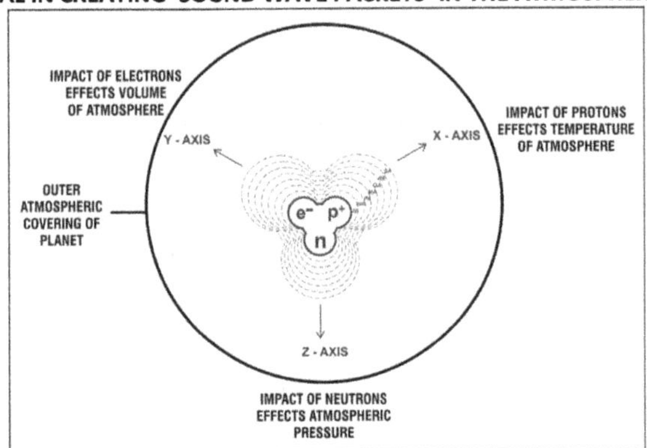

'SOUND WAVE PACKETS' EMITTED FROM MOUTH ARE MADE UP OF AIR WHICH CARRIES LETTERS AND WORDS IN GAS FORM AND ARE ACTIVE WITHIN ATMOSPHERE OF EARTH. THE HUMAN BODY INHALES OXYGEN AND RELEASES CARBON DIOXIDE DURING BREATHING. THE BODY EXHALES CARBON DIOXIDE, NITROGEN, DUST PARTICLES AND WATER VAPOUR ETC ALONG WITH SOUND WAVE PACKETS. 'SOUND WAVE PACKETS' ARE CREATED WITH LOW FREQUENCY POWER WAVES INSIDE THE ATMOSPHERE OF PLANET. THESE PACKETS CONTAIN HIGHER WAVELENGTH AND PROLIFERATE ALONG THREE AXES ON PLANETS. 'SOUND WAVE PACKETS' ARE EFFECTIVE WITHIN OZONE LAYER OF ATMOSPHERE AND ARE NOT ACTIVE OUTSIDE ATMOSPHERIC COVERING ON ANY PLANET. 'SOUND WAVE PACKETS' WILL NOT ACT ON SURFACE OF MOON, MARS AND MOONS OF OTHER PLANETS. 'POWER WAVE PACKETS' ARE CREATED DUE TO IMPACT OF ELECTRONS, PROTONS AND NEUTRONS ALONG THREE AXES INSIDE ATMOSPHERE OF PLANETS. POWER WAVE PACKETS ARE EMITTED BY LIVING ANIMALS AND HUMAN BEINGS AND THEY ARE CAPABLE TO AFFECT HUMAN BODY BECAUSE THEY ARE MADE UP OF ENERGY OF ELECTROMAGNETIC WAVES. POWER WAVES CONTAIN WAVES OF HIGHER WAVELENGTH WHEREAS ENERGY OF HUMAN BODY CONTAIN WAVES IN THE RANGE 4000 ANGSTROMS TO 7500 ANGSTROMS. ELECTROMAGNETIC WAVES IN THE RANGE 4000 ANGSTROMS TO 7500 ANGSTROMS CREATE BODY OF ALL LIVING BEINGS. POWER WAVES HAVING HIGHER WAVELENGTH ARE MORE POWERFUL THAN ELECTROMAGNETIC WAVES IN THE RANGE 4000 ANGSTROMS TO 7500 ANGSTROMS. EVERY ELEMENT CREATES ONE LETTER OR 'AKSHAR' AND 118 'AKSHARS' ARE CREATED IN TOTAL IN THE UNIVERSE WHICH TAKES PART IN CREATION OF HUMAN BODY AND LIFE FORMS. SOUND WAVES CREATE 118 ATOMIC PACKETS OF ATOMS OF ELEMENTS AS LETTERS WITHIN ATMOSPHERE OF PLANET EARTH. IN THE SOUND WAVE PACKET, MASS OF NEUTRON SHAPES CONSONANTS WHEREAS BOTH CHARGES SHAPE VOWELS. COMBINED IMPACT OF BOTH GIVES SHAPE TO *AKSHARAS* (LETTERS) AND *SHABDAS* (WORDS).

Fig. 5.15

The disturbance produced by a source of sound is not always a sine wave. A pure sine wave has a unique frequency but a disturbance of other wave form may have many frequency components in it. The compression and rarefaction in a sound wave is caused due to the back and forth motion of the particles of the medium. This motion is along the direction of propagation of sound and hence the sound waves are longitudinal. All directions perpendicular to the direction of propagation are equivalent and hence sound waves cannot be polarized.

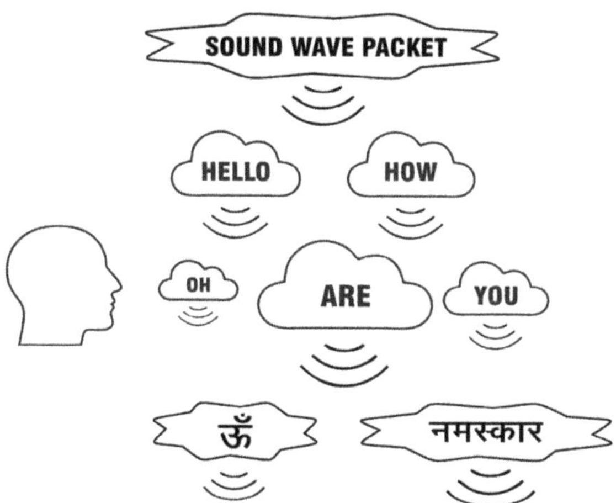

SOUND WAVE PACKETS COME OUT FROM MOUTH OF HUMAN BODY AND IT FLOATS IN AIR IN THE ATMOSPHERE. THE MOMENT LIPS ARE CLOSED THE WAVE PACKETS START FLOATING AND MOVING IN AIR IN THE ATMOSPHERE OF PLANET. THESE 'SOUND WAVE PACKETS' ACT INDEPENDENTLY AND EFFECT HUMAN BODY AND ALL LIVING BEINGS OF PLANET. THE 'SOUND WAVE PACKETS' CAN EXIST IN THE ATMOSPHERE ONLY AND BEYOND THAT THEY LOSE THEIR EXISTENCE BECAUSE THEY CAN NOT BE HEARD. SOUND WAVE PACKETS EFFECT ALL OBJECTS OF ENTIRE PLANET. 'SOUND WAVE PACKETS' ARE PRODUCED LIKE LIGHTNING IN THE ATMOSPHERE WHICH EXISTS FOR A FEW SECONDS OR MINUTES, SHOWS ITS IMPACT ON ALL MATERIALS WITHIN ATMOSPHERE AND VANISHES. ITS IMPACT IS VISIBLE AFTERWARDS ON ALL LIVING BEINGS, OBJECTS AND PLANET. IT VANISHES IN THE ATMOSPHERE AND SUB-ATOMIC PARTICLES MERGE WITH AIR OF ATMOSPHERE. 'POWER WAVE PACKETS' ARE CREATED DUE TO IMPACT OF ELECTRONS, PROTONS AND NEUTRONS ALONG THREE AXES INSIDE ATMOSPHERE OF PLANETS. POWER WAVE PACKETS ARE EMITTED BY LIVING ANIMALS AND HUMAN BEINGS AND THEY ARE CAPABLE TO AFFECT HUMAN BODY BECAUSE THEY ARE MADE UP OF ENERGY OF ELECTROMAGNETIC WAVES. SOUND WAVE PACKETS ARE MADE UP OF POWER WAVES IN THE FREQUENCY RANGE Of 256 Hz TO 512 Hz.

Fig. 5.16

Transmission of sound wave packets always need a medium and they cannot travel in vacuum. Sound waves constitute alternate compression and rarefaction pulses travelling in the medium. Sound waves are audible only if the frequency of alteration of pressure is between 20 Hz to 20,000 Hz. These limits are subjective and may vary slightly from person to person. An average human ear is not able to detect disturbance in the medium if the frequency is outside this range. Electronic detectors can detect waves of lower and higher frequencies as well. A dog can hear sound of frequency up to about 50 kHz and a bat up to about 100 kHz. The waves with frequency below the audible range are called infrasonic waves and the waves with frequency above the audible range are called ultrasonic waves.

MEDIUM	SPEED (m s^{-1})	MEDIUM	SPEED (m s^{-1})
Air (dry 0^{0}C)	332	Copper	3810
Hydrogen	1330	Aluminum	5000
Water	1486	Steel	5200

Table 5.4

Speed of sound is the distance travelled per unit time by a sound wave as it propagates through an elastic medium. Speed of sound at sea level is 340.29 meters per second. In dry air at 20^{0}C (68^{0}F), the speed of sound is 343.21 meters per second or one kilometer in 2.914 second. The speed of sound in an ideal gas depends only on its temperature and composition. The speed has weak dependence on frequency and pressure in ordinary air, deviating slightly from ideal behavior. In common everyday speech, speed of sound refers to the speed of sound waves in air. The speed of sound varies from substance to substance: sound travels very slowly in gases; it travels faster in liquids; and faster still in solids. For example, sound travels at 343.21 meter per second in air, it travels at 1484 meters per second in water and at 5,120 meters per second in iron. In an exceptionally hard material such as diamond, sound travels at 12,000 meters per second, which is around the maximum speed that sound will travel under normal conditions. Sound waves in solids are composed of compression waves (as in gases and liquids), but there is also a different type of sound wave called a shear wave, which occurs only in solids. These different types of waves in solids usually travel at different speeds, as exhibited in seismology. The 'Sound Wave Packets' behave like free flowing waves within the atmospheric covering of Planets.

The emission of colors in spectra shows fixed trend in light elements but shows fluctuation in heavy elements due to increase in number of neutrons and increase in atomic mass. The circumference of circle remains the same and shows value of 22 (11 + 11) whereas the diameter squeezes from 11 to 7 and falls in the folds of seven-color cycle during contraction of mass. The flame color of elements depends upon degree of ionization of the elements. As for example, Na (11) shows yellow color, K (19) shows violet color, Sr (38) shows red color and Ba (56) shows green color. The metallic octets of elements tend to show green color spectra. The elements and their isotopes having non-metallic trend tend to show light color (red, orange and yellow) spectra whereas elements and their isotopes having metallic trend tend to show dark color (blue, indigo and violet) spectra.

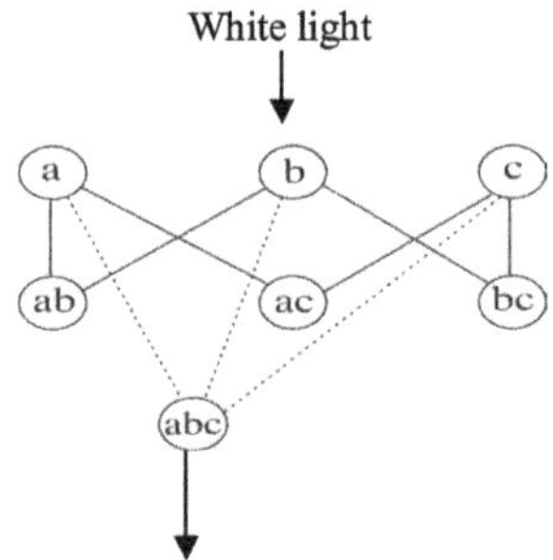

Dark energy is absorbed inside black matter

WHITE LIGHT CREATES THREE COLORS WHICH COMBINES WITH EACH OTHER AND CREATES FOUR MORE COLORS. IN THIS PROCESS SEVEN COLORS ARE CREATED FROM WHITE LIGHT IN TOTAL IN SPACE.

Fig. 5.17

154

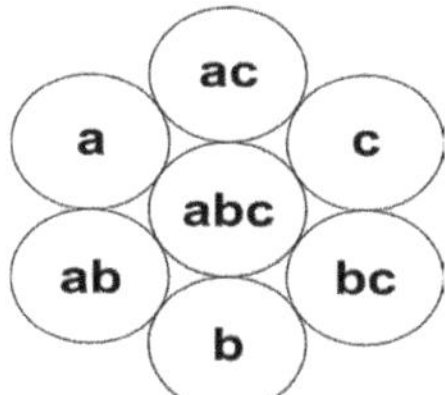

"SOUND WAVE PACKETS" ARE CREATED DUE TO INTERMINGLING OF SEVEN TYPES OF AUDIBLE SOUND WAVES. SOUND WAVE PACKETS ARE CREATED AND EMITTED FROM MOUTH IN THE PATTERN OF WORDS CREATED FROM LETTERS AND CHEMICAL COMPOUNDS CREATED FROM ATOMS OF ELEMENTS. SOUND WAVE PACKETS ARE EFFECTED BY PRESSURE, TEMPERATURE AND VOLUME OF THE LETTERS.

Fig. 5.18

The white light creates seven colors and colors maintain their identity and originality in the form of three colors, red, yellow and blue. These three colors by intermixing among themselves create four more colors, violet, orange, green and indigo. The color sequence finally merges in black region. Due to constant oscillatory movement and compression and rarefaction of waves in the space, seven colors move in alternate fashion. The overlapping of colors is observed in seven colors cycle. Colors carry energy of elements in ionized state as well as in normal state. During stage of creation the sequence of formation of color rays from white light takes place in arithmetic progression on following pattern :

1. Red colour rays   (a)
2. Yellow colour rays   (b)
3. Blue colour rays   (c)

Intermixing of above three colour rays produces all other colours. In total seven possibilities exist for creation in algebraic manner for separation of colour rays from these colours.

Red   Orange   Yellow   Green   Blue   Indigo   Violet
(a)   (ab)   (b)   (bc)   (c)   (abc)   (ac)

These seven colour rays are produced out of white light. The rainbow shows above sequence of seven colour rays. The alternating waves show following sequence of movement of colour rays.

a, ab, b, bc, c, abc, ac,
a, b, c, ac, ab, bc, abc,
a, c, ab, abc, b, ac, bc,
a, ab, b, bc, c, abc, ac.

On planets, red color substances, blue color substances and green color substances when mixed together produce white substance. The intermixing of red, green and blue atoms, molecules or compounds produces substances that look white in appearance. There are many probabilities of intermixing of electromagnetic waves in alternating fashion in space. In the alternate movement of waves, out of seven colours, the first, fourth and seventh colours are very important due to inherent energy. All the colours are moving and overlapping each other due to constant oscillatory movement of waves. The intermixing and overlapping of colour waves is seen in following manner: (i) alternate (leaving one colour). (ii) Leaving two colours, (iii) leaving three colours, (iv) leaving four colours, (v) leaving five colours. Intermixing leaving six colours jump will bring the combination back to initial sequence of colours. The colour staring from yellow colour shows that at two places the colour combination begins with yellow colour rays and ends at blue colour rays. It is not possible to get absolute white and absolute black in the shape of elements.

Mixing of red, green and blue produces white color but not white light. The storage and settlement of elements, compounds and mass particles on astral bodies takes place due to color

155

temperature and maximum mass with highest volume is supposed to sediment in red color region. White light first splits into three colors (a, b and c) and due to intermixing (ab, ac, bc and abc) creates seven colors in total. The seven stars of U. Minor and U. Major are interlinked to each other. In the zone of absorption, absorption bands are seen at different wavelengths. These absorption bands are like fingerprints that show position of planets in the ladder of energy of electromagnetic waves in every solar system. The inner black region of absorption maintains static equilibrium in planet. The intermixing and multiplication of seven colors with seven colors cycle produces a combination of 49 color crystals as follows:

		(a)	(ab)	(b)	(bc)	(c)	(abc)	(ac)
a	X =	a^2	a^2b	ab	abc	ac	a^2bc	a^2c
ab	X =	a^2b	a^2b^2	ab^2	ab^2c	abc	a^2b^2c	a^2bc
b	X =	ab	ab^2	b^2	b^2c	bc	ab^2c	abc
bc	X =	abc	ab^2c	b^2c	b^2c^2	bc^2	ab^2c^2	abc^2
c	X =	ac	abc	bc	bc^2	c^2	abc^2	ac^2
abc	X =	a^2bc	a^2b^2c	ab^2c	ab^2c^2	abc^2	$a^2b^2c^2$	a^2bc^2
ac	X =	a^2c	a^2bc	abc	abc^2	ac^2	a^2bc^2	a^2c^2

Out of 49 mixed color crystals mentioned above 7 colors show entity as individual color and rest show repetition of colors. Thus seven types of settlements of mass due to colors are produced in the shape of seven types of crystals symmetry in solid objects. There is possibility of further mixing of colors as 49 x 7 = 343 mixed colors. Out of 343 mixed colors, 230 color forms show their entity as 230 crystal forms on planets and stars. Out of 49 colors produced by intermixing of colors, 7 odd combinations as seven crystal forms are produced, 24 combinations in the form of pairs, 12 combinations in the form of quadruplets and 6 combinations in the form of equivalent crystals are produced. The details are given below:

<u>Formation of Seven odd combinations:</u>

a^2, a^2b^2, b^2, b^2c^2, c^2, $a^2b^2c^2$, a^2c^2

<u>Formation of 24 combinations in pairs:</u>

a^2b, ab, ac, a^2c,
a^2b, ab^2, a^2b^2c,
ab, ab^2, b^2c, bc,
b^2c, bc^2, ab^2c^2,
ac, bc, bc^2, ac^2,
a^2b^2c, ab^2c^2, a^2bc^2,

156

a^2c, ac^2, a^2bc^2.

<u>Formation of 12 combination in quadruplets:</u>

$abc^2, abc^2, abc^2, abc^2,$
$ab^2c, ab^2c, ab^2c, ab^2c,$
$a^2bc, a^2bc, a^2bc, a^2bc.$

<u>Formation of 6 similar combinations:</u>

abc, abc, abc, abc, abc, abc.

Seven colors create seven system in living beings. The black region acts as region of absorption and white region acts as region of emission. Seven systems develop due to contraction of mass under seven crystal systems inside living beings. Animals are created as astral bodies which take different shape as non-spherical astral bodies. The animals possess black matter in the core and centre of body and seven colors show impact on development of seven systems, organ and outer limbs.

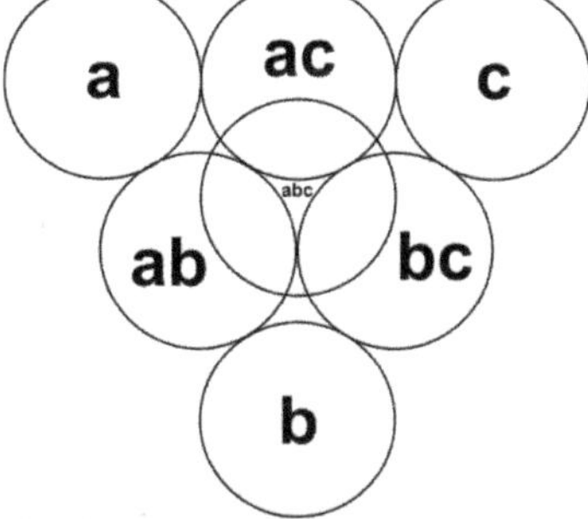

SEVEN TYPES OF *SWARAS* OR AUDIBLE SOUND WAVES COMBINE WITH EACH OTHER IN DIFFERENT FORMS AND CREATE COMPOUND WORDS AS "SOUND WAVE PACKETS". IT TAKES PLACE IN THE SIMILAR MANNER AS CHEMICAL COMPOUNDS ARE CREATED IN THE ATMOSPHERE OF EARTH AND COMPLEX WORDS ARE EMITTED FROM MOUTH OF HUMAN BEINGS. SOUND WAVE PACKETS ARE EFFECTED ALONG THREE AXES DUE TO PRESSURE, TEMPERATURE AND VOLUME. COLOR WAVES DISPERSE ALONG THREE AXES DURING CREATION AND SHOW THEIR IMPACT ON LIVING BEINGS ALONG THREE AXES. WHITE LIGHT INITIALLY CREATES RED, GREEN AND BLUE COLORS DUE TO PROMINENCE OF POSITIVELY CHARGED PARTICLES, NEUTRAL MASS PARTICLES AND NEGATIVELY CHARGED PARTICLES.

Fig. 5.19

The words are created by vocal cord and mouth parts of every animal under the guidance of nervous system and all body parts of animal and human being. The words are expression of a particular cause or sentiment with specific meaning for every animal. The words emitted by vocal cord and mouth of animal and human being effect the body parts and organs of every living body. The words are made up of wave packets of sound waves and show definite impact on body of every living being through energy of electromagnetic waves. The sound waves inherent in language create words or wave packets at particular frequency which acts as electromagnetic waves of low frequency effecting the body of living beings.Sound waves in the range 407.2 Hz to 439.5 Hz. (*Ma - Pa*) effect the growth and development of life forms, plants, animals and human body. The visible spectra from 4990 Angstrom to 5430 Angstrom improves the growth of muscles of life forms. Blue-green region of visible spectra is helpful in growth of cells and tissues.

Sound waves expand in circular orbit because expansion and contraction of neutral mass particles is seen in spherical orbits due to spherical time frame. Light waves move in elliptical orbit and stretch of orbit becomes elliptical because of contraction and expansion of charged particles, both electropositive and electronegative and charged particles tend to make the orbit egg-shaped. Elliptical orbit is egg-shaped and it is not completely elliptical. The maximum elliptical orbit on account of charges of elements is observed along one axis up to 7 point to the maximum. The growth of life forms is excellent at 18^0C on earth for all genus and species of land, water and air borne animals and plants.

If the size of atom decreases during ionization, it behaves as cation and cations have tendency to shift towards core of planet. The cations and anions of different elements having different atomic radius and different binding energy try to fit in 14 zones on human bodies. The fourteen ionic zones of human body show impact on 14 zones of space. Fourteen energy levels of cations and anions form 14 zones of electromagnetic waves in space. Out of 14 total zones, 7 anion zones actually exist in periphery of human body. So basically every human body maintains nine energy zones inside it (one non-metallic octet white zone + seven charges zone + one metallic octet black zone).

The energy of seven color electromagnetic waves ranging from 4000 Angstroms to 7500 Angstroms is absorbed in seven systems of living beings. The energy of white region above 7500 Angstroms of wavelength, which lies above seven colors, occupies the brain and tip of central nervous system in all living beings. The sound waves are longitudinal waves found roaming in the space. The light waves are transverse waves and they tend to make the orbit of astral bodies elliptical due to both charges being concentrated at two opposite polar points. The 'Sound Wave Packets' are shaped by vocal cords. They are emitted by mouths and behave as 'free moving water waves' in the atmosphere of a planet.

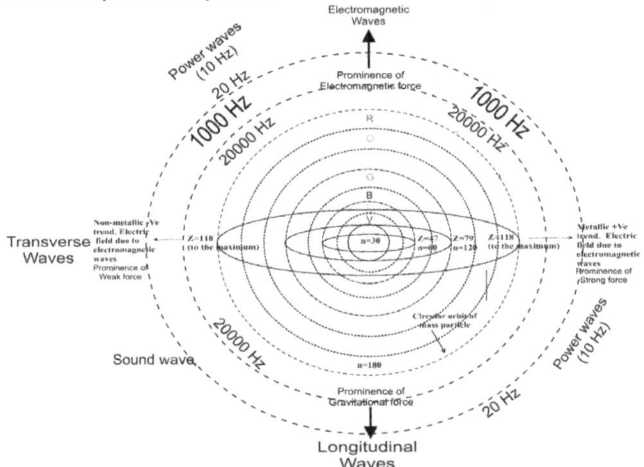

POWER WAVES IN THE FREQUENCY RANGE 256 Hz TO 512 Hz CREATE "SOUND WAVE PACKETS' OR LETTERS OR 'AKSHARS' LIKE ATOMS OF ELEMENTS WITHIN ATMOSPHERE OF PLANET EARTH. THE ENERGY OF ELECTROMAGNETIC WAVES OF THREE FUNDAMENTAL SUB-ATOMIC PARTICLES, i.e., ELECTRONS, PROTONS AND NEUTRONS CREATES ATOMS OF ELEMENTS OR LETTERS OR 'AKSHARS'. THE IMPACT OF FUNDAMENTAL PARTICLES

Fig. 5.20

'Sound Wave Packets' emitted from mouth contain gas with letters and words in gas form and are active within atmosphere of earth. The human body exhales carbon dioxide, some quantity of nitrogen gas along with other dust particles etc. The 'sound wave packets' come out with gases from mouth of body in the atmosphere and are transmitted to different places. On any planet having atmospheric covering, the movement of arrows, missiles, aeroplanes and ammunition above speed of sound should be forbidden because it will effect existence and survival of ozone layer covering around earth. Movement of any object above speed of sound will effect growth and survival of animals and human beings.

The sound produced at some point by a vibrating source travels in all directions in the medium if the medium is extended. The sound waves are, in general, three dimensional waves. For a small source, we have spherical layers of medium on which the pressure at various elements have the same phase at a given instant. The appearance of sound to human ear is characterized by three parameters, (a) pitch, (b) loudness and (c) quality. All the three are subjective description of sound though they are related to objectively defined quantities. Pitch is related to frequency, loudness is related to intensity and quality is related to waveform of sound waves. A musical scale is a sequence of frequencies which have a particularly pleasing effect on human ear. A widely used musical scale is a sequence of frequencies which have a particularly pleasing effect on human ear. A widely used musical scale, called diatonic scale, has eight frequencies covering an octave. Each frequency is called a note.

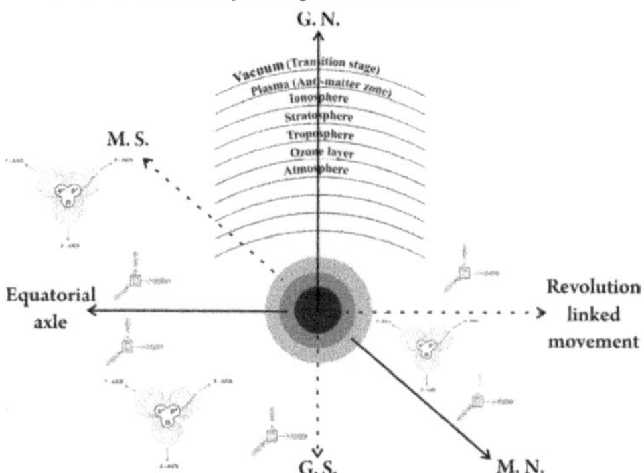

ATMOSPHERIC COVERING ON ANY PLANET. SOUND WAVE PACKETS WILL NOT ACT ON SURFACE OF MOON, MARS AND MOONS OF OTHER PLANETS. 'POWER WAVE PACKETS' ARE CREATED DUE TO IMPACT OF ELECTRONS, PROTONS AND NEUTRONS IN ATOMS ALONG THREE AXES INSIDE ATMOSPHERE OF PLANETS. POWER WAVE PACKETS ARE EMITTED BY LIVING ANIMALS AND HUMAN BEINGS AND THEY ARE CAPABLE TO AFFECT HUMAN BODY BECAUSE THEY ARE MADE UP OF ENERGY OF ELECTROMAGNETIC WAVES. POWER WAVES CONTAIN WAVES OF HIGHER WAVELENGTH WHEREAS ENERGY OF HUMAN BODY CONTAINS WAVES IN THE RANGE 4000 ANGSTROMS TO 7500 ANGSTROMS. ELECTROMAGNETIC WAVES IN THE RANGE 4000 ANGSTROMS TO 7500 ANGSTROMS CREATE BODY OF ALL LIVING BEINGS. POWER WAVES HAVING HIGHER WAVELENGTH ARE MORE POWERFUL THAN ELECTROMAGNETIC WAVES IN THE RANGE 4000 ANGSTROMS TO 7500 ANGSTROMS. ELECTROMAGNETIC ENERGY OF SEVEN COLORS CREATES CHARGED PARTICLES IN PLASMA MEDIUM IN SPACE WHICH GRADUALLY COMBINE WITH EACH OTHER TO PRODUCE SOLID PARTICLES AND THEN ATOMS OF ELEMENTS. IN THIS PROCESS ELECTROMAGNETIC ENERGY IS CONVERTED INTO ELECTRIC ENERGY. POSITIVELY CHARGED PARTICLES SHAPE AXIAL RATIOS AND NEGATIVELY CHARGED PARTICLES SHAPE AXIAL ANGLES IN CRYSTALS OF ATOMS OF ELEMENTS. DURING THIS PROCESS ELECTRIC ENERGY OF PARTICLES IS CONVERTED INTO CHEMICAL ENERGY STORED INSIDE ATOMS OF 118 ELEMENTS. AXES ATTACHMENT OF THREE FUNDAMENTAL PARTICLES INSIDE WAVES IS INSTRUMENTAL IN CREATING 'SOUND WAVE PACKETS' WITHIN ATMOSPHERE OF PLANETS.

Fig. 5.21

All the planets of any Solar system that maintain mean temperature between zero degrees Celsius to 100 degrees Celsius shall contain life forms. It is because water (H_2O) exists in three states, i.e., solid, liquid and gas state in this temperature range. The oxygen gas exists inside living beings in gas form, liquid form and solid form. The storage of O_2 inside living beings takes place in above three states, i.e., gas, liquid and solid state. Storage of water and oxygen in solid forms is least in living beings. Storage of H_2O and O_2 in liquid form is high in living beings. Storage of H_2O and O_2 in gas forms is high in living beings. As increases the storage of water and oxygen inside living beings so increases the size and age of living beings. Atmosphere develops around the planets that contain oxygen and water in solid, liquid and gas forms. Development and existence of atmosphere is compulsory for survival of multi-cellular living beings on planets. All the planets looking blue in color tend to develop atmosphere of oxygen gas and water around the planet. The atmosphere needs one covering layer to allow gases and liquids of atmosphere to survive on planet and atmosphere will be delineated along three axes by pressure, volume and temperature. The outer covering of earth called as ozone layer protects all the life forms from outside harmful radiations and it is compulsory for existence of living beings on any planet.

The sound waves are mechanical waves caused due to vibrations produced in any object placed in an elastic medium. Human being can hear vibrations of certain frequencies range only, i.e., 20 Hz to 20,000 Hz. This is called audible frequency range. The sound waves having frequency more than 20,000 Hz are called ultrasonic and waves having frequency less than 20 Hz are called infrasonic. The sound waves are further divided into two categories, (i) longitudinal waves and (ii) transverse waves. In the propagation of a longitudinal wave medium particles vibrate about their mean position in the direction of motion of the wave. When these medium particles come very close to each other it is called compression and when these particles move away it is called rarefaction.

Vocal language or oral language is produced as 'wave packet' by vocal cord as opposed to a sign language which is produced with body parts and organs. Spoken language is vocal language which comes out from mouth and different mouth parts during speaking as speech. A longitudinal wave can travel in all three medium, i.e., solids, liquids and gases. Speed of a longitudinal wave in a medium is given by, $V = \sqrt{E/d}$, where E is elasticity of the medium and d is its density. On the other hand in the propagation of transverse wave medium particles vibrate about their mean position perpendicular to the direction of motion of the wave. These waves can travel in solids and on liquid surface. Since gas molecules are relatively free from each other transverse waves are not possible in gases. The voice box in the mouth of human beings is one of the prominent sources of sound. It can produce sound waves having frequency range 100 - 1100 Hz. Different animals can also produce sound but of different frequency range. For example the mew of cat has frequency range 150-750 Hz and chirping of bird has frequency range, 2000 - 13000 Hz.

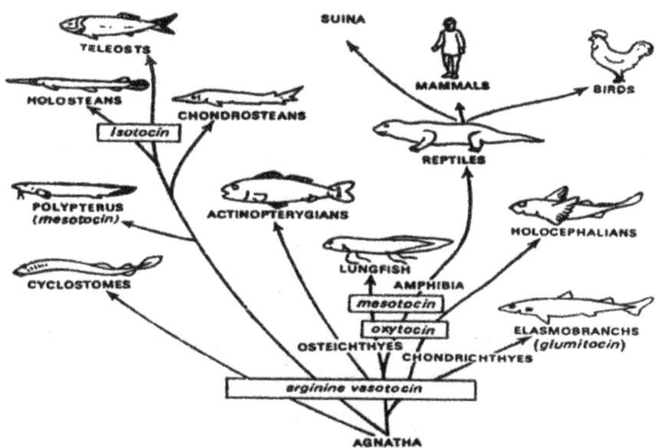

IMPACT OF HORMONES IS OBSERVED ON DEVELOPMENT OF MAJOR GROUPS OF VERTEBRATES. IT HELPS IN DEVELOPMENT OF CRANIAL NERVES, SPINAL NERVES, BODY SYSTEMS AND VOCAL CORDS OF ANIMALS. POWER WAVES IN THE FREQUENCY RANGE 256 Hz TO 512 Hz CREATE 'SOUND WAVE PACKETS' OR LETTERS OR 'AKSHARS' LIKE ATOMS OF ELEMENTS WITHIN ATMOSPHERE OF PLANET EARTH. THE SOUND WAVES INHERENT IN LANGUAGES CREATE WORDS OR WAVE PACKETS AT PARTICULAR FREQUENCY WHICH ACTS AS ELECTROMAGNETIC WAVES OF LOW FREQUENCY EFFECTING THE BODY OF LIVING BEINGS. SOUND WAVES IN THE RANGE 407.2 Hz TO 439.5 Hz. (Ma - Pa) OF SEVEN SURAS EFFECT THE GROWTH AND DEVELOPMENT OF LIFE FORMS, PLANTS, ANIMALS AND HUMAN BODY. THE VISIBLE SPECTRA FROM 4990 ANGSTROM TO 5430 ANGSTROM IMPROVES THE GROWTH OF MUSCLES OF ALL LIFE FORMS. BLUE-GREEN REGION OF VISIBLE SPECTRA IS MORE HELPFUL IN GROWTH OF CELLS AND TISSUES IN PLANTS AND ANIMALS.

Fig. 5.22

The sound is produced in a material medium by vibrating source. As the vibrating source moves forward, it compresses the medium past it, increasing the density locally. This part of the medium compresses the layer next to it by collisions. The compression travels in the medium at a speed which depends on the elastic and inertia properties of the medium. As the source moves back, it drags the medium and produces a rarefaction in the layer. The layer next to it is dragged back and thus the rarefaction pulse passes forward. In this way, compression and rarefaction pulses are produced which travel in the medium. Sound waves constitute alternate compression and rarefaction pulses travelling in the medium. The sound is audible only if the frequency of alteration of pressure is between 20 Hz to 20,000 Hz in case of human beings. The waves with frequency below audible range are called infrasonic waves and the waves with frequency above audible range are called ultrasonic waves. The compression and rarefaction in a sound wave is caused due to the back and forth motion of particles of the medium. This motion is along the direction of propagation of sound and hence sound waves are longitudinal.

The sound waves require medium for propagation and they are also called elastic or mechanical waves. These waves travel in the medium of matter waves through vibration of the medium particles about their mean positions. If the vibration of medium particles is along the

161

direction of propagation of the wave, they form compressions and rarefactions in the medium and the wave is called longitudinal wave, e.g., sound waves in air, solid and inside liquid. The longitudinal waves can travel in solid, liquid as well as in gas. On the other hand if the medium particles vibrate normal to the direction of propagation, forming crests and troughs, the wave is called transverse wave, e.g., solid waves in solid medium and in matter zones.

In the human body, breath enters spinal cord from two sides and acts as electropositive charge and as electronegative charge tubes. After passing through the inter-vertebral foramen, each spinal nerve separates into posterior and anterior branches. The posterior branch innervates the muscles and skin of the posterior portion of the body. The anterior branch innervates the limbs and the literal and anterior portions of the body. Spinal nerves in the thoracic and lumbar regions also have a visceral branch, which innervates internal organs. The meningeal branches, a small branch innervates the structures around the spinal cord. The brain and spinal cord being delicate structures are well protected by their location in bony cavities, i.e., skull and the vertebral column. They are covered by three membranes or meninzes namely (i) outer fibrous dura mater, (ii) middle arachnoid mater and (iii) inner vascular pia mater. The space between the arachnoid and pia maters contains a fluid, the cerebrospinal fluid that is also present in the ventricles of brain and central canal of the spinal cord.

The variety of sound waves production increases with increase in nerves and systems along three axes inside animal body. The central and mean temperature at 18^0 C is maintained in many bigger life forms. The living body will develop biggest size and store highest mass inside the outer covering at 18^0 C temperature. The atom of Oxygen (Z = 8) have the capacity to capture and store energy and transform the same inside living body by changing the form from gas state to liquid and then to solid state. During circulation of blood inside living body the energy is released during respiratory process and oxygen is converted into carbon dioxide which is released from living body along with voice and speech.

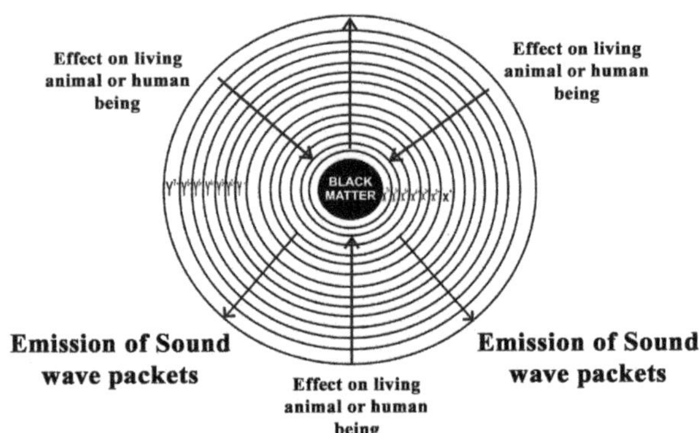

FORCES OPERATING INWARDS AND OUTWARDS ALONG THREE AXES ON ANIMALS AND HUMAN BEINGS ON PLANETS.

Fig. 5.23

Sound of bang or a big thud of collision is often heard in space. It is not sound wave and its impact is not observed on planets, stars and life forms. Sound waves are composed of seven types of radio waves with fixed wavelengths. Seven types of sound waves show significant impact on seven systems of life forms. Seven sound waves effect growth and development of body of life forms on planets. Life forms develop automatic on all planets and their size increases gradually with every round, period and group of movement of planets around stars.

The internal parts, organs and systems of life forms develop along three axes on the patterns of creation of elements in the periodic table. The external features of life forms depend upon pressure and gravity prevailing on planet and its atmosphere. It also depends upon volume and temperature of planet. The external features of life forms may show prominence along three axes during development or may show dominance of round time frame in outer covering or may show prominence of four forces in development of body parts of life forms. Atmosphere develops around the planets that contain oxygen and water in solid, liquid and gas forms. Development and existence of atmosphere is compulsory for survival of multi-cellular living beings on planets. During creation of elements, 118 elements are created in seven periods within 14 vertical rounds. Every element creates one letter or "Akshar" and 118 "Akshars" are created in total in the universe which take part in creation of human body, life forms, astral bodies, planets and stars. Sound waves are created as 118 "Atomic Packets" of atoms of elements called as letters or "Akshars".

All animal bodies in the universe are moving in perpetuity with regard to movement of astral bodies because time progresses and produces new generation of genus and species. Simultaneously time retrogresses and time can contract mass associated with 118 electrons, 118 protons and 180 neutrons to the maximum inside any animal body. The equilibrium of mass and energy is maintained by animal body along three axes by the movement of astral bodies due to daily changes, annual changes and long-term changes. Due to equatorial bulging of earth the animal forms on equator are biggest and largest in size and shape. The arctic area and Antarctica contain comparatively smaller living animals. The energy of electromagnetic waves is observed as energy of particles stored inside human bodies. Spinal cord and spinal nerves develop inside animal body and their number increases gradually reaching climax at 32. Thirty two pairs of spinal nerves are created on the pattern of 32 crystal classes inside advanced living animals and human beings.

The characteristics of living beings is observed along three axes in the manner of 32 characters (2 + 6 + 10 + 14), 12 characters and 16 characters (1 white character + 7 non-metallic character + 7 metallic character + 1 black character) on the pattern of movement of planets and stars. During course of evolution the intermixing of invertebrate and vertebrate characters and gradual evolution of mixed characters is observed which produces new genus and species.

Serial Number	Crystal Structure	Dominance and Number of Crystal Classes	Number of Spinal Nerves inside Body	Types of Nerves
1	Triclinic	2	2	One pair Coccygeal and one pair fused
2	Tetragonal	7	5	Sacral
3	Hexagonal	7	5	Lumbar
4	Trigonal	5	6	Thoracic
5	Cubic	5	6	- do -
6	Orthorhombic	3	4	Cervical
7	Monoclinic	3	4	- do -
	Total	32 Crystal Classes	32 pairs of Nerves	

Table 5.5

In the seven places of spinal cord and brain, four places (4 to 7) contain 32 pairs of spinal nerves (4 + 6 + 10 + 12). These 32 pairs of spinal nerves provide strength and stability to vertebrae, spinal cord, body parts and central nervous system. The central nervous system contains gray matter and white matter. The gray matter contains nerve cells and unmediated nerve fibres as well as neuroglia cells and fibres. The white matter contains myelinated nerve fibres, but no cell bodies; it also contains neuroglia cells and fibres. The brain contains about thousand nerves in cerebrum and cerebral cortex and they show mathematical arrangement. The nerves of brain merge into two lobes of cerebellum and form thalamus plexus and basal ganglion. Thirty-two pairs of spinal nerves are named and numbered according to the vertebra with which they are associated. They include eight pairs of cervical nerves, (i.e., 8 x 2 = 16 vocal cord nerves), twelve pairs of thoracic nerves, five pairs (ten) lumbar nerves, 6 (5 + 1) sacral nerves and two pairs of coccygeal nerves at the base of spinal cord.

Constant oscillation of waves and compression and rarefaction of waves contracts dark mass particles and makes the medium denser at some places and thinner at other places. This leads to birth of sound waves at some places and annihilation of sound waves at other place on planet. The pressure of atmosphere creates different types of animal life forms on planets. The creation of vocal cords and emission of 'Akshars' or sound waves depends upon pressure maintained by the planet. The atmospheric pressure of planet is controlled by neutrons of atoms of elements which create letters and words by contraction.

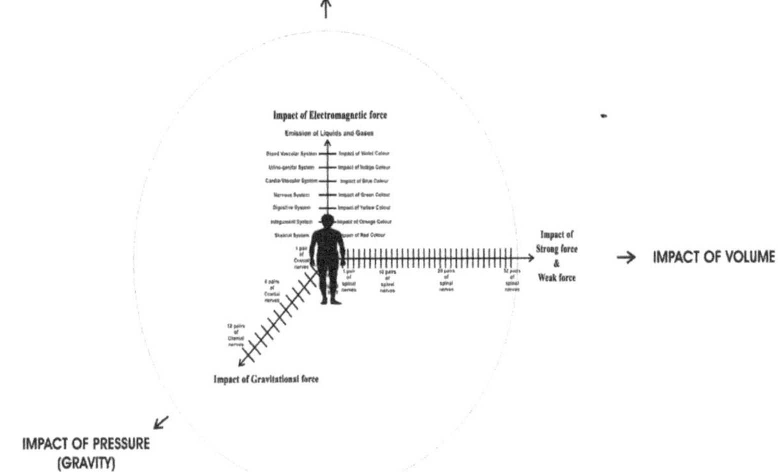

PRESSURE INCREASES INSIDE HUMAN BODY IN THE MULTIPLES OF TWELVE, TEMPERATURE IN THE MULTIPLES OF NINE AND VOLUME IN THE MULTIPLES OF 32 (2+6+10+14). ROUND OUTER COVERING OF BODY MAINTAINS THERMODYNAMIC EQUILIBRIUM ALONG THREE AXES. EVOLUTION OF CHARACTERS ALONG THREE AXES PRODUCES DIFFERENT TYPES OF ANIMALS ON PLANETS AND THERE IS GRADUAL INCREASE IN COMPLEXITY OF ORGANS AND SYSTEMS INSIDE ANIMALS AND HUMAN BEINGS.

Fig. 5.24

The living beings develop and exist as close thermodynamic systems on planets. Layer by layer deposition of elements, cells, soft tissues and hard tissues increases the size of living body along three axes on planets. In this process complex and bigger living body is produced and as big and tough is the body so long is the age of that life form. The growth and development of body may be different along three axes depending upon position of life form on planet. The impact of pressure, volume and temperature decides the size and shape of individual living being on planet

The extent of atmosphere of planet is controlled by pressure, temperature and volume along three axes. The sound waves in the low frequency range become equivalent to power waves and act as power waves. The sound waves emitted by animals and human beings are form of electromagnetic waves. The sound waves can convert into electromagnetic waves and act in similar manner in any medium in space. They show their impact on visible spectra (4000 Å to 7500 Å) of electromagnetic waves. The sound waves effect the growth and development of body parts in living animals and human beings. The electromagnetic waves having frequency between 256 Hz to 512 Hz effect body organs of living animals and human beings. The electromagnetic waves in the range 4000 Å to 7500 Å (frequency 4×10^{14} Hz $- 7.5 \times 10^{14}$ Hz) effect body organs of all living beings. The voice box in the mouth of human beings is one of the prominent sources of sound. It can produce sound waves having frequency range between 100-1100 Hz. Emission of sound wave packets and hearing by ear work in harmony and are controlled by nervous system.

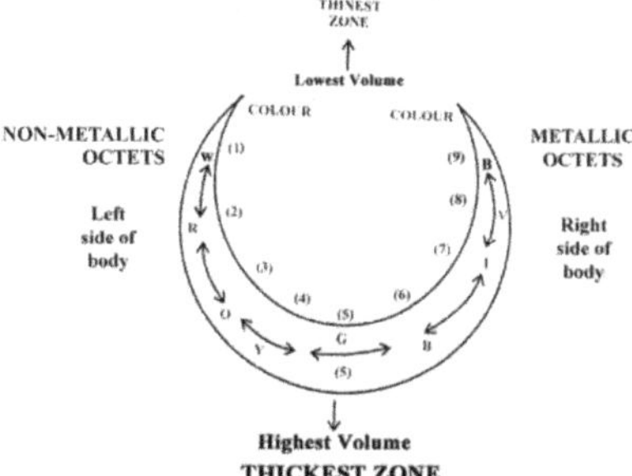

HORSE-SHOE SHAPED CYCLE OF SEDIMENTATION OF MATTER INSIDE ANIMAL BODY BASING ON STORAGE OF ENERGY OF NINE COLORS.

Fig. 5.25

Sound waves are composed of seven types of radio waves with fixed wavelengths. Seven types of sound waves show significant impact on seven systems of life forms. Seven sound waves effect growth and development of body of life forms on planets. In the universe, first emerges light waves from space having about infinite wavelength and least frequency. Then comes power waves in the lowest range of frequency. The power waves containing electromagnetic waves of lowest frequency in the range of about 50-600 Hz. behave as sound waves. The power waves emitted from vocal cords of animals in the range of 50-600 Hz. are heard in the atmosphere of earth and effect ear drum in the prevalent atmosphere. Then emerges radio waves in space with low frequency range of 3×10^4 - 3×10^7 Hz. in space. The transmission of sound waves takes place due to movement of three fundamental sub-atomic particles, i.e., electron (e-), proton (p+) and neutron (n) inside an atom. The sound waves propagate along three axes and effect body of living beings and human beings along three axes.

The highest evolved animal on any planet will develop twelve cranial nerves along one axis, seven body systems along second axis and thirty two spinal nerves along third axis. The mean temperature of planet varying between 0^0C to 18^0C creates water borne and dependent animals, e.g., invertebrates, Pisces, amphibians, whales, crocodiles etc. The mean temperature of planet varying between 18^0C to 36^0C produces hard and thick skinned animals, reptiles, dinosaurs and

165

elephants etc. Sound wave packets are created by sub-atomic particles of elements and show movement along three axes within atmosphere of planet.

The existence of continuous oxygen layer covering around planet is compulsory for regular exchange of oxygen by living beings on any planet. Thus planets having continuous and homogenous outer covering of atmosphere with oxygen all around maintain life forms in perpetuity. The existence of oxygen in three states, i.e., gas form, liquid form and solid form is compulsory for existence of life forms on any planet. Life forms develop on planets which maintain an outer covering of atmosphere between the temperature range zero degree to 100^0C. The life forms exist on blue planets, i.e., towards low wavelength of spectra. The life forms do not exist on red or white planets, i.e., towards higher wavelength of spectra. In the nine-planet system the planets closer to sun will be hottest and planets farthest from sun will be the coldest. The middle planet, which maintains a mean temperature of 18^0C, will tend to develop biggest atmosphere along with biggest life forms.

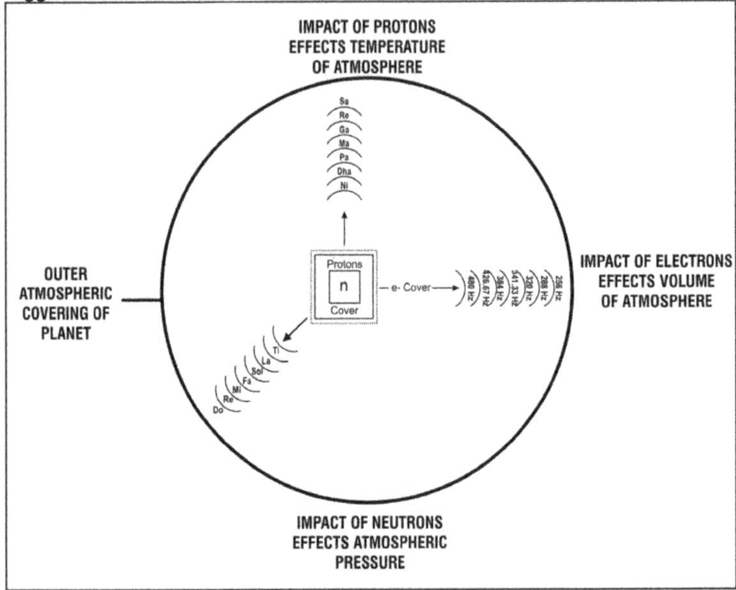

IN THE SOUND WAVE PACKETS OF WORDS OR SHABDAS, MASS OF NEUTRON SHAPES CONSONANTS WHEREAS BOTH CHARGES SHAPE VOWELS. COMBINED IMPACT OF MASS AND CHARGE GIVE SHAPE TO AKSHARAS (LETTERS) OR SHABDAS (WORDS). SUB-ATOMIC PARTICLES OF ATOM PROLIFERATE ALONG THREE AXES UPTO SEVEN POINTS AND CREATE SEVEN TYPES OF SOUND WAVE PACKETS. SOUND WAVE PACKETS MOVE FREELY WITHIN ATMOSPHERE INSIDE OZONE LAYER COVERING OF PLANET. POWER WAVES IN THE FREQUENCY RANGE 256 Hz TO 512 Hz CREATE SOUND WAVE PACKETS OR LETTERS OR 'AKSHARS' LIKE ATOMS OF ELEMENTS WITHIN ATMOSPHERE OF PLANET EARTH. THE ENERGY OF ELECTROMAGNETIC WAVES OF THREE FUNDAMENTAL SUB-ATOMIC PARTICLES, i.e., ELECTRONS, PROTONS AND NEUTRONS CREATES ATOMS OF ELEMENTS OR LETTERS OR 'AKSHARS'. THE IMPACT OF FUNDAMENTAL PARTICLES TAKES PLACE ALONG THREE AXES DUE TO PRESSURE, TEMPERATURE AND VOLUME EFFECT OF ATMOSPHERE. CREATION OF LETTERS LIKE ATOMS OF ELEMENTS ARE CONTROLLED BY TEMPERATURE, VOLUME AND PRESSURE ALONG THREE AXES ON PLANETS HAVING

ATMOSPHERE.'SOUND WAVE PACKETS' BEHAVE LIKE WATER WAVES FLOWING FREELY IN THE ATMOSPHERE OF PLANET.

Fig. 5.26

5.4 CREATION OF SEVEN *SWARAS*

Seven color electromagnetic waves produce seven 'swaras' or *suras* which are used in music and they show resemblance with voices of seven types of animals. The languages are created and produced by different animals and human beings depending upon their position, place, time and degree of evolution in any community. The degree of civilization of any community helps in developing and refining the language spoken by that community and determines the number of alphabets, consonants and vowels. The sound waves in the low frequency range become equivalent to power waves and behave as power waves. The animal life forms develop automatic on all planets where oxygen is available simultaneously in solid, liquid and gas forms. The growth of life forms is maximum at 18^0C mean temperature on planet under the prevalent pressure, volume and temperature. Life develops as unicellular organism and gradually converts into multi-cellular organism depending upon availability of 118 elements on planets.

'SOUND WAVE PACKETS' ARE PRODUCED LIKE ATOMS OF ELEMENTS WITHIN ATMOSPHERE OF PLANET. NUCLEUS OF ATOMS OF ELEMENTS IS ALWAYS SOLID IN STRUCTURE AND SEVEN TYPES OF NUCLEUS ARE FORMED INSIDE ATOMS. ELECTRONS AND PROTONS ARE NOT FOUND IN EMBEDDED FORM ON EDGES AND DIAGONALS RATHER THEY FORM A LAYER OF MASS AROUND SOLID BLACK NUCLEUS AND SEVEN TYPES OF CRYSTALS ARE PRODUCED. 'SOUND WAVE PACKETS' ARE PRODUCED AS VOICES IN GAS FORM EMITTED BY VOCAL CORDS OF HUMAN BEINGS. BOTH CHARGES TEND TO FORM VOWELS WHEREAS NEUTRAL MASS PARTICLES HELP CREATE CONSONANTS.

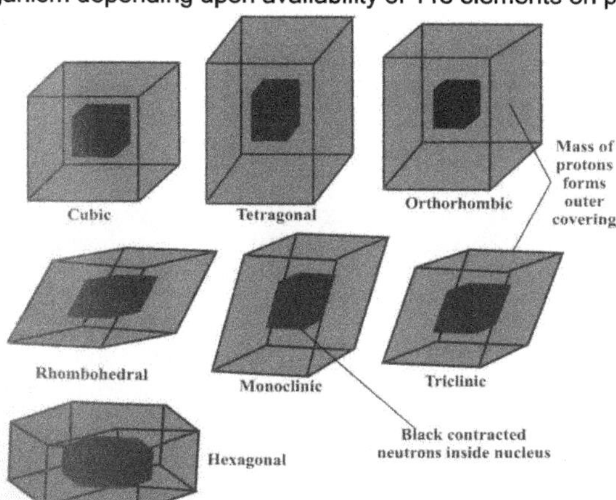

Fig. 5.27

On planets, the sound waves emitted from the vocal cord of animals and human beings and vibrations of wings of insects etc act as 'sound wave packets' with frequency equivalent to power waves within atmosphere of planet.

The spherical astral bodies, planets, living animals and human beings behave as accelerated charges because of their continuous motion and attachment with three stars and planets along three axes. The electromagnetic waves can propagate in vacuum and exhibit the phenomenon of interference, diffraction and polarization. Energy is basically white light, which acts through electromagnetic waves and when it strikes an astral body, it is either absorbed or emitted in the form of radiation. The electromagnetic waves below 4000 angstrom are fully absorbed by spherical astral bodies. The electromagnetic waves in the range 4000 angstrom to 7500 angstrom make this perceptible world of solid particles. The electromagnetic waves in the range 7500 angstrom and above are radiated. Power waves can form 'sound wave packets' due to three axes attachment of particles of atoms within atmosphere of a planet.

Sound wave packets are power waves containing neutral mass particles of smallest size with charged particles. Round wave packets in atmosphere containing neutral mass particles in it create sound waves in power wave region of electromagnetic waves. Sound wave packets are round or elliptical in shape controlled by three axes attachment within atmosphere. The +Ve charges and -Ve charges effect sound wave packets. Sound wave packets effect animal and human body along three axes. In the absence of charges, both +Ve and -Ve, it is unable to act in vacuum and in space. The sound waves are not audible in space, vacuum and in low density areas. In total seven possibilities exist in the separation of color rays and on similar lines seven sound waves are created from power waves in algebraic progression.

Red	Orange	Yellow	Green	Blue	Indigo	Violet
(a)	(ab)	(b)	(bc)	(c)	(abc)	(ac)
Sa (Do)	*Re (Re)*	*Ga (Mi)*	*Ma (Fa)*	*Pa (Sol)*	*Dha (La)*	*Ni (Ti)*

These seven color rays and seven sound waves are produced from energy of electromagnetic waves. On planets, red color substances, blue color substances and green color substances when mixed together produce white substance. The intermixing of red, green and blue atoms, molecules or compounds produces substances that look white in appearance. There are many probabilities of movement and intermixing of electromagnetic waves in alternating fashion in space. All the sound wave packets are moving and overlapping each other due to constant oscillatory movement of waves. The intermixing and overlapping of sound waves is seen in following manner: (i) alternate (leaving one). (ii) Leaving two, (iii) leaving three, (iv) leaving four, (v) leaving five. Intermixing leaving six waves jump will bring the combination back to initial sequence. The sound wave packets produce jumbled words like compounds of atoms of elements. The jumbled letters and words are created in the range 256 Hz. To 512 Hz. of electromagnetic waves.

POWER WAVES IN THE FREQUENCY RANGE 256 Hz TO 512 Hz CREATE "SOUND WAVE PACKETS' OR LETTERS OR 'AKSHARS' LIKE ATOMS OF ELEMENTS WITHIN ATMOSPHERE OF PLANET EARTH. IN SPACE, PARTICLES TAKE BIRTH AND ANNIHILATE EACH OTHR REGULARLY. THE PARTICLES ARE REFERRED TO AS "KSHAR" WHICH MEANS PERISHABLE. THE LETTERS CREATED BY ANIMALS AND HUMAN BEINGS ARE "AKSHAR" MEANING THAT THEY ARE NON-PERISHABLE. SOUND WAVE PACKETS OF ATOMS OF ELEMENTS ARE NON-PERISHABLE. THEY EFFECT HUMAN BODY SYSTEMS AND CAN BRING CHANGES IN BODY. SOUND WAVE LETTER PACKETS OR "AKSHARS" ARE MORE POWERFUL THAN SEVEN COLOR ELECTROMAGNETIC WAVES (4000 TO 7500 ANGSTROMS) WHICH ARE BUILDING BLOCKS OF HUMAN BODIES. AKSHARS FROM LETTER ONE TO 118 ACT AS BUILDING BLOCKS OF HUMAN BODY.

The upper four centres of spinal cord contain 32 pairs of spinal nerves which make the spinal cord highest evolved in human beings. In *Homo sapiens* the central nervous system is a modified tube consisting of brain, which gives rise to twelve pairs of cranial nerves and the spinal cord from which thirty-two pairs of spinal nerves emerge. The hollow portion of the tube is modified to form the ventricle cord and they contain cerebrospinal fluid. The brain stem comprises the medulla, pons and midbrain. The spinal cord is the downward continuation of the medulla. The upward breath through spinal cord and its tri-junction point makes the air enter spinal cord and takes the nervous impulse out from the body. The spinal cord retains extra air inside it and ageing stops for that time. The air inside spinal cord makes the body vital, fresh and increases the air holding capacity of the human body. The human body can stop disease, retain vitality and maintain the body alive for a longer period by retaining air inside the spinal cord. The spinal cord retains air inside it and has the capacity to stop time till the air remains inside the spinal cord.

During creation of elements, 118 elements are created in seven periods within 14 rounds. Every element creates one letter or "*Akshar*" and 118 "*Akshars*" are created in total in the universe which take part in creation of human body, life forms, astral bodies, planets and stars. Sound waves are created as 118 "Atomic Packets" of atoms of elements called as letters or "*Akshars*". Sound is produced in a material medium by a vibrating source in arithmetic progression. As the vibrating source moves forward it compresses the medium past it increasing the local density. This part of the medium compresses layer next to it by collisions. The compression travels in the medium at a speed which depends on the elastic and inertia properties of the medium. As the source moves back it drags the medium and produces a rarefaction in the layer. The layer next to it is then dragged back and thus the rarefaction pulse passes forward. In this way compression and rarefaction pulses are produced which travel in the medium. Sound waves are power waves.

The transmission of energy takes place due to contraction of circumference of waves in space. Wave motion is a mechanism by which the energy is transmitted from one point to other. The mass component inherent in the particles is instrumental in transferring the energy from one point to other. As much will be the stretch of diameter component in the wave and as much will be the value of diameter, so high and quick will be the transmission of energy in the medium from one point to other point. Thus, waves with highest circumference are better transmitters of energy as compared to the waves with smaller circumference.

The speed of compression of sound wave in solids is determined by the medium's compressibility, shear modulus and density. In fluid dynamics, the speed of sound in a fluid medium (gas or liquid) is used as a relative measure for the speed of an object moving through the medium. The ratio of speed of an object to the speed of sound in the fluid is called the object's Mach Number. Objects moving at speeds greater than Mach 1 are travelling at supersonic speeds. Sound waves emitted from vocal cords of animals and sound emitted due to movement of wings of animals are limited within seven types of waves. These sound waves are effective within atmosphere of any planet. Power waves in the frequency range 256-512 Hertz are not audible in space because they are not responded by nerves of animals and human beings. The audible nerves of animals and human beings can recognise waves in the frequency range 256-512 Hertz of power waves within atmosphere of planets. Central nervous system is effective within three axes attachment of animals and human body inside atmospheric covering of planet which is bound by pressure, temperature and volume of body along three axes. The objects moving with speed greater than Mach 1 or objects moving with supersonic speeds should be banned because they are harmful to living beings on earth. High speed causes damage to atmospheric ozone covering and will allow harmful radiation to enter the atmosphere of earth. The velocity of objects, aircrafts, missiles and rockets moving with higher velocity above Mach 1 needs to be regulated on earth.

Different animals produce sound waves in different frequency range. The mew of cat has frequency range between 150-750 Hz and chirping of bird has frequency range between 2000-13000 Hz. The sound waves emitted by different animals effect the entire gamut of life forms on planets in different frequency ranges because sound waves convert into electromagnetic waves. The sound waves emitted by animals restrict the growth and development of all animals within visible spectra (4000Å to 7500Å) of electromagnetic waves on all planets of universe. A musical scale is a sequence of frequencies which have a particularly pleasing effect on human ear. A widely used musical scale is a sequence of frequencies which have a particularly pleasing effect on human ear. A widely used musical scale, called diatonic scale, has eight frequencies covering an octave. Each frequency is called a note. Vocal cord of animals is designed in such a manner that it can emit sound wave packets as alphabets having low frequency. Human brain cells or neurons can imagine and visualize Pole Star or other distant stars in least time due to capacity of brain cells to stretch and contract in least time. Brain cells of human being have the capacity to reach from one point to another in least time due to stretching and contraction of brain cells.

On planet earth, growth pattern having fixed thermodynamic equilibrium is effective at particular pressure, volume and temperature of 18^0C. The pressure, volume and temperature may vary on other planets and other planets may produce different types of life forms depending upon their growth pattern along three axes. The highest evolved animals will show development of seven systems along one axis, twelve body parts along second axis and 32 teeth and spinal nerves (2+6+10+14) along third axis. The life forms develop close thermodynamic systems on planets. The continuity of above conditions along with outer covering layer of oxygen on planets creates different life forms during evolution. The impact of pressure, volume and temperature may vary on other planets depending upon stage of evolution of life forms on that planet.

Sound waves are longitudinal waves. The particles of medium are pushed and pulled along the direction of propagation of sound. If the disturbance produced as wave passes along direction of wave propagation, the wave is called longitudinal wave. All the waves cannot be characterized as either longitudinal or transverse. A very common example of wave that is neither longitudinal nor transverse is wave on the surface of water. On water surface the waves are produced because the water particles move in elliptic or circular path as the wave passes through them. The elliptic motion has two components, i.e., both along and perpendicular to the direction of propagation of wave.

BLACK REGION	VIOLET	INDIGO	BLUE	GREEN	YELLOW	ORANGE	RED	WHITE REGION
Zero^0 C Tempe-rature of living being	Mean Temp 4^0C. Biggest life forms are produced	Mean Temp10^0C Bigger life forms are produced	Mean Temp 18^0C	Mean Temp 25^0C	Mean Temp 30^0C	Mean Temp 35^0C	Mean Temp 50^0C to 100^0C	High Temperature of Living being up to 100^0C

Table 5.6

The existence and survival of life forms on planets depends upon mean temperature which varies between -4^0C to 100^0C. The survival of life forms is lowest at solid water (ice) level at -4^0C and at gaseous water (Vapor) level at 100^0C. The existence and survival of life forms is highest at liquid water level. The biggest life forms contain highest quantum of liquid oxygen inside multi-cellular living beings on any planet. The living animals absorb non-metallic oxygen molecules in the form of gas. The atom of oxygen contains eight protons, eight electrons and eight neutrons in atom and makes existence as non-metallic octet. The stable non-metallic octet of oxygen helps in storing liquid oxygen inside living beings and sustains life forms on planets.

Power wave packets are created due to impact of electrons, protons and neutrons along three axes inside atmosphere of planets. These wave packets are guided by volume, temperature and pressure along three axes within atmosphere of earth. Power wave packets are emitted by living animals and human beings and they are capable to affect living body because they are made up of energy of electromagnetic waves. Power waves contain waves of higher wavelength whereas living beings are created by waves in the range 4000 Angstroms to 7500 Angstroms. Electromagnetic waves in the range 4000 Angstroms to 7500 Angstroms create body of all living beings. Power waves having higher wavelength are more powerful than electromagnetic waves in the range 4000 Angstroms to 7500 Angstroms. The elements occupy particular position on planet and exist in different layers on planets. The longitudinal waves expand in space and create non-metallic octets and on similar pattern create sound waves. The speed of sound is the highest in granite having metallic octets and lowest in non-metallic octets.

Atomic theory of sound waves is based on periodic table of elements. Intermixing of sound waves create letters and words on the pattern of compounds of elements within atmosphere of planet. The creation of words along three axes is observed in similar manner as observed in periodic table of elements. 118 elements of periodic table are equivalent to 118 letters spoken by animals and human beings. The creation of 32 pairs of spinal nerves in human beings are effected by elements created in the vertical group of 32 elements. Twelve pairs of cranial nerves are created on the pattern of twelve parts of ecliptic in blocks of elements of periodic table. Words are created in jumbled form on the pattern of nine colors cycle due to prominence of electromagnetic force. Ancient people on earth had very good idea about science and technology. The human intelligence with present level of knowledge about science was available on earth about 43.2 lakh years ago. Speed of sound and its impact on ozone layer protection was known to them. They did not allow any body to fire arrows and shots above speed of sound. Firing of missiles, movement of aircrafts and ammunition above speed of sound was prohibited on earth.

Swaras are created like seven elements of periodic table and are emitted from mouth of human beings. These are:

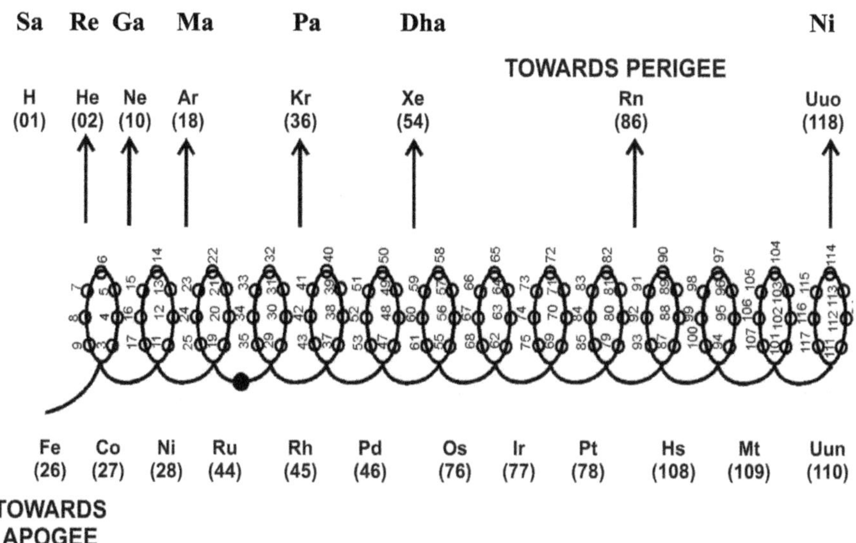

(The numbers indicate atomic numbers of elements)

FOURTEEN ROUNDS OF MOVEMENT CREATE 118 ELEMENTS ON PLANETS AND STARS. PRECESSIONARY MOVEMENT CAUSES CREATION OF 118 ELEMENTS IN FOURTEEN ROUNDS DUE TO IMPACT OF STARS OF URSAE MINOR AND URSAE MAHOR IN OUR STAR DYNASTY. CYCLIC (SPIRAL) MOVEMENT OF ENERGY TAKES PLACE IN FOURTEEN ROUNDS AND CREATES 118 ELEMENTS IN THE UNIVERSE IN CYCLIC MANNER

SEVEN SWARAS

The significance of seven Swaras (lyrical voices of classical music) is that they are created by vocal cord and instruments. These are

(a) **Shadaja means SA** (Agni Deva): Shadaja (SA) is the rapturous sound of peacock when rain clouds gather in the sky.

(b) **Rishabha means RE** (Brahma Devta): Rishabha (RE) is the bellowing of a cow when her calf is separated from her.

(c) **Gandhar means GA** (Sarasvati): Gandhara (GA) is the bleating of a goat in a flock.

(d) **Madhyam means MA** (God Mahadeva): Madhyama (MA) is the cry of a heron.

(e) **Panchama means PA** (Goddess Laxmi): Panchama (PA) is the sound of Indian Kokila (Nightingale) in spring.

(f) **Dhaivata means DHA** (Lord Ganesha): Dhaivata (DHA) is the neighing of a horse.

(g) **Nishad means NI** (Sun God): Nishada (NI) is the trumpeting of an elephant.

These are seven basic units or '*sur*' in Music. The wave on a string is caused by displacement of particles of the string. These displacements are in the direction perpendicular to the direction of propagation of wave. If the disturbance produced in a wave has a direction perpendicular to the direction of propagation of wave, the wave is called transverse wave. The wave on a string is transverse wave. Light waves are transverse waves. The electric field changes its value with space and time and the changes are propagated in space. The direction of electric field is perpendicular to the direction of propagation of light when light travels in free space. The waves carry mass particles which store energy inside themselves. Inside the atoms and matter zones of astral bodies, the energy of electromagnetic waves is contracted with mass particles and act as particles. Life forms grow, develop and exist as close thermodynamic systems on planets. The impact of pressure, volume and temperature decides the size and shape of individual living beings on planets.

$$\boxed{NI\ \ SA\ \ RE\ \ GA\ \ MA\ \ PA\ \ DHA}$$
$$\boxed{DHA\ \ NI\ \ SA\ \ RE\ \ GA\ \ MA\ \ PA}$$
$$\boxed{PA\ \ DHA\ \ NI\ \ SA\ \ RE\ \ GA\ \ MA}$$
$$\boxed{MA\ \ PA\ \ DHA\ \ NI\ \ SA\ \ RE\ \ GA}$$
$$\boxed{GA\ \ MA\ \ PA\ \ DHA\ \ NI\ \ SA\ \ RE}$$
$$\boxed{RE\ \ GA\ \ MA\ \ PA\ \ DHA\ \ NI\ \ SA}$$
$$\boxed{SA\ \ RE\ \ GA\ \ MA\ \ PA\ \ DHA\ \ NI}$$

SEVEN SWARAS ARE CREATED IN ASCENDING ORDER OF ELECTROMAGNETIC WAVES AND THEY CREATE LYRICAL VOICES. WORDS ARE CREATED FROM LETTERS AS 'WAVE PACKETS' BY VOCAL CORDS OF ANIMALS AND HUMAN BEINGS IN THE MULTIPLES OF 7 X 7. ARRANGEMENT OF LETTERS INTO 32 X 16 = 512 LETTERS IN JUMBLED FORM CREATES MANY WORDS WHICH EFFECT HUMAN BODY. CREATION OF WORDS AS 'WAVE PACKETS' TAKES PLACE DUE TO THREE AXES ATTACHMENT OF ANIMALS AND HUMAN BODIES. IT IS THREE AXES ATTACHMENT OF THREE FUNDAMENTAL PARTICLES INSIDE WAVES THAT CREATES 'SOUND WAVE PACKETS' IN THE ATMOSPHERE OF PLANETS.

Fig. 5.29

Depending upon emergence of 32 nerves from vertebral column the human body shows attachment with different waves by 32 nerves and they are observed as 32 consonant letters spoken by human beings. These 32 consonant letters are controlled by 16 cervical nerves which relate to 16 vowel letters. The vowels create sound and produce 16 types of sound waves in human beings. Thus vowels and consonants in total create 32 x 16 = 512 types of sound waves. Svaras are associated with seven body Chakras or knots inside spinal cord of human body. Muladhara is associated with Sa Swara, Svadhisthana is associated with Re Swara, Manipuraka is associated with Ga Swara, Anahata is associated with Ma Swara , Visuddha is associated with Pa Swara, Ajna is associated with Dha Swara and Saharashara is associated with Ni Swara.

Analysis of sound waves, recording and monitoring can be taken up with various instruments and methods, e.g., palatograph, kymograph, oscillograph, ink-writer, mingograph, chromograph, spectrograph, speech-stretcher, pattern play back, formant graphic machine etc. Sound waves exist and remain effective within atmosphere of planet. Outside atmosphere in space the human voice is not audible. In vacuum and space, the communication is observed through nerve cell which have the capacity to contract and expand. The contraction and expansion of nerve cells connects our senses, nervous system and memory with distant parts of universe within fraction of seconds through different frequencies of electromagnetic waves.

The transmission of sound waves takes place due to movement of three fundamental sub-atomic particles, i.e., electron (e-), proton (p+) and neutron (n) inside an atom of element. The sound waves propagate along three axes and effect body of living beings and human beings along three axes.

The intermixing of seven colors and seven sound waves or *Swaras* produce a combination of forty nine *Swaras* as follows:

SA	x	(a)	(ab)	(b)	(bc)	(c)	(abc)	(ac)
	=	SA-SA	SA-RE	SA-GA	SA-MA	SA-PA	SA-DHA	SA-NI

RE	x	(a)	(ab)	(b)	(bc)	(c)	(abc)	(ac)
	=	RE-SA	RE-RE	RE-GA	RE-MA	RE-PA	RE-DHA	RE-NI
GA	x	(a)	(ab)	(b)	(bc)	(c)	(abc)	(ac)
	=	GA-SA	GA-RE	GA-GA	GA-MA	GA-PA	GA-DHA	GA-NI
MA	x	(a)	(ab)	(b)	(bc)	(c)	(abc)	(ac)
	=	MA-SA	MA-RE	MA-GA	MA-MA	MA-PA	MA-DHA	MA-NI
PA	x	(a)	(ab)	(b)	(bc)	(c)	(abc)	(ac)
	=	PA-SA	PA-RE	PA-GA	PA-MA	PA-PA	PA-DHA	PA-NI
DHA	x	(a)	(ab)	(b)	(bc)	(c)	(abc)	(ac)
	=	DHA-SA	DHA-RE	DHA-GA	DHA-MA	DHA-PA	DHA-DHA	DHA-NI
NI	x	(a)	(ab)	(b)	(bc)	(c)	(abc)	(ac)
	=	NI-SA	NI-RE	NI-GA	NI-MA	NI-PA	NI-DHA	NI-NI

Out of 49 types of sound waves *Swaras* produced by intermixing of seven original sound waves, 7 odd combinations as seven solidified forms, 24 combinations in the form of pairs, 12 combinations in the form of quadruplets and 6 combinations in the form of equivalent waves are produced. Out of 49 mixed sound waves mentioned above, 7 show entity as individual sound waves and rest show repetition and mixing of sound waves. There is possibility of further mixing of sound waves as 49 x 7 = 343 mixed jumbled words. Out of 343 mixed sound wave *Swaras*, 230 sound wave forms show their entity as 230 crystal forms on planets and stars.

Intermixing and overlapping of sound wave *Swaras* takes place in many ways along three axes. Sound wave *Swaras* mix and create jumbled words which acts along three axes. Some of the probabilities of intermixing are given below:

SA =   SA-SA-SA   SA-RE-SA   SA-GA-SA   SA-MA-SA
         SA-PA-SA   SA-DHA-SA   SA-NI-SA

RE =   RE-SA-RE   RE-RE-RE   RE-GA-RE   RE-MA-RE
         RE-PA-RE   RE-DHA-RE   RE-NI-RE

GA =   GA-SA-GA   GA-RE-GA   GA-GA-GA   GA-MA-GA
         GA-PA-GA   GA-DHA-GA   GA-NI-GA

MA =   MA-SA-MA   MA-RE-MA   MA-GA-MA   MA-MA-MA
         MA-PA-MA   MA-DHA-MA   MA-NI-MA

PA =   PA-SA-PA   PA-RE-PA   PA-GA-PA   PA-MA-PA
         PA-PA-PA   PA-DHA-PA   PA-NI-PA

DHA =   DHA-SA-DHA   DHA-RE-DHA   DHA-GA-DHA   DHA-MA-DHA
         DHA-PA-DHA   DHA-DHA-DHA   DHA-NI-DHA

NI   =   NI-SA-NI   NI-RE-NI   NI-GA-NI   NI-MA-NI
         NI-PA-NI   NI-DHA-NI   NI-NI-NI

Proliferation of sound wave *Swaras* can take place along three axes in many more ways as mentioned below:

SA-MA-SA x MA-NI-MA x NI-MA-NI
RE-PA-RE x GA-DHA-GA x MA-PA-MA
NI-DHA-NI x SA-PA-SA x GA-NI-GA
DHA-MA-DHA x RE-GA-RE x PA-RE-PA

There are many more probabilities of intermixing of sound wave *Swaras* and creation of words effective along three axes. Intermingling may take place in many ways and production of sound wave *Swaras* depends upon the capability of vocal cord of animals to produce different types of waves on planet. *Swara* sound is produced in a material medium by a contraction and rarefaction of waves. The vibrating source of wave moves forward and compresses the medium past it, thus increasing the local density. This part of the medium compresses layer next to it by collisions. The compression travels in the medium at a speed which depends on the elastic and inertia of the medium. As the source moves back it drags the medium and produces a rarefaction in the layer. The layer next to it is then dragged back and thus the rarefaction pulse passes forward. In this way compression and rarefaction pulses are produced which travel in the medium.

Sound waves are made up of power waves. In space, power waves of electromagnetic waves act as sound waves. On planets, the sound waves emitted from the vocal cord of animals and human beings and vibrations of wings of insects etc act as 'sound wave packets' having frequency equivalent to power waves and their impact is observed on ear along three axes. The sound waves emitted by thunder and collision of astral bodies and planets in space act as thud and noise and do not have wavelength equivalent to power waves of electromagnetic waves. Formation of Sanskrit alphabets shows that it is based upon a clear understanding of sound waves.

Voice is the sound produced by humans and animals from their mouths and oral organs. It is generated by flow of air consisting mostly of O_2 and CO_2 from the lungs with fixed pressure under the supervision of vocal cord. Emission of languages vary from person to person and are effected by mouth parts, teeth, tongue and lips. Many disorders of voice are also noticed which involve problems related with pitch, loudness and quality of voice. Pitch of sound may be high or low depending upon frequency of sound waves. Loudness is perceived as volume or amplitude of the sound wave but quality refers to character or distinctive attributes of sound wave. Vocal apparatus may become impaired in case the nerves controlling larynx are impaired due to physiological reasons. Hearing by ear may also become impaired due to accident or pressure on ear or by dislocation of nerves.

IMPACT OF SOUND WAVES AND EQUIVALENT ELECTROMAGNETIC WAVES ON ANIMALS AND HUMAN BEINGS

SYM-BOL	INDIAN NAME	WESTE-RN NAME	FREQU-ENCY OF SOUND WAVE (in Hz.)	FREQUE-NCY OF ANIMAL SOUND WAVE (in Hz.)	TYPES OF WAVE	ELECTRO-MAGNETIC WAVE (in Å)	WAVE LENGTH OF EQUIV-ALENT POWER WAVES (in Meters)	ELECTRO-MAGNETIC WAVE (in Meters)
(1)	(2)	(3)	(4)	(5)	(6)	(7)	(8)	(9)
			10-20	10 Hz.	Power wave		$1 \times 10^7 - 10^{20}$	
			20 Hz.	Vocal cord of Cats	- do -		$1 \times 10^4 - 1 \times 10^7$	
			20 Hz.	Vocal cord of Animals	- do -		- do -	
C	Sa	Do	256	Vocal cord of Human Beings	Sound wave		$1 \times 10^4 - 1 \times 10^7$	
D	Re	Re	324.7	- Do -	Sound wave		- do -	
E	Ga	Mi	363.4	- Do -	Sound wave		- do -	
F	Ma	Fa	407.2	- Do -	Sound wave		- do -	
G	Pa	Sol	439.5	- Do -	Sound wave		- do -	
A	Dha	La	464.3	- Do -	Sound wave		- do -	
B	Ni	Ti	491.5	- Do -	Sound wave		- do -	

C_1	Sa	Do	512	- Do -	Sound wave			
				1100 Hz.	- do -			
			$3 \times 10^4 - 3 \times 10^8$	Vocal cord of Birds	Radio wave		$1 - 10^4$	$1 - 10^4$
				Vocal cord of Animals	- do -		$1 - 10^{-1}$	$1 - 10^{-1}$
			$3 \times 10^8 - 3 \times 10^9$ 20000 Hz.	Vibration of Insects	Micro wave			$3 \times 10^{-1} - 3 \times 10^{-5}$
			$3 \times 10^9 - 4 \times 10^{14}$	Vibration of Insects	Infra red	10000 Å	$1 \times 10^{-4} - 1 \times 10^{-7}$	$3 \times 10^{-5} - 7.5 \times 10^{-7}$
			4×10^{14}	Vibration of body and wings of Insects	Red	7500 Å		7.5×10^{-7}
				- Do -	Orange	6560 Å		
				- Do -	Yellow	6030 Å		
				- Do -	Green	5430 Å		
				- Do -	Blue	4990 Å		
				- Do -	Indigo	4650 Å		
			7.5×10^{14}	- Do -	Violet	4280 Å		4.0×10^{-7}
			$8 \times 10^{14} - 1 \times 10^{16}$		UV	4000 Å		$4 \times 10^{-7} - 3 \times 10^{-8}$
			$1 \times 10^{16} - 3 \times 10^{19}$		X – ray			$3 \times 10^{-8} - 1 \times 10^{-10}$
			$3 \times 10^{19} - 5 \times 10^{20}$		γ - ray			$1 \times 10^{-10} - 6 \times 10^{-13}$

Table 5.7

177

The smallest time frame emerges in vacuum state and time frame increases gradually in size in plasma, gas, liquid and finally in solid state. The solid state shows biggest time frame in the universe in the shape of biggest red stars. At this stage the Circumference/Diameter ratio becomes equal to 22/7 along three axes and time frame develops highest stretch as biggest red star in the universe. The smallest particles may gradually reduce in size and merge in space as absolute zero having zero circumference. Contraction of waves is observed due to stretching and contraction of circumference of mass particles from 22/11 to 22/7 in space. The compression and rarefaction of matter waves in space creates strings under black, seven colors and white regions. The change in contraction of circumference of creates different types of waves and particles. The diameter varying from 22/11 to 22/7 creates waves whereas diameter varying between 22/7 to 22/2.2 creates particles. Human brain has the capacity to contract and expand waves of different diameters and in this process can perceive about the details of distant stars and star dynasties. The imagination acting through neurons of human brain cells can reach Pole Star or other distant stars in no time due to capacity of brain cells to stretch and contract in less time.

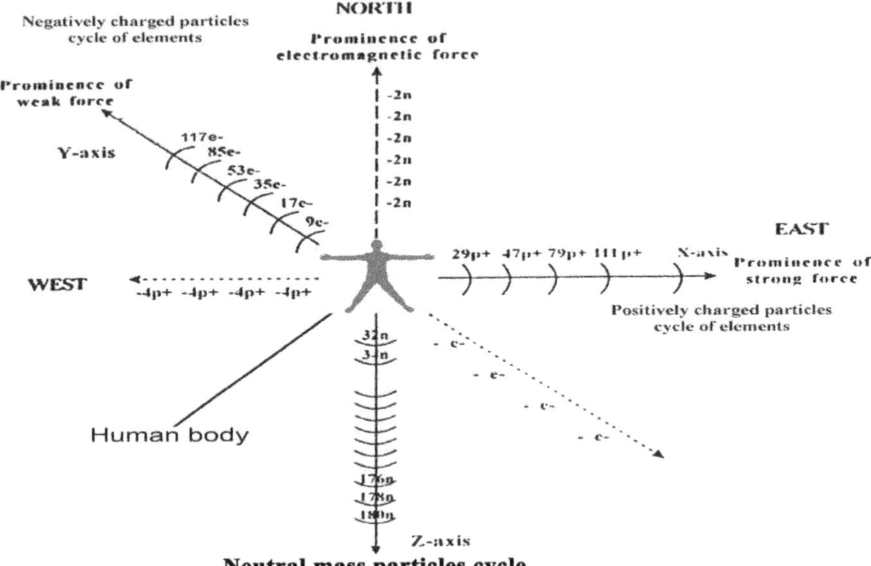

EVOLUTION OF HUMAN BODY ON PLANETS TAKES PLACE AUTOMATIC BY 118 ELEMENTS UNDER THE COMBINED IMPACT OF FOUR FORCES. THE HUMAN BODY ACTS AS ELECTROMAGNET CONTAINING BLACK ELEMENT IN THE CENTRE OF BODY.

Fig. 5.30

In the universe, four forces are equal and act simultaneously on every mass particle moving in space. Four forces act in four directions on all the atoms of elements in the universe. The impact of weak force creates -Ve particles, impact of strong force creates +Ve particles, impact of gravitational force creates neutral neutron particles and impact of electromagnetic force is observed as anti-neutron pull on atoms of elements. The forces act in four directions and create different elements with specific characteristics.

In the past knowledge and intelligence among human being was transmitted from one generation to other by '*SHRUTI*' (VERSE SPEAKING BY *GURU* AND LISTENING BY *SHISHYAS*) and '*SMRITI*' (TO MEMORISE). The means of communication, i.e., ALPHABETS, VOWELS, CONSONANTS, VERSE, SCIENTIFIC COMMUNICATION, PAPER WRITING and TRANSMISSION was least and it developed gradually on planet. Structure of atom was known to ancient people and it was preserved in the form of idols, statues, edicts, golden structures and stories from one generation to another by '*SHRUTI*' and '*SMRITI*'. Ancient civilization had clear idea about atomic structure and movement of ions in seven shells of colors. Development of non-metallic and metallic ions takes place in fourteen (seven + seven) color regions in fourteen matter zones inside planets and stars in arithmetic progression and it was transmitted through stories. SANSKRIT VISHWAVIDYALAYAH (SANSKRIT UNIVERSITY) or GURUKUL existed in many parts of the world where students used to learn, speak verses, listened from *Gurus* (*Shruti*) and memorised (*Smriti*) the verses for posterity in Gurukul.

'Power wave packets' exist as electromagnetic waves at certain wavelength and frequency inside body of living beings. One particular electromagnetic wave at particular wavelength acts as soul and attaches each individual with other individual through seven colors visible spectra and white and black regions. The electromagnetic waves of seven colors create all living beings and attach each and every living being with other living beings. In sound producing animals the sound waves act as check and balance over animals' growth, movement and migrations and behave as soul. It appears that movement pattern of astral bodies, planets and stars has been depicted in different manner in many scriptures, epics and books of concentration. The stories of different gods, goddesses, human being and places are actually stories of creation of planets and stars, equilibrium in space and destruction. The planetary stories are depicted in different manner in different epics and books and we get traces of evolution and life cycle of astral bodies, planets and stars during cyclic movement of energy in the universe. Chanting of words made up of different letters by living beings have definite impact on their body. The languages effect all body systems and bring changes inside body. It is the reason that many communities forbid people speaking bad and non-sense words. Expression from mouth involves energy transformation and speaking unhealthy words are forbidden in many societies and communities.

If the sound waves expressed through words are channelized properly and scientifically it can cure diseases and bring profound changes inside body parts and organs of human body. The movement of words along three axes is observed in similar manner as observed in periodic table of elements. The 118 elements of periodic table are equivalent to 118 words spoken by living beings. The creation of 32 pairs of spinal nerves are effected by elements created in the vertical group of 32 elements created within 32 classes of crystal symmetry. Twelve pairs of cranial nerves are created on the pattern of twelve blocks of elements of periodic table. The wave packets of sound waves are like capsules of medicine diagnosed for particular disease or ailment which can be cured through chanting of particular language. The sound waves act in the multiples of 32 (16 x 2) in *Devanagari* script effecting body systems. Sanskrit language having alphabets in the multiples of 32 effect body and body systems by mantras (chanting), letters, words and combination of words. Sanskrit language and its letters, if combined in the manner that it effects particular body part of human beings, has curative effect on human body and diseases can be cured by use of the language.

The means of communication, i.e., alphabets, vowels, consonants, verses, scientific knowledge, writing on dry leaves and barks and transmission through papers developed gradually on planet. During passage of time, fragments of knowledge became visible in different pockets throughout the world in many forms. Shruti and Smriti helped in development and spread of science and knowledge and human life grew to normal state during course of time. There may be change in magnetic axis of attraction of nine planets system due to reshuffling in relation to sun, twelve constellation of stars and Pole Star along three axes. Knowledge and intelligence will pass from one generation to another by 'SHRUTI' (VERSE SPEAKING AND LISTENING) and 'SMRITI' (MEMORISING) in human beings. Our ancestors and fore fathers were more intelligent than us. They knew how to preserve sacred things for posterity, e.g., structure of atoms, creation of planets and stars through Ramayana and Mahabharata, limit of speed of sound and ozone layer etc. through *Shruti* and *Smriti*. Ancient people used to chant '*Mantras*' and make sacrificial camp fires (*Havanas*) during worship.

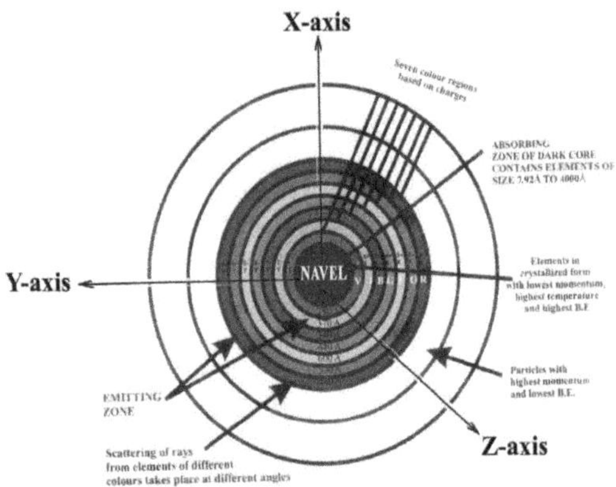

MOVEMENT OF ANIMALS AND HUMAN BEINGS TAKES PLACE ALONG THREE AXES AND CENTRE OF THREE AXES PASSES THROUGH NAVEL OF THE BODY. IMPACT OF SOUND WAVES IS OBSERVED ON BODY ALONG THREE AXES.

Fig. 5.31

The 'sound wave packets' are emissions of vocal cord and body parts of animals and human beings and these are controlled by central nervous system. The words are created by vocal cord and mouth parts of every animal under the guidance of nervous system and all body parts of animal and human being. The words are expression of a particular cause or sentiment with specific meaning for every animal. The words emitted by vocal cord and mouth of animals and human beings effect the body parts and organs of every living body. The words are made up of wave packets of sound waves and show definite impact on body of every living being through energy of electromagnetic waves. The sound waves inherent in language create words or wave packets at particular frequency which acts as electromagnetic waves of low frequency effecting the body of living beings. The words, expression and outcome of sound waves directly and indirectly relates to growth and development of human body. Human beings express their thought, feelings and ideas verbally to each other through a series of movements that change and mould the basic tone created by voice into specific and purposeful sounds which can be decoded. Speech is the outcome of coordinated muscle action in the brain, head, neck, chest and spinal cord. Speech production is a gradual process that requires regular practice by children in human being. During the process children learn how to regulate the muscles of mouth for producing sound and speech that can be understood by everybody.

The left nostril of human body inhales air and passes air to right bottom of spinal cord. The right nostril of human body inhales air and passes air to left bottom of spinal cord. The air accumulated at the bottom of spinal cord goes upwards and enters inside spinal cord and drags the fluid of spinal cord upwards. As much the spinal fluid moves inside cord so much the nerves of lower limbs and body become numb in character. The lower body parts become bereft of spinal fluid and faces of nerves inside spinal cord turn upwards. Due to control of will power on human body the spinal liquid is kept upwards and retained inside spinal cord for longer life period by human beings.

Mass extinctions took place on earth many times. Human life with present level of knowledge about science, atoms and electronic theory existed on earth earlier and traces of scientific works and nomenclature are available at many places throughout the world. Magnetic South Pole, which passes through earth, is located near Canada, probably the reason of naming Canada. White light contains electromagnetic energy which fills up entire space and creates fourteen anti-matter zones due to anti-neutron pull of atoms of elements. Stripped electrons of Fe from core areas of planets and stars shift towards crust and outside vacuum areas and create anti-matter zones in space. Due to stripping of electrons, the crystals of Fe^{7+} in core area become deformed crystal lattices and remains in molten super dense state. The core with deformed lattices acts as super conductor in molten state having very high temperature. The stripped electrons of Fe from core create a zone of negative charge and negative energy around planets and stars in vacuum. Repulsion among stripped electrons create fourteen anti-matter zones around every planet and star in space. Stripping of electrons from Fe atoms changes the domain in atoms and they face towards north direction in magnetic rods or bar magnets. Human life has flourished for the second or third time on earth after wobbling, reshuffling and destruction of some moons and planets of our solar system.

The voice type of human being classifies voice of singer by vocal range, vocal weight, tessitura, vocal timbre, vocal transition points like breaks and lifts and vocal register. Voice classification is an important instrument for singers, composers, venues and listeners for categorizing vocal properties and associating their roles with voices. The choral singers can be classified into voice parts based on their vocal range. Solo singers can be classified into voice types based on their tessitura, where voice becomes more comfortable for most of the time.

Vedic Sanskrit is the language of Veda and Vedas were written in Sanskrit. The Vedas contain hymns and incantations called *Samhitas* for theological and philosophical guidance for priests of Vedic religion. It was believed to be direct revelation to seers among early ages. Four chief collections are the Rig Veda, Sam Veda, Yajur Veda, and Atharva Veda. Cycle of creation and dissolution of planets and stars was memorized in the form of stories of Ramayana and Mahabharata and transmitted to posterity. People knew about impact of sound waves, magnet, four forces and impact of colors on living beings. Ancient works state about scientific activities like:

(a) MOVEMENT OF PLANETS AND STARS AROUND FOURTEEN '*MANUS*' OR FOURTEEN STARS OF URSAE MINOR AND URSAE MAJOR DURING CREATION AND DISSOLUTION OF PLANETS AND STARS.

(b) PRESERVATION OF SUB-ATOMIC PARTICLES IN TEMPLES AND RELIGIOUS STRUCTURES IN THE SHAPE OF ELECTRON (FEMALE GODDESS), PROTON (MALE POSITIVELY CHARGED GOD) AND NEUTRON PARTICLES (NEUTRAL BLACK GOD).

(c) RAMAYANA IS THE STORY OF CREATION OF PLANETS AND STARS DURING *TRETA* YUGA. CYCLE OF CREATION IS DEPICTED IN THE FORM OF STORY OF GODS AND GODDESSES.

(d) MAHABHARATA IS THE STORY OF CREATION OF PLANETS AND STARS IN CYCLIC MANNER IN OUR STAR DYNASTY DURING *DWAPARA* YUGA.

(e) ***Raghukul rit sada chali aai, pran jaye par vachan na jahin'.*** IT MEANS THAT SOUND WAVE PACKETS OR WORDS EMITTED THROUGH VOCAL CORDS OF HUMAN BEINGS ARE MORE POWERFUL THAN ENERGY OF SEVEN COLOR ELECTROMAGNETIC WAVES THAT CREATES HUMAN BODY AND BODY PARTS.

DURING RESHUFFLING AND WOBBLING OF PLANET EARTH IN THE PAST, ABOUT 99.99 PERCENT OF THE SUPER STRUCTURE ALONG WITH POPULATION FINISHED WITHIN THREE DAYS. IMPACT WAS MORE ON URBAN AND CIVILIZED AREAS AND LESS ON ISLANDS, ISOLATED COASTAL PATCHES, MOUNTAIN TOPS, ICE COVERINGS AND REMOTE AREAS. CIVILIZATION PROSPERED AGAIN ON PLANET AND REMNANTS OF KNOWLEDGE AND INTELLIGENCE PASSED FROM ONE GENERATION TO ANOTHER BY *SHRUTIS* AND *SMRITIS*. THE MEANS OF COMMUNICATION, i.e., ALPHABETS, VOWELS, CONSONANTS, VERSE, SCIENTIFIC KNOWLEDGE, WRITING ON DRY LEAVES AND BARKS AND TRANSMISSION THROUGH PAPERS DEVELOPED GRADUALLY ON PLANET. DURING PASSAGE OF TIME, FRAGMENTS OF KNOWLEDGE BECAME VISIBLE IN DIFFERENT POCKETS THROUGHOUT THE WORLD IN MANY FORMS. SHRUTI AND SMRITI HELPED IN DEVELOPMENT AND SPREAD OF SCIENCE AND KNOWLEDGE AND HUMAN LIFE GREW TO NORMAL STATE DURING COURSE OF TIME. IN FUTURE, WOBBLING OF PLANETS AND MOONS WILL EFFECT SURFACE AREA, DESTROY ALL SUPER STRUCTURES AND MAY CALM DOWN AFTER 7 OR 30 OR 365 DAYS (ONE REVOLUTION OF EARTH AROUND SUN). THE DOWN FALL OF CIVILIZATION AND NEXT CATASTROPHE MAY BE EXPECTED AGAIN AT THE TIME OF RESHUFFLING IN OUR SOLAR SYSTEM. THERE MAY BE CHANGE IN THE MAGNETIC AXIS OF ATTRACTION OF NINE PLANETS SYSTEM DUE TO RESHUFFLING IN RELATION TO SUN, TWELVE CONSTELLATION OF STARS AND POLE STAR ETC. KNOWLEDGE AND INTELLIGENCE WAS PRESERVED IN THE FORM OF IDOLS, STATUES, EDICTS, GOLDEN STRUCTURES AND STORIES. IN THE PAST, KNOWLEDGE AND INTELLIGENCE AMONG HUMAN BEING WAS TRANSMITTED FROM ONE GENERATION TO OTHER BY 'SHRUTI' (VERSE SPEAKING AND LISTENING) AND 'SMRITI' (MEMORISE). THE MEANS OF COMMUNICATION, i.e., ALPHABETS, VOWELS, CONSONANTS, VERSE, SCIENTIFIC KNOWLEDGE, PAPER WRITING AND TRANSMISSION WAS LEAST AND IT DEVELOPED GRADUALLY ON PLANET. STRUCTURE OF ATOM WAS KNOWN TO ANCIENT PEOPLE AND IT WAS PRESERVED IN THE FORM OF IDOLS, STATUES, EDICTS, GOLDEN STRUCTURES AND STORIES FROM ONE GENERATION TO ANOTHER BY 'SHRUTI' AND 'SMRITI'. ANCIENT CIVILIZATION HAD CLEAR IDEA ABOUT ATOMIC STRUCTURE AND MOVEMENT OF IONS IN SEVEN SHELLS OF COLORS WAS WELL KNOWN TO THEM. DEVELOPMENT OF NON-METALLIC AND METALLIC IONS TAKES PLACE IN FOURTEEN (SEVEN + SEVEN) COLOR REGIONS IN FOURTEEN MATTER ZONES INSIDE PLANETS AND STARS IN ARITHMETIC PROGRESSION AND IT WAS TRANSMITTED THROUGH STORIES OF KRISHNA AND GOPIS. CYCLE OF CREATION AND DISSOLUTION OF PLANETS AND STARS WAS MEMORISED IN THE FORM OF STORIES OF RAMAYANA AND MAHABHARATA. PEOPLE KNEW ABOUT IMPACT OF SOUND WAVES, MAGNET, FOUR FORCES AND IMPACT OF COLORS ON LIVING BEINGS.

Science and religion are two faces of the same coin. Science can be seen, visualized, perceived, experimented and tested on the surface of earth, solar system, star dynasty and in the universe. Scientific experiments can be observed on planets and stars and different theories can be correlated with each other in the universe. Religion is perceived as faith, concentration of power, feeling and attachment with living beings, astral bodies and forces existing in the universe. Religion acts as devotion and attaches every living being with other living being through energy of electromagnetic waves in the universe. Religion acts as concentration of power and attaches every living organism with other living organism through four forces acting on every element of human body on the planet.

7

CREATION OF SANSKRIT LETTERS AS ELEMENTS

All the sciences in the universe develop in association with different branches of science. Nothing develops in isolation and nothing can survive in isolation in the universe. Thirty two consonant letters, thirty two pairs of spinal nerves, thirty two teeth in mouth which shape language, thirty two classes of crystal symmetry, thirty two vertical groups of elements in Periodic table and thirty two nerves shown by *Kundalini Shakti* in human body are inter-related to each other and exhibit interaction amongst themselves. Human body language is definitely related to different nerves of nervous system, 'sound wave packets' made up of electromagnetic waves, crystal symmetry developed due to contraction of mass and atoms and elements of Periodic Table.

Letters are created as 'Sound Wave Packets' having mass as 32 consonant letters within atmosphere of planet earth. Four forces show impact on 32 classes of crystal symmetry and seven crystal systems can be divided into four groups of 2, 6, 10 and 14 crystals as mentioned below :

2 crystals	-	2 Triclinic crystals
6 crystals	-	6 (3 monoclinic + 3 orthorhombic) crystals
10 crystals	-	10 (5 cubic + 5 trigonal) crystals
14 crystals	-	14 (7 tetragonal + 7 hexagonal) crystals

The impact of four forces takes place in equal quantum on all the planets and stars. Equal application of four forces keeps the planets and stars hanging in balance in equilibrium in space and does not allow lop-sided growth in any direction. Individual charges exist temporarily in isolated form on any astral body, planet and star. The +Ve charge of particle and -Ve charge of particle conjugate with each other alongewith neutrons to form atoms during particles interaction. The strong force is formed due to electropositive charge of particle whereas weak force is the outcome of electronegative charge of particle. Thus, affect of strong force and weak force works together to create atoms in fourteen groups.

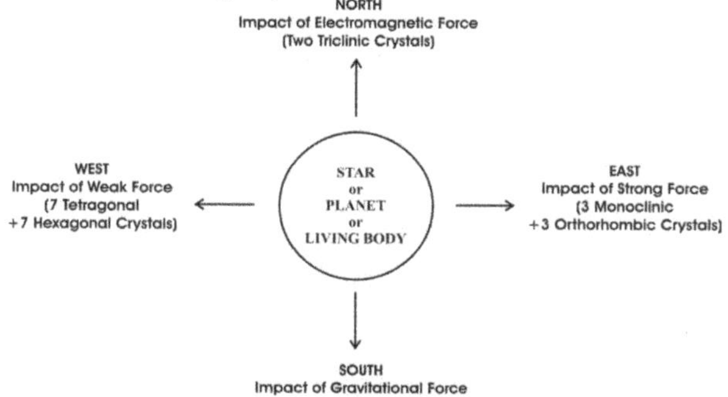

IMPACT OF FOUR FORCES IS OBSERVED ON 32 PAIRS OF SPINAL NERVES, 32 TEETH AND 32 CLASSES OF CRYSTAL SYMMETRY OF ELEMENTS IN PERIODIC TABLE ON PLANETS, STARS, ASTRAL BODIES AND LIVING BEINGS. FERROMAGNETIC AXLE CREATED BY ATOMS OF $^{56}_{28}Fe$ ESTABLISHES LINKS BETWEEN MICROWORLD OF ELEMENT WITH MEGA-WORLD OF PLANETS AND STARS IN THE UNIVERSE.

Fig. 6.1

Several efforts have been made for documenting different languages of the world and it is ascertained that about 7000 distinct languages are common in the world. The letters, words and languages in the world are genetically related to one another because they are created as atoms of elements from which animals and human bodies are created on planet. Languages are not uniformly distributed around the world as animals and human beings show diversity in distribution and languages also show diversity in speaking. In some civilizations, their language contains 118 letters in total basing upon periodic table of elements. In ceremonial occasions, they use 118 number as auspicious number. Sixteen vowel letters can be divided into one white + seven colors + seven colors + one black letter. Thirty two consonant letters can be divided into two letters in north direction + six letters in east direction + 10 letters in south direction + 14 letters in west direction.

The accumulation of positively charged particles (p+) takes place along one axis, negatively charged particles (e-) along second axis and neutral mass particles (n) along third axis. The fusion of smaller nuclides into bigger nucleus and creation of heavy elements due to nucleosynthesis takes place due to combined effect of rotation, revolution and precession on planets and stars. The cycle of nucleosynthesis accompanied with contraction of matter inside fourteen zones increases temperature inside core of planets and stars. The element nucleosynthesized in black region with highest binding energy and highest crystalline structures like cubic crystals shift to core of planets and stars. The peripheral portion is occupied by elements created in seven colors regions having less binding energy and less compact crystals with low level of symmetry. In total 118 elements are created along three axes by this movement:

1   **PERIODS: IMPACT OF ROTATION-LINKED MOVEMENT ON CREATION OF 118 ELEMENTS DUE TO ELECTROMAGNETIC FORCE. CREATION OF ELEMENTS IN SEVEN PERIODS DUE TO ROTATION-LINKED MOVEMENT. PERIODS CREATE ELEMENTS WITHIN 32 CLASSES OF CRYSTAL SYMMETRY.**

2   **ROUNDS: IMPACT OF PRECESSION-LINKED MOVEMENT ON CREATION OF 118 ELEMENTS DUE TO STRONG FORCE AND WEAK FORCE. CREATION OF ELEMENTS IN FOURTEEN ROUNDS DUE TO PRECESSION-LINKED MOVEMENT. ROUNDS CREATE ELEMENTS DUE TO DOMINANCE OF ANIONS AND CATIONS.**

3   **BLOCKS: IMPACT OF REVOLUTION-LINKED MOVEMENT ON CREATION OF ATOMS OF 118 ELEMENTS WITH 180 NEUTRONS DUE TO GRAVITATIONAL FORCE. CREATION OF ELEMENTS IN TWELVE BLOCKS DUE TO REVOLUTION-LINKED MOVEMENT. BLOCKS CREATE ELEMENTS DUE TO DEPOSITION OF NEUTRONS IN EVERY 30 DEGREES PARTS OF CELESTIAL SPHERE DURING MOVEMENT BY DOMINANCE OF GRAVITATIONAL FORCE.**

The elements with fixed electromagnetic energy are basic constituents of all astral bodies and elements only make room inside core of astral bodies as dense mass and contracted black matter. The accumulation of sub-atomic particles produces elements with different characteristics on planets and stars. Genealogy of astral bodies, planets and stars shows three axes attachment due to contraction of sub-atomic particles under the impact of four types of particle interaction inside 118 elements. On every astral body, planet and star, nucleosynthesis of 118 atoms of elements takes place along three axes due to rotation-linked movement, precession-linked movement and revolution-linked movement in periods, rounds and blocks. Impact of four forces create 118 elements and it is observed on movement of planets, stars in the star dynasty.

(a) Electromagnetic Force: In every star dynasty, the nine planets system is controlled by electromagnetic force bound by nine colors cycle. Nine planets system is controlled by twenty seven asterisms which are guiding force for all the objects on any star dynasty. These 27 asterisms are Ashwini, Bharani, Krittika, Rohini, Mrigashirsha, Ardra, Punarvasu, Pushya, Ashlesha, Magha, Purva Phalguni, Uttara Phalguni, Hasta, Chitra, Swati, Vishakha, Anuradha, Jyeshtha, Moola, Purva Ashadha, Uttara Ashadha, Shravana, Dhanishta, Shatabhisha, Purva Bhadrapada, Uttara Bhaadrapada and Revati. They are spread at a distance of $13^{0}20'$ around all stars. The asterisms are controlled by 27th letter of consonant '*Ram*' and move in the multiple of 27. Any astral body, planet, star or living being or living body can not survive beyond 27 and it is the reason '*Ram*' becomes essential for their survival due to 27 asterisms in space. It is pronounced as *Ra + Am* (fifteenth letter of vowel) and commonly called as *Ram*.

(b) Gravitational Force: Neutron particles in atoms of elements spread to 180 neutrons in total are controlled by gravitational force. Neutron particles in twelve blocks create 118 elements in total in every cycle of element creation. These twelve blocks are represented by twelve zodiac signs in every stara dynasty. These are Aries, Taurus, Gemini, Cancer, Leo, Virgo, Libra, Scorpio, Sagittarius, Capricorn, Aquarius and Pisces.

(c) Strong Force and Weak Force: They create 118 elements within fourteen stars cluster of star dynasty within 7 + 7 groups in every cycle of element creation.

The elements are nucleosynthesized as electromagnetic constants on numerical basis. The cycle of creation of elements moves rounds after round and creates 118 elements on any astral body to the maximum. The atoms of elements are created as integers within 32 classes of crystal symmetry. The elements are created in seven periods and can contain 32 elements to the maximum in any period. 32 classes contain seven types of crystal system with solid nucleus inside atoms. The consonants are created in 32 pairs of spinal nerves and maintain their originality within spinal cord.

1st Matter Zone	2nd Matter zone	3rd Matter zone	4th Matter zone	5th Matter zone	6th Matter zone	7th Matter zone	8th Matter zone	9th Matter zone	10th Matter zone	11th Matter zone	12th Matter zone	13th Matter zone	14th Matter zone
V	I	B	G	Y	O	R	V	I	B	G	Y	O	R
e-	2 e-												⟶
3 e-	4 e-	5 e-	6 e-	7 e-	8 e-								⟶
9 e-	10 e-	11 e-	12 e-	13 e-	14 e-	15 e-	16 e-	17 e-	18 e-				⟶
19 e-	20 e-	21 e-	22 e-	23 e-	24 e-	25 e-	26 e-	27 e-	28 e-	29 e-	30 e-	31 e-	32 e-

CREATION OF ELEMENTS TAKES PLACE BY COMBINATION OF ELECTRONS AND PROTONS IN FOURTEEN COLORS GROUP WITHIN 32 CLASSES (2 + 6 + 10 + 14) OF CRYSTAL SYMMETRY.

Table 6.1

Elements with pure color are produced in the initial rounds of creation of elements when n/p ratio is less. The n/p ratio increases in elements of later rounds and elements with dark colors, e.g., dark hue, dark gray, gray, steel gray etc are produced due to high level of intermixing of colors. Core area of stars and planets contain elements, compounds and matter in black region and peripheral area contains elements and compounds of light color and white region. The color effect is seen due to compression and rarefaction of waves. The white light and black (dark) matter maintain balance among each other. The energy of electromagnetic waves forms seven regions having seven crests and seven troughs due to seven valence electrons of elements.

Electromagnetic wavelengths from about zero angstrom to 4000 angstrom are absorbed by mass particles and mass particles look black in appearance and behave as dark matter particles. Electromagnetic waves from 4000 angstrom to 7500 angstrom absorb seven colors in particles of elements and mass particles and matter behave like particles in this wavelength range. The electromagnetic waves above 7500 angstroms make the particles behave as waves and they look white and lose their three-dimensional shape.

It can be said that universe is composed of white light and colorless mass particles, big and small. In black region and in white region the elements behave as neutral elements. The transverse waves are absorbed and accumulated in metallic octet and in core of astral body, e.g., electric waves. The longitudinal waves expand in space and create non-metallic octets, e.g., sound waves. The speed of sound is the highest in granite having metallic octets and lowest in non-metallic octets. Emission spectrum of atomic hydrogen shows the trend of compression of waves and particles of smaller sizes and wavelengths towards black end of spectra. Energy levels show gradual increase in squeezing of maximum waves per cm towards dark and black region of spectra. 'Sound Wave Packets' are made up of sub-atomic particles of atoms of elements and behave as free flowing water waves in the atmosphere of planet.

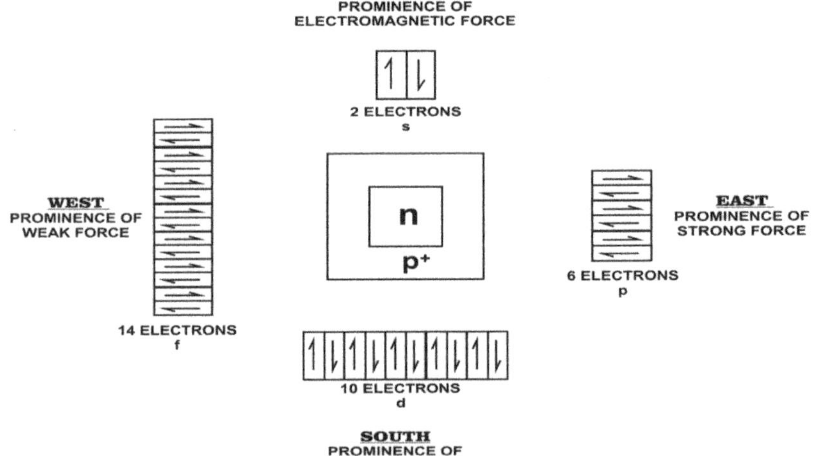

ELEMENTS ARE CREATED WITHIN 32 CRYSTAL CLASSES ON THE PATTERN OF s, p, d f AND 118 ELEMENTS ARE CREATED IN TOTAL IN SEVEN PERIODS. THE HIGHEST NUMBER OF ELEMENTS OR LETTERS CONTAINED IN ONE PERIOD IS EQUAL TO 32.

Fig. 6.2

186

COLOR-CRYSTAL CYCLE OF ELEMENTS

THE ENERGY OF ELECTROMAGNETIC WAVES IN THE RANGE OF SEVEN COLORS, i.e., 4000 Å TO 7500 Å CONVERTS INTO ELECTRIC ENERGY AND CREATES SEVEN COLORS IN ARITHMETIC PROGRESSION. THE ELECTRIC ENERGY PRODUCES OPPOSITELY CHARGED PARTICLES, i.e., e^- AND p^+. BOTH CHARGED PARTICLES ENCAPSULATE NEUTRAL MASS PARTICLES AND PRODUCE SOLID NUCLEUS IN CRYSTALLIZED FORM IN ATOMS. THE STRUCTURE OF ATOM SHOWS THAT POSITIVELY CHARGED PARTICLES SHAPE AXIAL RATIOS AND CONTRACT DARK MATTER PARTICLES INSIDE NUCLEUS THROUGH AXIAL RATIOS WHEREAS NEGATIVELY CHARGED PARTICLES SHAPE AXIAL ANGLES OF NUCLEUS. THE ENERGY OF ELECTROMAGNETIC WAVES IS STORED INSIDE SEVEN CRYSTALS SYSTEM DUE TO POSITIVE CHARGE AND NEGATIVE CHARGE OF THE ATOM OF ELEMENTS.

1st Matter zone	2nd Matter zone	3rd Matter zone	4th Matter zone	5th Matter zone	6th Matter zone	7th Matter zone	8th Matter zone	9th Matter zone	10th Matter zone	11th Matter zone	12th Matter zone	13th Matter zone	14th Matter zone
V	I	B	G	Y	O	R	V	I	B	G	Y	O	R
X^{7+}	X^{6+}	X^{5+}	X^{4+}	X^{3+}	X^{2+}	X^{+}	Y^{-}	Y^{2-}	Y^{3-}	Y^{4-}	Y^{5-}	Y^{6-}	Y^{7-}
TRIC LI क	TRI CLI ख	············											➤
MON OC ग	MO NO C घ	MO NO C ङ	ORTH ORH च	ORTH ORH छ	ORTH ORH ज	············							➤
TRIG ON झ	TRI GON अ	TRI GON ट	TRIG ON ठ	TRIG ON ड	CU BIC ढ	CU BIC ण	CU BIC त	CU BIC थ	CU BIC द	············			➤
TETR AG ध	TET RAG न	TET RAG प	TETR AG फ	TETR AG ब	TETR AG भ	TET RAG म	HE XAG य	HE XAG र	HE XAG ल	HE XAG व	HE XAG श	HE XAG ष	HEX AG स

CREATION AND MOVEMENT OF ELEMENTS TAKES PLACE IN CYCLIC MANNER IN THE GROUP OF FOURTEEN WITHIN 32 CLASSES (2 + 6 + 10 + 14) OF CRYSTAL SYMMETRY. THE ELEMENTS ARE ACCOMODATED IN FOURTEEN MATTER ZONES OF ALL PLANETS AND STARS. SEVEN CRYSTALS SYSTEM DISPERSE INTO THIRTY-TWO CLASSES OF CRYSTAL SYMMETRY DUE TO IMPACT OF FOURTEEN CHARGES ZONES OF MATTER INSIDE ALL PLANETS AND STARS. THIRTY-TWO CRYSTAL CLASSES CONTAIN TRICLINIC (2), ORTHORHOMBIC (3), MONOCLINIC (3), TRIGONAL (5), CUBIC (5), TETRAGONAL (7) AND HEXAGONAL (7) CRYSTALS WHICH FINALLY MAKE ROOM INTO FOURTEEN IONIZATION ZONES OF MATTER INSIDE PLANETS AND STARS. CONTRACTION OF MASS IN GEOMETRIC PROGRESSION PRODUCES SEVEN CRYSTALS SYSTEM AND STORES MATTER INSIDE PLANETS AND STARS. CRYSTALS TEND TO AGGREGATE MASS IN THE MULTIPLES OF $1^3 : 2^3 : 4^3$ ALONG THREE AXES THROUGH AXIAL RATIOS INSIDE PLANETS AND STARS. CONTRACTION OF MASS THROUGH AXIAL ANGLES IN THE RANGE 90^0 TO 120^0 PRODUCES SEVEN CRYSTALS SYSTEM. SEVEN CRYSTALS SYSTEM MOVE IN TWELVE BLOCKS AND PRODUCE $7 \times 12 = 84$ TYPES OF CRYSTALS DURING EVERY REVOLUTION OF PLANETS AND STARS ALONG ONE AXIS.

Table 6.2

The white light splits into seven colors and these colors are created with fixed wavelengths in alternating pattern. Rainbow shows same sequence of colors with expansion of waves in the same proportion. The contraction of mass inside elements takes place in similar ratio with similar sequence of colors. The crest portion of wave develops negatively charged particles whereas the trough portion settles as mass with positive charge. The electromagnetic energy up to 4000 Angstrom of electromagnetic waves is stored as "black stored energy" or "dark energy" inside solid crystals of particles, elements and astral bodies. The electromagnetic waves above 4000

Angstrom, constituting seven color waves, microwaves and radio waves etc disperse energy in different forms in space. The electromagnetic energy above 4000 Angstrom is released due to emission of radiation of different colors by planets and stars.

IT CAN BE CORRELATED THAT ATOMIC STRUCTURE WAS WELL KNOWN TO ANCIENT PEOPLE AND FORMATION OF ASTRAL BODIES IN DIFFERENT PERIODS OF TIME IN CYCLIC MANNER IS EVIDENT FROM OLD STORIES. CYCLE OF CREATION OF ELEMENTS AND ATOMIC STRUCTURE WAS WELL KNOWN TO PEOPLE ON EARTH ABOUT FORTY FOUR LAKHS YEARS AGO. HUMAN LIFE WITH PRESENT LEVEL OF INTELLIGENCE EXISTED ON EARTH EARLIER.

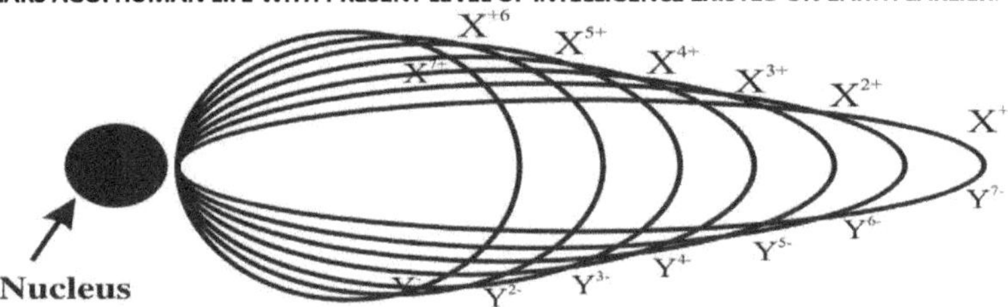

DEVELOPMENT OF NON-METALLIC AND METALLIC IONS TAKES PLACE IN SEVEN COLOR REGIONS IN FOURTEEN MATTER ZONES INSIDE PLANETS AND STARS. ELLIPTICITY OF ORBIT DEVELOPS DUE TO FORMATION OF ANIONS (Y^-, Y^{2-}, Y^{3-}, Y^{4-}, Y^{5-}, Y^{6-}, Y^{7-}) AND CATIONS (X^+, X^{2+}, X^{3+}, X^{4+}, X^{5+}, X^{6+}, X^{7+}) IN THE ATOMS OF ELEMENTS IN ARITHMETIC PROGRESSION. GRADUAL INCREASE IN ELLIPTICITY OF EGG-SHAPED ORBIT TAKES PLACE UP TO SEVEN POINTS TO THE MAXIMUM DUE TO IONISATION IN AN ATOM. BLACK NEUTRON IS CONTRACTED INSIDE NUCLEUS OF ATOM OF ELEMENT. DEVELOPMENT OF ANIONS HAVING –Ve CHARGE AND CATIONS HAVING +Ve CHARGE TAKES PLACE IN ATOMS OF 118 ELEMENTS. ANCIENT PEOPLE USED TO PRESERVE THEIR KNOWLEDGE AND INTELLIGENCE IN THE FORM OF IDOLS, EYES OF STATUES, TEMPLES AND IN CENTRES OF FAITH.

SET OF THREE FUNDAMENTAL PARTICLES, i.e., PROTON (+Ve CHARGED PARTICLE, p+), ELECTRON (-Ve CHARGED PARTICLE, e-) AND NEUTRON (^{27}Vm CONTRACTED AS 'RAM', n) CREATE ATOM OF ELEMENT WHICH IS BASIC UNIT OF LIFE AND ASTRAL BODIES AND WHICH IS IMMORTAL IN THE UNIVERSE. IN THE ABOVE PICTURE, EYES OF BLACK GOD HAVE BEEN DEPICTED AS ROUND STRUCTURE AS NEUTRON ^{27}Vm MASS UNIT CONTRACTED AS RAM) WHICH IS SQUEEZED BY –Ve CHARGED AND +Ve CHARGED PARTICLES OF ATOM. EYES OF THE MALE AND FEMALE SHOW ELLIPTICITY EQUIVALENT TO SEVEN CATIONS AND SEVEN ANIONS DUE TO POSITIVE CHARGE AND NEGATIVE CHARGE RESPECTIVELY. IT SEEMS THAT ANCIENT PEOPLE HAD CLEAR IDEA ABOUT CATIONS AND ANIONS AND THEIR ELLIPTICITY DUE TO BOTH CHARGES. STRUCTURE OF ATOM WAS KNOWN TO ANCIENT PEOPLE AND IT WAS PRESERVED IN THE FORM OF IDOLS, STATUES, EDICTS, GOLDEN STRUCTURES AND STORIES FROM ONE GENERATION TO ANOTHER BY 'SHRUTI' (VERSE SPEAKING AND LISTENING) AND 'SMRITI' (MEMORISE). ATOM STANDS FOR 'A-TAM'. TAM MEANS TO FINISH AND A-TAM MEANS THE MATTER WHICH CAN NOT BE DESTROYED. AGGREGATION OF NEUTRON PARTICLES MAY CREATE HIGHLY COMPACTED ENERGETIC BIGGEST NEUTRON STAR LIKE STRUCTURES. ANCIENT CIVILIZATION HAD CLEAR IDEA ABOUT ATOMIC STRUCTURE AND MOVEMENT OF IONS IN SEVEN SHELLS OF COLORS WAS WELL KNOWN TO THEM.

Fig. 6.3

The sub-atomic particles and elements which contain electromagnetic energy from zero angstrom to 4000 angstrom look black in appearance and occupy every nook and corner of space in universe and it is the reason that space looks dark and black in appearance. The sub-atomic particles which contain energy from 4000 angstrom to 7500 angstrom provide seven color appearances and create 118 elements. They absorb radiation up to 7500 angstrom and emit rays of seven respective colors. The sub-atomic particles and molecules of elements and compounds which contain electromagnetic energy from 7500 angstrom and above look white in appearance and occupy peripheral portion of planets and stars.

On water surface the waves are produced because the water particles move in elliptic or circular path as the wave passes through them. The elliptic motion has two components, i.e., both

188

along and perpendicular to the direction of propagation of wave. The 'Sound Wave Packets' also behave as water waves within atmosphere of planet.

Laws of physics, creation of 118 elements and cyclic evolution of life forms due to rotation, revolution and precession along three axes is same everywhere in all solar systems and star dynasties in the universe. Life forms develop automatic on all planets and their size increases gradually with every round, period and group of movement of planets around stars. Smaller life forms evolve initially from hard coat bacteria preserved on planet and their size increases gradually on bigger planets.

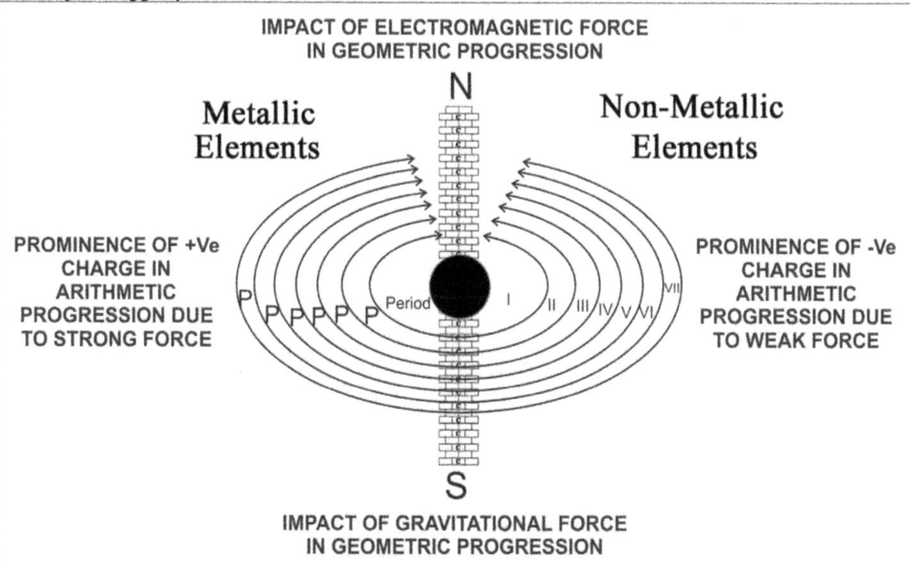

FERROMAGNETIC POLAR AXLE ACTS AS STRAIGHT ELECTROMAGNET AND ROTATION OF PLANETS AND STARS ON AXIS NUCLEOSYNTHESIZES ELEMENTS IN SEVEN PERIODS AS OBSERVED IN CREAM SEPARATOR. FIRST PERIOD CREATES TWO ELEMENTS, SECOND AND THIRD EIGHT ELEMENTS EACH, FOURTH AND FIFTH EIGHTEEN ELEMENTS EACH AND SIXTH AND SEVENTH PERIOD CREATES THIRTY TWO ELEMENTS EACH DURING CYCLE OF CREATION. MATTER SETTLES INSIDE ALL ASTRAL BODIES WITHIN THIRTY TWO CLASSES OF CRYSTAL SYMMETRY.

Fig. 6.4

Contraction and storage of mass with energy of electromagnetic waves takes place in the multiples of "√m x Energy of Electromagnetic waves in the range 4000 Å to 7500 Å x 10^2" as unit of existence of matter in the universe. This unit creates set of "three fundamental particles, i.e., e-, p+ and n" in the atoms of elements. Contraction of mass and energy of electromagnetic waves inside atoms of elements creates 118 elements on planets and stars in the universe. Matter exists in the form of elements and stores energy of electromagnetic waves above 4000 Å. Matter is stored inside planets and stars in the form of elements. Anti-matter does not exist in the form of elements and does not exist inside planets and stars. Anti-matter exists as waves or 'debt' in space and occupies anti-matter zones of space where planets and stars move. Classification of elements can be taken up in fourteen rounds.

											He (2)
H (1) Initial Element											
ROUND I →				Li (3)	Be (4)	B (5)	C (6)	N (7)	O (8)	F (9)	Ne (10)
ROUND II →				Na (11)	Mg (12)	Al (13)	Si (14)	P (15)	S (16)	CI (17)	Ar (18)
ROUND III →				K (19)	Ca (20)	Sc (21)	Ti (22)	V (23)	Cr (24)	Mn (25)	
	Fe (26)	Co (27)	Ni (28)								
ROUND IV →				Cu (29)	Zn (30)	Ga (31)	Ge (32)	As (33)	Se (34)	Br (35)	Kr (36)
ROUND V →				Rb (37)	Sr (38)	Y (39)	Zr (40)	Nb (41)	Mo (42)	Tc (43)	
	Ru (44)	Rh (45)	Pd (46)								
ROUND VI →				Ag (47)	Cd (48)	In (49)	Sn (50)	Sb (51)	Te (52)	I (53)	Xe (54)
ROUND VII →				Cs (55)	Ba (56)	La (57)	Ce (58)	Pr (59)	Nd (60)	Pm (61)	
ROUND VIII →				Sm (62)	Eu (63)	Gd (64)	Tb (65)	Dy (66)	Ho (67)	Er (68)	
ROUND IX →				Tm (69)	Yb (70)	Lu (71)	Hf (72)	Ta (73)	W (74)	Re (75)	
	Os (76)	Ir (77)	Pt (78)								
ROUND X →				Au (79)	Hg (80)	Ti (81)	Pb (82)	Bi (83)	Po (84)	At (85)	Rn (86)
ROUND XI →				Pr (87)	Ra (88)	Ac (89)	Th (90)	Pa (91)	U (92)	Np (93)	
ROUND XII				Pu (94)	Am (95)	Cm (96)	Bk (97)	Cf (98)	Es (99)	Fm (100)	
ROUND XIII				Md (101)	No (102)	Lr (103)	Rf (104)	Db (105)	Sg (106)	Bh (107)	
ROUND XIV	Hs (108)	Mt (109)	Ds (110)	Rg (111)	Cn (112)	Nh (113)	Fl (114)	Mc (115)	Lv (116)	Ts (117)	Og (118)

(Figures in the bracket indicate atomic numbers)

THERE IS ALWAYS CONTINUITY OF CREATION OF 118 ELEMENTS IN THE UNIVERSE ON THE PATTERN OF CREATION OF PLANETS AND STARS.

Table 6.3

.   The cycle of nucleosynthesis of elements moves in fourteen groups due to precession of earth around fourteen stars. The electromagnetic force plays prominent role in creation of elements in fourteen (7+7) colors group. The metallic octet zone and non-metallic octet zone also contain elements and they generally remain in neutral forms. If the elements loose electrons during ionization, they tend to show metallic character and shift towards black region. If the elements gain electrons during ionization, they tend to show non-metallic character and shift towards white region. On any human body, charged particles show prominence of positively

190

charged particles at one end and prominence of negatively charged particles at the other end. Periodic Table of elements is cyclic creation of elements on continuous basis starting from atomic number 1 and ending at 118. During creation of elements, 118 elements are created in seven periods within 32 classes of crystal symmetry.

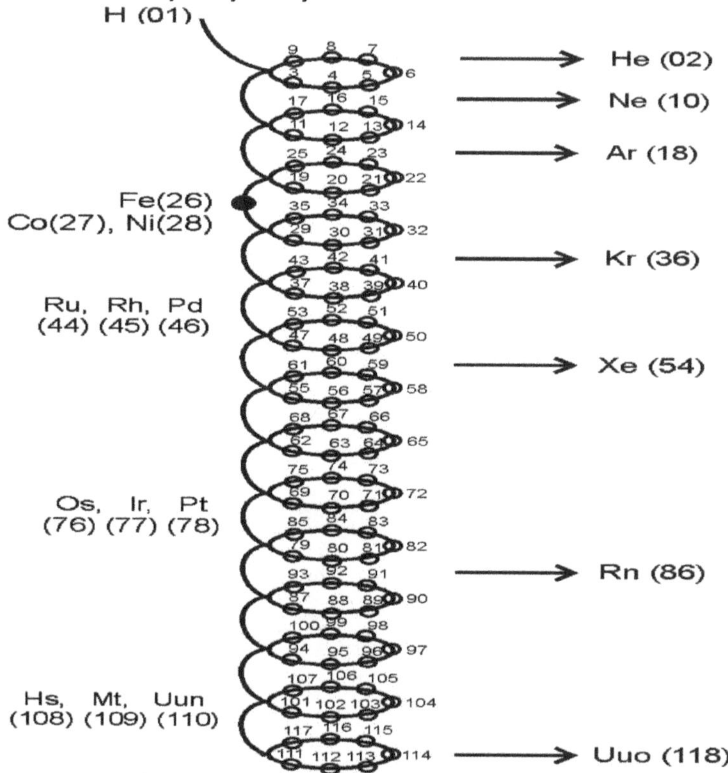

(The numbers indicate atomic numbers of elements)

CYCLIC (SPIRAL) MOVEMENT OF ENERGY TAKES PLACE IN FOURTEEN ROUNDS AND CREATES 118 ELEMENTS IN THE UNIVERSE IN CYCLIC MANNER. SEVEN COLOR CYCLE STORES ENERGY OF ELECTROMAGNETIC WAVES INSIDE ELEMENTS OF ELEMENT CYCLE ON CONTINUOUS BASIS. PERIODIC TABLE OF ELEMENTS IS A CLOSE CHAIN CONTINUOUS CYCLE AND NEVER AN OPEN CHAIN CYCLE. IN THE PROCESS, TWELVE METALLIC ELEMENTS ARE SEPARATED ON ONE SIDE AND SEVEN NON-METALLIC OCTETS ON OTHER SIDE. THE ENERGY OF ELECTROMAGNETIC WAVES IN THE RANGE OF SEVEN COLORS, i.e., 4000 Å TO 7500 Å CONVERTS INTO ELECTRIC ENERGY. THE ELECTRIC ENERGY PRODUCES OPPOSITELY CHARGED PARTICLES, i.e., e⁻ AND e⁺ INITIALLY AND THEN PRODUCES BIGGER PARTICLES (e⁻ AND p⁺). BOTH CHARGED PARTICLES ENCAPSULATE NEUTRAL MASS PARTICLES AND PRODUCE SOLID NUCLEUS IN CRYSTALLIZED FORM IN ATOMS. THE STRUCTURE OF ATOM SHOWS THAT POSITIVELY CHARGED PARTICLES SHAPE AXIAL RATIOS AND CONTRACT DARK MATTER PARTICLES INSIDE NUCLEUS THROUGH AXIAL RATIOS WHEREAS NEGATIVELY CHARGED PARTICLES SHAPE AXIAL ANGLES OF NUCLEUS. IN THIS PROCESS, A 'SET OF THREE FUNDAMENTAL PARTICLES' PRODUCES ATOMS OF 118 ELEMENTS ON ALL PLANETS AND STARS. CONTRACTION OF MASS STORES ENERGY OF ELECTROMAGNETIC WAVES INSIDE ATOMS OF ELEMENTS IN

FOURTEEN MATTER ZONES OF PLANETS AND STARS. COMPOSITION OF ELEMENTS INSIDE ALL PLANETS AND STARS IS THE SAME AND DEPOSITION OF ELEMENTS TAKES PLACE IN ABOVE MENTIONED MANNER. THE ELEMENTS FROM Z=27 TO Z= 118 CREATED IN LATER ELEVEN ROUNDS TEND TO MOVE AWAY FROM CENTRE, CORE AND MANTLE OF PLANETS AND STARS. CYCLE OF PRECESSION AND MOVEMENT TAKES PLACE IN FOURTEEN ROUNDS OF ELEMENT CYCLE WITHIN CONTROL OF URSAE MAJOR AND URSAE MINOR. THERE IS ALWAYS CONTINUITY OF CREATION OF 118 ELEMENTS WITHIN SEVEN COLORS CYCLE IN THE UNIVERSE.

Fig. 6.5

Star clusters in the multiples of fourteen are observed with different solar systems in space As for example, U. Minor and U. Major maintain fourteen stars cluster in Milky Way Star Dynasty. Cycle of nucleosynthesis produces 32 vertical groups of elements on the patterns of 32 classes of crystal symmetry due to impact of strong force and weak force. 32 types of elements are produced within fourteen rounds during evolutionary ladder of ascendance of colors.

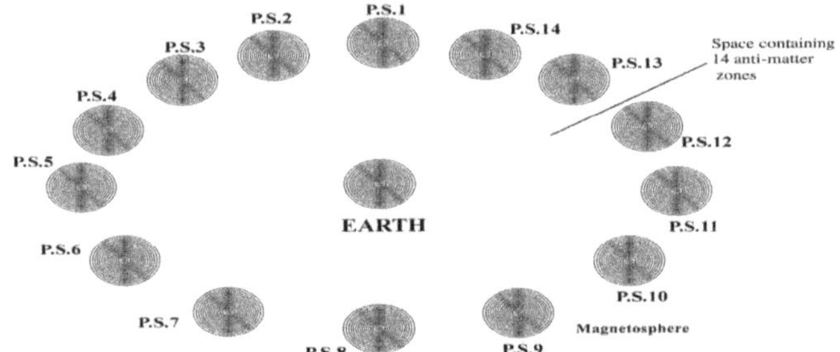

MOVEMENT OF FOURTEEN STARS IN SPACE COMPELS FOR AGGREGATION OF FOURTEEN ATOMS OF $^{56}_{26}Fe$ IN THE FORM OF FERROMAGNETIC ROD OR AXLE INSIDE PLANETS AND STARS DURING EVOLUTION. CYCLE OF NUCLEOSYNTHESIS CREATES 118 ELEMENTS IN FOURTEEN ROUNDS IN ASCENDING ORDER OF COLORS. CYCLE OF PRECESSION AND MOVEMENT OF EARTH TAKES PLACE AROUND FOURTEEN STARS OF U. MINOR AND U. MAJOR IN FOURTEEN ANTI-MATTER ZONES IN 360,000 YEARS (25,714.285 X 14 YEARS = 360,000 YEARS) CYCLE. REPULSION AMONG FOURTEEN STARS OF URSAE MAJOR AND URSAE MINOR CAUSES CYCLE OF PRECESSION IN OUR STAR FAMILY OF SEVEN COLORS. FOR EVERY ACTION THERE IS EQUAL AND OPPOSITE REACTION IN ASTRAL BODIES. COMPACTION OF ATOMS OF Fe IN THE MULTIPLES OF 14 INSIDE FERROMAGNETIC AXLE COMPELS FOR MOVEMENT OF PLANETS AND STARS AROUND 14 ADJOINING STARS IN SPACE. REPULSION AMONG STARS CAUSES EARTH TO MOVE IN 360,000 YEARS CYCLE OF PRECESSION IN SPACE. DIVISION OF TIME PERIOD DEVELOPED IN THE MULTIPLES OF HUNDRED BY FOURTEEN GIVES THE VALUE OF MOVEMENT OF EVERY STAR IN SPACE. 1000/14 = 71.43 YEARS AND ITS MULTIPLES IS THE TIME PERIOD OF MOVEMENT OF EVERY POLE STAR AROUND CENTRAL STAR. EARTH COMPLETES ONE CYCLE OF PRECESSION IN 3,60,000 YEARS MOVING AROUND FOURTEEN STARS IN ANTI-MATTER ZONES OF U. MINOR AND U. MAJOR IN SPACE. FOURTEEN ANTI-MATTER ZONES AROUND PLANETS AND STARS LOOK LIKE 'SHADOW OR DEBT' AND EXIST SO LONG AS PLANETS AND STARS SURVIVE IN SPACE. CONTRACTION OF NEUTRON PARTICLES CAUSES 'MASS DEFECT' IN ATOMS OF ELEMENTS. THE MASS DEFECT CREATES "DEBT OR SHADOW OR VACUUM" IN EQUAL PROPORTION IN SPACE WHICH FORMS ANTI-MATTER ZONES AROUND PLANETS AND STARS. CONTRACTION OF NEUTRON PARTICLES IN ROOT VALUES, i.e., ^2V, ^3V, ^{14}V, ^{84}V,...MASS UNITS STORES MATTER INSIDE PLANETS AND STARS. SIMILARLY, DUE TO CONTRACTION AND SQUEEZING, VACUUM OR ANTI-MATTER DEVELOPS AROUND PLANETS AND STARS IN SQUARE, CUBE AND MULTIPLE VALUES, i.e., 10^2, 10^3, 10^{14}, 10^{84}... TIME UNITS AND CREATES FOURTEEN ANTI-MATTER ZONES AROUND ALL SPHERICAL ASTRAL BODIES. IMPACT OF STRONG FORCE AND WEAK FORCE CREATES CYCLE OF PRECESSION AND MOVEMENT OF ELEMENT CYCLE TAKES PLACE IN FOURTEEN ROUNDS UNDER CONTROL OF URSAE MAJOR AND URSAE MINOR. THERE IS ALWAYS CONTINUITY OF CREATION OF 118 ELEMENTS ON ALL PLANETS AND STARS IN THE UNIVERSE.

Fig. 6.6

192

Life forms will exist on nine planets system of any solar system. Multi-cellular living beings thrive well on blue planets having atmospheric covering. In the cycle of colors, blue color is third in sequence and planet which occupies third place in sequence of planets from central star, i.e., sun will tend to develop life forms. All spherical planets of any solar system may develop life forms provided mean temperature of the planet is 18^0C and it maintains cover of ozone layer around planet. All planets having 18^0C temperature show highest proliferation of multi-cellular life forms.

ELECTROMAGNETIC WAVES FROM 4000Å TO 7500Å ARE ABSORBED OR EMITTED AS CHARGED PARTICLES IN THE FORM OF SEVEN COLORS IN ATOMS OF ELEMENTS, COMPOUNDS AND ASTRAL BODIES. ELECTROMAGNETIC WAVES ABOVE 7500Å ARE EMITTED IN THE FORM OF MICROWAVES, RADIO WAVES, COLORLESS PARTICLES AND WHITE OBJECTS IN SPACE.

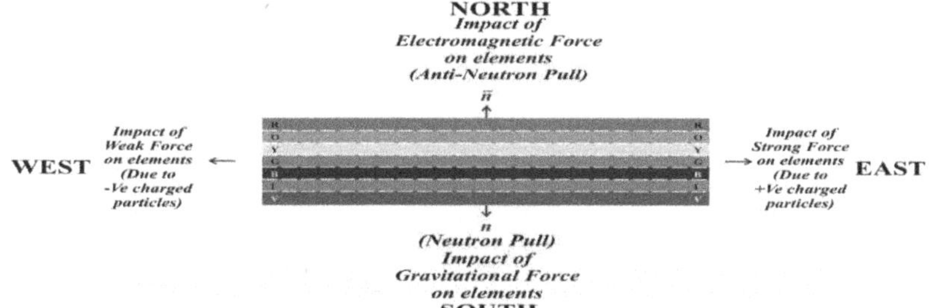

FOUR DIRECTIONS AT RIGHT ANGLES TO EACH OTHER CREATE FOUR FORCES AND AFFECT ALL THE MASS PARTICLES, MATTER, PLANETS, STARS AND ASTRAL BODIES DURING CREATION WITHIN SEVEN COLORS CYCLE. SPACE LOOKS DARK AND BLACK IN APPEARANCE. IT CAN BE SAID THAT ALL THE PARTICLES, ELEMENTS AND ASTRAL BODIES IN SPACE ABSORB ALL INCIDENT RAYS AND LOOK BLACK. ELECTROMAGNETIC RAYS UPTO 4000 Å IS ABSORBED AS DARK ENERGY INSIDE SUB-ATOMIC PARTICLES, ATOMS AND THREE DIMENSIONAL OBJECTS IN SPACE. ELECTROMAGNETIC WAVES FROM 4000 Å TO 7500 Å ARE ABSORBED OR EMITTED AS CHARGED PARTICLES IN THE FORM OF SEVEN COLORS IN ATOMS OF ELEMENTS, COMPOUNDS AND ASTRAL BODIES. ELECTROMAGNETIC WAVES ABOVE 7500 Å ARE EMITTED IN THE FORM OF MICROWAVES, RADIO WAVES, COLORLESS PARTICLES AND WHITE OBJECTS IN SPACE.

Fig. 6.7

Due to churning with straight electromagnet inside planet and star as churning axle, crystals under 32 classes of symmetry are produced in seven periods on every planet and star. Due to prominence of electropositive charge at one end and electronegative charge at other end, churning of mass particles takes place in space and elements with different characteristics are produced. During solidification of crystals, positive charge under impact of strong force shapes axial ratios while negative charge under impact of weak force shapes axial angles. The nucleus of every atom is solid in structure that is produced in crystallized forms of 2 crystals (triclinic) + 6 crystals (monoclinic and orthorhombic) + 10 crystals (rhombohedral and cubic) + 14 crystals (hexagonal and tetragonal) under 32 vertical columns. The elements spread in 32 classes of vertical columns and produce elements in gas, liquid or solid forms.

PERIODIC TABLE OF ELEMENTS

PROMINENCE OF METALLIC TREND (+ Ve Elements)   (ENERGY OF ELECTROMAGNETIC WAVES FROM 4000 Å to 7500 Å)   **PROMINENCE OF NON-METALLIC TREND (- Ve Elements)**

Columns 1–16:

PERIODS	1	2	3	4	5	6	7	8	9	10	11	12	13	14	15	16
PERIOD I	H 1															
PERIOD II	Li 3			Be 4				B 5				C 6				
PERIOD III	Na 11				Mg 12				Al 13					Si 14		
PERIOD IV	K 19	Ca 20		Sc 21		Ti 22		V 23		Cr 24		Mn 25		Fe 26		Co 27
PERIOD V	Rb 37	Sr 38		Y 39		Zr 40		Nb 41		Mo 42		Tc 43		Ru 44		Rh 45
PERIOD VI	Cs 55	Ba 56	La 57	Ce 58	Pr 59	Nd 60	Pm 61	Sm 62	Eu 63	Gd 64	Tb 65	Dy 66	Ho 67	Er 68	Tm 69	Yb 70
PERIOD VII	Fr 87	Ra 88	Ac 89	Th 90	Pa 91	U 92	Np 93	Pu 94	Am 95	Cm 96	Bk 97	Cf 98	Es 99	Fm 100	Md 101	No 102

Columns 17–32:

PERIODS	17	18	19	20	21	22	23	24	25	26	27	28	29	30	31	32
PERIOD I																He 2
PERIOD II	N 7				O 8				F 9							Ne 10
PERIOD III			P 15				S 16				Cl 17					Ar 18
PERIOD IV	Ni 28		Cu 29		Zn 30		Ga 31		Ge 32		As 33		Se 34		Br 35	Kr 36
PERIOD V	Pd 46		Ag 47		Cd 48		In 49		Sn 50		Sb 51		Te 52		I 53	Xe 54
PERIOD VI	Lu 71	Hf 72	Ta 73	W 74	Re 75	Os 76	Ir 77	Pd 78	Au 79	Hg 80	Tl 81	Pb 82	Bi 83	Po 84	At 85	Rn 86
PERIOD VII	Lr 103	Rf 104	Db 105	Sg 106	Bh 107	Hs 108	Mt 109	Ds 110	Rg 111	Cn 112	Nh 113	Fl 114	Mc 115	Lv 116	Ts 117	Og 118

(Figures indicate atomic number of elements nucleosynthesized in cyclic manner in seven periods)

THIRTY TWO CLASS OF CRYSTAL SYMMETRY CREATE ELEMENTS IN SEVEN PERIODS. THE ELEMENTS CREATED IN LEFT AND RIGHT SIDE OF TABLE OCCUPY PERIPHERAL PORTION WHILE ELEMENTS CREATED IN THE MIDDLE OF TABLE OCCUPY CORE AND MANTLE OF PLANETS AND STARS IN THE UNIVERSE. THE ELEMENTS MOVE INSIDE PLAENTS AND STARS AND THEIR ACTUAL POSITION IS DECIDED BY COLOR-CRYSTAL CYCLE. THE ELECTROMAGNETIC ENERGY ASSOCIATED WITH ELEMENTS DECIDES THE POSITION OF NON-METALLIC AND METALLIC ELEMENTS ON PLANETS AND STARS. ALL THE ELEMENTS OCCUPY DIFFERENT POSITIONS UNDER THIRTY-TWO VERTICAL COLUMNS AND SEVEN PERIODS OF TABLE AND MAKE ROOM INSIDE PLANETS AND STARS OWING TO THEIR ROTATION, REVOLUTION AND PRECESSION MOVEMENT ALONG THREE AXES IN SPACE.

Table 6.4

PERIODIC TABLE OF ELEMENTS

PROMINENCE OF METALLIC TREND (32 CLASSES OF CRYSTAL SYMMETRY) PROMINENCE OF NON-METALLIC TREND

PERIODS	Hex	Hex	Hex	Hex	Hex	Hex	Hex	Tet	Tet	Tet	Tet	Tet	Tet	Tet	Cub	Cub	Cub	Cub	Cub	Tgn	Tgn	Tgn	Tgn	Tgn	Ort	Ort	Ort	Mon	Mon	Mon	Tri	Tri
PERIOD I	Tri																															Tri
PERIOD II	Ort	Ort																									Ort	Mon	Mon	Mon	Tri	Tri
PERIOD III	Ort	Ort																									Ort	Mon	Mon	Mon	Tri	Tri
PERIOD IV	Cub	Cub															Cub	Cub	Cub	Tgn	Tgn	Tgn	Tgn	Tgn	Ort	Ort Ort	Ort	Mon	Mon	Mon	Tri	Tri
PERIOD V	Cub	Cub															Cub	Cub	Cub	Tgn	Tgn	Tgn	Tgn	Tgn	Ort	Ort	Ort	Mon	Mon	Mon	Tri	Tri
PERIOD VI	Hex	Hex	Hex	Hex	Hex	Hex	Hex	Tet	Tet	Tet	Tet	Tet	Tet	Tet	Cub	Cub	Cub	Cub	Cub	Tgn	Tgn	Tgn	Tgn	Tgn	Ort	Ort	Ort	Mon	Mon	Mon	Tri	Tri
PERIOD VII	Hex	Hex	Hex	Hex	Hex	Hex	Hex	Tet	Tet	Tet	Tet	Tet	Tet	Tet	Cub	Cub	Cub	Cub	Cub	Tgn	Tgn	Tgn	Tgn	Tgn	Ort	Ort	Ort	Mon	Mon	Mon	Tri	Tri

THIRTY TWO CLASSES OF CRYSTAL SYMMETRY SETTLE IN CONCH SHELL MANNER: Tri – Triclinic (2) , Mon – Monoclinic (3) , Ort – Orthorhombic (3) Tgn – Trigonal (5) , Cub – Cubic (5) , Tet – Tetragonal (7) , Hex – Hexagonal (7).

ALL THE ELEMENTS MOVE WITHIN 32 CRYSTAL CLASSES OF CRYSTAL SYMMETRY AND THEY FIT IN 32 VERTICAL GROUPS OF ELEMENTS. THE ELEMENTS MAY SHOW DIFFERENT TYPES OF CRYSTAL SYMMETRY DEPENDING UPON THEIR POSITION IN SEVEN NON-METALLIC ZONES AND SEVEN METALLIC ZONES INSIDE ALL PLANETS AND STARS. THE ELEMENTS CREATED IN LEFT SIDE OF TABLE HAVE HIGHER CRYSTAL SYMMETRY AND OCCUPY CORE AND MANTLE PORTION WHILE ELEMENTS CREATED IN THE RIGHT OF TABLE HAVE LOWER CRYSTAL SYMMETRY AND OCCUPY PERIPHERAL PORTION IN CONCH SHELL MANNER ON PLANETS AND STARS IN THE UNIVERSE. ALL THE ATOMS OF ELEMENTS CAN EXHIBIT SEVEN TYPES OF CRYSTAL STRUCTURE DEPENDING UPON PRESSURE, VOLUME AND TEMPERATURE OF ALL ASTRAL BODIES, PLANETS AND STARS. CRYSTAL FORMATIONS TAKE PLACE IN CYCLIC MANNER DEPENDING UPON CHARGES OF THE ATOMS OF ELEMENTS.

Table 6.5

POSITION OF ELECTRONS MASS (DOTS REPRESENT e-) IS SHOWN IN SEVEN SHELLS AND SUB-SHELLS IN NON-METALLIC ELEMENTS. THE MASS OF ELECTRONS FORM SHELLS AROUND SOLID NUCLEUS LIKE PEELS OF LEMON OR ORANGE OR ECHOES OF SOUND WAVES. THE SHELLS ARE ELLIPTICAL OR EGG-SHAPED IN NON-METALS. ELECTROMAGNETIC ENERGY OF SEVEN COLORS CREATES CHARGED PARTICLES IN PLASMA MEDIUM IN SPACE WHICH GRADUALLY COMBINES WITH EACH OTHER TO PRODUCE SOLID NUCLEUS AND THEN ATOMS OF ELEMENTS. IN THIS PROCESS ELECTROMAGNETIC ENERGY IS CONVERTED INTO ELECTRIC ENERGY. POSITIVELY CHARGED PARTICLES SHAPE AXIAL RATIOS AND NEGATIVELY CHARGED PARTICLES SHAPE AXIAL ANGLES IN CRYSTALS OF ATOMS OF ELEMENTS. DURING THIS PROCESS ELECTRIC ENERGY OF PARTICLES IS CONVERTED INTO CHEMICAL ENERGY WHICH IS STORED INSIDE ATOMS.

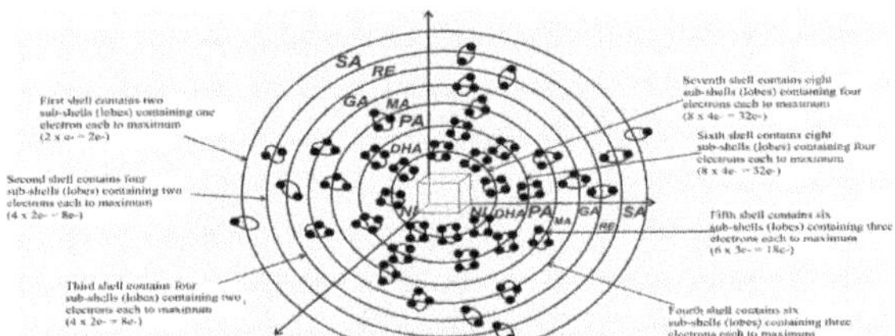

'SOUND WAVE PACKETS' EMERGE AS VIBRATIONS OR ECHOES AND EFFECT BODY PARTS ON PLANETS. THE ECHOES CAN PROLIFERATE UP TO SEVEN POINTS ON THE PATTERN OF IONIZATION OF ATOMS OF ELEMENTS. THE LETTERS ARE CREATED ON THE PATTERN OF ATOMS OF ELEMENTS AND WORDS ARE CREATED LIKE COMPOUNDS HAVING JUMBLED CONFIGURATIONS.

Fig. 6.8

196

DIVISION OF CELESTIAL SPHERE IN PARTS	CREATION OF LETTERS IN CIRCULAR AND ELLIPTICAL ORBITS DUE TO CONTRACTION AND EXPANSION IN GEOMETRIC AND ARITHMETIC PROGRESSION																															
	1	2	3	4	5	6	7	8	9	10	11	12	13	14	15	16	17	18	19	20	21	22	23	24	25	26	27	28	29	30	31	32
CIRCULAR ORBIT VARYING FROM ONE TO NINE (1 + 7 + 7 + 1)	1 A अ		2 AA आ		3 E इ		4 I ई		5 U उ		6 OO ऊ		7 R HI ऋ		8 R HI ॠ		9 LR I ऌ		10 LR EE ॡ		11 E ए		12 AI ऐ		13 O ओ		14 AU औ		15 AM अं		16 A H अः	
CIRCULAR ORBIT VARYING FROM ONE TO TWENTY FOUR (24)					1 K क	2 KH ख	3 G ग	4 GH घ	5 ANG ङ	6 CH च	7 CHH छ	8 J ज	9 JH झ	10 EIN ञ	11 T ट	12 TH ठ	13 D ड	14 DHA ढ	15 N ण	16 T त	17 TH थ	18 D द	19 DH ध	20 N न	21 P प	22 PH फ	23 B ब	24 BH भ				
ELLIPTICAL ORBIT VARYING FROM ONE TO THIRTY TWO (2+6+10+14)	1 K क	2 KH ख	3 G ग	4 GH घ	5 ANG ङ	6 CH च	7 CHH छ	8 J ज	9 JH झ	10 EIN ञ	11 T ट	12 TH ठ	13 D ड	14 DHA ढ	15 N ण	16 T त	17 TH थ	18 D द	19 DH ध	20 N न	21 P प	22 PH फ	23 B ब	24 BH भ	25 M म	26 Y य	27 R र	28 L ल	29 V व	30 SH श	31 SH ष	32 SA स

CREATION OF LETTERS IN CIRCULAR AND ELLIPTICAL ORBITS TAKES PLACE DUE TO CONTRACTION AND EXPANSION IN GEOMETRIC AND ARITHMETIC PROGRESSION. ORBITS ARE CIRCULAR DUE TO CONTRACTION IN GEOMETRIC PROGRESSION. ELLIPTICITY OR ORBIT DEVELOPS DUE TO FORMATION OF ANIONS (Y^-, Y^{2-}, Y^{3-}, Y^{4-}, Y^{5-}, Y^{6-}, Y^{7-}) AND CATIONS (X^+, X^{2+}, X^{3+}, X^{4+}, X^{5+}, X^{6+}, X^{7+}) IN THE ATOMS OF ELEMENTS IN ARITHMETIC PROGRESSION. ORBITS BECOME ELLIPTICAL DUE TO ARRANGEMENT OF ATOMS IN 2 + 6 + 10 + 14 = 32 ATOMS IN EVERY PERIOD OF CREATION. VOWELS OCCUPY SIXTEEN BLOCKS AND CONSONANTS OCCUPY 24 BLOCKS IN CIRCULAR ORBITS. 24 STANDS FOR FOUR TYPES OF SPINAL NERVES (THORACIC, LUMBAR, SACRAL AND COCCYGEAL) WHICH PRODUCES 24 CONSONANT LETTERS FROM *KA* TO *BHA*. CONSONANTS EXPAND UP TO 32 BLOCKS WHEN THE ORBIT BECOMES ELLIPTICAL IN SHAPE AND PRODUCE 32 LETTERS FROM *KA* TO *SA*.

Table 6.6

197

The hub and liver are composed primarily of compounds of black $^{56}_{26}Fe$ element. The north pole of bar magnet and magnetic needle points towards Geographic South and is called North Pole of magnet. The human body is composed of many elements and abundance of elements inside body depends upon period of rotation, revolution and precession of earth. The prominence of either of the forces on human being leads to creation of human being with different characteristics. In the human being contraction of cells and tissues and accumulation of mass is seen along three axes. The creation of organs and smaller parts of organs takes places along three axes. The development and production of smaller cells and smaller organs etc. takes place in the multiples of 9 along one axis due to rotation linked movement, 12 along second axis due to revolution linked movement and 14 along third axis due to precession linked movement. Every element creates one letter or "*Akshar*" and 118 "*Akshars*" are created in total in the universe which takes part in creation of human body, life forms, astral bodies, planets and stars. "Atomic Packets of Sound waves" which are 16 + 32 in number are created from atoms of elements called as letters or "*Akshars*" in human body.

Every turn of spherical astral body on its axis adds mass of H (Z = 1) having mass of $(9.11 \times 10^{-31}$ Kg. $+ 1.672 \times 10^{-27}$ Kgs.) + He (Z = 2) having mass of $(2 \times 9.11 \times 10^{-31}$ Kg. $+ 2 \times 1.672 \times 10^{-27}$ Kgs. $+ 2 \times 1.675 \times 10^{-27}$ Kgs.) + Li (Z = 3) having mass of $(3 \times 9.11 \times 10^{-31}$ Kg. $+ 3 \times 1.672 \times 10^{-27}$ Kgs. $+ 4 \times 1.675 \times 10^{-27}$ Kgs.) +.................Uuo (Z = 118) having mass of $(118 \times 9.11 \times 10^{-31}$ Kg. $+ 118 \times 1.672 \times 10^{-27}$ Kgs. $+ 180 \times 1.675 \times 10^{-27}$ Kgs.) Mass Units inside it. Fusion of atoms of elements increases mass of planets and stars with every movement till biggest red star is produced. The shortfall or abnormality of creation of elements from Z = 1 to Z = 118 is replenished within one movement of earth around Pole Star in 25,714.285 years. Gradually plenty of sub-atomic particles from space are assimilated and utilized in creation of atoms of elements by fusion process inside planets and stars.

Block I of ecliptic coincides with month of March, Block II with April, Block III with May, Block IV with June, Block V with July, Block VI with August, Block VII with September, Block VIII with October, Block IX with November, Block X with December, Block XI with January and Block XII with February every year. Mass particles have tendency to move in circular orbits. The time is interwoven with space and both exist together in the universe.

Chemical properties of elements are periodic functions of their atomic numbers whereas physical properties of elements are periodic functions of their atomic masses. 118 elements are created in different rounds, groups and periods and position of elements in core, mantle and crust area varies from one astral body to other astral body due to rotation, revolution and precession of spherical astral bodies. The impact of four forces decides the position of individual elements in core, mantle and crust portion of astral body. The sedimentation of elements and compounds takes place layer by layer on astral bodies due to rotation, revolution and precession. A solid astral body cannot exist in the universe if it does not contain Ba (Z=56) which contains four protons on every edge and diagonal of its atom.

Radio waves and power waves having very less frequency are absorbed inside planets and stars and they behave as radio wave towers. Human beings having less frequency sound wave act as radio wave towers and transmit and respond to waves in the frequency range 256 Hz to 512 Hz. Seven colors with their inherent energy are often referred to as seven horses in space. Horses signify horse power and are associated with energy of seven colors in space.

Vacuum medium transmits energy from one place to other due to contraction of waves and without the help of particles. The transmission of energy takes place due to contraction of circumference of waves of every 'wave packet' in space. Wave motion is a mechanism by which the energy is transmitted from one point to other. The mass component inherent in the particles is instrumental in transferring the energy from one point to other. As much will be the stretch of diameter component in the wave and as much will be the value of diameter, so high and quick will

198

be the transmission of energy in the medium from one point to other point. Thus, waves with highest circumference are better transmitters of energy as compared to the waves with smaller circumference.

The quantification of universal features can precisely be done with two parameters, i.e., circumference and diameter. Increase in density of the medium and application of different forces contract the diameter of particles in different directions. The particles being squeezed in different angles produces geometrically shaped structures with Circumference / Diameter ratio varying between √10 to √16. This ratio of particles produces seven crystal systems. Similarly, elliptical orbit and orbital expansion can also be measured with these parameters. Circumference as outer covering stands for time and changes in outer covering effects the storage of mass inside any object. The particles of smaller size produce crystals of smaller size as compared to particles of larger size, which produces crystals of bigger size with more mass component.

The spherical astral bodies that can produce life forms in our solar system are Venus, Earth, Europa, Titan or any other spherical astral body, which is created in blue / violet region of colors. The probability of life on Mars is less because it is a red planet. The impact of white region, seven colors and black region produces nine regions inside human body and their impact is observed through energy of electromagnetic waves. The week days are divided into seven days keeping in view the impact of seven colors on seven body systems of living body.

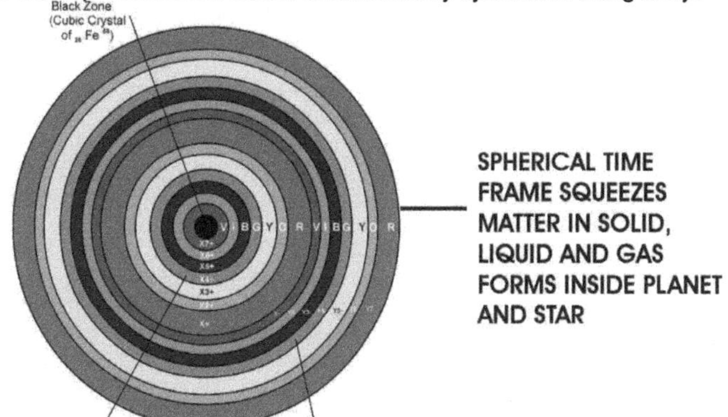

EXISTENCE OF ATOMS AND IONS IN FOURTEEN MATTER ZONES INSIDE PLANETS AND STARS. THE CORE OF PLANETS AND STARS CONTAIN $_{26}^{56}Fe$ AS BLACK METALLIC OCTET. TIME PERIOD OF MOVEMENT OF PLANETS AND STARS ALONG THREE AXES WILL ALWAYS BE DIFFERENT FROM EACH OTHER. PLANETS AND STARS BOUND TO EACH OTHER ALONG THREE AXES MOVE CONTINUOUSLY IN THE STAGE OF EQUILIBRIUM IN SPACE. ROTATION-LINKED MOVEMENT SHOWS LOW TIME PERIOD OF MOVEMENT, REVOLUTION-LINKED MOVEMENT SHOWS HIGH TIME PERIOD OF MOVEMENT AND PRECESSION-LINKED MOVEMENT SHOWS HIGHEST TIME PERIOD OF MOVEMENT IN SPACE.

Fig. 6.9

The presence of H_2O in all three states, i.e., gas state (moisture), liquid state (water) and solid state (solid compounds having water molecules attached with them) is compulsory for existence of life forms on planets. Life forms develop on planets which maintain an outer covering of atmosphere between the temperature range zero degree to 100^0 C. The life forms exist on blue planets, i.e., towards low wavelength of spectra. The planets and their moons arrange themselves according to nine-color cycle around the sun and form nine-planet system. In the nine-planet system the planets closer to sun will be hottest and planets farthest from sun will be the coldest. The middle planet, which maintains a mean temperature of 18^0 Celsius, will tend to develop biggest atmosphere along with biggest life forms.

Existence of life on planets depends upon availability of oxygen in solid, liquid and gas forms inside living beings. As high is the availability and retention of oxygen in liquid form inside any living being so high is the existence of life forms on that planet. The oxygen element tries to make room in three forms inside life forms and has the capability to change forms inside living body. It can be said that life exists on planets due to liquid oxygen only. It is the molecular oxygen in gas, liquid and solid form that creates and sustains life forms on planets. Under high pressure and low temperature, oxygen element $_8O^{16}$ can be liquefied. The liquid oxygen is slightly blue in color and has boiling point of -183^0C. The molecular oxygen has melting point of 54.4 K and boiling point of 90.2 K. The prominence of liquid oxygen on earth and on similar planets provides blue appearance to the planet from outside.

The planets whose circumference upon diameter ratio is either less than 22/7 or more than 22/7 along all the three axes have probability of developing life forms. Such planets have ridges, hills and furrows and tend to contain atmosphere in the temperature range 0^0C to 100^0C.

The wave on a string is caused by displacement of particles of the string. These displacements are in the direction perpendicular to the direction of propagation of wave. If the disturbance produced in a wave has a direction perpendicular to the direction of propagation of wave, the wave is called transverse wave. The wave on a string is transverse wave. Light waves are transverse waves. The electric field changes its value with space and time and the changes are propagated in space. The direction of electric field is perpendicular to the direction of propagation of light when light travels in free space. Sound waves are longitudinal waves. The particles of medium are pushed and pulled along the direction of propagation of sound. If the disturbance produced as wave passes along the direction of wave propagation, the wave is called longitudinal wave. All the waves cannot be characterized as either longitudinal or transverse. A very common example of wave that is neither longitudinal nor transverse is wave on the surface of water.

The animal body or human body can survive in dead condition on ice and cold areas of planets for 25,714.285 years. The body parts do not disintegrate on ice in frozen conditions. The corpse will remain intact for some time and then deterioration will commence from feet portion. The central nervous system retains oxygen, devours time and do not allow deterioration of body. The body well preserved on ice in frozen condition can be brought to life and can be made alive by adding breath in the body.

The evolution of life forms will be different on all planets and their characteristics will be decided by existence of atmosphere, oxygen and water in different proportions on different planets. A planet which contains plenty of mammals, reptiles and dicotyledonous trees may contain less number of non-vertebrates, grasses and herbs. Other planet may contain plenty of herbs, shrubs, insects and fishes but may not contain bigger trees, reptiles and mammals. The availability of different genera and species depends on stage of evolution of planets in relation to other planets and stars in space. The existence of gas layer around planets is compulsory for absorption of all radiation other than visible spectra and survival of body of life forms.

It is observed during aerobic upward pressure where nerves at seven places inside spinal cord drag air towards brain and tends to weaken connection with peripheral nervous system. The peripheral nerves become almost non-functional for some time due to dragging of air inside spinal cord of human beings. The concentration of extra air in brain and spinal cord refreshes central nervous system and makes human body young in age. The moment concentration of air inside brain and spinal cord decreases, the nerves tend to gain normal posture and efficiency along with consciousness of peripheral nervous system is restored. The above mentioned seven nerve centres inside spinal cord are not visible from outside the body. In human beings, suction pressure of air drags nerves from bottom of body, i.e., legs towards top and head of body. Thus head portion contains bigger and massive network of nerves as compared to leg portion.

The left nostril of human body inhales air and passes air to right bottom of spinal cord. The right nostril of human body inhales air and passes air to left bottom of spinal cord. The air accumulated at the bottom of spinal cord goes upwards and enters inside spinal cord and drags the fluid of spinal cord upwards. As much the spinal fluid moves inside cord so much the nerves of lower limbs and body become numb in character. The lower body parts become bereft of spinal fluid and faces of nerves inside spinal cord turn upwards. Due to control of will power on human body the spinal liquid is kept upwards and retained inside spinal cord for longer period by human beings. Every nerve of the brain of animal body has link with one star group in the universe at particular wavelength of electromagnetic wave. The planets and stars group are created for every wavelength of electromagnetic waves and in similar manner nerves are created inside human body having attachment with energy of electromagnetic waves.

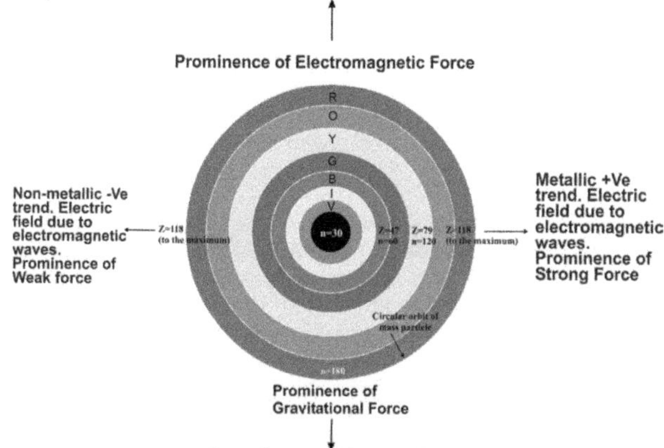

'POWER WAVE PACKETS' ARE CREATED DUE TO IMPACT OF ELECTRONS, PROTONS AND NEUTRONS ALONG THREE AXES INSIDE ATMOSPHERE OF PLANETS. POWER WAVE PACKETS ARE EMITTED BY MOUTH OF ANIMALS AND HUMAN BEINGS AND THEY ARE CAPABLE TO AFFECT HUMAN BODY BECAUSE THEY ARE MADE UP OF ENERGY OF ELECTROMAGNETIC WAVES. POWER WAVES CONTAIN WAVES OF HIGHER WAVELENGTHS IN THE RANGE $1 \times 10^4 - 1 \times 10^7$ METERS WHICH ARE RECEIVED AND INTERPRETED BY EAR AND BRAIN. ELECTROMAGNETIC WAVES IN THE RANGE 4000 ANGSTROMS TO 7500 ANGSTROMS CREATE BODY OF ALL LIVING BEINGS. POWER WAVES HAVING HIGHER WAVELENGTH ARE MORE POWERFUL THAN ELECTROMAGNETIC WAVES IN THE RANGE 4000 ANGSTROMS TO 7500 ANGSTROMS.

Fig. 6.10

This process of inhaling air through bottom end of spinal cord makes the lower part of body numb and numbness continues till the air of breath is retained upwards inside spinal cord. The breath can be retained upwards inside spinal cord by will power of animals and human beings. The coiled nerves of spinal cord become straight and spinal fluid goes upwards till breath of human beings is stopped for certain period. The oxygen in gas, liquid or solid form stored inside spinal fluid provides energy to human body and stops the impact of time by preserving human body. The moment human being releases breathe by relaxing will power the spinal fluid comes down inside spinal cord and nerves again become active. The numbness inside nerves and human body vanishes and human being starts taking normal breath through nostrils. The process of inhaling air through bottom end of spinal cord or say "opposite breath" through bottom of spinal cord helps human beings in retaining and preserving spinal fluid, spinal cord, brain and human body. The air stored inside spinal cord refreshes human body, stops ageing and preserves entire human body (*susumna bhakhshayate samayah*).

By artificial methods and in artificial incidences, e.g., videotapes and tape-recorded incidences, we see time as instance, which is repeating itself. In artificial recorded instances, we see time reversing and retrogressing. In natural conditions, the time progresses as well as retrogresses. The element created with prominence of metallic trend occupies centre of human body whereas elements created with prominence of non-metallic trend shift to periphery of body. This is due to prominence of high attraction at centre and gradual depletion of attraction towards periphery. The cycle of will power pulls air upwards inside spinal cord and energy towards white color region from black region. It tries to drag human body and contents of spinal column including bone marrow from basal hip portion towards brain portion. It pulls energy towards red and white region of energy of electromagnetic waves. There is gradual increase in number of nerves from base of spinal cord upwards towards brain.

The concentration of power due to electropositive charge with mass expands body and helps in development of tumor and fats inside body, expands the organs and cancerous growth of body parts and organs. The concentration of power due to electronegative charge with mass reduces growth of body and helps in development of tall, lean and thin body parts with least fat inside body.

Energy associated with seven color electromagnetic waves creates positively charged particles and negatively charged particles in plasma medium in space. The oppositely charged particles combine to form crystals and energy of electromagnetic waves is converted into electrical energy of particles. Positively charged particles shape axial ratios whereas negatively charged particles shape axial angles in crystals of elements thus electric energy converts into chemical energy. Chemical energy of atoms is stored with particles inside elements. Nucleus of atoms of elements is always solid structure created by charged particles and stores neutral mass particles inside it. In this process, energy of electromagnetic waves is stored inside elements. In the stage of equilibrium during nucleosynthesis of elements on planets and stars, the energy of seven colors plays distinct role.

The fertile planets can sustain life forms and examples are Earth, Venus and Io (satellite of Jupiter) and many other moons etc. A planet or astral body, which maintains fourteen zones, will obviously emit radiation with very high energy. The highly energetic particles in non-metallic zones show blue color emission. Life develops automatically on all planets where oxygen is available simultaneously in solid, liquid and gas forms. Life develops as unicellular organism and gradually develops into multi-cellular organism depending upon availability of 118 elements on planet. The invertebrates and vertebrates may develop on all planets, e.g., Venus, Mars, Europa, Io, Titan, moons of planets and all other planets as and when oxygen and water appears simultaneously in solid, liquid and gas forms on planets. Life forms develop automatic on all planets and their size increases gradually with every round, period and group of creation of elements on planets around stars. Smaller life forms evolve initially on every planet and their size increases gradually on bigger planets. Evolution of bigger life forms does not take place overnight on any planet.

Planets are bound to each other like family members in a family and play their role like male planet, female planet , father, mother, son and daughter etc. Depending upon many factors and forces, the planets stagnate at various points of equilibrium in the shape of elements. These factors decide the abundance of elements on different planets and role of a planet changes according to its position in any solar system. As for example, a man or woman takes birth as child, attains stable body by 26 years, attains high position by 26, 47 and 79 years and dies by 118 years. In the similar manner role of a planet changes from time to time. In case of accidents / artificial change / transition periods the planets keep moving till they enter stage of static equilibrium of any solar system. During stage of equilibrium the orbital ellipticity, inclination, time period of movement and number of satellites of planets becomes fixed and these factors decide the elemental abundance of any planet.

Atmospheric covering around planet allows sound waves to move with highest velocity. Coldest area of planet maintain surface temperature between 0^0C to 40^0C and contains biggest life forms, e.g. whales, Bear and Hippo etc. Below Zero degree centigrade solidification of water increases and that reduces the size of animals. The thermodynamic equilibrium is fixed by the status of planet. The planets which are not fully compact and which show high volcanic activity etc. may act as fertile planets because they have better chances of developing atmosphere. The fertile planets can sustain life forms and examples are Earth, Venus and Io (satellite of Jupiter) and many other satellites etc.

The spherical planets looking blue and emitting blue radiation will have probability of developing life forms and atmosphere. Spherical planets having highest number of ridges, furrows, mountains and deep trenches will have probability of developing more life forms. The planets having flat compacted round outer structure will have lesser probability of developing life forms due to their fully round structures. Multi-cellular life forms may develop on planets of solar system provided they have average temperature of 18^0C, which helps growth of living beings.

All spherical planets of any solar system or dynasty may develop life forms provided mean temperature of the planet is 18^0C. The stars, comets and asteroids etc. will never contain multi-cellular life forms. A planets having 18^0C temperature show highest proliferation of multi-cellular life forms. The planets, which develop life forms, will have highly undulated surface for water storage and maintenance of mean temperature at 18^0C. The planets having maximum flat surfaces may not develop life forms. The maintenance of three states, i.e. solid, liquid and gas form of water is essential for developing multi-cellular life forms on spherical planets. The existence and survival of life forms on planets depends upon mean temperature which varies between -4^0C to 100^0C. The survival of life forms is lowest at solid water (ice) level at -4^0C and at gaseous water (Vapor) level at 100^0C. The existence and survival of life forms is highest at liquid water level. The biggest life forms contain highest quantum of liquid oxygen inside multi-cellular living beings on any planet. The living plants and animals absorb non-metallic oxygen molecules in the form of gas. The atom of oxygen contains eight protons, eight electrons and eight neutrons in atom and makes existence as non-metallic octet.

Theoretically, round time frame can expand to infinite extent and orbits of movement can expand to infinite extent. Similarly round time frame can contract to lowest extent of singularity encapsulating dense mass in smallest crystalline forms. However, in practice expansion of round time frame is limited within 14 colors (7+7) anti-matter zones of electromagnetic waves in space and fourteen colors (7+7) matter zones of elements stored inside planets and stars.

Due to churning with straight electromagnet in the core of planet and star as churning rod, 32 classes of crystal systems are produced in seven periods on every planet and star. Due to prominence of electropositive charge at one end and electronegative charge at other end, churning of mass particles takes place in space and elements with different characteristics are produced. Due to constant compression and rarefaction of waves in space, mass particles are churned out in three-dimensional geometrical forms. The solid nucleuses are created in 32 crystalline classes in elements under seven periods during movement of planets and stars. During creation of elements, 118 elements are created in seven periods within 14 vertical rounds. Every element creates one letter or "Akshar" and 118 "Akshars" are created in total in the universe which take part in creation of human body, life forms, astral bodies, planets and stars. Sound waves are created as 118 "Atomic Packets" of atoms of elements called as letters or "Akshars".

The multi-cellular life forms can exist on planets only and they cannot exist on meteorites, asteroids and stars. The planets, which develop life forms, will have highly undulated surface for water storage and maintenance of mean temperature at 18°C. The planets having maximum flat surfaces may not develop life forms. The maintenance of three states, i.e., solid, liquid and gas form of water is essential for developing multi-cellular life forms on spherical planets.

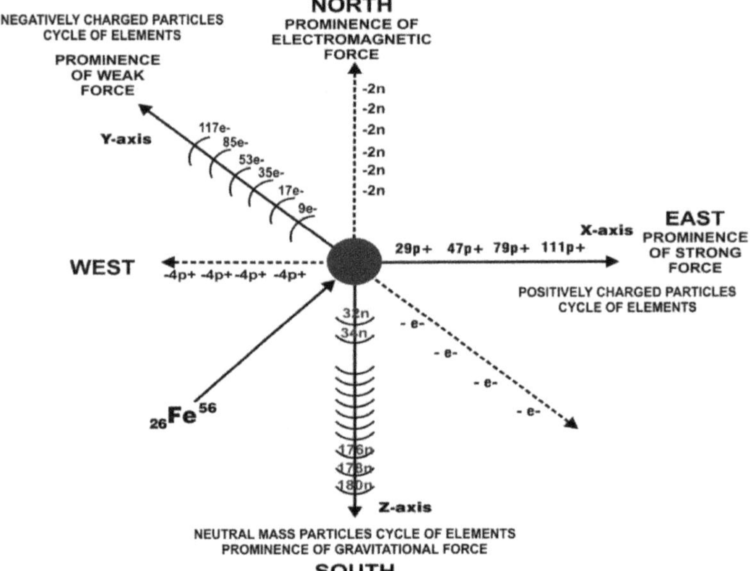

118 ELEMENTS ARE CREATED IN TOTAL BY NUCLEOSYNTHESIS OF THREE SUB-ATOMIC PARTICLES ALONG THREE AXES INSIDE ATOMS OF ELEMENTS ON PLANETS AND STARS. STAR AND PLANET ACT AS ELECTROMAGNET AND CAN CREATE 118 ELEMENTS TO THE MAXIMUM IN THE UNIVERSE.

Fig. 6.11

The animals of blue and dark colors are biggest and largest in size and mass and contain high quantity of compact solid mass. The animals of white, red, yellow and light colors are smaller in size, lighter and less compact in size. Unlike planets and stars, all animals and living beings contain an outer body covering which stores mass inside the body under seven systems. An outer covering is compulsory for all living beings. The central temperature at 18^0 centigrade is maintained in many bigger life forms. The living body will develop biggest size and store highest mass inside the outer covering at 18^0 centigrade which is maintained in many bigger life forms. The living body will develop biggest size and store highest mass inside the outer covering at 18 degrees centigrade temperature.

In case we compare astral bodies with living beings than we find that animals behave like planets, which absorbs all the electromagnetic radiations coming from space and do not emit any radiation from itself. The absorption of electromagnetic waves of higher energy tends to control

204

more and more mass of nucleus. They produce metallic octets, non-metallic octets and crystalline octets. Mass of electrons is observed as energy of seven color electromagnetic waves in ionized forms. In ionized form of elements the electrons behave as waves. The higher will power tends to contract human body in squares and spherical shape due to impact of round time frame.

The life forms exist on blue planets, i.e., towards low wavelength of spectra. The human being do not exist on red or white planets, i.e., towards higher wavelength of spectra. In a solar system, many planets surround the centrally located star. These planets and their moons arrange themselves according to nine-color cycle around the sun and form nine-planet system. In the nine-planet system the planets closer to sun will be hottest and planets farthest from sun will be the coldest. The middle planet, which maintains a mean temperature of 18^0 Celsius, will tend to develop biggest atmosphere along with human beings.

SURROUNDING STARDUST, METEORITES, ETC FALL ON PLANET DUE TO ATTRACTION AND PROMINENCE OF FUSION OF ELEMENTS.

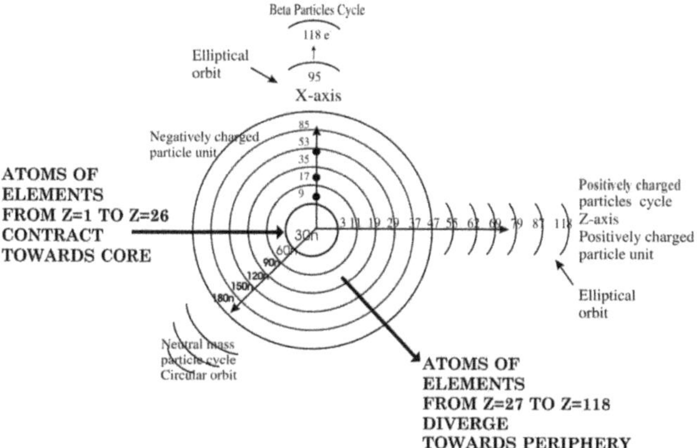

COMPOSITION OF ATOMS OF ELEMENTS INSIDE ALL PLANETS AND STARS IN THE UNIVERSE IS SAME AND DEPOSITION OF ELEMENTS TAKES PLACE IN ABOVE MENTIONED MANNER. SURROUNDING METEORITES, ASTEROIDS, PROTO-MOONS ETC ARE REPELLED AWAY DUE TO REPULSION AND PROMINENCE OF FISSION TREND IN ELEMENTS. EMISSION OF RAYS TAKES PLACE ALONG THREE AXES FROM PLANETS AND STARS. LAWS OF PHYSICS AND CHEMISTRY WILL NEVER BREAK DOWN DURING COLLISION, BANG, CRUNCH, COLLAPSE, WOBBLING AND DEATH OF ASTRAL BODIES, PLANETS AND STARS. LAWS OF PHYSICS CONTINUE FOREVER IN ALL DIRECTIONS AND WILL NEVER CHANGE AT ANY POINT OF TIME IN THE UNIVERSE.

Fig. 6.12

The time machine and time frame never reaches infinity. The time frame halts somewhere at some point in case of every planet and star and enters static equilibrium (t^{eq}). Time frame in practice never reaches either t^0 or t^{00}. The time frame halts somewhere at some point in case of every planet and star and enters stage of static equilibrium (t^{eq}). Time frame never reaches either t^0 or t^{00} on any astral body. Sound waves effect human body and its impact is observed along three axes as follows:

(a) Every day change: It relates to rotation of earth about its axis. The elements created from atomic number one to 26 belong to this category. In case their abundance ratio is disturbed on earth it replenishes within 24 hours (one rotation about its axis). It is linked to rotation of planet about its axis in 24 hours. The loss or gain made by elements from atomic number one to atomic number 26 shall be replenished in 24 hours.

205

(b) Annual change: It relates to revolution of earth around sun in one year. In case the element abundance ratio of elements created with atomic number 27 to 79 is disturbed, it replenishes within 365.25 days of one year due to revolution of earth around sun. It is linked to revolution of planet around sun in 365.256 days. The loss or gain made by elements from atomic number 27 to atomic number 79 shall be replenished in 365.25 days.

(c) Long term change: It relates to period of precession and movement of planets around pole star in cyclic manner. In case the element abundance ratio of elements created with atomic number 80 to 108 is disturbed, it takes 25,714.285 years to replenish back to normalcy. It is linked to precession of planet in 25,714.285 years. The loss or gain made by elements from atomic number 87 to atomic number 118 shall be replenished in full time period of precession.

All the animal body show three types of movement due to their attachment with three controlling stars and planets along three axes respectively. The period of movement decides the distance of animal body with three controlling astral bodies. The movement of animal body maintains status quo of abundance of elements on animal body and loss and gain in elemental abundance is compensated in the fixed time period.

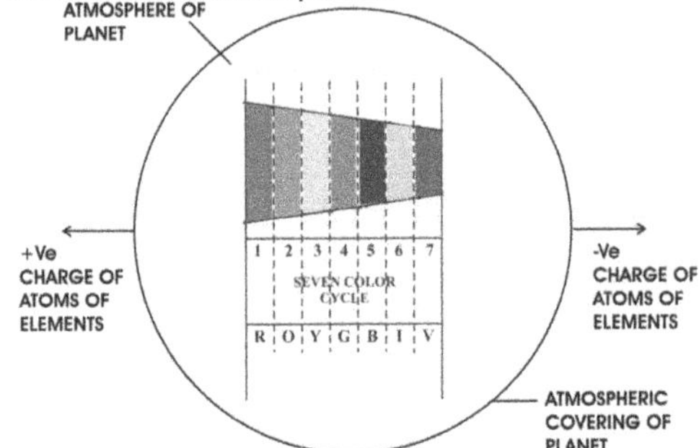

THE INNER MASS OF PARTICLES OF DIFFERENT CIRCUMFERENCES GETS LOCKED INTO 360⁰ TIME FRAME (24 HOURS FIXED TIME OF DAY IN SEVEN DAYS WEEK). POWER WAVES IN THE FREQUENCY RANGE 256 Hz TO 512 Hz CREATE 'SOUND WAVE PACKETS' OR LETTERS OR 'AKSHARS' LIKE ATOMS OF ELEMENTS WITHIN ATMOSPHERE OF PLANET EARTH. THE ENERGY OF ELECTROMAGNETIC WAVES OF THREE FUNDAMENTAL SUB-ATOMIC PARTICLES, i.e., ELECTRONS, PROTONS AND NEUTRONS CREATES ATOMS OF ELEMENTS OR LETTERS OR 'AKSHARS'. THE IMPACT OF FUNDAMENTAL PARTICLES TAKES PLACE ALONG THREE AXES DUE TO PRESSURE, TEMPERATURE AND VOLUME EFFECT OF ATMOSPHERE. PROTONS EFFECT TEMPERATURE, NEUTRONS EFFECT PRESSURE AND ELECTRONS CONTROL VOLUME OF LETTERS OR 'AKSHARS' WITHIN ATMOSPHERE OF PLANET. CREATION OF LETTERS LIKE ATOMS OF ELEMENTS ARE CONTROLLED BY TEMPERATURE, VOLUME AND PRESSURE ALONG THREE AXES ON PLANETS HAVING ATMOSPHERE. THESE POWER WAVE PACKETS ARE EMITTED BY VOCAL CORDS OF ANIMALS AND HUMAN BEINGS AND INSTRUMENTS OF HUMAN BEINGS ON PLANET BUT THEY WILL FAIL TO EXIST ON PLANETS AND STARS HAVING NO ATMOSPHERE.

Fig. 6.13

Life exists in unicellular forms as bacteria, virus, yeast, mycoplasma or unicellular structures within hard coat on astral bodies for infinite periods. It is transported, exported or imported through meteorites, asteroids, moons, planets and stars etc from time to time. The hard coat protects unicellular life forms for billions of years in dormant forms. The moment it gets congenial environment, it proliferates and produces different life forms through binary fission. Multi-cellular life forms cannot exist on any astral body unless supported by oxygen and water in solid, liquid and gas forms covered by ozone layer. Life forms in dormant stage are integral part of our universe and they proliferate the moment they get congenial atmosphere.

As the elements are created in fixed numerical order in the same manner letters and words are created in numerical order. The words contain waves of particulars wavelength and have impact like astral bodies. The elements are created as integers or whole numbers in numerical order. In the similar manner letters are also created in every living being in fixed numerical order. The expansion of time is directly proportional to expansion of mass inside astral bodies. The orbit of element becomes elliptical from atomic number 2 and onwards but the fission trend remains suppressed due to increasing binding energy of the element cycle which reaches its climax at atomic number 26. From atomic number 27 and onwards the fission trend in elements increases in ascending order subject to different equilibrium constants of elements.

TATVA – VIJNAN UDYAAN
(PERIODIC TABLE OF ELEMENTS)

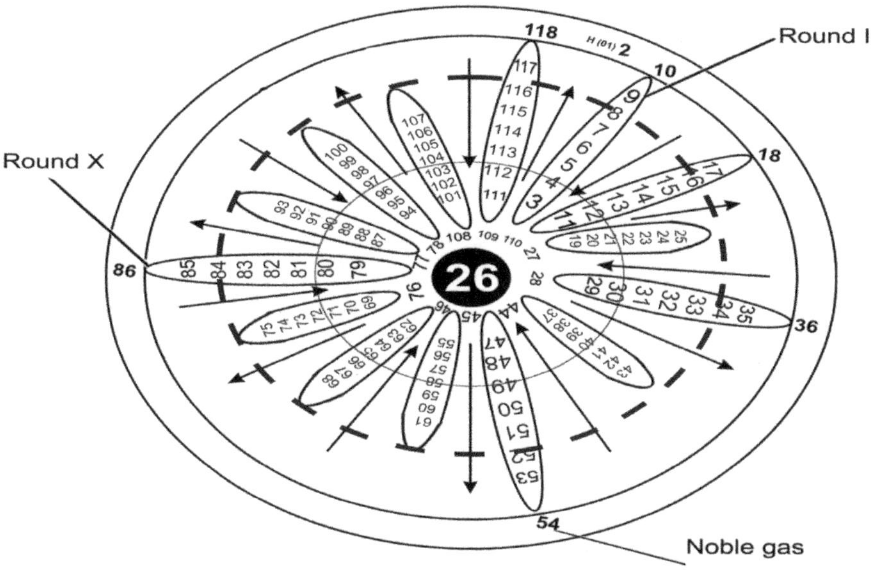

ELEMENTS CREATED IN FOURTEEN ROUNDS OCCUPY DIFFERENT POSITIONS INSIDE PLANETS AND STARS. METALLIC ELEMENTS OCCUPY CORE WHEREAS NON-METALLIC ELEMENTS SHIFT TOWARDS PERIPHERY. THE ATOMS OF ELEMENTS KEEP CIRCULATING IN LAYERS INSIDE PLANETS AND STARS DURING COURSE OF NUCLEOSYNTHESIS.

Fig. 6.14

In our solar system, many planets and moons of planets maintain environment which are congenial for existence of life forms. These planets and moons contain hills, furrows, soil, water and oxygen retaining capacity in different forms and may develop atmosphere and layer of oxygen covering around planet. In our solar system, Venus, Titan, Europa and many other moons of planets can develop life forms provided they occupy a position where temperature varies between zero degrees Celsius to 100 degrees Celsius. During reshuffling of planets and moons of

207

planets of our solar system, these moons and planets may occupy positions where temperature varies between zero degrees Celsius to 100 degrees Celsius and may develop life forms. Generally the inner planets occupying third to fifth positions from Sun in the electromagnetic wavelength range violet to blue-green color (4000 Angstrom to 5430 Angstrom) will maintain above temperature range and may develop life forms.

Physically the energy of electromagnetic waves varies between 4000 Å to to 7500 Å inside animals and human beings. Chemically the charge and mass of matter waves varies between the smallest particles, i.e., e-, p+ and neutron to highest particles having 118e-, 118p+ and 180 neutrons in elements. The color cycle compels elements to settle inside fourteen matter zones of planets and stars. The color-crystal cycle tries to restrict the number of elements created on planets to 118 elements. The quantification of universal features can precisely be done with two parameters, i.e., circumference and diameter. Increase in density of the medium and application of different forces contract the diameter of particles in different directions. The particles being squeezed in different angles produces geometrically shaped structures with C/D ratio varying between $\sqrt{10}$ to $\sqrt{16}$. This ratio of particles produces seven crystal systems.

In the elements seven color component is provided by +Ve charge and -Ve charge particles of particles. Mass particles roam around as black and dark particles in space. It is captured by +Ve charged particles and -Ve charged particles and result is creation of elements by nucleosynthesis. The energy associated with different colors have the capacity to nucleosynthesize different elements in numerical order and settle them inside the animal and human bodies.

"*Kaal Chakra*" stands for disc of time period of movement due to revolution-linked movement of planets and stars. The planets, which are oblate spheroid in shape, develop life forms. The planets, which revolve around sun in clockwise direction, develop equatorial bulge due to accumulation of mass of elements and their poles become flattened. Such oblate spheroids can develop atmosphere and can contain life forms. The atmosphere of a spherical astral body is created by prominence of gas state and liquid state on astral body. These two states retain mass in floating form and wave motion is high in these two states. The wave motion increases gradually in plasma and other state in space. The planets generally develop a protective covering with liquid and gas states around them in case of earth and ozone layer forms an outer covering and retains mass in gas and liquid form in atmosphere. As much will be the prominence of these two states on any planet so thick will be the layer of atmosphere on that planet and mean temperature will be about 18^0 C. the planets may contain an outer protective layer or may not contain any layer. The planets, which contain liquid oxygen in any form, will automatic develop living beings as seen in case of planet earth.

The colors may disperse in many ways and their mixing may create different color combinations but they finally make room inside planets and stars in the multiples of 16 only. The planets and stars contain one outer white region, seven colored non-metallic region, seven colored metallic region and one central black region. In smaller astral bodies they are visible in nine color regions. Light waves are made up of particles and waves. Seven stars of U. Major and seven stars of U. Minor create fourteen zones for elements in space as fourteen anti-matter zones. Fourteen rounds of elements creation shows the impact of outer compaction of crystals by fourteen crystals inside astral body and consequent expansion of mass in fourteen equivalent zones in space being observed as fourteen stars cluster.

The elements produce ions of seven colors according to energy of ions. The black region possesses highest temperature and energy and ions of dark color shift towards centre of human body. The ions of light color possess lesser energy on planet as compared to dark color and occupy peripheral portion of human body.

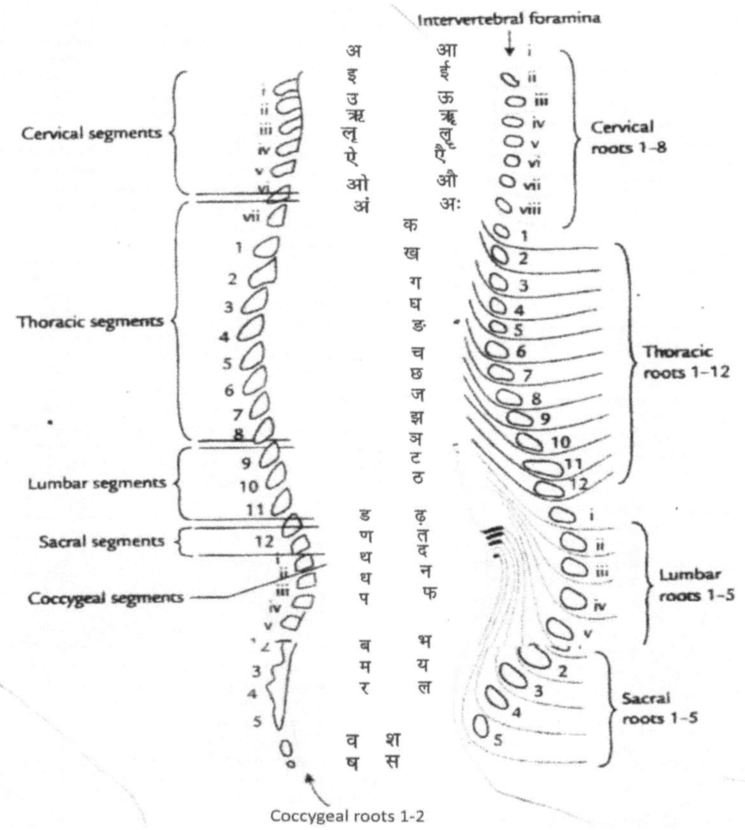

THE SEGMENTS OF SPINAL CORD INSIDE BODY AND SPINOUS PROCESSESS OF THE VERTEBRAE ARE SHOWN ABOVE. VOCAL CORD BEGINS PRODUCTION OF VOICE OF VOWELS AND CONSONANTS STARTING FROM KA…..KAA…..KI…..KEE…..KU…..KOO…..KRI…..KREE…..KLRI…..KLREE…..KE…..KAI….KO…..KAU…..KAM…..KAH IN HUMAN BEINGS. FIRST CONSONANT LETTER KA MULTIPLIED WITH SIXTEEN VOWEL LETTERS PRODUCES SIXTEEN TYPES OF SOUND WAVES. INFANTS IN HUMAN BEINGS AT THE TIME OF BIRTH CRY AND MAKE A SOUND OF "K……A…….R……A…….H…….N…….A…….H". OR "K……A…….H…….A". OR "K……A…..R….A……N…..AH". OR "K……A…….N……AH". THE EMISSION OF FIRST LETTER OF SOUND WAVE PACKET, i.e., KA TAKES PLACE FROM THORACIC NERVE. IT BEGINS FROM A…..AA AND ENDS AT 16TH POSITION OF CERVICAL NERVE, i.e., AN….. AH IN CERVICAL NERVES OF HUMAN BODY. THE INFANT BEGINS UTTERING OF LANGUAGE FROM FIRST CONSONANT OF SPINAL NERVES ('KA') AND ENDS AT LAST SIXTEENTH VOWEL ('AH') OF CERVICAL NERVES NEAR THROAT. THE LAST POINT, COCCYX IS CALLED AS TAILBONE WHICH IS SMALL TRAINGULAR BONE LOCATED AT THE BOTTOM OF SPINE. IT IS COMPOSED OF FOUR FUSED COCCYGEAL VERTEBRA OR SPINAL BONES. THESE FOUR FUSED VERTEBRAE ACT AS BASE OF SPINAL CORD IN HUMAN BEINGS AND CONTAIN TWO PAIRS OF COCCYGEAL NERVES IN FUSED FORM. CRY OF INFANTS BORN IN AFRICA AND CRY OF INFANTS BORN IN AUSTRALIA AT THE TIME OF BIRTH HAVE SAME TONE OF UTTERING, i.e.,…. KA….. KHA……AR……AN……AH……AH.

Fig. 6.15

209

In the human body, four types of teeth are produced inside human mouth which form 32 teeth in total. Thirty two teeth help in formation and emission of different letters and words from mouth. The extent and diversity of languages in the world are many and vary with time and place. The linguists have tried to study all languages of the world at different places. It depends upon the scientific structure of animal body, atmosphere and movement pattern of planet. Evolution of nerves and central nervous system plays significant role in production of voices, letters, alphabets and languages. Language is the product of Spinal nerves and Cervical nerves inside body. Vowels are produced by cervical nerves whereas consonants are produced by spinal nerves of nervous system. Every animal has different parts, organs and systems and variation of characteristics of planet along three axes decides the development of languages on planet. The letters develop in the sequence of creation of atoms of elements on earth and on the pattern of development of nervous system in animals and human beings.

Creation of words takes place just like formation of compounds of elements. The atoms of elements combine to form different compounds and in similar manner vowels and consonants combine to create words or '*shabdas*' or compound letters on planets. The atoms of elements combine to form different types of compounds as follows:

$$CuSO_4 + Fe \longrightarrow FeSO_4 + Cu$$
Copper Sulphate　Iron　　　　Ferrous Sulphate　　Copper

$$AgNO_3 + NaCl \longrightarrow AgCl + NaNO_3$$
Silver Nitrate　Sodium Chloride　　Silver Chloride　Sodium Nitrate

$$Zn(OH)_2 + H_2SO_4 \longrightarrow ZnSO_4 + 2H_2O$$
Zinc Hydroxide　Sulphuric Acid　　Zinc Sulphate　Water

$$C_{12}H_{22}O_{11} + H_2O \longrightarrow C_6H_{12}O_6 + C_6H_{12}O_6$$
Sucrose　　Water　　　　Glucose　　Fructose

$$NH_2CONH_2 + H_2O \longrightarrow 2NH_3 + CO_2$$
Urea　　　Water　　　　Ammonia　Carbon Dioxide

Sanskrit words are formed by the process of taking verb roots and basic noun and converting them into complex and expressive words. Creation of sound wave packets or letters or '*Akshars*' with the help of mass of electrons, protons and neutrons makes the letters and words audible and non-perishable like atoms of 118 elements. The wave packets hit the drum of our ear and seven types of letters or jumbled words are perceived by our nervous system. The storage and settlement of elements, compounds and mass particles on astral bodies takes place due to temperature and maximum mass with highest volume is supposed to sediment in red color region. In the zone of absorption, absorption bands are seen at different wavelengths. These absorption bands are like fingerprints that show position of planets in the ladder of energy of electromagnetic waves in every solar system.

The sound waves cannot travel in vacuum but in space they are observed as equivalent to power waves of electromagnetic waves. Sound waves are called longitudinal waves because the particles of the medium vibrate in the direction of propagation of waves. Ultrasonics are the frequencies which are greater than 20,000 Hz whereas infrasonics are frequencies which are lesser than 20 Hz. In human beings the sound waves on striking the ear drum make it vibrate exactly the same way as the given sound emitting object. The bones in the middle ear starts vibrating when the ear drum vibrates. It helps in magnifying the vibrations. When the magnified vibrations reach the cochlea in the inner ear, the fluid in it starts vibrating. These vibrations are picked up by sensor receptors and are converted into electrical signals. These electrical signals then travel to brain which interprets sound waves under seven classes.

Compounds are created from atoms of elements and in the similar manner Letters or '*Akshars*' combine to form different types of complex Words as follows:

अधि + इ (आ) + प + अयू + ति > अध्यापयति

क्री + प + अय + ति > क्रापयति

जि (जा) + प + अय + ति > जापयति

आ	+ पु	+ ल्यप्	आपूय	पवित्र कर
आ	+ मुष्	+ ल्यप्	आमूष्य	चुराकर
प्र	+ अश्	+ ल्यप्	प्राश्य	खाकर
आ	+ प्री	+ ल्यप्	आप्रीय	खुशकर
प्र	+ सू	+ ल्यप्	प्रसूय	जनकर
वि	+ भी	+ ल्यप्	विभीय	डरकर
आ	+ दा	+ ल्यप्	आदाय	लेकर
वि	+ हा	+ ल्यप्	विहाय	छोड़कर

संयुक्ताक्षर में 'ऋ' का 'अरू' हो जाता है। जैसे— स्मृ + य + ते > स्मर्यते।

दीर्घ ऋकार के स्थान में 'ईर्' हो जाता है। जैसे— कृ + य + ते > कीर्यते

जृ + य + ते > जीर्यते

VOWELS AND CONSONANTS OF SANSKRIT LANGUAGE CREATE DIFFERENT COMPOUND WORDS WHICH CARRY DIFFERENT MEANING AND EFFECT BODY PARTS.

Table 6.7

The availability of elements on planets decides the size, shape and number of life forms in cyclic manner on planets. The planets possessing solid oxygen and solid water in isolated or combined form with other elements develop life forms on the surface of planets. The planets possessing liquid oxygen and liquid water in isolated or combined form with other elements develop life forms inside water and on surface.

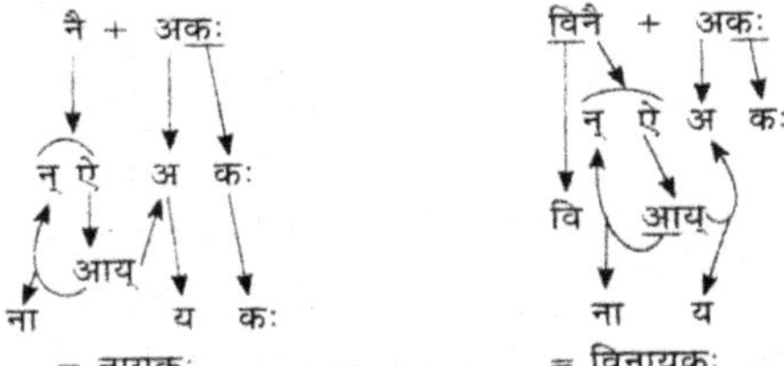

WORDS ARE CREATED AS 'SOUND WAVE PACKETS' BY INTERMIXING OF VOWELS AND CONSONANTS.

Fig. 6.16

Multi-cellular life forms may develop on planets of solar system provided they have medium temperature, which helps growth of living beings. The planet must maintain adequate pressure for

211

growth, maintain oxygen layer and ozone layer for protection and must have sufficient water and fluid medium for circulation throughout astral body and inside plants and animals. A planet which is not having congenial atmosphere and temperature at present may develop the same in future if planetary sequence in solar system changes in future. As for example, Europa or Venus may develop life forms and atmosphere like earth in future provided the sequence of planets changes in future and they get congenial environment.

The speed of sound in gas, liquid and solid medium can be expressed in terms of its pressure, temperature, volume and density. As wave travels in a medium, energy is transported from one part of the space to another part. The intensity of sound wave is defined as the average energy crossing a unit cross-sectional area perpendicular to the direction of propagation of the wave in unit time. It may also be stated as the average power transmitted across a unit cross-sectional area perpendicular to the direction of propagation. The impact of pressure, volume and temperature decides the size and shape of individual living being on planet. Every living being maintains individual thermodynamic equilibrium on planets. The thermodynamic equilibrium of living body depends upon four forces and combined action of pressure (p), volume (v) and temperature along three axes on living body.

The loudness of sound that we feel is mainly related to the intensity of sound. It also depends on the frequency to some extent. The appearance of sound to a human ear is characterized by three parameters, i.e., pitch, loudness and quality. All the three are subjective description of sound though they are related to objectively defined quantities. Pitch is related to frequency, loudness is related to intensity and quality is related to the wave form of sound waves.

(a) PITCH AND FREQUENCY: Pitch of a sound is that sensation by which we differentiate the sounds of buffalo voice, male voice and female voice. We say that a buffalo voice is of low pitch, a male voice has higher pitch and a female voice has still higher pitch. This sensation primarily depends on the dominant frequency present in the sound. Higher the frequency, higher will be the pitch and vice versa.

(b) LOUDNESS AND INTENSITY: The loudness that we sense is related to the intensity of sound though it is not directly proportional to it. Our perception of loudness is better correlated with the sound level measured in decibels.

(c) QUALITY AND WAVE FORM: A sound generated by a source may contain a number of frequency components in it. Different frequency components have different amplitudes and superposition of them results in the actual waveform. The appearance of sound depends on this waveform apart from the dominant frequency and intensity. We differentiate between the sound from a drum set and that from dumbbell by saying that they have different quality. A musical sound has certain well defined frequencies which have considerable amplitude. These frequencies are generally harmonics of a fundamental frequency. Such a sound is particularly pleasant to the ear. On the other hand, a noise has frequencies that do not bear any well defined relationship among themselves.

When there exists a discontinuity in the medium, the wave gets reflected. When a sound wave gets reflected from a rigid boundary, the particles at the boundary are unable to vibrate. Thus a reflected wave is generated which interferes with the oncoming wave to produce zero displacement at the rigid boundary. At these points (zero displacement) the pressure variation is maximum. Thus a reflected pressure wave has the same phase as the incident wave. That means a compression pulse reflects as a compression pulse and a rarefaction pulse reflects as a rarefaction pulse. A sound wave is also reflected if it encounters a low pressure region. A practical example is when a sound wave travels in a narrow open tube. When the wave reaches an open end it gets reflected. The force on the particles there due to the outside air is quite small and hence the particles vibrate with increased amplitude. As a result the pressure there remains at the average value. Thus the reflected pressure wave interferes destructively with the oncoming wave. There is a phase change of π in the pressure wave when it is reflected by an open end. That means a compression pulse reflects as a rarefaction pulse and vice versa.

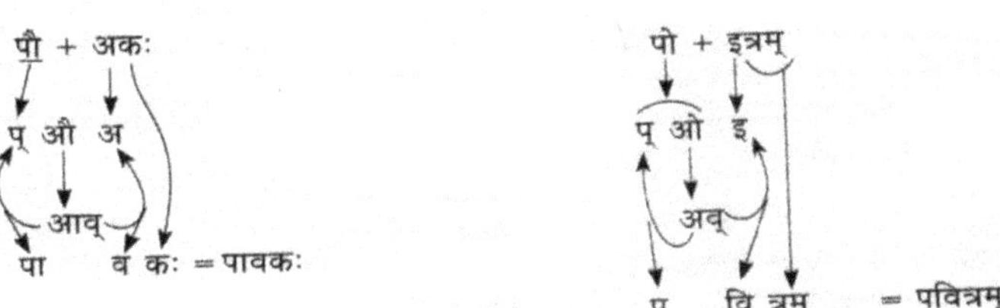

WORDS ARE CREATED AS 'SOUND WAVE PACKETS' BY INTERMIXING OF VOWELS AND CONSONANTS.
Fig. 6.17

The principle of superposition of sound waves is observed when two or more waves pass through the same region of a medium and the resultant disturbance is equal to the sum of disturbances produced by individual waves. Depending upon the phase difference the waves can interfere constructively or destructively leading to a corresponding increase or decrease in the resultant intensity. While discussing the interference of two sound waves, it is advised that the waves be expressed in terms of pressure change. The resultant change in pressure is the algebraic sum of the changes in pressure due to individual waves.

SOUND LEVELS	DECIBELS
Minimum audible sound	0 dB
Whispering (at 1 meter)	10 dB
Normal talk (at 1 meter)	60 dB
Maximum tolerable sound	120 dB

Table 6.8

Standing waves can be produced in air columns trapped in tubes of cylindrical shape. Organ pipes are such vibrating air columns. A closed organ pipe is a cylindrical tube having an air column with one end closed. Sound waves are sent in by a source vibrating near the open end. An ingoing pressure wave gets reflected from the fixed end. This inverted wave is again reflected at the open end. After two reflections it moves towards the fixed end and interferes with the new wave sent by the source in that direction.

DIFFRACTION

When waves are originated by a vibrating source, they spread in the medium. If the medium is homogeneous and isotropic the waves from a point source have spherical wave fronts, the rays going in all directions. Far from the source the wave fronts are nearly planes. The shape of the wave front is changed when the wave meets an obstacle or an opening in its path. This leads to bending of the wave around the edges. For example, if a small cardboard is placed between a source of sound and a listener, the sound beyond the cardboard is not completely stopped, rather the waves bend at the edges of the cardboard to reach the listener. If a plane wave is passed through a small hole (an opening in large obstacle) spherical waves are obtained on the other side as if the hole itself is a source sending waves in all directions. Such bending of waves from an obstacle or an opening is called diffraction.

Diffraction is a characteristic property of wave motion and all kinds of waves exhibit diffraction. The diffraction effects are appreciable when the dimensions of openings or the obstacles are comparable or smaller than the wavelength of the wave. If the opening or obstacle is large compared to the wavelength, the diffraction effects are almost negligible. The frequency of audible sound ranges from about 20 Hz to 20 kHz. Velocity of sound in air is around 332 m s^{-1}. The wavelength of audible sound in air thus ranges from 16 m to 1.6 cm. Quite often the wavelength of sound is much larger than the obstacles or openings and diffraction is prominently displayed.

SONIC BOOMS

A supersonic plane travels in air with a speed greater than the speed of sound in air. It sends a cracking sound called sonic boom which can break glass dishes, window panes and even cause damage to buildings. The spherical wave fronts intersect over the surface of a cone with the apex at the source. Because of constructive interference of a large number of waves arriving at the same instant on the surface of the cone, pressure waves of very large amplitude are sent with the conical wave front. Such waves are one variety of shock waves. As the tiny source moves it drags the cone with it. When an observer on ground is intercepted by the cone surface, the boom is heard. There is a common misconception that the boom is produced at the instant the speed of plane crosses the speed of sound and once it achieves the supersonic speed it sends no further shock wave. The sonic boom is not a onetime affair that occurs when the speed just exceeds the speed of sound. As long as the plane moves with a supersonic speed, it continues to send the boom.

AEKALABYA

AEKLABYA, A JUNGLE BOY FIRED ARROW ABOVE VELOCITY OF SOUND WHICH EFFECTED PLANET. AEKLABYA FIRED ARROW ABOVE VELOCITY OF SOUND TO SUCH AN EXTENT THAT BARKING SOUND OF DOG WAS NOT HEARD. HIS ARROW SHOTS STOPPED BARKING SOUND OF DOG AND SOUND OF OTHER PERSONS OF THE AREA. HIS GREATEST SKILL OF ARCHERY WAS EVIDENCED BY PEOPLE AND ANIMALS OF THE FOREST AREA. FIRING OF ARROW WITH SPEED ABOVE VELOCITY OF SOUND IS HARMFUL FOR PLANET EARTH. ARROWS, MISSILES, AIRCRAFTS TRAVELLING WITH SPEED ABOVE SPEED OF SOUND ARE DETRIMENTAL FOR LIFE, OZONE LAYER, ATMOSPHERE AND PLANET EARTH.

The speed of compression of sound wave in solids is determined by the medium's compressibility, shear modulus and density. The ratio of speed of an object to the speed of sound in the fluid is called the object's Mach Number. Objects moving at speeds greater than Mach 1 are said to be travelling at supersonic speeds. The increase in speed of sound have harmful effect on body and will reduce the growth and development of body. Any device, machine, arms, ammunition and supersonic appliance emitting sound waves above Mach 1 needs to be banned within atmosphere of earth.

Ancient people had very good idea about science and present level science was known to them about forty three lakh years ago on earth. Speed of sound and ozone layer protection was known to them. They did not allow any body to fire shots above speed of sound. Firing of missiles, movement of planes and ammunition above speed of sound was prohibited on earth. Aeklabya was a Bhil boy of forest area and with his constant practice he learnt the art of firing arrows above velocity of sound. He fired shots and arrow above speed of sound to such an extent that it crossed speed of sound. Once while he was practicing firing of arrow, dogs started barking and disturbed in his practice. He filled up the mouth of dog by firing arrows and stopped velocity of sound. He stopped barking sound of dog and violated the norms of planet. Dog was unable to bark. Dog ran for his survival and reached before Arjun and Dronacharya. Guru Dronacharya did not allow any body to fire arrows above velocity of sound to save earth. He found that activities of Aeklabya was detrimental for survival of ozone layer of earth. He found that Aeklabya was firing shots and arrows above speed of sound then survival of earth will be at stake. He asked Aeklabya to surrender his thumb so that he cannot fire any more arrow above speed of sound in future and planet Earth could be saved. Movement of appliances above speed of sound will affect growth of animals and human beings and will deplete ozone layer around earth.

A musical scale is a sequence of frequencies which have a particularly pleasing effect on the human ear. A widely used musical scale, called diatonic scale, has eight frequencies covering an octave. Each frequency is called a note. In the houses proper case is required to be taken for absorption and reflection of sound waves. The sound waves can reach a listener directly from the source as well as after reflection from a wall or the ceiling. This leads to echo which is heard after an interval of hearing the first sound. This echo interferes with the next sound signal affecting the clarity. Another effect of multiple reflection is the reverberation. A listener hears the direct sound, sound coming after one reflection, after two reflections and so on. The time interval between the successive arrival of the same sound signal keeps on decreasing. The intensity of signal also decreases gradually. The vocal cords of animals and human beings produce sound waves as 'wave packets'. The frequency of wave packets emitted by different animals varies from one animal to other and constitutes building blocks of different languages. Most of the languages show independent origin and maintain their individual character at many isolated places and pockets on earth.

Voice, letters, alphabets and Language is produced due to impact of Spinal nerves and Cervical nerves by vocal cords inside Life forms. The impact of sound waves is observed as power waves. During creation of life forms with seven color electromagnetic waves, it is observed that sound waves are more powerful in action than electromagnetic waves. There is a saying that

"Raghukul rit sada chali aai, pran jahin par vachan na jahin". The meaning of the same is that sound waves are more powerful and act more vigorously on living body than seven color electromagnetic waves that creates body of living beings. The seven color waves constituting the body may perish but sound waves acting as power waves will not perish and will exist on earth. 'Sound Wave Packets' are a form of power waves emitted from vocal cords of human body as 'wave packets' of lower frequency. It is the most scientific language emitted from nerves of human body. It is emitted from human body and often it is referred to as "Immortal Language". Its impact persists for generations and effects all human beings on earth through electromagnetic waves emitted from mouth.

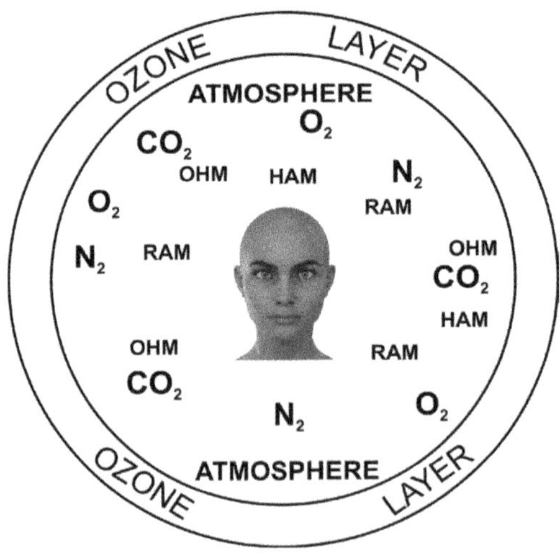

216

'SOUND WAVE PACKETS' CAN EXIST IN THE ATMOSPHERE ONLY AND BEYOND THAT IN SPACE THEY LOSE THEIR EXISTENCE BECAUSE THEY CAN NOT BE HEARD. 'SOUND WAVE PACKETS' EFFECT ALL OBJECTS INSIDE PLANET BUT THEY FAIL TO EXIST IN SPACE. 'SOUND WAVE PACKETS' ARE PRODUCED LIKE LIGHTNING IN THE ATMOSPHERE WHICH EXISTS FOR A FEW SECONDS OR MINUTES, SHOWS ITS IMPACT ON ALL MATERIALS WITHIN ATMOSPHERE AND VANISHES. ITS IMPACT IS VISIBLE AFTERWARDS ON ALL LIVING BEINGS, OBJECTS AND PLANET. IT VANISHES IN THE ATMOSPHERE AND SUB-ATOMIC PARTICLES MERGE WITH AIR OF ATMOSPHERE. SOUND WAVES IN POWER WAVES REGION CAN CONVERT INTO SEVEN COLOR ELECTROMAGNETIC WAVES AND SHOW IMPACT ON SPHERICAL BODIES AND LIFE FORMS. EXPANSION OF PARTICLES AND ELEMENTS TAKES PLACE IN SEVEN COLORS (4000 TO 7500Å) INSIDE ATOMS OF ELEMENTS. MAXIMUM EXPANSION OF PARTICLES CAN TAKE PLACE UPTO 7500Å INSIDE ELEMENTS STORED IN SEVEN COLOR REGIONS INSIDE HUMAN BODIES. POWER WAVES IN THE FREQUENCY RANGE 256 Hz TO 512 Hz CREATE "SOUND WAVE PACKETS' OR LETTERS OR 'AKSHARS' LIKE ATOMS OF ELEMENTS WITHIN ATMOSPHERE OF PLANET EARTH. THE ENERGY OF ELECTROMAGNETIC WAVES OF THREE FUNDAMENTAL SUB-ATOMIC PARTICLES, i.e., ELECTRONS, PROTONS AND NEUTRONS CREATES ATOMS OF ELEMENTS OR LETTERS OR '*AKSHARS*'. THE IMPACT OF FUNDAMENTAL PARTICLES TAKES PLACE ALONG THREE AXES DUE TO PRESSURE, TEMPERATURE AND VOLUME EFFECT OF ATMOSPHERE. PROTONS EFFECT TEMPERATURE, NEUTRONS EFFECT PRESSURE AND ELECTRONS CONTROL VOLUME OF LETTERS OR 'AKSHARS' WITHIN ATMOSPHERE OF PLANET. CREATION OF LETTERS LIKE ATOMS OF ELEMENTS ARE CONTROLLED BY TEMPERATURE, VOLUME AND PRESSURE ALONG THREE AXES ON PLANETS HAVING ATMOSPHERE.

Fig. 6.18

Speed of sound higher than Mach one is harmful for life on earth. The speed of compression of sound wave in solids is determined by the medium's compressibility, shear modulus and density. In fluid dynamics, the speed of sound in a fluid medium is used as a relative measure for the speed of an object moving through the medium. The ratio of speed of an object to the speed of sound in the fluid is called the object's Mach Number. Objects moving at speeds greater than Mach 1 are said to be travelling at supersonic speeds. 'Sound Wave Packets' emitted from mouth are made up of waves which carry letters and words in gas form and are active within atmosphere of planet earth. The human body inhales oxygen and releases carbon dioxide through breathing. The body exhales carbon dioxide, nitrogen gas and water vapour along with other dust particles etc. The 'sound wave packets' come out with gases from mouth of body and spread in the atmosphere. These waves are guided by pressure, temperature and volume along three axes within atmosphere. Four fused vertebrae at the base of spinal cord in human beings contain four coccygeal nerves in fused form. The infants at the time of birth cry with new and fresh nerves. The infants of different countries at different places cry in similar tone at the time of birth and have same tone of uttering as, K....A.....KHA.....AR....R.....AM......AH.....AH, starting from first consonant letter 'KA' and ending at last vowel letter 'AH'.

The transmission of sound waves depends upon temperature, pressure and volume of atmosphere of planet. It changes form due to density of the medium of planet. The human ear can detect wide range of frequencies. Frequencies from 20 to 20,000 Hz are audible to human ear. Any sound with frequency below 20 Hz is called as Infrasound and any sound wave with frequency above 20,000 Hz is called as Ultrasound. All planets having atmosphere, water in gas form, liquid water and solid water contain life forms on it. The width and elemental composition of the atmospheric layer varies on every astral body and depends upon:

(a) Stage of equilibrium of planet,
(b) Elemental composition of planet,
(c) Magnetic balance along three axes,
(d) Relative position of planets under nine planets system,
(e) Compulsory outer layer of planet with oxygen,
(f) Planets adhering towards blue color end and emitting blue color,
(g) Planets maintaining fourteen non-metallic and metallic zones in itself,

(h) Planets emitting blue color due to high electronegative charge of elements in their ionosphere have higher probability of sustaining life and atmosphere.

(i) Planets maintaining average temperature of 18^0C.

Sound waves are produced by collisions among astral bodies, lightning and thunder and its impact is observed on planets and life forms. During formation of spherical astral bodies, planets and stars, plenty of metallic elements and metallic octets (X^{7+}) of elements are created and contracted inside core, mantle and crust. In this process a lot of positively charged particles are concentrated with elements inside spherical astral bodies, planets and stars especially in core. It causes imbalance between positive charge and negative charge in space. To counter the above imbalance a lot of negatively charged particles with non-metallic elements and non-metallic octets (Y^{7-}) develop due to ionization in space.

The following factors are compulsory for development of life forms and creation of letters (*Aksharas*) and words (*Shabda*) on any planet in any solar system in the universe:

1. Ozone layer around planet,
2. Availability of Oxygen in three states, i.e.,solid, liquid and gas state on planet,
3. Availability of Water in three states, i.e.,solid, liquid and gas state on planet,
4. Goldie-lock zone around planet containing life forms.
5. Continuous movement of planet in fixed time period of movement due to Rotation linked movement, Precession linked movement and Revolution linked movement.

The universe contains plenty of hot and cold zones at the same time and there is every possibility of existence of many "Goldi-lock zones" in space. Life will exist on many congenial planets in different parts of the universe within ladder of evolution.

HOT STAR AND COLD MOON APPEAR EQUAL IN SIZE FROM EARTH. THEY WILL BE OPPOSITE IN MAGNITUDE OF TEMPERATURE IN GOLDI-LOCK ZONE. THEIR DISTANCE VARIES FROM EARTH AND THEIR SIZE IS ALSO DIFFERENT. FROM EARTH BOTH APPEAR EQUAL IN SIZE.

Fig. 6.19

Life exists in unicellular forms as bacteria, virus, yeast, spores, mycoplasma or unicellular structures within hard coat on astral bodies for infinite periods. It is transported, exported or imported through meteorites, asteroids, moons, planets and stars etc from time to time from one place to another in space. The hard coat protects DNA and amino acids in unicellular life forms for billions of years in dormant forms. The moment it gets congenial environment, it proliferates and produces different life forms through binary fission. Multi-cellular life forms cannot exist on any astral body unless supported by oxygen and water in solid, liquid and gas forms covered by ozone layer. The outer ozone layer maintains a balance among pressure, volume and temperature on planet along three axes. The outer covering of planet and atmosphere helps in development of life forms along three axes on planets. Life forms in dormant stage are integral part of our universe and they proliferate the moment they get congenial atmosphere. Equal temperature of star on one side and planet on other side leads to production of ozone layer around planet.

Goldi-lock zone is the area which contains hot star and cold moon at such a distance that their heat and cold is equal on planet earth. It is evident from the visible size of star, i.e., Sun and moon which looks equal from earth irrespective of their actual size and distance in space. Such situation provides equal quantum of heat and cold on middle planet and allows growth of maximum number of life forms on planet earth. The planet containing life forms maintains distance with sun (star) and moon (planet) in such a manner that heat and cold is equal and it allows life to exist on planet. The size of sun and moon appears to be equal to each other irrespective of their original size and distance from the central planet. The emission / absorption ratio (E/A) of radiation of sun is equal to absorption / emission ratio (A/E) of moon in the Goldi-lock zone. If size of sun increases, heat will increase on that planet and xerophytes, desert and desert animals will be produced in plenty. If size of moon increases, cold waves will increase on planet and hydrophytes, water animals and water bodies will be produced in plenty. In the astral bodies, absorption of radiation and emission of radiation is common phenomenon. During evolution of astral bodies, the meteorites, asteroids, comets and planets absorb radiation. These astral bodies have E /A below one and they increase in size by grabbing mass of moving particles in space. The astral bodies having E /A below one create planets and gradually by increase in size create biggest red planets. Existence of Goldie-lock zone proves that our universe is 'living universe' and will not become extinct.

VERY HOT ZONE IN SPACE ◄·········	HOT ZONE IN SPACE ◄·········	GOLDI-LOCK ZONE IN SPACE	COLD ZONE IN SPACE, ISM ·········►	VERY COLD ZONE IN SPACE ·········►
Star, Supernovae	Star	Cold Planet having one hot star and one cold planet on both sides	Coldest Planets, Asteroids,	Coldest Planets, Asteroids, meteorites,
Star, Pole Star	Star	Earth	Titan, Europa, cold moons,	Icy Planets
Virus, Bacteria within Hard Coat, Spores,	Virus, Bacteria within Hard Coat, Spores,	Life Forms, Animals, Plants, Human Beings,	Smaller Life Forms, Spores, Virus, Bacteria within Hard Coat	Virus, Bacteria within Hard Coat, Spores,
Unicellular Organisms	Unicellular Organism	Multi-cellular Organisms	Unicellular, bi-cellular, tetra-cellular and smaller Multi-cellular aquatic Organisms. Titan, Europa, Mars and other cold planets may develop smallest aquatic life forms.	Unicellular Organisms

Table 6.9

Every life form is a time machine controlled equally by hot and +Ve charged elements along with cold and -Ve charged elements inherent in it. Sun represents hot and +Ve charges of elements whereas moon represents cold and -Ve charges of elements on earth. The distance of sun and moon from earth are such that both appear to be equal in size from earth and provide equal quantum of heat and cold to earth within Goldi-lock zone. Their individual sizes and distances are different from each other but from earth both appear to be equal in size. It is true for all planets having life forms inherent on it.

The growth and development of parts and systems of human beings always takes place in the multiples of nine along one axis, twelve along second axis and fourteen along third axis. The development of parts in the multiples of nine includes one white region + seven color regions of systems + one black region. The production of organs in the multiples of twelve due to gravitational force includes twelve parts of body. The creation of seven metallic regions produces bones, cartilages, hard muscles, hard tissues and stony parts whereas creation of seven non-metallic regions produces soft muscles, veins, arteries, soft tissues, pores, air sacs, liquid exudates and gas emissions. The pressure, volume and temperature of life forms varies on every planet and its impact is observed on shape, size and external features of living beings on planets. All the planets looking blue in color tend to develop atmosphere of oxygen gas and water around the planet. The outer covering of earth called as ozone layer protects all the life forms from outside harmful radiations and it is compulsory for existence of living beings on any planet. The atmosphere needs one covering layer to allow gases and liquids of atmosphere to survive on planet and atmosphere will be delineated along three axes by pressure, volume and temperature. The contraction and expansion takes place along three axes in the following manner:

(a) Contraction of matter along three axes: The impact of movement of planet on animal body or human body is observed along three axes. The inner features and characteristics of body systems contract matter and develop parts of body along three axes.

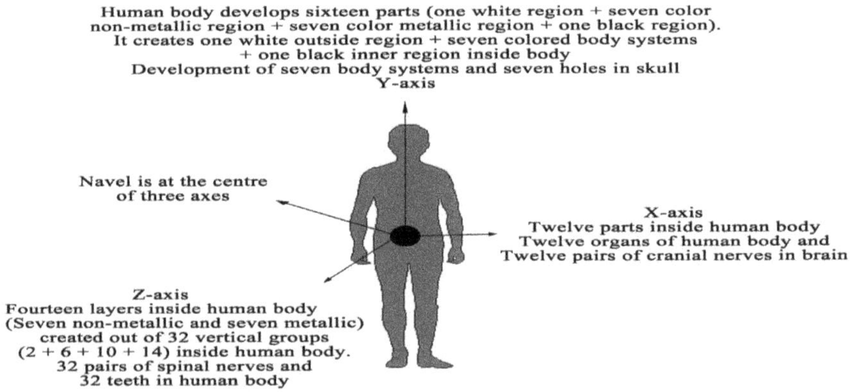

CONTRACTION OF MATTER AND DEVELOPMENT OF CHARACTERS, BODY PARTS, SYSTEMS AND ORGANS TAKES PLACE IN THE MULTIPLES OF 9, 12 AND 32 INSIDE LIVING HUMAN BODY ALONG THREE AXES. IMPACT OF SOUND WAVES SHAPES THE DEVELOPMENT OF CHARACTERS, BODY PARTS, SYSTEMS AND ORGANS IN THE MULTIPLES OF 12 BLOCKS, 14 MATTER ZONES AND 9 SYSTEMS INSIDE HUMAN BODY ALONG THREE AXES. DEVELOPMENT OF ATMOSPHERIC COVERING ALL AROUND WITH THREE AXES ATTACHMENT IS THE BIGGEST ARBITER FOR EXISTENCE AND SURVIVAL OF LIFE FORMS ON PLANETS.

Fig. 6.20

Creation of elements in the periodic table along three axes testifies development of elements on the above pattern in the universe. Life forms will not develop on stars because stars have high temperature, show high radiation of energy and lack atmosphere. The spherical planets looking blue and emitting blue radiation will have probability of developing life forms and atmosphere. Spherical planets having highest number of ridges, furrows, mountains and deep trenches will have probability of developing more life forms. The planets having flat compacted round outer structure will have lesser probability of developing life forms due to their fully round structures.

Multi-cellular life forms will develop on planets of solar system provided they have mean temperature of 18^0C with oxygen and water for growth of different living beings on earth.

(b) Expansion of matter along three axes: The impact of movement of planet, animal body or human body is observed along three axes. The outer characters of body systems and parts expand mass and develop along three axes. The life forms develop on planets under the combined impact of pressure, volume and temperature. Every planet, which has congenial atmosphere for development of life forms, produces outer ozone layer around planet and maintains oxygen and water in gas form, liquid form and solid forms simultaneously. In this process impact of pressure, volume and temperature is observed on all life forms:

1. **Impact of pressure and equilibrium:** Increase or decrease in pressure on life forms is perceived due to impact of gravitational force along one axis.

2. **Impact of temperature and equilibrium:** Increase or decrease of temperature on life forms is observed due to impact of electromagnetic force along second axis.

3. **Impact of volume and equilibrium:** Increase or decrease in volume is observed on life forms due to combined impact of strong force and weak force along third axis.

The growth of animal body halts at certain equilibrium point of age and starts deteriorating after that age. The inter-relationship among pressure, temperature and volume of living body changes on planets depending upon their status and three axes attachment.

(Change in temperature)
Temperature changes in multiples of 16 parts due to Electromagnetic Force (One white region + seven colors region + black region)

(Change in volume)
Volume changes in the multiples of 14 (32 vertical groups of Periodic Table) due to combined effect of Strong Force and Weak Force

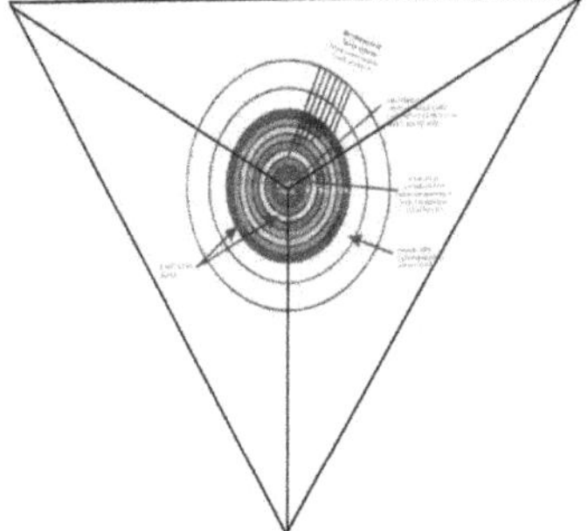

High pressure due to mass and density (Change in pressure)
Pressure changes in the multiples of 12 (12 blocks of elements due to Gravitational Force)

CREATION OF ATMOSPHERE AROUND PLANET IS COMPULSORY FOR EXISTENCE OF LIFE FORMS ON ANY PLANET. EXPANSION OF MATTER AND DEVELOPMENT OF PLANETS, STARS, ASTRAL BODIES, CHARACTERS, BODY PARTS, SYSTEMS AND ORGANS IS EFFECTED BY TEMPERATURE, PRESSURE AND VOLUME IN THE MULTIPLES OF 9, 12 AND 32 RESPECTIVELY INSIDE EVERY ASTRAL BODY AND LIVING BODY ALONG THREE AXES. IMPACT OF COLORS HELPS IN DEVELOPMENT OF SEVEN SYSTEMS INSIDE HUMAN BODY. CENTRAL BLACK HUB AS CORE IN HUMAN BODY ABSORBS ELECTROMAGNETIC WAVES INSIDE HUMAN BODY. THE IMPACT OF PRESSURE, VOLUME AND TEMPERATURE DECIDES THE SIZE AND SHAPE OF INDIVIDUAL LIVING BEING ON PLANETS. THE SIZE AND SHAPE OF LIFE FORMS ALONG THREE AXES DEPENDS UPON TIME PERIOD OF ROTATION, REVOLUTION AND PRECESSION OF THAT PARTICULAR PLANET. EXISTENCE OF HARDENED CELLS, FLUIDS AND

221

GASES IN DIFFERENT SYSTEMS, PARTS AND ORGANS AROUND BLACK HUB OF ANIMAL BODY MAINTAINS THERMODYNAMIC EQUILIBRIUM COVER OF LIVING BODY ALONG THREE AXES.

Fig. 6.21

The deposition and retention of cells takes place in layers inside life forms in cyclic manner. Evolution of characters e.g. organs, outgrowth, depression, symmetry and development of nerves and organs etc depends upon three axes attachment of animal body. The humans possess black mass in the center of body and seven colors show impact on development of seven systems, organs and outer limbs. The highest energy is stored in black region of body part of human body. Solid crystals form solid skeleton and bones in the multiples of seven, e.g. seven vertebrae. Seven holes in skull are created by seven color energy and seven systems remain in muscular, liquid and gas forms.

In the animals and human beings contraction of cells and tissues and their accumulation is observed along three axes. The formation of organs and their division into smallest parts takes place along three axes producing monoblastic, diploblastic and triploblastic parts. The development of parts and organs etc takes place in multiples of 7 x 7 along one axis, 9 x 9 along second axis and 12 x 12 along third axis. Stellar atmospheres are characterized by equilibrium in radiation.

The nucleosynthesis of elements, creation of compounds, synthesis of nucleic acids, formation of cells, tissues, organs and seven systems take place automatic in life forms during cycle of evolution of life forms. The most developed life forms are created under the combined impact of fourteen stars cluster, constellation of twelve stars and nine planets system. The existence of continuous oxygen layer covering around planet is compulsory for regular exchange of oxygen by living beings on any planet. Thus planets having continuous and homogenous outer covering of atmosphere with oxygen all around maintain life forms in perpetuity. The existence of oxygen in three states, i.e., gas form, liquid form and solid form is compulsory for existence of life forms on any planet. Life forms develop on planets which maintain an outer covering of atmosphere between the temperature range zero degree to 100^0C. The life forms exist on blue planets, i.e., towards low wavelength of spectra. The life forms do not exist on red or white planets, i.e., towards higher wavelength of spectra. In a solar system, many planets surround the centrally located star. These planets and their moons arrange themselves according to nine colors cycle around the sun and form nine planet system. The middle planet, which maintains a mean temperature of 18^0C, will tend to develop biggest atmosphere along with biggest life forms.

8

CONTROL OF DISEASES THROUGH LANGUAGE

Human being and life forms with present level of intelligence existed on earth about 43,20,000 years ago. The contraction of nerve cells gives extra powers to human brain to perceive and visualize things and imagination can reach better depths in vacuum medium. Vacuum medium connects every individual with other individual through contraction and expansion of nerve cells of brain. Sanskrit letters and words are outcome of different nerves of human body and their uttering from mouth in any form effects human body. The emission either as vowel, consonant, word or poem or chanting of *mantra* comes from nerves of body and effects all human being within atmosphere of our earth.

Soul exists as concentration of power in the form of electromagnetic energy of elements inside living body. In case of human being the soul can be perceived as concentration of power with oxygen element which provides vital breath of air for circulation of energy. The oxygen element acts as carrier of energy (*Prana Vayu*) for human beings and all animals and stores the energy of electromagnetic waves. Human brain is subject of neuroscience which responds to languages, vocal cord and signals passed by nerves in the body. The human beings may develop personal languages controlled by vocal cord which is used within lifetime of that individual. It uses linguistic resources, i.e., categories, construction and distinctions available in vocal cord during processing information from all senses.

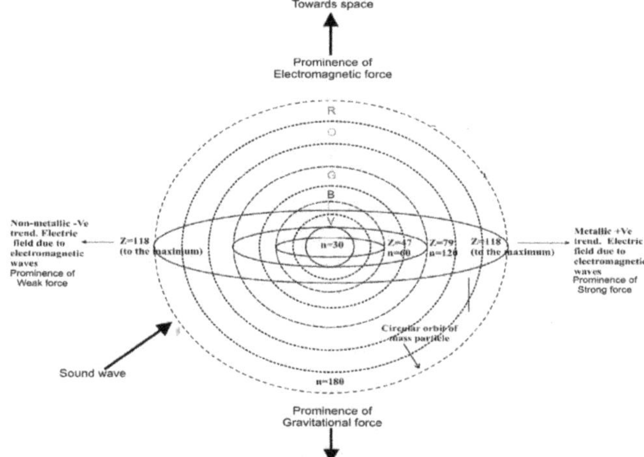

SOUND WAVES CAN CONVERT INTO ELECTROMAGNETIC WAVES OF 4000Å TO 7500Å AND SHOW IMPACT ON HUMAN BODIES. MAXIMUM EXPANSION OF WAVES INTO PARTICLES CAN TAKE PLACE FROM 4000Å TO 7500Å INSIDE ELEMENTS AND CREATE DIFFERENT TYPES OF ANIMAL BODIES.

Fig. 7.1

A planet must maintain adequate pressure for growth, maintain oxygen layer and ozone layer for protection and must have sufficient water and fluid medium for circulation throughout astral body and inside animals. Human brain controls understanding and contributions of

223

language during thinking and formation with learning and experience. Many old languages are well structured cultural objects which we inherit from generations work as our biological inheritance and persist in societies as guiding force of human brains and human beings.

Stretching of electromagnetic waves is accompanied with dilation of time. As much wave is stretched, so much time dilates and expands as outer covering of matter. Similarly, contraction of waves is accompanied with squeezing of time and contraction of time. Time makes outer surface of human body round in shape and its impact is observed on growth of inner body parts along three axes. The internal parts, organs and systems of life forms develop along three axes on the patterns of creation of elements in the periodic table. The external features of life forms may show prominence along three axes during development or may show dominance of round time frame in outer covering. The highest evolved animals will show development of seven systems along one axis, twelve body parts along second axis and 32 teeth and 32 pairs of spinal nerves (2+6+10+14) along third axis.

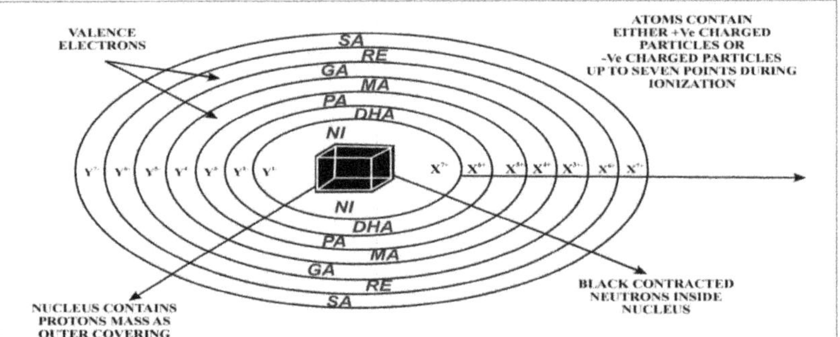

'SOUND WAVE PACKETS' EMERGE IN ARITHMETIC PROGRESSION AS VIBRATIONS OR ECHOES AND EFFECT HUMAN BODY PARTS ON PLANETS. THE ECHOES CAN PROLIFERATE UP TO SEVEN POINTS ON THE PATTERN OF IONIZATION OF ATOMS OF ELEMENTS. THE LETTERS ARE CREATED ON THE PATTERN OF ATOMS OF ELEMENTS AND WORDS ARE CREATED LIKE COMPOUNDS HAVING JUMBLED CONFIGURATIONS. ELLIPTICITY OF ORBIT DEVELOPS DUE TO FORMATION OF ANIONS (Y^-, Y^{2-}, Y^{3-}, Y^{4-}, Y^{5-}, Y^{6-}, Y^{7-}) AND CATIONS (X^+, X^{2+}, X^{3+}, X^{4+}, X^{5+}, X^{6+}, X^{7+}) IN THE ATOMS OF ELEMENTS IN ARITHMETIC PROGRESSION. ANIONS PLAY SIGNIFICANT ROLE IN PRODUCTION OF SOUND WAVES BY VOCAL CORD OF ANIMALS AND HUMAN BEINGS.

Fig. 7.2

The chanting of words, emission of words and sound from mouth of human body depends upon nerves of nervous system and every letter and word effects particular nerve and organ of human body. The impact of sound waves can cure and affect body parts and systems and affect whole body. The combination of letters and words effect body parts and have the capacity to improve or harm body parts. The audible range of sound waves will be different for different animals on different planets. The sound waves are equivalent to their corresponding electromagnetic waves, i.e., power waves. So the sound waves of animals and human beings are more powerful than electromagnetic waves of seven colors (4000Å -7500Å) that constitute and make animal and human body. The sound waves effect animal body like power waves and sound waves can last longer like power waves in the atmosphere. The sound waves will not perish and on the patterns of power waves it will affect animal body with impact on future growth and development. The sound waves of animal body effect present time and will affect the body in future because power waves last longer in atmosphere.

The impact of sound wave packet or Swara, *Sa* (256 Hz.) effects skeletal system under impact of red color. Similarly, the impact of sound wave packet or Swara, *Re* will effect integument system under impact of orange color. The impact of sound wave packet or Swara, *Ga* will effect digestive system under impact of yellow color. The impact of sound wave packet or Swara, *Ma* (407.2 Hz.) will effect nervous system under impact of green color. The impact of sound wave packet or Swara, *Pa* will effect cardio-vascular system under impact of blue color. The impact of sound wave packet or Swara, *Dha* will effect urino-genital system of body under impact of indigo color. The impact of sound wave packet or Swara, *Ni* will effect blood circulatory system under impact of violet color. The contraction of circumference upon diameter ratio from 22/11 to 22/5.5 tends to change the wavy character of nerve cells to solidified nerve cells. The strong and stout nerve cells transmit the message from human brain to body parts. Regular contraction and expansion of nerve cells inside human brain connects the central nervous system with vacuum, astral bodies and planets in space.

7.1 SKELETAL SYSTEM

Skeletal system is effected by pronunciation of '*Sa*' sound wave packets carrying mass particles. The impact creates and strengthens bones and cures diseases and abnormalities related to bones. The impact of red color brings significant improvement in the skeletal system. The movement of organs and locomotion of entire body is based on the presence of bones to which muscles are attached constituting a system of lever action. The skeletal system is constituted by the bones and cartilages. It is supporting and protective in function. The skeletal system is created in '*Sa*' sound wave region and the anomalies of skeletal system and bones can be solved through its application on bones. It increases the energy content of system thus bringing the skeletal system to normalcy. There are many Mantras developed by scholars for cure of diseases and for skeletal system it is given below:

"Om Ghrini Suryaya Namah".

Impact of sound waves is observed on formation of stout body parts, systems, secretion of hormones and creation of organs. Organs of the body are affected by sound waves and disorders associated with bones and cartilages are cured by application of sound waves. Particular sound wave creates and controls particular system. Due to '*Sa*' Sound waves packet or Swara, bones constitute basic frame of body and afford protection to many vital organs. They also serve as great reservoir for minerals especially phosphorus and calcium etc. They contain bone marrow which acts as haemopoietic organ and is main site for reticulo-endothelial cells. There are two hundred and eight bones in the human body. Solidity and strength of bones takes place due to this sound wave. The impact is clearly observed on healing of bone related problems. The compound words created by vowels and consonants of chanting effect and penetrate skeletal system and bring the system to normal state.

7.2 INTEGUMENT SYSTEM

Integument system is affected by sound wave packet or Swara carrying particles called '*Re*' and its impact is observed on hard tissues, cartilages and soft tissues in combined manner. The hard tissues settle towards center of living body whereas soft tissues occupy peripheral portion of body. The impact creates and strengthens integument system and cures diseases and abnormalities related to skin and soft tissues. All the movements of human body are effected by muscles. They cover bony parts of skeleton in almost every part of body and provide the organism its normal external shape. They help in movement of limbs, locomotion and liberation of heat and energy. It is made up of skin which is mainly protective, sensory and secretory in function. It is composed of various muscles and is responsible for external and internal movements of the body and body parts.

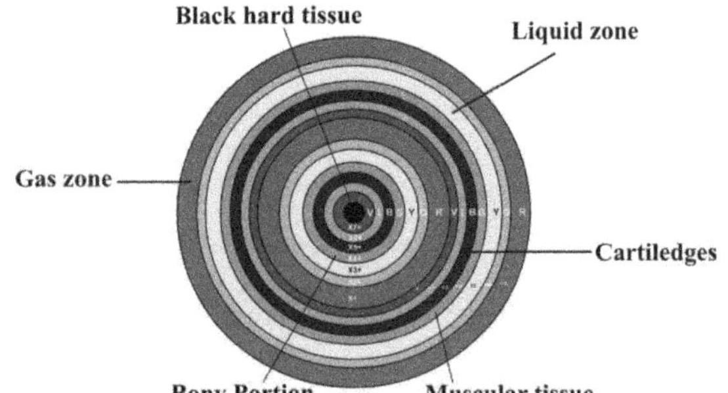

BLACK HARD TISSUES, BONES, CARTILEDGES, TISSUES, LIQUIDS AND GASES ARE DISTRIBUTED IN FOURTEEN ZONES INSIDE HUMAN BODY.

Fig. 7.3

The integumentary system is created in sound wave packet '*Re*' region and anomalies of integuments can be solved by its application on animal or human body. Cells after division are differentiated and by the end of embryonic development all varieties of the cells are formed in the young adult body. The phenomenon by which the cells assume different forms and functions is called cell differentiation. Initially all the cells are more or less similar but during development they become gradually different from one another to perform various functions and sound waves play significant role in development of skin. There are many Mantras developed by scholars for cure of diseases related to Integument system and some are given below:

Om, Jay Jay Sri Sudarshana,
Vande Kashim Guham Gangam,
Bhawanim Manikarnikam

The impact of orange color improves skin and integument system significantly. The entire structural and functional organization of a cell is according to genes it possessed. In each variety of cells only a specific part of the genotype (all the genes of and individual) is operational and the remaining part of the genotype is inactive. Thus different specific parts of the genotype are active in different types of cells. This variable gene activity or gene suppression is only physical basis of cell differentiation. The cells group together form tissues. These tissues perform different specialized functions. Based on the location and function, the animal tissues are classified into four types. All the tissues are of regular occurrence in the body of a vertebrate and many of them can be seen in the invertebrates too. Integument system includes skin, muscles, hair and other outgrowths which provide cover to living body from all around and develop due to sound wave packet or Swara, '*Re*'. The cover of skin maintains thermodynamic equilibrium of the living body. It regulates osmoregulation and exchange of gases and water inside the body. The hair, hair-like outgrowth and other appendages on the outer cover of body of living being help in regulating temperature and maintaining thermodynamic equilibrium of life forms. The pores, stomata, smaller holes and outlets on the body of living beings help in osmoregulation and control of water balance of living body. They help in exchange of gases inside living body and in this process regulate seven systems and help in food metabolism and synthesis of energy. The compound words created by vowels and consonants of chanting effect and penetrate nerves of integument system and bring the system to normal state.

226

7.3 DIGESTIVE SYSTEM

Digestive system is effected by sound wave packet carrying mass particles packet or Swara, '*Ga*'. It creates and strengthens digestive system and cures diseases and abnormalities related to digestive organs. The digestive system deals with digestion, absorption and utilization of food. The process of digestion takes place with the help of enzymes present in oral cavity and gastro-intestinal tract. The end products of digestion are mostly absorbed from small intestine which helps in the growth and repair of tissues and liberation of heat and energy. The unabsorbed food residue is passed out through lower part of large intestine. In this system many glands, e.g., salivary glands, liver, pancreas, and other intestinal glands and their secretions play prominent role in the process of digestion. All forms of chemical and energy transformation taking place inside body are termed as metabolism. The oxidation of food stuffs which produces energy is known as catabolism whereas the opposite process which uses energy is termed as anabolism. It includes alimentary canal and digestive glands. The ingestion, digestion and absorption of food and ejection of fecal matter take place by this system. The digestive enzymes and system are created in sound waves packet '*Ga*' region and anomalies of digestive system can be solved through it. The impact of yellow color brings improvement in the working of digestive system.

The energy content of sound wave letter packet or Swara '*Ga*' tries to bring the system to normalcy. All living systems require constant replenishment of energy giving and building material for work, growth, maintenance and repair. The organisms get the materials from their environment in the form of foodstuffs which principally include carbohydrates, fats, proteins, minerals vitamins and water. The basic function of gastrointestinal system is to transfer food and water from external environment to internal environment for subsequent distribution to the cells of the body by circulatory system. Reticulo-endothelial system consists of reticulum cells, endothelial cells and some wandering cells. The reticulum cells are present in the spleen, lymph nodes and bone marrow and endothelial cells are present in the blood sinuses of spleen and bone marrow etc. The wandering cells are present in the blood stream. The main function of cells of this system are phagocytosis, formation of anti-bodies, formation and destruction of red blood corpuscles etc.

The lymphoid tissue consists of lymphoid cells, lymphatic channels and lymph nodes. The lymphoid tissue is distributed throughout the body, e.g., lymph nodes, pharyngeal tonsil, spleen, in mucous membrane of small intestine and vermiform appendix etc. The lymphatic vessels are thin-walled channels containing valves and lymph can flow in one direction only. Most of the food consumed is made up of complex substance which cannot cross the cell membrane. Gastrointestinal system ensures that complex and insoluble food substances are transformed into simpler, soluble and diffusible forms suitable for absorption into the body for further utilization. This break down process of food called digestion is brought about by enzymes in digestive juices secreted into the alimentary tract. The final products of digestion cross the cell membrane of the intestinal tract to enter the circulation by the process called absorption. The digestive enzymes gradually increase inside human body and so increase the deposition of fats, oils and lipids inside human body. Various Mantras have been developed by scholars for cure of diseases and some are given below:

"Augustyam Kumbhakaranam Cha Shanim Cha Bad Vaanalam,

Aahaar Paripakartham Smerad Bhimam Cha Pancham."

The compound words created by vowels and consonants of chanting effect and penetrate parts and organs of digestive system and bring the system to normalcy. The deposition of matter inside life forms stores energy of electromagnetic waves inside crystals of atoms of elements. The sound wave '*Ga*' helps the process of digestion and absorption of the foodstuffs along the digestive tract aided by its movement. The movement is a component of the gastrointestinal triad (secretion, absorption and movement) and finally results in elimination of the unabsorbed remains from the anal end. The digestive system relates to intake of food and exit of waste materials from the body parts of human beings. The complexity of organs increases in human beings. The human beings maintain full system of digestion which adds strength and energy to the body. The human beings have most elaborate digestive system and energy intake is also the highest.

7.4 NERVOUS SYSTEM

Nervous system is effected by sound wave packets with mass particle packet or Swara called '*Ma*' and its impact is observed on nervous tissues in combined manner. The nervous system becomes hardy from outside and inner portion is hollow and filled up with cerebro-spinal fluid. The impact of sound wave creates and strengthens nervous system and cures diseases and abnormalities related to nerves. The system consists of central or somatic nervous system, autonomic nervous system and special senses. The central nervous system consists of cerebrum, cerebellum, brain stem and spinal cord. The ventricles in the cerebrum, brain stem and central canal of the spinal cord contain cerebro-spinal fluid. There are twelve pairs of cranial nerves and 32 pairs of spinal nerves. The last pair of spinal nerve is fused and is not visible. The central nervous system is mainly concerned with higher intellectual properties, maintains muscle tone and regulates posture and equilibrium. The autonomic nervous system consists of sympathetic and parasympathetic nerves. They control secreting glands and involuntary muscles etc. Hypothalamus is the high centre for autonomic nervous system. Besides other functions, hypothalamus plays an important role in regulation of body temperature and controls the functions of different endocrine glands. The contraction of nerve cells gives extra powers to human brain to perceive and visualize things and imagination can reach better depths in vacuum medium. Vacuum connects every individual with another individual through contraction and expansion of nerve cells of brain.

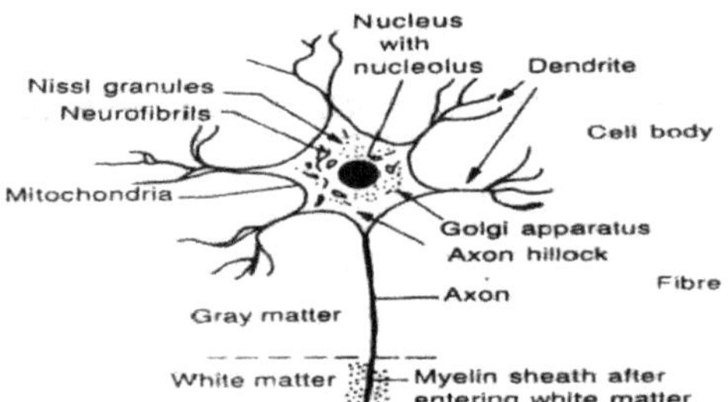

SOUND WAVE '*Ma*' EFFECTS GROWTH AND DEVELOPMENT OF NERVOUS SYSTEM INSIDE BODY. THE FUNCTION OF NERVE FIBRE IS TO CONDUCT NERVE IMPULSE. THE ENTIRE ACTIVITY OF THE NERVOUS SYSTEM DEPENDS UPON ABILITY OF THE NERVES TO TRANSMIT IMPULSES AND CONVEY INFORMATION FROM ONE SITE TO ANOTHR IN THE BODY. EXCITABILITY AND CONDUCTIVITY ARE TWO OUTSTANDING PHYSIOLOGICAL PROPERTIES OF THE NERVE FIBRES. APPLICATION OF THE SAME IMPROVES NERVES RESPONSE IN THE BODY.

Fig. 7.4

During evolution the highest developed mammal will maintain 32 pairs of spinal nerves. The lowest coccygeal nerves near base of spinal cord appear to be fused. The spinal nerves are formed by the union of dorsal and ventral roots shortly after they leave the spinal cord. Each spinal nerve has afferent (sensory) and efferent (motor) fibres. In general efferent come from the ventral root and afferents go into the dorsal root. Thus, all spinal nerves are mixed nerves because they carry both sensory and motor impulses. Left side of the spinal cord carries electronegative charge whereas right side of the spinal cord carries electropositive charge. After passing through the inter-vertebral foramen, each spinal nerve separates into posterior and anterior branches. The posterior branch innervates the muscles and skin of the posterior portion of the body. The anterior branch innervates the limbs and the literal and anterior portions of the body.

The emission of letters from vocal cord through mouth is like pressing one button of piano or harmonium. It effects the nerves of that particular organ and transmits impulse to brain. Sixteen Cervical nerves control vowels and effect vocal cord. At the time of emission of voice of letters, the cervical nerves modify the letters with either of the sixteen vowels and produce particular sound as voice.

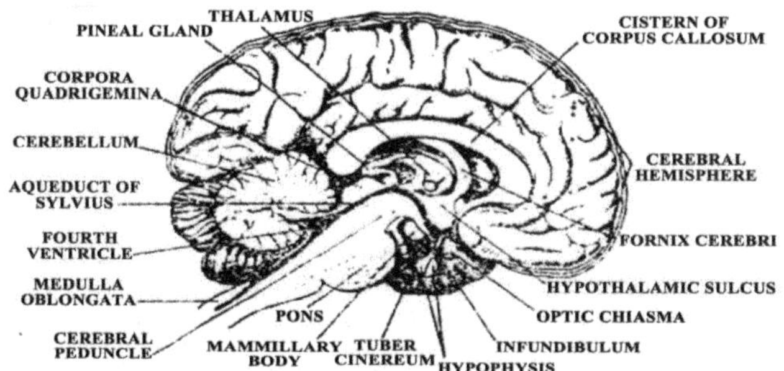

DIAGRAMMATIC REPRESENTATION OF MEDIAN SAGITTAL SECTION OF BRAIN STEM.

Fig. 7.5

Spinal nerves in the thoracic and lumbar regions also have a visceral branch, which innervates internal organs. The meningeal branches, a small branch innervates the strictures around the spine, membrane, ligaments, and blood vessels of the cord itself. The lumbar, sacral and coccygeal nerves leave the spinal cord before its termination at the level of the first lumbar veretebra and extend downwards inside the vertebral canal in the subarachnoid space below this level. Out of the above seven places, four places contain 32 pairs of spinal nerves (4 + 6 + 10 + 12). These 32 pairs of spinal nerves provide strength and stability to vertebrae, body parts and central nervous system. Impact of sound wave packet or Swara 'Ma' strengthens nervous system of human body.

Strong nerve cells transmit the message from human brain to body parts. Regular contraction and expansion of nerve cells inside human brain connects the central nervous system with astral bodies, planets and stars in space. The sense organs mainly consist of taste, smell, vision and hearing. It comprises of brain, spinal cord, cranial and spinal nerves and autonomic nervous system. This system controls and coordinates different activities of the various body parts. It includes sense organs such as eyes, ears, nose, tongue and skin. The organs of this system receive senses and convey the same to nervous system. It is formed of ductless gland whose secretions are known as hormones, which influence various metabolic processes of the body. Hormones act as chemical messengers. The impact of green color improves nerves response significantly and makes nervous system effective.

The central nervous system is affected by sound wave packet or Swara '*Ma*' and anomalies of this system can be solved through its application because its energy tries to bring it to normalcy. They resemble smooth muscle cells and are involuntary. These cells arise from the ectoderm instead of mesoderm. Myofibroplast cells resemble fibroplasts but contain action and myosin arranged as in smooth muscle and are contractile. In fact myofibroblasts are specialized contractile fibroblasts. The contraction of wounds is caused by the shortening of myofibroblasts. Pericyte cells are found around capillaries and venules. They contain actin and myosin. Pericytes can give rise to myofibroplasts and to mesenchyma, which can differentiate into fibroblasts and can form new blood vessels.

Autonomic system is that part of nervous system which controls the activity of viscera. Its actions are generally unconsidered and independent of "will". Consequently, the motor processes are all reflex actions. Control by the autonomic system is mostly homolateral. Like the somatic system it has got a spinal and cranial outflow. Certain special nerve centre situated in the medulla, pons and midbrain are included in this system. Other higher centres like hypothalamus, thalamus, corpus striatum and cerebrum control this system. These activities of the somatic and autonomic system always run parallel. It is because at every important level of the nervous system there are free intercommunications between these two systems. Cerebrum controls both these systems. Although involuntary, yet the system is not altogether beyond voluntary control. It can be classified in three ways:

1. Anatomical – According to the situation of outflow:
      (b) Craniosacral (cranial III, VII, IX, X and sacral 2-4)
      (c) Thoracolumbar (thoracic 1-12 and lumber 1-3)
2. Functional - According to the nature of function
      (a) Sympathetic - Same as thoracolumbar
      (b) Parasympathetic - same as craniosacral

The parasympathetic reactions are usually localised reactions and the sympathetic reactions are concerned with mass reactions. The parasympathetic activity results in slowing of the heart and increase in the peristaltic and glandular activities of the gut: these conserve the energies. Sympathetic activity results, for example, in constriction of the cutaneous arteries (with consequent increase in the blood supply to the heart, brain and muscle), acceleration of the heart and increase of blood pressure, contraction of the sphincters and lessening of the peristalsis of the gut; these mobilize body energies for dealing with emergencies. These two actions are functionally opposite. Broadly speaking functions of sympathetic are catabolic, while those of parasympathetic are anabolic in nature.

3. Chemical. According to the chemical substances liberated.
      (a) Adrenergic. Those producing norepinephrine or epinephrine at the nerve endings. Include only the postganglionic fibres of sympathetic except to sweat glands.
      (b) Cholinergic. Those producing acetylcholine. Include (a) the whole of parasympathetic- both preganglionic and postganglionic fibres, (b) all preganglionic sympathetic fibres, and (c) those postganglionic sympathetic fibres which supply the sweat glands.

The adrenergic fibres produce epinephrine or norepinephrine at the nerve endings, whereas cholinergic fibres produce acetylcholine both at the synapses (ganglia) as well as at the nerve endings. The parasympathetic receptors may be excitatory, as in glands and in smooth muscle cells of the alimentary canal or inhibitory, as in the heart. Sympathetic B-receptors in blood vessels (when present) are not innervated, but in other kinds of receptor cell, such as the heart, they are thought to be innervated and may be excitatory. Autonomic reflexes are very important in the control of the viscera. Like some of the somatic reflex arcs the autonomic reflex arc also contains three neurons, e.g. afferent, connector and efferent (excitor or effector) neurons. There are many Mantras developed by scholars for cure of diseases and some are given below:

Om dyau shanty rantariksha gwam shantih
Prithivi shanty rapah shanty
Rosha dhyaya shantih,
Vanas ptyah shantih vishwe dewah shanty
shanty brahma shantih
sarwag mam shantih , shanty reva shantih
Sa ma shanty redhi
Ohm shanty shanty shantih.

In the somatic system the afferent neurons lie in the posterior root ganglia or their cranial homologues. In the autonomic system they also lie in the posterior root ganglia. The connector neurons in the somatic system are found in the posterior horn cells. But in the autonomic system they are found in the lateral horn cells. In the somatic system the effector neurons are situated in the anterior horn cells. But in the autonomic system they are not present in the central nervous system at all. They lie outside the central nervous system in the form of various ganglia. The presence of peripheral ganglia is the characteristic feature of the autonomic system. In the sympathetic system the ganglia lie away from viscera supplied. But in the parasympathetic system they lie in or near the viscera. Hence, the parasympathetic system exerts a more localized action than the sympathetic system.

Autonomic functions like the control of the elasticity of blood vessels, sweating, gastro-intestinal, genito-urinary, respiratory and cardiac functions are reflex maintained. Autonomic reflexes are qualitatively similar to somatic ones and mostly they are polysynaptic. However, because of the interneuron located in the spinal cord, the integrity of the spinal cord is essential for regulating the autonomic reflex area. Efferent postganglionic fibres that run in gray rami communicates to the spinal nerves innervate vasoconstrictor fibres to blood vessels, motor fibres to the arrectores pilorum muscles in the areas supplied by the corresponding spinal nerves, and secretomotor fibres to the sweat glands. Those efferent postganglionic fibres accompany motor nerves to voluntary muscles are presumably distributed only to blood vessels supplying the muscles. Those fibers which run in the viscera and other structures are related to vasoconstriction, dilatation of pupils and of bronchioles, movements of the alimentary tract and the urinary bladder (relaxation of muscle walls and contraction of sphincters), glandular secretion and so on.

7.4.1 IMPACT OF AEROBIC PRACTICES

The contraction of waves or cells or atoms inside living body and change in their circumference and diameter connects the spherical body with global bubbles which are contracting and expanding in vacuum medium. Neurons and brain cells of animals have the capacity to contract and expand and in this manner they attach themselves with cells, atoms and round bodies of vacuum medium in space. Depending upon the capacity of contraction and expansion the brain cells of animals and human beings connect themselves with global bubbles, global spherical time frame, global mind and global consciousness. The contraction and expansion of cells is noticed in plants, trees, animals and human beings under the impact of electromagnetic waves. The impact of aerobic practices tends to change mass from solid state to gas state. It tends to increase the flow of oxygen gas inside spinal cord.

The cycle of will power pulls air and energy towards white region from black region. It tries to drag the animal body and contents of spinal column including bone marrow from basal hip portion towards brain portion. It pulls energy towards red and white side of energy of electromagnetic waves. There is gradual increase in the number of nerve from base of spinal cord upwards. The increase is gradual from local life forms to higher animals and it is highest in human beings. Human beings having highest number of nerves and due to gravitation matter outside and inside is pulled towards the brain. The spinal cord of human having grey matter inside and white matter outside are more advanced than the spinal cord of animals having white matter inside and grey matter outside. In all the life forms black mass and black matter stores highest quantum of energy with wavelength raining from zero to 4000 Å. The energy in black region is stored in the center of the nucleus and hub of life forms. The energy of seven color electromagnetic waves ranging from 4000 Å to 7500 Å is absorbed in seven systems of living beings. The energy of white region above 7500 Å of wavelength, which lies above seven colors, occupies the brain and tip of central nervous system in all living beings.

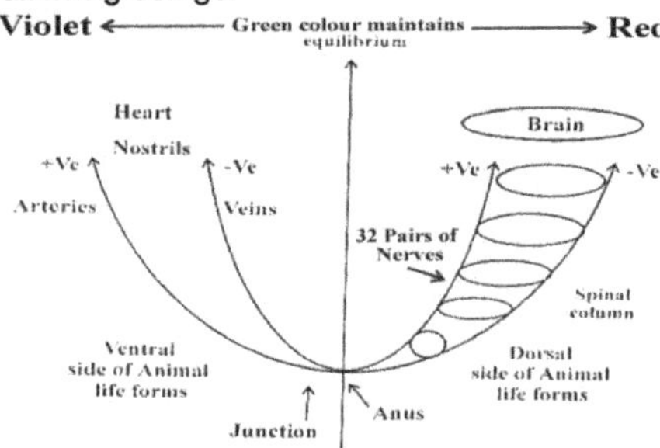

COMBINATION OF BREATH FROM LEFT AND RIGHT SIDE OF NOSTRILS NEAR BASE OF SPINAL CORD AND ANUS TENDS TO UNITE AND CHANNELIZE BREATH INSIDE SPINAL CORD. THE UNITED BREATH ENTERS SPINAL CORD AND LIFTS CEREBROSPINAL FLUID UPWARDS TOWARDS BRAIN.

Fig. 7.6

The spinal nerves are formed by the union of dorsal and ventral roots shortly after they leave the spinal cord. Each spinal nerve has afferent (sensory) and efferent (motor) fibres. In general efferent come from the ventral root and afferents go into the dorsal root. Thus, all spinal nerves are mixed nerves because they carry both sensory and motor impulses. Left side of the spinal cord carries electronegative charge whereas right side of the spinal cord carries electropositive charge. After passing through the intervertebral foramen, each spinal nerve separates into posterior and anterior branches. The posterior branch innervates the muscles and skin of the posterior portion of the body. The anterior branch innervates the limbs and the literal and anterior portions of the body. Spinal nerves in the thoracic and lumbar regions also have a visceral branch, which innervates internal organs. The meningeal branches, a small branch innervates the strictures around the spine, membrane, ligaments, and blood vessels of the cord itself. The lumbar, sacral and coccygeal nerves leave the spinal cord before its termination at the level of the first lumbar vertebra and extend downwards inside the vertebral canal in the subarachnoid space.

The human body is created by geometrical structures and circle or sphere is the points of distinction between waves and particles because circular outline stands for time frame. The mass and matter, whose axial angles vary from 0^0 to 15^0 along three axes maintain circular or wavy outline and behave as waves. Matter having axial angles from 90^0 to 120^0 along three axes make the intercepts flat and elongated thus converting waves in to geometrical particles. The human body contains black metallic centre having matter in the shape of elements of black matter. The black metallic centre is surrounded by fourteen crystal systems all around where cubic crystals occupy core portion and triclinic crystals tend to occupy peripheral portion in spherical astral body. The seven crystal systems are covered by seven liquid zones all around which are again covered

232

by seven gaseous zones and finally by seven ionic zones in any spherical astral body. Beyond ionic zones are found electromagnetic waves of seven colors having different wavelengths. Major functions of the nervous system are:

1. To detect changes in situations which affect the body because these changes must be sensed before they can be understood, this function is termed sensory function or sensation.
2. To initiate and control the activities of tissues which require and extrinsic stimulus to function. Examples are the contraction of voluntary and smooth muscles and the secretory processes of glands. Since positive action is produced this is called a motor function.
3. To coordinate the activities of units, parts or entire organs with other structures.
4. To conduct the impulses generated in nerve cells to or away from the central nervous system. The transmission and distribution of nerve impulses originating in its cells are basic to all functions of the nervous system.
5. To store oxygen inside spinal cord and increase the longevity of human body by killing time and protecting the body with oxygen stored inside nervous system.
6. To minimize the ageing effect on human body by storage of liquid oxygen inside spinal cord and brain. The nervous system becomes fresh, repairs the loss of neurons etc quickly and keeps the human body alive and long lasting. The moment oxygen inside spinal cord and brain is finished the human body tends to collapse and decay.

The breath enters spinal cord from two sides and acts as electropositive charge and as electronegative charge tubes. After passing through the intervertebral foramen, each spinal nerve separates into posterior and anterior branches. The posterior branch innervates the muscles and skin of the posterior portion of the body. The anterior branch innervates the limbs and the literal and anterior portions of the body. Spinal nerves in the thoracic and lumbar regions also have a visceral branch, which innervates internal organs. The meningeal branches, a small branch innervates the structures around the spinal cord. The brain and spinal cord being delicate structures are well protected by their location in bony cavities, i.e., skull and the vertebral column. They are covered by three membranes or meninzes namely (i) outer fibrous dura mater, (ii) middle arachnoid mater and (iii) inner vascular pia mater. The space between the arachnoic and pia maters contains a fluid- the cerebrospinal fluid that is also present in the ventricles of brain and central canal of the spinal cord. The spinal nerves emerge from spinal cord and concentration of nerves like nodes inside spinal cord and brain is observed at following seven places:

1. Extension of Brain   - Cerebrum or cerebral cortex having $32 \times 16 = 512 \times 2$
   'SAHASRASAR' $= 1024$ nerves $\times 10^2 \times 10^2 \times 10^2 = 1024,000$ types of nerves and its multiples.

2. Two lobes of cerebellum   - Thalamic plexus basal ganglion
   (2 nerves)
   'OHM'

3. Back side of Neck and vocal   - Throat - cervical plexus. Cervical Plexus innervates neck, chord (16 nerves)   throat and vocal cord and contains 16 nerves.
   'HAM'

4. In heart and lungs   - Heart plexus- Thoracic
   (12 nerves)   Brachial Plexus connects thoracic portion, chest and arm
   YAM'   and contains 12 nerves in heart plexus.

5. Coeliac   - Axis plexus - lumbar
   (10 nerves)   (in liver and abdomen). Lumbar Plexus innervates the liver
      'RAM'   and adjoining naval areas and contains 10 nerves in celiac
      and axis plexus. It is found in pairs of five affecting both sides of body.

6. Behind genitals   - Hypogastric pelvic - sacral
   (6 nerves)   - Pubic Nerves. Sacral Plexus connects the pelvic and
      'VAM'   genital regions and contains 6 nerves out of which some are fused.

7. Base of spinal cord   - Base or Pelvic plexus - Coccygeal.
   (4 nerves)   - In the perineum Coccygeal Plexus innervates the
      'LAM'   pelvic region and basal portion near anus and thighs and
      contains 4 nerves which are fused in pelvic plexus in the perineaum.

Out of the above seven places, four places contain 32 pairs of spinal nerves (4 + 6 + 10 + 12). These 32 pairs of spinal nerves provide strength and stability to vertebrae, body parts and central nervous system. The central nervous system contains gray matter and white matter. The gray matter contains nerve cells (cell bodies) and unmediated nerve fibres as well as neuroglia cells and fibres. The white matter contains myelinated nerve fibres, but no cell bodies; it also contains neuroglia cells and fibres. The brain contains about thousand nerves in cerebrum and cerebral cortex and they show mathematical arrangement. The nerves of brain merge into two lobes of cerebellum and form thalamus plexus and basal ganglion. Thirty-two pairs of spinal nerves are named and numbered according to the vertebra with which they are associated. They include eight pairs of cervical nerves, (8 x 2 = 16 vocal cord nerves), twelve pairs of thoracic nerves, 5 pairs of lumbar nerves, 5 pairs of sacral nerves and two coccygeal nerves at the base of spinal cord.

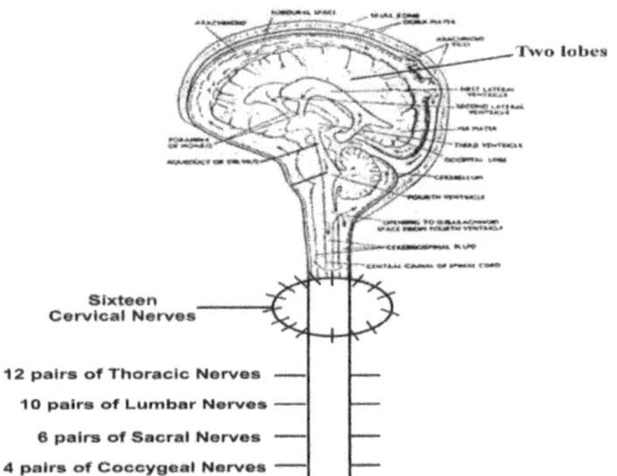

LONGITUDINAL SECTION PASSING THROUGH SPINAL CORD OF HUMAN BEING SHOWS NUMBER OF NERVES AROUND THE SPINAL CORD. VOWELS INSIDE HUMAN BODY ARE CREATED BY SIXTEEN CERVICAL NERVES OF THROAT PORTION. THE NERVES BELOW CERVICAL NERVES ARE DOUBLE IN NUMBER, I.E., THIRTY TWO AND THEY CREATE CONSONANTS INSIDE HUMAN BODY. INCREASE IN OXYGENATION OF SPINAL CORD INCREASES ENERGY AND METABOLISM OF LIVING HUMAN BODY. HIGH CONTENT OF OXYGEN MAKES HUMAN BODY LAST LONGER AND INCREASES LIFE SPAN OF ALL LIVING BEINGS. IF OXYGEN SUPPLY INSIDE SPINAL CORD IS INCREASED ARTIFICIALLY THE HUMAN BODY WILL HAVE HIGHER ENERGY AND LONGER LIFE PERIOD OF SURVIVAL.

Fig. 7.7

The genetic structure of normal tissue cell and the cancer cell (malignant neoplasm) are different. The differences between them are quantitative rather than qualitative. They concern their functional potentialities and behaviour rather their requirements and constitution. The normal tissue and cancerous tissue cannot be separated easily. The neoplasm does not obey normal growth limits and does not obey the feedback mechanism which normally controls the cellular growth and reproduction. The growth of cancer cells is not controlled and they can grow and proliferate without any limit. These cells compete with normal cells for the available nutrition inside body. When the number of cancer cells increase to high extent they draw all nutrition. As a result normal cells suffer from non-availability of nutrition and death ensures. For example, the cells of normal epidermis combine to form a tissue whereas the cancer cells which arise in the precursors of white blood cells (Leukaemia) are individual. Due to their rapid mobility the cancer cells spread through the body and do not combine to form a tissue. When the overgrowth of tissue proceeds without any regard to the surrounding tissues or the requirement of organism as a whole, this excessive usually progressive and purposeless process is known as neoplasm or new growth.

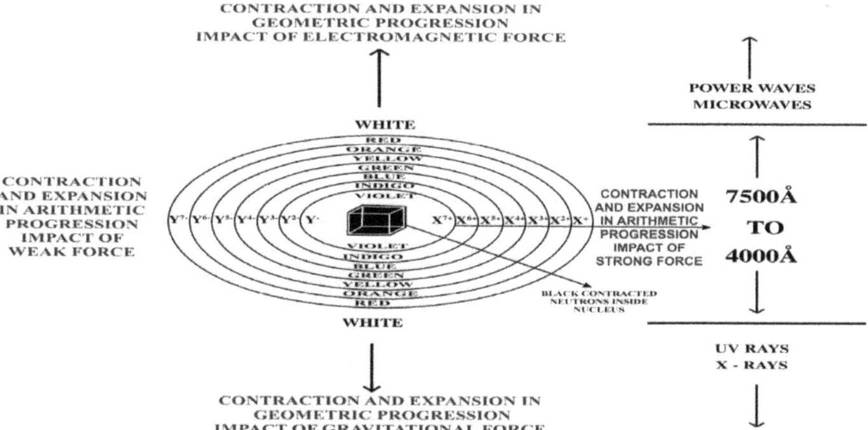

ECHO OF SPEECH OF HUMAN LETTERS AND WORDS CAN PROLIFERATE UPTO SEVENTH POINT OF IONIZATION IN THE ATMOSPHERE DURING SPEAKING AND SHOUTING. IT EFFECTS HUMAN BODY AND BRING CHANGES IN THE BODY. CHANTING OF *MANTRAS* AND *SLOKAS* BY HUMAN BEING AND THEIR ECHOES EFFECT ENTIRE COMMUNITY ON EARTH. CONTRACTION AND EXPANSION IS EFFECTED DUE TO WEAK FORCE AND STRONG FORCE IN ARITHMETIC PROGRESSION. CONTRACTION AND EXPANSION IS EFFECTED DUE TO ELECTROMAGNETIC FORCE AND GRAVITATIONAL FORCE IN GEOMETRIC PROGRESSION. SIMULTANEOUS ACTION OF FOUR FORCES LEADS TO CREATION OF ATOMS OF 118 ELEMENTS ON ASTRAL BODIES. DEVELOPMENT OF NON-METALLIC AND METALLIC IONS TAKES PLACE IN SEVEN COLOR REGIONS IN FOURTEEN MATTER ZONES INSIDE PLANETS AND STARS. ELLIPTICITY OF ORBIT DEVELOPS DUE TO FORMATION OF ANIONS (Y^-, Y^{2-}, Y^{3-}, Y^{4-}, Y^{5-}, Y^{6-}, Y^{7-}) AND CATIONS (X^+, X^{2+}, X^{3+}, X^{4+}, X^{5+}, X^{6+}, X^{7+}) IN THE ATOMS OF ELEMENTS IN ARITHMETIC PROGRESSION. THE MOTHER FIGURE ACTS AS – Ve CHARGE AND HELPS IN DEGENERATION OF CANCEROUS CELLS FROM HUMAN BODY. THE ECHO OFHUMAN LETTERS AND WORDS CAN PROLIFERATE UPTO SEVENTH POINT OF IONIZATION OF ELEMENTS IN THE ATMOSPHERE DURING SPEAKING AND SHOUTING. IT CAN EFFECT HUMAN BODY AND BRING CHANGES IN THE BODY. CHANTING OF *MANTRAS* AND *SLOKAS* BY HUMAN BEING AND THEIR ECHOES EFFECT ENTIRE COMMUNITY ON EARTH.

Fig. 7.8

Voice, speech, letters, alphabets and Language is produced due to impact of Spinal nerves and Cervical nerves by vocal cords inside Life forms. Vowels are produced by impact of cervical nerves whereas consonants are produced by spinal nerves of nervous system. Movement of waves and creation of negatively charged particles and positively charged particles inside atoms of elements takes place in arithmetic progression. The -Ve particles and +Ve particles move in elliptical orbits of seven color regions of electromagnetic waves. The lobes of brain contain neurons which can contract and expand like vacuum medium and maintains balance of energy with black matter. Vacuum can be detected and perceived by stretching of a bubble or matter wave.

The central nervous system consists of cerebrum, cerebellum, brain stem and spinal cord. The ventricles in the cerebrum, brain stem and central canal of the spinal cord contain cerebro-spinal fluid. The central nervous system is mainly concerned with higher intellectual properties, maintains muscle tone and regulates posture and equilibrium. The autonomic nervous system consists of sympathetic and parasympathetic nerves. They control secreting glands and involuntary muscles etc. Hypothalamus is the high centre for autonomic nervous system. Besides other functions, hypothalamus plays an important role in regulation of body temperature and controls the functions of different endocrine glands. The contraction of nerve cells gives extra powers to human brain to perceive and visualize things and imagination can reach better depths in vacuum medium. Vacuum medium connects every individual with another individual through contraction and expansion of nerve cells of brain.

Regular contraction and expansion of nerve cells inside human brain connects the central nervous system with vacuum, astral bodies, planets and stars in space. The sense organs mainly consist of taste, smell, vision and hearing. It comprises of brain, spinal cord, cranial and spinal nerves and autonomic nervous system. This system controls and coordinates different activities of various body parts. It includes sense organs such as eyes, ears, nose, tongue and skin. The organs of this system receive senses and convey the same to nervous system. It is formed of ductless gland whose secretions are known as hormones, which influence various metabolic processes of the body. Hormones act as chemical messengers. The central nervous system is affected by green color and anomalies of this system can be solved through application of green color because energy of yellow color tries to bring it to normalcy.

7.4.2 EFFECT OF WILL POWER ON LANGUAGE

The will power relates to upward pull of breath, dragging of air towards brain from lower part of body and retention of breath with determination inside body in consonance with other body parts of human body. The power fixes movement and destination of body and compels entire body to work with fixed aim towards fixed goal. The will power controls breath, intake of air inside body in desired manner and circulates the same towards fixed goal. The pull of breath joins the air of left and right nostrils at the base of spinal cord and this pull pushes the cerebro-spinal fluid towards brain. The cerebro-spinal fluid ascends from bottom of spinal cord towards brain. The process of uplifting cerebro-spinal fluid from lower part of spinal cord towards brain pulls the neurons and takes out the nervous activities of neurons of spinal nerve from the body parts. As a result the outer body parts become senseless, numb and cool bereft of nerve control and cerebro-spinal fluid. When normal breath is regained by human being, the cerebro-spinal fluid comes down from brain to spinal cord and spinal nerves naturally join body parts again. The lower and outer body parts again become warm, active and gain normal sense.

Higher the will power more pronounced becomes the loudness and hardiness of tone of language. Emphasis on emission of consonants increases loudness with forceful effect due to binding energy. The nervous tissue in general develops from ectoderm of the embryo, but microgliocytes arise from mesoderm of the embryo. The special properties of cells of nervous tissue are excitability and conductivity. Excitability is the ability to initiate nerve impulse in response to stimuli (changes outside and inside the body). Conductivity means the ability to transmit a nerve impulse (potential change in membrane of a nerve cell). The reaction is called response. The response may be sensation, such as pain or some activity such as muscle contraction or glandular secretion. A neuron is a structural and functional unit of the nervous tissue and hence the nervous system. Certain neurons may almost equal the length of body itself. The neurons with longer processes (projections) are the longest cells in the body. Human nervous system has about 100 billion neurons, majority of the neurons occur in the brain.

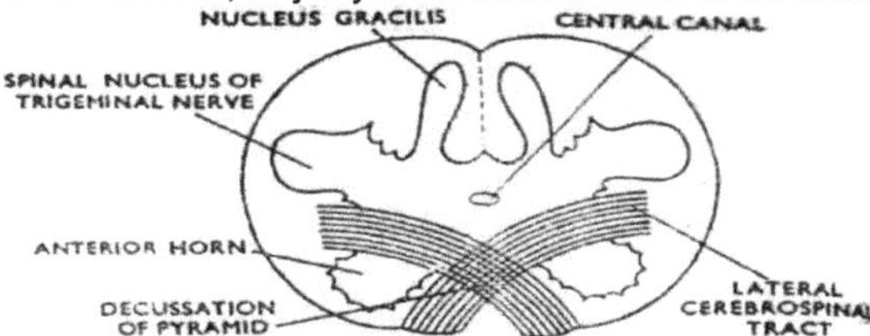

PICTURE OF DORSAL ASPECT OF MEDULLA AT THE LEVEL OF EFFERENT DECUSSATION OF PYRAMIDS (CEREBROSPINAL FIBRES)

Fig. 7.9

The impact of will power tries to contract and reduce the number of alphabets of animals and human beings and increases the loudness for forceful effect due to binding energy. The will power of animals affects all the activities of life forms and the highest level of impact of will power is seen in human beings. The lower life forms can also exercise will power and they do exercise but their will power is feeble as compared to human beings. The effect of will power drags high breath inside animals towards brain and due to higher energy value pituitary gland releases more secretions which increase kinetic energy of living animals. The increase in will power increases solidification trend in animals towards centre and drags ionization towards seventh point of solidification creating black metallic octet of X^{7+} in the center. All the animals and human beings possess will power and their will power is their highest concentration of energy. The concentration of nerves and central nervous system leads to united action of nerves and brain in one direction in every living being. The concentrated power of brain becomes the will power of that animal and human being.

The sound waves are equivalent to their corresponding electromagnetic waves, i.e., power waves. So the sound waves of human beings are more powerful than electromagnetic waves of seven colors (4000Å -7500Å) that constitute the human body and create human body parts. The sound waves effect human body like power waves and sound waves can last longer like power waves in the space. The sound waves will not perish and on the patterns of power waves it will affect human body with impact on future growth. The sound waves of animal body effect the present time and will affect the body in future also because power waves last longer in the space. Due to power waves the big size stars act like microwave or power wave towers which effect and control human body that is made up of electromagnetic waves of visible spectra. It is the reason that sound waves are considered to be more powerful than electromagnetic waves which shapes and constitutes human body.

The chanting of words, emission of words and sound from mouth of human body depends upon spinal nerves and cervical nerves of nervous system and every letter and word effects particular nerve and organ of human body. The impact of sound waves can cure and affect body parts and systems and can affect whole body. The combination of letters and words effect body parts and have the capacity to improve or harm body parts. The audible range of sound waves will be different for different animals on different planets. The sound waves are equivalent to their corresponding electromagnetic waves, i.e., power waves. So the sound waves emitted by animals and human beings are more powerful than electromagnetic waves of seven colors (4000 Å -7500 Å) that constitute and make animal and human body. The sound waves effect animal body like power waves and sound waves can last longer like power waves in the space. The sound waves will not perish and on the patterns of power waves it will affect animal body with impact on future growth and development. The sound waves of animal body effect the present time and will affect the body in future also because power waves last longer.

Power and energy exists as electromagnetic waves at certain wavelength and frequency. One particular electromagnetic wave at particular wavelength acts as brain power or soul and attaches each individual with other individual through seven colors visible spectra and white and black regions. The electromagnetic waves of seven colors create all living beings and attach each and every living being with other living beings. In sound producing animals the sound waves act as check and balance over animals' growth, movement and migrations and behave as soul.

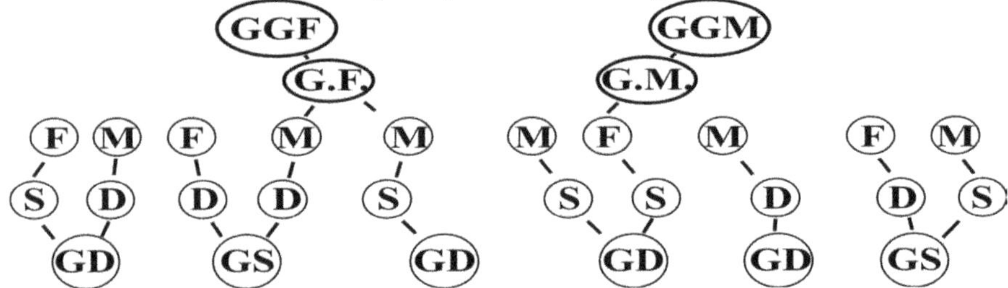

GGF	: Great Grand Father	GGM	: Great Grand Mother
GF	: Grand Father	GM	: Grand Mother
F	: Father	M	: Mother
S	: Son	D	: Daughter
GD	: Grand Daughter	GS	: Grand Son

ALL LIVING BEINGS INCLUDING HUMAN BEINGS ARE INTER-RELATED TO EACH OTHER THROUGH ENERGY OF ELECTROMAGNETIC WAVES. POWER WAVES IN THE FREQUENCY RANGE 256 Hz. TO 512 Hz. CREATE SEVEN TYPES OF SOUND WAVES. ELECTROMAGNETIC WAVES IN THE FREQUENCY RANGE 4×10^{14} Hz. TO 7.5×10^{14} Hz. CREATE ALL LIVING BEINGS ON PLANETS.

Fig. 7.10

The sound waves of animals and human beings form a circular outer covering around their planets like power waves range in space. The sound waves become more powerful than the visible spectra range that creates 118 elements and forms astral bodies, planets, stars, animal bodies and human beings. The sound waves when repeated at fixed wavelength with particular purpose become vow and being repeated time and again effect the body parts of human body. The length, width and breadth of human beings vary along three axes and if it increases along one axis it reduces and compensates along rest two axes. The age and longevity of human beings and life forms never reaches infinity because its components start degenerating and decomposing at certain age level and perish finally. The effect of will power drags all the breath in human beings towards brain and due to higher energy value pituitary gland releases secretions which increases kinetic energy of the human body. The increase in will power increases solidification in animals and human beings and drags ionization of elements towards seventh point in compounds.

Blue planets with atmospheric covering act as thermodynamic equilibrium of planet guided by pressure due to gravity, volume and temperature along three axes. Creation of new life forms depends upon balance of pressure, temperature and volume along three axes inside atmospheric

238

covering. Different new genus and species with new variety of life forms will take birth and will tend to become hardy and resistant to prevailing pressure due to gravity, volume and temperature of planet. The cycle of birth, existence and extinction of different genus and species of life forms will continue forever on planets in every solar system. Life with present level of intelligence, knowledge and science existed in cyclic manner on earth 43,20,000 years ago.

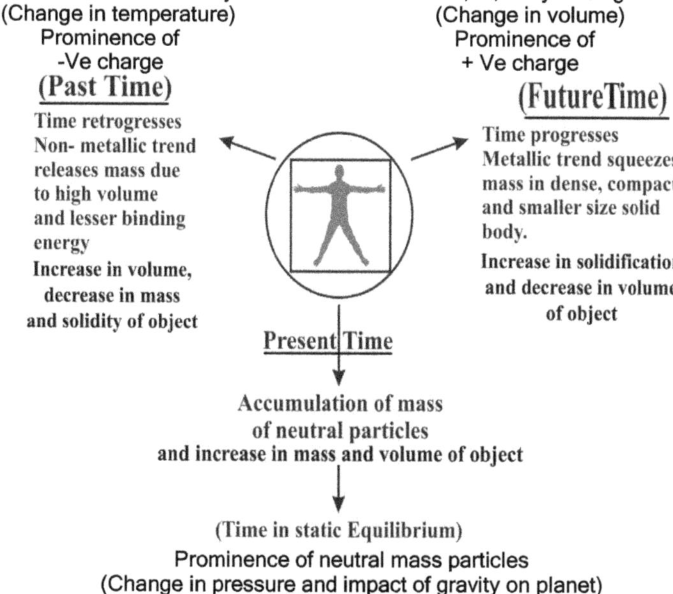

LIVING BEINGS MAINTAIN BALANCE ALONG THREE AXES AS TIME MACHINE AND LANGUAGE EFFECT GROWTH OF BODY ALONG THREE AXES. THE IMPACT OF PRESSURE, VOLUME AND TEMPERATURE DECIDES THE SIZE AND SHAPE OF INDIVIDUAL LIVING BEING ON PLANETS.

Fig. 7.11

Energy exists everywhere in every particle and brain, body of animal or human being, air, water, solid etc in the form of energy of electromagnetic waves. Brain power is associated with energy of all particles, sub-atomic particles, elements, astral bodies, plants and animals in the universe. Chanting and *Mantras* are diagnosis of your requirements for particular purpose and as is the requirement so is diagnosis.

The will power makes body strengthy, aligned and straight. Will power strengthens concentration and will power of animal body and human body and gives stimulus to body for working in any particular direction or situation. Will power directs every part of body and system to work in a particular manner and particular direction. Will power can control and cure diseases of body. It forces and compels the body organs to act according to desired will of brain. Obviously, the instruction is given by brain to body organs and systems for work. The secretions of glands and physiology of body acts in tune to instructions of brain and cures diseases of body as dictated by will power. Will power is life force and will power brings body energy to normalcy. Will power is the actual life force and has the capacity to cure all diseases.

239

It is observed during aerobic upward pressure that nerves at seven places inside spinal cord drag air towards brain and tends to weaken connection with peripheral nervous system. The peripheral nerves become almost non-functional for some time due to dragging of air inside spinal cord of human beings. The concentration of extra air in brain and spinal cord refreshes central nervous system and makes human body younger in age. The moment concentration of air inside brain and spinal cord decreases, the nerves tend to gain normal posture and efficiency along with consciousness of peripheral nervous system is restored. The above mentioned seven nerve centers inside spinal cord are not visible from outside the body. In human beings, suction pressure of air drags nerves from bottom of body, i.e., legs towards top and head of body. Thus head portion contains bigger and massive network of nerves as compared to leg portion.

CONTRACTION AND CONVERSION OF WAVES INTO MASS PARTICLES AND STORAGE OF MATTER INSIDE BRAIN CELLS SHOWS THAT HUMAN NERVOUS SYSTEM IS CONNECTED WITH VACUUM MEDIUM, ASTRAL BODY, PLANETS AND STARS IN SPACE. TWO PARAMETERS OF ANY OBJECT, i. e., CIRCUMFERENCE AND DIAMETER DECIDE THE SHAPE AND SIZE OF EVERY OBJECT WITH MASS IN THE UNIVERSE. CONTRACTION AND EXPANSION OF NERVE CELLS INSIDE BRAIN CAN CHANGE FROM ELEVEN DIMENSIONS TO THREE DIMENSIONS AND CREATE MEDIUM WHICH INCREASES THE POWER OF IMAGINATION OF BRAIN OF HUMAN BEINGS. CONTRACTION AND EXPANSION OF NERVE CELLS INSIDE HUMAN BRAIN IMPROVES THE IMAGINATION AND PERCEPTION OF HUMAN BRAIN AND CONNECTS HUMAN BODY WITH VACUUM MEDIUM IN SPACE. IMAGINATION OF HIGHER ANIMALS AND HUMAN BEINGS CAN REACH DISTANT PARTS OF STAR DYNASTIES WITHIN FRACTION OF SECONDS.

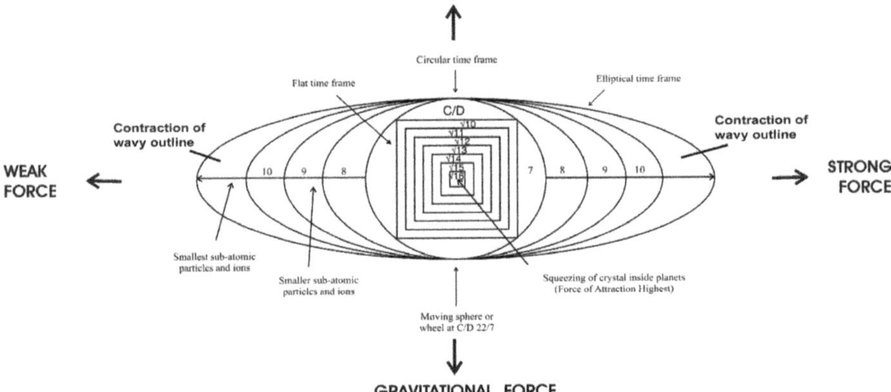

CONTRACTION AND EXPANSION OF MATTER WAVES IN HIGH VACUUM LEADS TO CRYSTALLIZATION AND FORMATION OF THREE-DIMENSIONAL PARTICLES IN SPACE. CONTRACTION AND CONVERSION OF WAVES INTO MASS PARTICLES AND STORAGE OF MATTER INSIDE PLANETS AND LIFE FORMS TAKES PLACE DUE TO SQUEEZING OF CIRCUMFERENCE AND DIAMETER OF WAVES ALONG THREE AXES. DURING CONTRACTION OF WAVES INTO SMALLER PARTICLES, WAVY PARTICLES EXHIBIT ZERO TO ELEVEN DIMENSIONS. THE SHAPE AND SIZE OF OBJECTS AND ASTRAL BODIES VARIES FROM GEOMETRICAL STRUCTURES, SQUARES, CUBES, SPHERES TO ELLIPTICAL EGG-SHAPED STRUCTURES. THE ORBIT, ORBITAL STRETCH AND ORBITAL ELLIPTICITY OF THEIR MOVEMENT VARIES FROM PLANETS TO STARS. FINALLY, IT IS SPHERICAL TIME FRAME WHICH DECIDES THE SHAPE OF HUMAN BODY

Fig. 7.12

PRANAYAM (BREATH AIR + CHANGE IN DIMENSIONS)

Change in dimensions of the Oxygen Molecule inside human body is called Pranayam (Prana + Aayam). Air taken during breath or oxygen gas controls life inside living body and remains in gas form on planets. The gas changes dimension from round or spherical to solid to dumb bell shape and finally splits into two spherical forms. Dimensions change form between one to eleven dimensions and create gas, liquid and solid state forms in the universe. For all life forms, existence of oxygen element in all the three states, i.e., gas, liquid and solid forms is essential and life forms thrive with all three states inside it on any planet. Change in dimensions brings changes in body and human body takes proper three dimensional shape suitable for existence.

In Kundalini Shakti (Serpent Power) process of inhaling air through bottom end of spinal cord makes the lower part of body numb and numbness continues till the air of breath is retained upwards inside spinal cord. The breath can be retained upwards inside spinal cord by will power of animals and human beings. The coiled nerves of spinal cord from bottom become straight and spinal fluid goes upwards till breath of human beings is stopped for certain period. The oxygen in gas, liquid or solid form stored inside spinal fluid provides energy to human body and stops the impact of time by preserving human body. The moment human being releases breath by relaxing will power, the spinal fluid comes down inside spinal cord and nerves again become active. The numbness inside nerves and human body vanishes and human being starts taking normal breath through nostrils. The process of inhaling air through bottom end of spinal cord or say "opposite breath" through bottom of spinal cord helps human beings in retaining and preserving spinal fluid, spinal cord, brain and human body. The air stored inside spinal cord refreshes human body, stops ageing and preserves entire human body.

The changes in two parameters, i.e., circumference and diameter decide the transformation of waves into particles and particles into waves. The changes in axial angles help in conversion of wavy outer covering into flat outer covering and vice versa. All the sub-atomic particles exist, as solid particles in the wavelength range zero angstrom to 7500 angstrom. Above 7500 angstrom, the sub-atomic particles tend to melt, lose their identity and convert into waves. The mass of electrons in the wavelength range 4000 angstroms to 7500 angstroms behaves as wave in non-metallic elements and as particle in case of metallic elements during ionization of atoms. A wavy circular particle converts into geometrically shaped crystals at transition or crystallization temperature point. The mass particles when bound by circular wavy outline and not limited by axial ratios and axial angles show wavy nature. The mass particles, when reach crystallization point, separate out of liquid medium duly delineated by axial ratios and axial angles and thus solid particles are created.

The sense organs mainly consist of taste, smell, vision and hearing. It comprises of brain, spinal cord, cranial and spinal nerves and autonomic nervous system. This system controls and coordinated the different activities of the various body parts. It includes sense organs such as eyes, ears, nose, tongue and skin. The organs of this system receive senses and convey the same to nervous system. It is formed of ductless gland whose secretions are known as hormones, which influence various metabolic processes of the body. Hormones act as chemical messengers. The central nervous system is affected by green color and anomalies of this system can be solved through application of green color because energy of yellow color tries to bring it to normalcy. They resemble smooth muscle cells and are involuntary. These cells arise from the ectoderm instead of mesoderm. Myofibroplast cells resemble fibroplasts but contain action and myosin arranged as in smooth muscle and are contractile. In fact myofibroblasts are specialized contractile fibroblasts. The contraction of wounds is caused by the shortening of myofibroblasts. Pericyte cells are found around capillaries and venules. They contain actin and myosin. Pericytes can give rise to myofibroplasts and to mesenchyma, which can differentiate into fibroblasts and can form new blood vessels. The power of imagination and change in circumference and diameter ratio of waves helps in contraction of mass inside human body.

RETROGRESSION OF TIME IN ROOT VALUES CONTRACTS WAVES AND MASS CREATES DIFFERENT STATES OF MATTER

STAGES	<C/D>	STATES OF MATT-ER	TEMPER ATURE	SHAPE	TRANS-MISSION OF ENERGY	TIME AND SPACE RELATI-ONSHIP	COL-OUR RANGE	VOLUME	DENSITY
Stage of tran-sition	Above √4 to 22/9	Vacuum and Plasma	Kinetic energy very high	Waves	By waves	Outer covering and inner contents	White	Highest volume and least mass	Lowest density
	22/9 to π	-do-	Kinetic energy high	-do-	-Do-	-Do-	-Do-	Higher volume and lesser mass	Lower density
	π	Gas	Kinetic energy moderate	-do-	Mass particle to mass particle	Outer covering and inner mass	White to Red	-do-	-do-
	π to √10	Fluid	Kinetic energy less and potential energy moderate	Wave like	-Do-	-Do-	-Do-	High volume and less mass	Low density
Star /Planet (Stage of bound energy)	√10 to √16	Solid	Potential energy stored inside crystal (Maximum energy stored is crystals of highest atomic numbers)	Solid crystals (discrete particles)	Solid crystal to solid crystal	Mass fixed in three dimens-ional crystals	Seven colors	Planets in equilibri um	Planets in equilibr-ium with fixed density
Stage of tran-sition	√17 to √484	Super dense to Binary star	-do-	Any shape betwe en C/D ratio √17 to √484	-Do-	Outer covering and inner contents	Black	Lowest volume and highest mass	Higher density

Table 7.1

The energy of electromagnetic waves below 4000 Å is absorbed inside three-dimensional dark matter particles (DMP) in space. The movement of dark matter particles in this wavelength range is free and they are not absorbed inside 14 matter zones of planets and stars. They constitute γ-rays, x-rays and UV rays depending upon frequency of their movement in space. They can pass through astral bodies, planets and stars without any obstruction. The energy of electromagnetic waves in the wavelength range 4000 Å to 7500 Å is absorbed inside DMP which

242

is contracted inside nucleus in the shape of neutrons. The neutrons are captured and contracted by force inside nucleus of elements by colored particles in the wavelength range 4000 Å to 7500 Å. These elements constitute visible spectra in space.

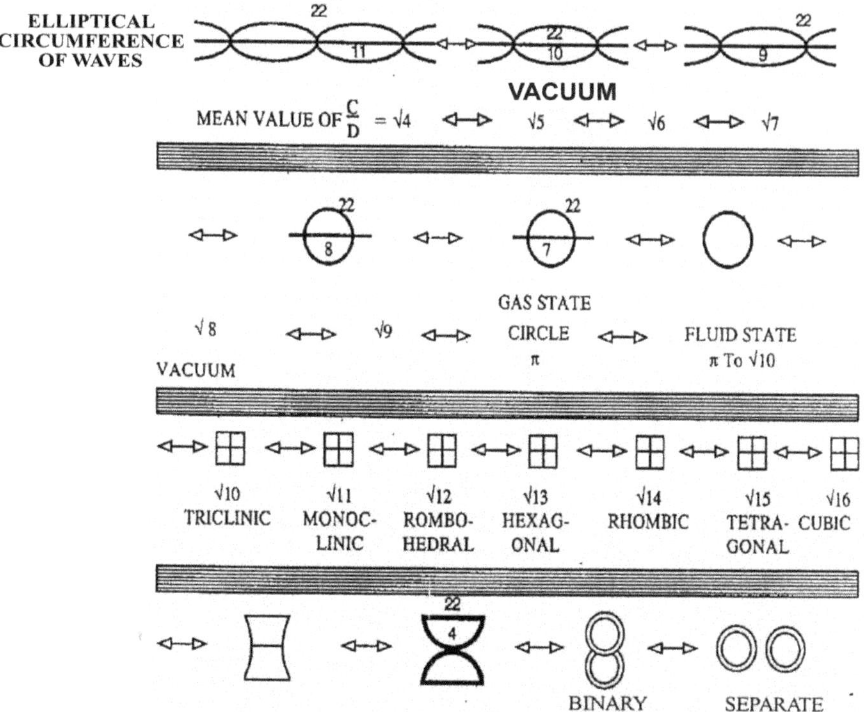

CONVERSION OF WAVES INTO PARTICLES TAKES PLACE DUE TO CHANGE IN CIRCUMFERENCE AND DIAMETER AND SHOWS REDUCTION IN DIMENSION FROM ELEVEN TO THREE DIMENSIONS IN CYCLIC MANNER. MATTER WAVES HAVING VERY HIGH ELLIPTICAL CIRCUMFERENCE CONTRACT MASS TO PRODUCE THREE DIMENSIONAL MASS PARTICLES AND CRYSTALS. INCREASE IN WILL POWER INCREASES THE SOLIDIFICATION TREND OF CELLS INSIDE NERVOUS SYSTEM AND MAKES PERSON ROBUST AND STRONG IN VOICE.

Fig. 7.13

The nervous tissue in general develops from the ectoderm of the embryo, but the microgliocytes arise from the mesoderm of the embryo. The special properties of the cells of the nervous tissue are excitability and conductivity. Excitability is the ability to initiate nerve impulse in response to stimuli (changes outside and inside the body). Conductivity means the ability to transmit a nerve impulse (potential change in membrane of a nerve cell). The reaction is called response. The response may be sensation, such as pain or some activity such as muscle contraction or glandular secretion. A neuron is a structural and functional unit of the nervous tissue and hence the nervous system. Certain neurons may almost equal the length of body itself.

Thus neurons with longer processes (projections) are the longest cells in the body. Human nervous system has about 100 billion neurons, majority of the neurons occur in the brain. Fully formed neurons never divide and remain in interphase throughout life. Shortly after birth, new neurons do not develop. Certain neurons have flask shaped cytons and are called Purkinje cells, which occur in cerebellum of the brain.

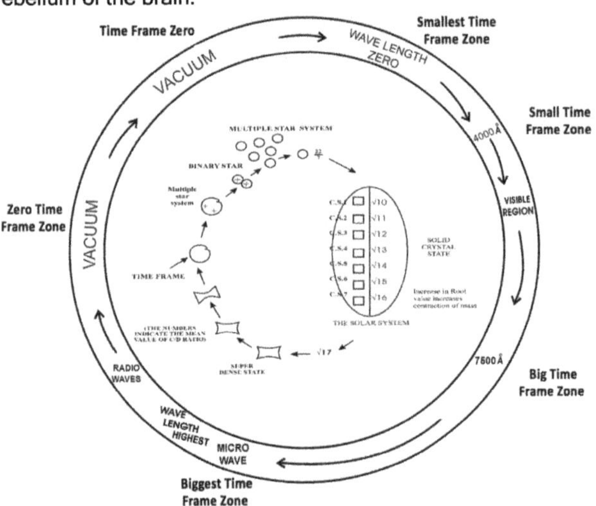

CYCLIC MOVEMENT OF MASS PARTICLES AND ENERGY IN DIFFERENT STATES OF MATTER IN THE UNIVERSE. CONVERSION OF WAVES INTO PARTICLES DUE TO CHANGE IN CIRCUMFERENCE AND DIAMETER SHOWS CHANGES IN DIMENSION FROM ELEVEN TO THREE DIMENSIONS IN CYCLIC MANNER.

Fig. 7.14

Increase in will power of human being increases the solidification trend of cells in the nervous system. It makes voice strong and body robust due to contraction of mass inside cells of human body. The contraction and expansion of any object can be measured with the help of two parameters, i.e., circumference and diameter of the object which can squeeze mass from eleven dimensions to three dimensions in space. The human brain has capability to contract the diameter of elliptical cell from 11 to 7 and then to 5.5 units inside circumference of cell of 22 units. The contraction of cells of neurons helps human brain to pass through ether medium and thought process of human brain with the help of neuron cells can perceive the movement pattern of planets and stars. The human brain with the help of neuron cells can perceive cyclic movement of energy in the universe. The atmosphere of a spherical astral body is created by prominence of gas state and liquid state on astral body. These two states retain mass in floating form and wave motion is high in these two states.

In case of earth ozone layer forms an outer covering and retains mass in gas and liquid form in atmosphere. As much will be the prominence of these two states on any planet so thick will be the layer of atmosphere on that planet and temperature of highest growth will vary between 0^0C to 36^0C and mean temperature showing maximum growth will be 18^0C. The planets may contain an outer protective layer or may not contain any layer. The planets, which contain solid, liquid and gaseous oxygen in any form, will automatic develop living beings as seen in case of planet earth.

In a planet as high is the compaction of crystals and increase of mass content in solid state so less is the atmospheric content of that planet. Similarly, a planet with more voids and containing crystals of lesser symmetry in mantle and crust portion has chances of developing thicker atmosphere around it. In a stellar atmosphere, which is generally neutral the radiating atoms experience a changing electric field produced by the passing electrons, protons, ions and atoms. Precisely the planet having all the three states of matter inherent in it can develop atmosphere around it. The planets having solid, liquid and gas states inherent in it only can show atmosphere around them. The planets closer to emission of blue color will tend to retain atmosphere in itself because emission of blue color rays shows presence of all the sixteen zones inside spherical astral body. The emission of blue color rays will preferably be seen by ions of non-metallic elements. The Hemoglobin (Hb) in red corpuscles of blood carries oxygen to the tissues.

$$Hb(s) \quad + \quad O_2(g) \quad = \quad Hb\,O_2(s)$$

The Oxygen combines with hemoglobin of blood to form oxy- hemoglobin which then move to tissues. Partial pressure of oxygen being low in the tissues, some of the $HbO_2(s)$ changes to Hb giving up the oxygen. When the blood returns to lungs, the partial pressure of oxygen being high, equilibrium favors the formation of more oxy- hemoglobin. It is the liquid oxygen that sustains multi-cellular life forms in the shape of plants and animals on planets. The multi-cellular life forms, which do not contain liquid oxygen inside them, fail to exist on planets and decay. Planets showing emission of red color may not develop atmosphere in itself. It is not compulsory that all the planets will have atmosphere of their own. The layers of planets, which produce continuous spectrum, absorption line spectrum and the emission line spectrum are together said to constitute the planetary atmosphere. The ions of elements having highest electronegative charge and containing highest quantum of energy will emit blue color rays on any astral body. On the contrary, ions of elements having highest electropositive charge containing highest quantum of energy will emit red color rays. Life forms will exist on oblate spheroid planets only because spherical planets show three-axis attachment, fourteen color regions and regular movement along three axes.

$$CO_2\,(g) \quad + \quad H_2O\,(l) \quad = \quad H_2CO_3\,(aq) \quad = \quad H^+\,(aq) \quad + \quad HCO_3^-\,(aq)$$

The blood removes CO_2 from the tissues during circulation. Carbon dioxide dissolves in the blood in the tissues since the partial pressure of CO_2 is high. However in the lungs, where the partial pressure of CO_2 is low, it is released from the blood. The spherical planets albedo should be equal to about one. The life forms will fail to exist on irregular astral bodies, irregularly shaped planets and on stars. The albedo of planet should be equal to one. The albedo of a planet is the ratio of sun's energy reflected by the planet to that incident on it. The Venus planet will have maximum probability of developing atmosphere and life forms because the internal features of Venus are very close to that of earth. The albedo of Venus is 0.85. The atmosphere may contain convective envelope or radiative envelope or both. The atmosphere of planet may contain outer protective layer or may not contain any protective envelope at all. The atmospheric width of planets may be thin or thick as compared to their radii. The temperature, pressure, density and volume of the atmospheric content vary from planet to planet. The width and elemental composition of the atmospheric layer varies on every planet and depends upon:

(a) Stage of equilibrium of planet,

(b) Elemental composition of planet,

(c) Magnetic balance along three axes,

(d) Relative position of planets under nine planets system,

(e) Compulsory outer layer with oxygen,

(f) Planets adhering towards blue color end and emitting blue color,

(g) Planets maintaining all the sixteen zones in itself,

(h) Planets emitting blue and indigo color due to high electronegative charge of elements in their ionosphere have higher probability of sustaining life and atmosphere.

(i) Planets maintaining mean temperature of 18^0 C which varies between 0^0 C to 36^0 C.

Stellar atmospheres are characterized by equilibrium in radiation. Some planets develop radiation equilibrium by maintaining constancy of mass of planets, i.e., mass lost by radiation is compensated by mass gained due to movement of planet. The conduction of energy under crystal layers, convection of energy at the surface of planet and radiation in the top layers of the atmosphere leads to development of thermodynamic equilibrium by every planet. Life forms exist on planets only and not on stars. The color-temperature cycle decides the existence of life forms on planets and highest proliferation of growth is seen at 18^0C. The nine planets system developed around every star or Sun depends upon nine-color energy cycle.

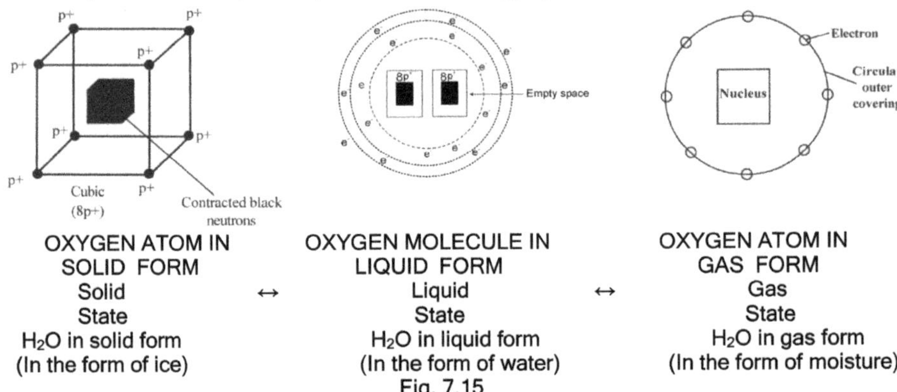

OXYGEN ATOM IN SOLID FORM	OXYGEN MOLECULE IN LIQUID FORM	OXYGEN ATOM IN GAS FORM
Solid State	↔ Liquid State ↔	Gas State
H_2O in solid form (In the form of ice)	H_2O in liquid form (In the form of water)	H_2O in gas form (In the form of moisture)

Fig. 7.15

All life forms commonly contain solid state, liquid state and gas state. Highest proliferation of life forms is seen in liquid state in the temperature range 0^0C to 100^0C. The water with lowest temperature produces biggest life forms whereas water with highest temperature produces smallest life forms. Life forms do not thrive well in solid state and gas state of water. The planets that maintain continuous, surface temperature between 0^0 to 100^0C along with protective ozone covering layer contain life forms. All the bigger and smaller planets, which can retain liquid oxygen inside life forms, will contain life forms. Obviously the planet containing outer protective layer of oxygen will have better chances to contain life forms on that planet. All spherical astral bodies, which are emitting blue color radiation contain atmosphere around them and have probability of containing life forms. Depending upon space and time relationship the mass and matter can be categorized into two types of astral bodies, which emit or absorb electromagnetic waves.

BLACK REGION	VIOLET	INDIGO	BLUE	GREEN	YELLOW	ORANGE	RED	WHITE REGION
Zero^0 C Tempe-rature of living being	Mean Temp 4^0C Biggest life forms are produced	Mean Temp10^0C Bigger life forms are produced	Mean Temp 18^0C	Mean Temp 25^0C	Mean Temp 30^0C	Mean Temp 35^0C	Mean Temp 50^0C to 100 ^{0}C	High Tempe-rature of Living being up to 100^0C

Table 7.2

The presence of H_2O in all three states, i.e., gas state (moisture), liquid state (water) and solid state (solid compounds having water molecules attached with them) is compulsory for existence of life forms on planets. Life forms develop on planets which maintain an outer covering of atmosphere between the temperature range zero degree to 100^0 C. The life forms exist on blue planets, i.e., towards low wavelength of spectra. The life forms do not exist on red or white planets, i.e., towards higher wavelength of spectra.

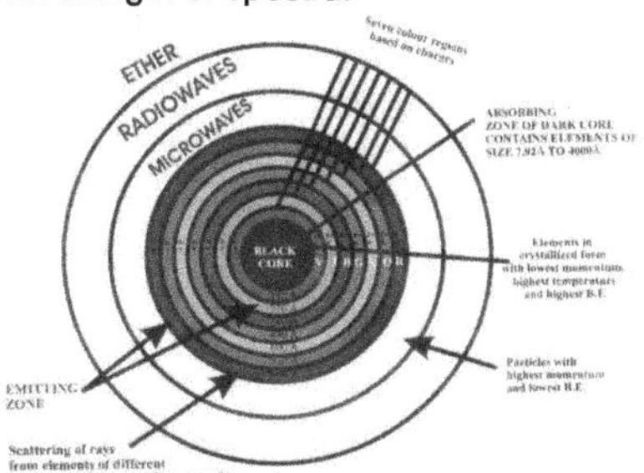

**ABSORPTION OF AIR, CIRCULATION IN BODY AND
CONTRACTION IN SEVEN ZONES INSIDE HUMAN BODY**

Fig. 7.16

Existence of life on planets depends upon availability of oxygen in solid, liquid and gas forms inside living beings. As high is the availability and retention of oxygen in liquid form inside any living being so high is the existence of life forms on that planet. The oxygen element tries to make room in three forms inside life forms and has the capability to change forms inside living body. It can be said that life exists on planets due to liquid oxygen only. It is the molecular oxygen in gas, liquid and solid form that creates and sustains life forms on planets. Under high pressure and low temperature, oxygen element $_8O^{16}$ can be liquefied. The liquid oxygen is slightly blue in color and has boiling point of -183⁰C. The molecular oxygen has melting point of 54.4 K and boiling point of 90.2 K. The prominence of liquid oxygen on earth and on similar planets provides blue appearance to the planet from outside.

The element created with prominence of metallic trend occupies centre of human body whereas elements created with prominence of non-metallic trend shift to periphery of body. This is due to prominence of high attraction at centre and gradual depletion of attraction towards periphery. The cycle of will power pulls air upwards inside spinal cord and energy towards white region from black region. It tries to drag human body and contents of spinal column including bone marrow from basal hip portion towards brain portion. It pulls energy towards red and white region of energy of electromagnetic waves. There is gradual increase in number of nerves from base of spinal cord upwards towards brain.

7.5 CARDIO-VASCULAR SYSTEM

Cardio-vascular system is effected by sound wave packet carrying mass particle packet or Swara called '*Pa*' and its impact with higher energy creates and strengthens cardio-vascular system and cures diseases and abnormalities related to respiration. The system consists of heart and blood vessels. Heart is situated inside thoracic cage and consists of four chambers. The right atrium receives impure blood through large veins from upper and lower regions of the body. The right atrial blood through an opening known as atrio-ventricular opening passes into the right ventricle. From right ventricle arises the pulmonary trunk. The pulmonary trunk divides and breaks

247

up into capillaries in the lungs. Due to contraction of right ventricle blood is carried to the lungs. This course is known as pulmonary or lesser circulation. In the alveoli of lungs the impure blood gives off carbon dioxide and takes up oxygen and gets purified in the process.

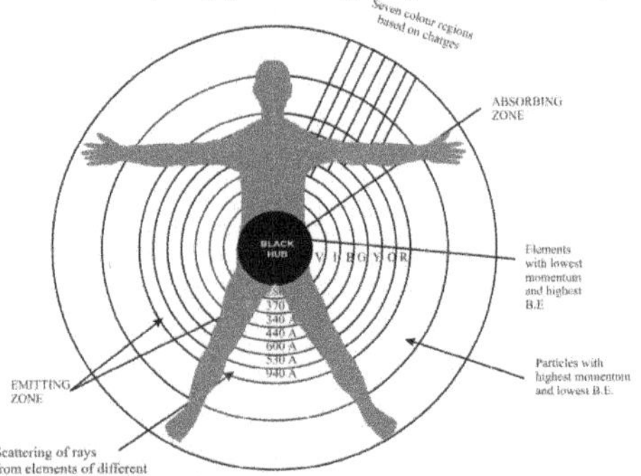

HUB OF HUMAN BODY CONTAINS COMPOUNDS OF BLACK Fe ELEMENT WHICH GRADUALLY DECREASES TOWARDS PERIPHERAL AREAS OF BODY. IN THE EMISSION OF SOUND WAVES HUB PLAYS A DOMINANT ROLE AND LANGUAGE RELATED TO HUB IS THE STRONGEST. ATOMIC THEORY OF SOUND WAVES IS BASED ON PERIODIC TABLE OF ELEMENTS. INTERMIXING OF 'SOUND WAVE PACKETS OR LANGUAGES' CREATE WORDS ON THE PATTERN OF COMPOUNDS OF ELEMENTS WITHIN ATMOSPHERE OF PLANET.

Fig. 7.17

The pure blood from the lungs is carried through pulmonary veins to the left atrium and through atrio-ventricular opening to the left ventricle. From the left ventricle arises a large artery known as aorta. The left ventricle contracts and pure blood is pumped out to aorta. The aorta and its arterial branches which break up into capillaries carry pure blood to head and neck regions, superior and inferior extremities, thorax, abdomen and trunk. The impure blood from different regions of the body is carried by veins provided with valves into the right atrium. This course of circulation is called systemic or major circulation. The right atrium sends blood to right ventricle and the cycle is repeated. There are about five litres of blood in adult human body and human heart beats 71.4 times per minute. Cardio-vascular system includes all organs related to respiration, lungs, alveoli, exchange of air, heart beat, control of breathing, blood pressure and balance of the body. The impact of blue color brings improvement in the working of cardio-vascular system. There are many verses or Mantras developed by scholars for cure of diseases and some are given below:

Lord Dhanavantari carries pot of nectar and helps restore cardiac functions through this Mantra:

"Om Tat Purusaya vidamahe amrita kalasa hastya dheemahi tanno Dhanavantari Prachodayatah."

The respiratory organs consist of nasal passage, nasopharynx and oropharynx laryngopharynx, larynx, trachea, bronchi and two lungs on each side of body. The lungs consist of bronchioles and alveoli. The alveoli are thin-walled and blood capillaries remain in partition between adjacent alveoli. Through the endothelial lining of alveoli and the endothelial lining of capillaries, CO_2 diffuses into alveoli and from the alveoli O_2 diffuses into blood remaining in capillaries. The impure blood becomes pure and is distributed through arterial system into

248

different parts of the body. Mitochondria is the powerhouse and controls yield of energy. Mitochondria becomes more strengthened due to chanting and religious concentration due to will power. ATP is the carrier of chemical energy and cycle of energy continues inside body. The exchange of gases and metabolism inside body keeps the body in thermodynamic equilibrium due to impact of sound wave '*Pa*'. The compound words created by vowels and consonants during chanting effect and penetrate the nerves of system and bring the system to normalcy.

7.6 URINO-GENITAL SYSTEM

Urino-genital system is effected by sound wave packet carrying mass particles packet or Swara called '*Dha*' and its combined impact is observed on urino-genital system in combined manner. The impact creates and strengthens urino-genital system and cures diseases and abnormalities related to genital organs. The sound wave helps in development of gonads in pairs and excretion of water. The human beings have well developed male and female sexual organs and offspring are produced through sexual reproduction. It consists of kidneys, ureters, urinary bladder, urethra and sex organs. It removes metabolic waste from the body. The reproductive system comprises male and female reproductive organs. Human reproductive organs include testes, epididymes, vasa deferentia, seminal vesicles, penis, uterus and vagina etc. The reproductive system is responsible for the multiplication of organisms. The urino-gential system is created by sound waves '*Dha*' and anomalies of this system can be solved by it. The compound words created by vowels and consonants of chanting effect and penetrate the urino-genital system and bring the system to normal state. There are many Mantras or verses created by scholars for cure of diseases and some are given below:

Om sri kamakhyaye namah
Om klim kamadevaya namah

The inter-relationship between space and time create electric and magnetic fields, which produces electromagnetic waves that travel even in particle-free space. The electromagnetic waves are those waves in which electric and magnetic fields vary in relation to each other and control formation of ions. The sound wave '*Dha*' cures the abnormalities of urino-genital system of body. The impact of indigo color increases sexual activity and vigor and improves the urino-genital system.

7.7 BLOOD CIRCULATORY SYSTEM

Blood circulatory system is effected by sound wave packet having mass particles packet or Swara called '*Ni*' and its combined impact is observed on circulatory system in combined manner. The respiratory organs consist of nasal passage, nasopharynx and oropharynx, laryngopharynx, larynx, trachea, bronchi and two lungs on each side of body. The lungs consist of bronchioles and alveoli. The alveoli are thin-walled and blood capillaries remain in partition between adjacent alveoli. Through the endothelial lining of alveoli and the endothelial lining of capillaries, CO_2 diffuses into alveoli and from the alveoli O_2 diffuses into blood remaining in capillaries. The impure blood becomes pure and is distributed through arterial system into different parts of the body. The application of violet color increases circulation and checks the diseases concerned with circulatory system. There are many Mantras developed by scholars for cure of diseases and some are given below:

Om so hum,
Keurinam harakirit jushtam chaturbhujam pashawarabhayanim
Shrini vahantam ganapam trinetram sachamarashtri yugalen yuktam.

Impact of sound wave '*N*' cures the abnormalities of this system and its effect is observed on formation of body parts, systems, secretion of hormones and creation of organs. The blood circulatory system in invertebrates is less developed and gradual increase in formation of advanced circulatory system takes place in vertebrates. The compound words emitted through vowels and consonants of chanting effect and penetrate the system and bring the system to normal state.

Various types of voice production are known as vocal registers. The exact number of vocal registers is disputed within the field of singing. The science identifies four types of registers, i.e.. whistle register, falsetto register, modal register and vocal fry register. Vocal range plays prominent role in classifying singing voices into voice types and two terms are confused with each other. The voice type is particular kind of human voice perceived as having many qualities and characteristics Vocal range is one of those characteristics. The other prominent factors are vocal weight, vocal tessitura, vocal timbre, vocal transition points, physical characteristics, speech level, and vocal registration etc. All the above factors combined together are used to categorize singers voice into particular type of singing voice or voice type.

Imagination through human brain cells can reach Pole Star or other distant stars in no time due to capacity of brain cells to stretch and contract in least time. All the body cells cannot contract and expand to such a high extent and cannot perceive the extreme ends of star dynasty and universe in least time. The vacuum medium can be perceived by stretching of elliptical cell to circular or crystalline cells but it cannot transfer the materials from one place to other place in universe. Brain cells of human beings have the capacity to reach from one point to another in no time due to stretching and contraction of brain cells. Vocal range is the span from lowest to highest note that particular voice can produce. But it does not relate with the vocal range when it is discussed in the context of singing and shouting by human being.

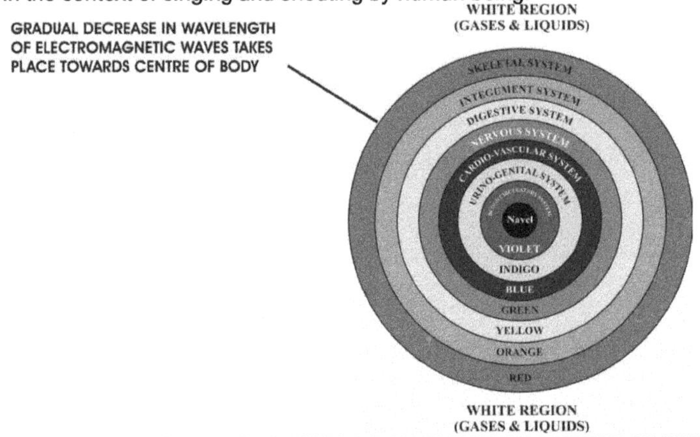

IMPACT OF SEVEN COLORS ALONG WITH WHITE AND BLACK REGION IS OBSERVED ON NINE BODY SYSTEMS OF HUMAN BODY ALONG ONE AXIS. NINE COLORS ARE LINKED TO ENERGY OF ELECTROMAGNETIC WAVES AND HELP IN DEVELOPMENT OF NINE SYSTEMS OF BODY PARTS OF HUMAN BEINGS. TIME INDUCES THE TENDENCY OF ROUNDNESS IN ALL BODY PARTS AND SYSTEMS OF HUMAN BODY. TIME FRAME TRIES TO MAKE OUTER SURFACE, INNER SURFACE AND OUTGROWTHS SPHERICAL IN SHAPE.

Fig. 7.18

INDIAN NAME	WESTERN NAME	FREQUENCY OF SOUND (in Hz.)	FREQUENCY OF ANIMAL SOUND (in Hz.)	TYPES OF WAVE	WAVE LENGTH OF EQUIVALENT POWER WAVES (in Meters)	ELECTRO-MAGNETIC WAVES EFFECTING LIVING BODY	ANIMAL BODY SYSTEMS
(1)	(2)	(3)	(4)	(5)	(6)	(7)	(8)
		10-20	10 - 20	Power wave	$1 \times 10^7 - 10^{20}$		White region, gas, liquid and outer peripheral organs
			Vocal cord of animals 20	- do -			-do-
Sa	Do	256	Vocal cord of Humans	Sound wave	- do -	Red (7500 Å)	Skeletal System
Re	Re	324.7	- Do -	Sound wave	- do -	Orange (6560 Å)	Integument System
Ga	Mi	363.4	- Do -	Sound wave	- do -	Yellow (6030 Å)	Digestive System
Ma	Fa	407.2	- Do -	Sound wave	- do -	Green (5430 Å)	Nervous System
Pa	Sol	439.5	- Do -	Sound wave	- do -	Blue (4990 Å)	Cardio-vascular System
Dha	La	464.3	- Do -	Sound wave	- do -	Indigo (4650 Å)	Urino-genital System
Ni	Ti	491.5	- Do -	Sound wave	- do -	Violet (4280 Å)	Blood circulatory System
Sa	Do	512	- Do -	Sound wave			Black region containing black parts in the centre of body
			Vocal cord of animals 1100	- do -			-do-
		$3 \times 10^4 - 3 \times 10^8$	Vocal cord of Birds	Radio wave	$1 \quad - 10^4$		-do-
			20000	- do -	$1 - 10^{-1}$		-do-
		$3 \times 10^8 - 3 \times 10^9$	Voice of Insects	Micro wave	$3 \times 10^{-1} - 3 \times 10^{-5}$		-do-
		$3 \times 10^9 - 4 \times 10^{14}$	Sound of wings of Insects	Infra red	$1 \times 10^{-4} - 1 \times 10^{-7}$		-do-

IMPACT OF SOUND WAVES ON BODY SYSTEMS OF ANIMALS AND HUMAN BODY
IMPACT OF LETTERS, VOWELS, CONSONANTS AND WORDS CREATED FROM LETTERS EFFECTS ALL THE NERVES, BODY SYSTEMS AND BODY PARTS OF LIVING BODY. PROPER CREATION AND APPLICATION OF WORDS MAY CURE DISEASES AND BRING PROFOUND CHANGES INSIDE LIVING BODY. THE SOUND WAVES SHOW DEFINITE CORRELATIONS WITH COLOR WAVES OF DIFFERENT WAVELENGTHS AND POWER WAVES AND BOTH ARE CREATED IN ARITHMETIC PROGRESSION. CHANTING OF WORDS CREATED FROM LETTERS EFFECTS ALL THE NERVES AND BODY PARTS OF LIVING BODY.

Table 7.3

Atmosphere develops around the planets that contain oxygen and water in solid, liquid and gas forms. Development and existence of atmosphere is compulsory for sound wave packets and survival of multi-cellular living beings on planets. All the planets looking blue in color tend to develop atmosphere of oxygen gas and water around the planet. The atmosphere needs one covering layer to allow gases and liquids of atmosphere to survive on planet and atmosphere will be delineated along three axes by pressure, volume and temperature. The outer covering of earth called as ozone layer protects all the life forms from outside harmful radiations and it is compulsory for existence of living beings on any planet.

The pressure, volume and temperature of life forms vary on every planet and its impact is observed on shape, size and external features of living beings on planets. All the planets looking blue in color tend to develop atmosphere of oxygen gas and water around the planet. The atmosphere needs one covering layer to allow gases and liquids of atmosphere to survive on planet and atmosphere will be delineated along three axes by pressure, volume and temperature. The outer covering of earth called as ozone layer protects all the life forms from outside harmful radiations and it is compulsory for existence of living beings on any planet. The impact of movement of planet, animal body or human body is observed along three axes. The inner features and characteristics of body systems contract matter and develop parts of human body along three axes.

A.   Impact of Electromagnetic Force on white region, seven colors region and Black region during creation of nine systems inside human body (along one axis).

The electromagnetic force is instrumental in creating 14 matter zones inside every planet and living body. It is observed finally in the form of one peripheral white region + seven colors region + central black region inside living body. Every human body contains nine systems controlled by colors cycle on planets.

1. **Gases and liquids   – Effect of white light   (Wavelength above 7500Å)**
2. **Skeletal system – Effect of sound wave packet or Swara *Sa* (256 – 288 Hz.)   – Sunday,**
3. **Integument system – Effect of sound wave packet or Swara *Re* (288–320 Hz.) – Monday,**
4. **Digestive system– Effect of sound wave packet or Swara *Ga* (320 – 341.33 Hz.) – Tuesday,**
5. **Nervous system –Effect of sound wave packet or Swara *Ma* (341.33 – 384 Hz.) – Wednesday,**
6. **Cardio-vascular system – Effect of sound wave packet or Swara *Pa* (384 – 426.67 Hz.) – Thursday,**
7. **Urinogenital system –Effect of sound wave packet or Swara *Dha* (426.67 – 480 Hz.) – Friday,**
8. **Blood circulatory system – Effect of sound wave packet or Swara *Ni* (480 – 512 Hz.) – Saturday.**
9. **Black central hub   – Effect of deposition of black matter**

The planet must maintain adequate pressure for growth, maintain oxygen layer and ozone layer for protection and must have sufficient water and fluid medium for circulation throughout astral body and inside plants and animals. A planet which is not having congenial atmosphere and temperature at present may develop the same in future if planetary sequence in solar system changes in future. As for example, Europa or Venus may develop life forms and atmosphere like earth in future provided the sequence of planets changes in future and they get congenial environment. Such planets have ridges, hills and furrows and tend to contain atmosphere in the temperature range 0^0C to 100^0C.

The existence and survival of life forms on planets depends upon mean temperature which varies between $-4^0 C$ to 100^0C. The survival of life forms is lowest at solid water (ice) level at -4^0C

and at gaseous water (Vapor) level at 100⁰C. The existence and survival of life forms is highest at liquid water level. The biggest life forms contain highest quantum of liquid oxygen inside multi-cellular living beings on any planet.

B. Impact of Gravitational Force on creation of twelve pairs of cranial nerves in Brain inside human body (along second axis).

The gravitational force accumulates matter in geometrical patterns and creates 12 blocks of matter during revolution of planet around central star. The impact of gravitational force creates twelve pairs of cranial nerves in brain of human beings. The cranial nerves are bound by round time frame due to movement of planet around central star and they can be depicted on round time frame.

The plants, trees, animals, human beings and all life forms behave as close thermodynamic systems under fixed pressure, volume and temperature on any planet. The thermodynamic equilibrium of life forms on planets changes when pressure, volume and temperature changes on any planet. Layer by layer deposition of elements, cells, soft tissues and hard tissues increases the size of living body along three axes on planets. In this process complex and bigger living body is produced and as big and tough is the body so long is the age of that life form. The impact of pressure, volume and temperature decides the size and shape of individual living being on planet. Every living being maintains individual thermodynamic equilibrium on planets. The thermodynamic equilibrium of living body depends upon four forces and combined action of pressure (p), volume (v) and temperature along three axes on living body.

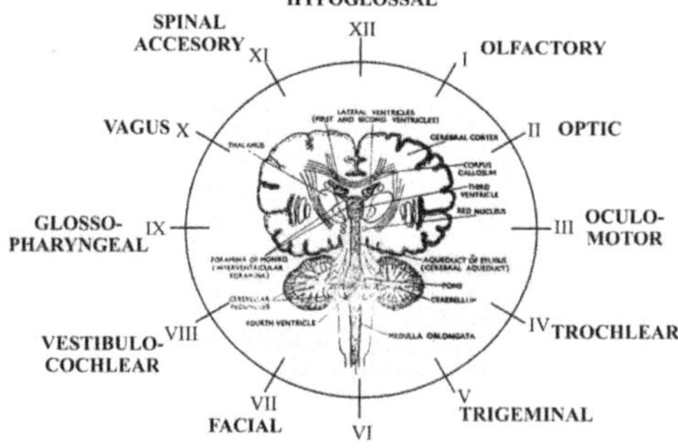

CREATION OF BODY PARTS DUE TO GRAVITATIONAL FORCE ALONG SECOND AXIS INSIDE HUMAN BODY. CORONAL SECTION THROUGH CEREBRAL HEMISPHERE AND BRAIN STEM SHOWS THAT SPHERICAL BRAIN INSIDE SKULL IS CONTROLLED BY TWELVE PAIRS OF CRANIAL NERVES.

Fig. 7.19

Development of ferromagnetic axles along three axes inside animals, tetrapods and human beings increases their movement along three axes on planets. Life forms grow, develop and exist as close thermodynamic systems on planets. The impact of pressure, volume and temperature decides the size and shape of individual living beings on planets. All such spherical astral bodies, which are emitting blue color radiation contain atmosphere around them and have probability of containing life forms. The animals and human beings of blue and dark colors are biggest and largest in size and mass and contain high quantity of compact solid mass. The animals and human beings of white, red, yellow and light colors are smaller in size, lighter and less compact in volume and size. Unlike planets and stars, all plants, animals and living beings contain an outer body covering which stores mass inside the body under seven systems. An outer covering is compulsory for all living beings for maintaining thermodynamic equilibrium. The outer covering helps in temperature regulation inside body of living beings.

C. Combined impact of Strong Force and Weak Force on creation of thirty two pairs of spinal nerves inside human body (along third axis).

The combined effect of strong force and weak force create 32 vertical groups of elements in the periodic table. The creation of elements is linked to 32 crystal classes and its impact is observed on human body in the form of creation of 32 pairs of spinal nerves inside body. Heart is linked with North Pole Star due to precession linked movement of earth in space. The progress of time is observed in the multiples of 10 and 10^3 / 14 stars period of movement = 71.4 beats per minute of pulse in human beings. Human body shows thirty one pair of spinal nerves. In fact, 31st and 32nd pair of spinal nerves are fused and show one nerve. It shows degenerating trend in human body along one axis. Along other two axes, i.e., twelve pairs of cranial nerves and nine body systems the body does not show any degeneration. It can be correlated with degeneration of Pluto, the ninth planet of our solar system, which justifies that our solar system is entering degenerating stage in the ladder of evolution.

SPINAL CORD CONTAINS 32 (31 + 1) PAIRS OF SPINAL NERVES INSIDE VERTEBRAL COLUMN. SOME LOWEST SPINAL NERVES ARE FUSED AND NOT VISIBLE PROMINENTLY

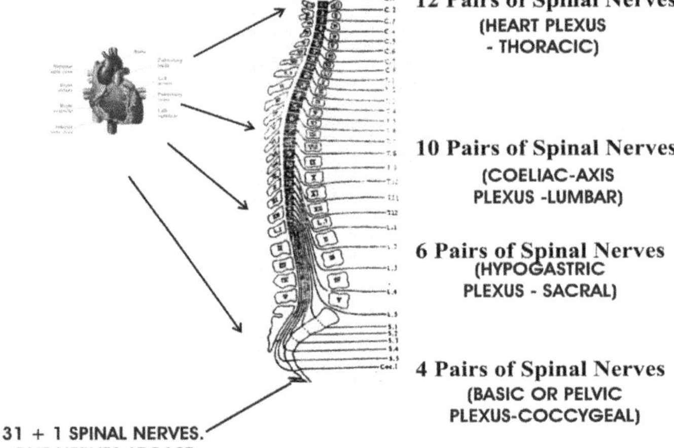

FOUR CENTRES FROM BOTTOM HAVE BEEN REFERRED AS 'LAM', 'VAM', 'RAM', 'YAM' OF VERTEBRAL COLUMN AND SPINAL CORD. ABOVE FOUR IS FIFTH KNOT CALLED AS 'HAM' WHICH CONTAINS SIXTEEN CERVICAL NERVES. FIFTH KNOT OF SPINAL CORD PRODUCES SIXTEEN VOWELS FROM VOCAL CORD N CASE OF HUMAN BEINGS. ABOVE FIFTH CENTRE IS SIXTH CENTRE KNOWN AS 'OHM' WHICH CONTAINS TWO CEREBRAL HEMISPHERES. CREATION OF SPINAL NERVES ALONG THIRD AXIS DUE TO COMBINED ACTION OF STRONG FORCE AND WEAK FORCE ON HUMAN BODY. SPINAL NERVES IN THE MULTIPLES OF 14 (2 + 6 + 10 + 14 = 32 SPINAL NERVES) ARE GUIDED BY HEART OF HUMAN BODY. ITS IMPACT IS OBSERVED ON 1000 / 14 = 71.43 PULSES PER MINUTE OF HUMAN BODY. FIGURE SHOWS SEGMENTS OF SPINAL CORD WITH REFERENCE TO BODY AND SPINOUS PROCESSES OF THE VERTEBRAE.

Fig. 7.20

254

The audible range of sound waves will be different for different animals on different planets. The sound waves are equivalent to their corresponding electromagnetic waves, i.e., power waves. So, the sound waves of human beings are more powerful than electromagnetic waves of seven colors (4000Å -7500Å) that constitute the human body and create human body parts. The sound waves effect human body like power waves and sound waves can last longer like power waves in the space. The sound waves will not perish and on the patterns of power waves it will affect human body with impact on future growth. The sound waves of animal body effect present time and will affect the body in future also because power waves last longer in the space. Due to power waves the big size stars act like microwave or power wave towers which effect and control human body that is made up of electromagnetic waves of visible spectra. It is the reason that sound waves are considered to be more powerful than electromagnetic waves which shapes and constitutes human body.

PLANETS AND STARS HANG IN BALANCE IN SPACE ATTACHED TO EACH OTHER DUE TO ANTI-CLOCKWISE AND CLOCKWISE MOVEMENTS (ONE PORTION OF STAR DYNASTY FACING TOWARDS OUR SOLAR SYSTEM)

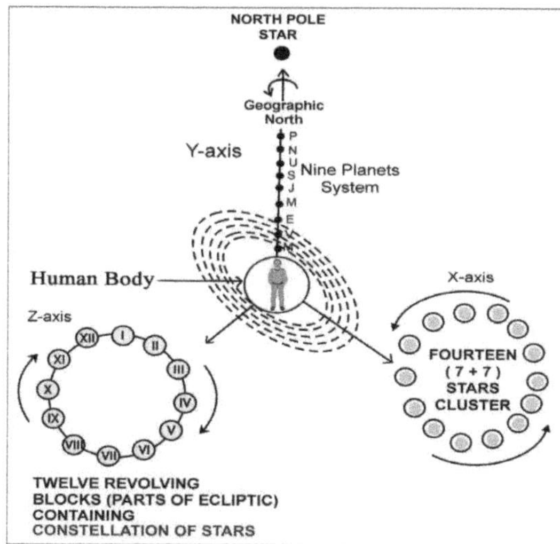

HUMAN BODY IS ATTACHED TO FOURTEEN STARS CLUSTER, TWELVE BLOCKS OF STAR CONSTELLATIONS AND NINE PLANETS SYSTEM ALONG THREE AXES DUE TO EFFECT OF MAGNETIC FIELD ON HUMAN BODY. NO PLANET IS LOCATED ON EDGE AND NO PLANET OR STAR IS LOCATED IN CENTER OF STAR DYNASTY. ALL THE PLANETS AND STARS ARE MOVING RELATIVE TO EACH OTHER ALONG THREE AXES AND ARE ATTACHED THROUGH TWO STARS CLUSTER ALONG TWO AXES AND NINE PLANETS SYSTEM ALONG THIRD AXIS RESPECTIVELY. HUMAN BODY IS ATTACHED TO FOURTEEN STARS CLUSTER. CONSTELLATION OF TWELVE STARS AND NINE PLANETS SYSTEM ALONG THREE AXES DUE TO EFFECT OF MAGNETIC FIELD ON HUMAN BODY.

Fig. 7.21

7.8 CREATION OF COMPOUND WORDS FROM LETTERS AND CHANTINGS

The growth and development of parts and systems of living beings always takes place in the multiples of nine along one axis, twelve along second axis and fourteen along third axis. The development of parts in the multiples of nine includes one white region + seven color regions of systems + one black region. The production of organs in the multiples of twelve due to gravitational force includes twelve parts of body. The creation of seven metallic regions produces bones, cartilages, hard muscles, hard tissues and stony parts whereas creation of seven non-metallic regions produces soft muscles, veins, arteries, soft tissues, pores, air sacs, liquid exudates and gas emissions. Intermixing and overlapping of sound wave packets takes place in many ways along three axes. 'Sound wave packets or Akshars' mix and create jumbled words which acts along three axes.

There are many probabilities of intermixing of sound wave packets of *Akshara* and creation of jumbled words effective along three axes. Intermingling may take place in many ways and production of sound wave packets depends upon the capability of vocal cord of animals to produce different types of waves on planet. Jumbled and complex sound wave packets can control action, movement and diseases of human beings due to their profound effect on human body systems. The impact of sound waves can be used for curing diseases of human bodies along three axes. *Mantras* are prayers to gods and goddesses created for their worship. *Mantras* are created with combination of different words in Sanskrit for specific purposes and different mantras are used for different purposes on human body. Some of the chanting of verses, poems and uttering (mantras) are mentioned below:

"Ohm Bhurbhuvah...............pra chodyat"

"Ohm trayam bakam............maa..... mritat"

These verses and many others effect human body and can cure diseases of body. As for example, uttering of words and sentences in Sanskrutam will effect body parts.

O my God. Make my body disease free and give me long life.

Ohm Ishwarah. Aham Sharir Nihrog bhawatu, evam aham ayushman bhavati:

O my Father God. Make my body disease free and give me long life.

O my Mother God. Make my body disease free and give me long life.

Ohm Mateya Eeshwarah. Aham Sharir Nihrog bhawatu, evam aham ayushman bhavami:

The intermixing of sound wave packets can take place in many ways along three axes. Sound wave packets mixture can create words which acts along three axes on human body. Different types of vocal production can be observed by human beings. The human voice can produce different types of languages using physiological processes of larynx.

The sound waves of animals and human beings form a circular outer covering around their planets like power waves range in space. The sound waves in many communities are associated with chanting and uttering. The sound waves when repeated at fixed wavelength with particular purpose become vow and being repeated time and again effects the body parts of human body. The metals, stones and any mixed material of particular shape is used by the animal body for stabilizing the works and sentiments of particular place. The chain, ring, instruments and tools of different shape and sizes can be used by persons for gaining particular wish achieved.

BIBLIOGRAPHY AND REFERENCES

Elements of Spectroscopy,

Modern College Zoology,

Sanskrit Vyakaran aur Rachna,

Text Book of Human Physiology,

Text Book of Languages,

Text Book of Sanskrit,

Text Book of Sound,

Text Book of Spectroscopy,

Text Book of Chemistry,

Text Book of Electro-Magnetism,

Text Book of Physics.

INDEX